CONCEPTUAL AND PRACTICAL RESEARCH AND STATISTICS FOR SOCIAL WORKERS

CONCEPTUAL AND PRACTICAL RESEARCH AND STATISTICS FOR SOCIAL WORKERS

By Francis K. O. Yuen

California State University, Sacramento

SAN DIEGO

Bassim Hamadeh, CEO and Publisher
Kassie Graves, Vice President, Editorial
Amy Smith, Senior Project Editor
Celeste Paed, Associate Production Editor
Jess Estrella, Senior Graphic Designer
Stephanie Kohl, Licensing Coodinator
Natalie Piccotti, Director of Marketing
Jamie Giganti, Director of Academic Publishing

Cover image: Copyright © 2019 iStockphoto LP/DrAfter123.
            Copyright © 2019 iStockphoto LP/DrAfter123.
            Copyright © 2019 iStockphoto LP/DrAfter123.

Printed in the United States of America.

3970 Sorrento Valley Blvd., Ste. 500, San Diego, CA 92121

To my esteemed colleagues:

   Dr. Gregory Skibinski, who gave me the inspiration to write this book, and
   Dr. John T. Pardeck, who gave me the encouragement to publish.

To my wonderful family, which has given me the unconditional support to pursue my goals.

To my students, who have given me the reasons to complete this book.

BRIEF CONTENTS

DETAILED CONTENTS

Chapter 3. Human Diversity, Ethical Considerations, and Protection of Human Subjects   25

Chapter 4. Conceptualization and Measurement (Terms of Endearment)   43

Chapter 5. Qualitative Research and Quantitative Research (Yin and Yang) 71

Chapter 9. Data Collection Instruments and Development (the Tools)   165

Chapter 10. Needs Assessment, Program Planning, and Program Evaluation (What and What Happens)   199

LIST OF FIGURES

LIST OF TABLES

LIST OF BOXES

PREFACE

"If we knew what we were doing it wouldn't be research."
—Albert Einstein

This is a basic research and statistics core textbook for undergraduate and graduate social work students. Using everyday language and examples from the profession, humor and mapping, and the students' own intuition, this book aims to develop competency in the application of research and statistics toward social work practice and vice versa (Council on Social Work Education, 2015, Competency 4: engage in practice-informed research and research-informed practice). Written from the research-practitioner perspective, this book intends to present key information intuitively, logically, and in manageable amounts. Students will incrementally develop a sense of mastery and confidence that will lead to understanding and competency.

Promoting research and statistics literacy and proficiency among social workers, while minimizing the potential math anxiety, is a major task for the social work profession. This book intends to contribute to that effort by offering the following features:

- This book follows a learner-centered, intuitive, needs-driven, and results-oriented emphasis. "Beginning with the end in mind," "KISS—keep it simple, sweet," "Tell the stories," "Trust your instinct," and "It is only statistics" are the book's mottos.
- It is organized into sections and chapters that are logically connected. Following the cognitive mapping structure of research and statistics (i.e., Figure 1.1, A Brief Visual Map of Research and Statistics for Social Workers and Table 11.5, Common Statistics and Choice of Statistics Chart), students will be able to easily gauge where they are in the learning

of the research process and the competency that they have acquired. It is similar to going on a road trip equipped with a GPS to the destination.

- Learning research (and particularly statistics) is like learning how to ride a bike. One cannot master the skills by only reading the how-to books. It takes practice and, of course, falling down and occasionally scraping knees. This book uses examples, charts, figures, and exercises that guide students in gaining hands-on experience to enhance their learning.
- Actual social work research and statistical analysis examples are used.
- This book also uses strategic repetitions and reminders to refresh students on various related subjects. The learning of research and statistics is not a linear but a spiral process where "two steps forward one step back" is not a discouragement or failure but an expected progression.
- The layout of the book could be easily converted by instructors into a course syllabus.

This book has two main sections: research and statistics. The structure of the book follows the basic research process that moves from research questions to research designs, data collection methods, data collection instruments, and data analyses (statistics) to reporting and dissemination of findings. This book reminds readers to be cognizant of the need to know "where you are going, for what purpose, and how to get there." This will allow readers to stay focused and guide their choice of proper research design and statistical methods based on the intent of the research. This logical approach will support students in unfolding the connected branches of research and statistics systematically.

Following the book's motto of "beginning with the end in mind," students are expected to achieve the following learning outcomes from the book:

- Understand the key methodological, ethical, and logical concepts in research and statistics for social work practice.
- Show knowledge of the research processes, including various research designs and methodologies.
- Demonstrate abilities in data collection approaches and instrument development.
- Become familiar with basic needs assessment and program evaluation.
- Develop a mental map of basic statistics for social work research.
- Exhibit capacity in choosing the appropriate statistics.

- Interpret statistic outputs and draw conclusions related to the research question and hypotheses.
- Become a producer of social work research beyond being a consumer.

THE IMPETUS FOR THIS BOOK

Dr. Gregory Skibinski was a gifted social worker, researcher, and professor. Along with the late Dr. John T. Pardeck, they were my "writing buddies" and dear friends. Dr. Skibinski's effective teaching style, great heartland humor, and charisma made him the students' favorite teacher. He was drafting a statistics book that integrated his plain and intuitive ways of understanding statistics with his wit and years of practice wisdom when his life was cut short by illness. This book is written to continue and to honor his legacy. Although I was not able to recover and include much of his writing, I have prepared this book in his spirit.

ACKNOWLEDGMENTS

Many colleagues, friends, and students have contributed to the completion of this book. Much appreciation goes to Dr. Lois Lowe who not only proofread the draft but also used old-fashioned hand calculations to cross-check all the statistical results. Dr. Serge Lee and Dr. Maria Dinis of California State University, Sacramento, Division of Social Work, gave valuable comments on my first draft. The division's writing specialists, David Reynolds and Rik Keller, did the difficult initial editing for me. Kassie Graves, vice president, and Amy Smith, project editor at Cognella Academic Publishing have been amazingly patient, supportive, and helpful. There are also others in the remarkable Cognella team. Peter Labella served as a brilliant development editor for the manuscript, helping me to make much-needed improvements. Haley Brown and Celeste Paed provided outstanding support for the development of active learning materials and the final copyediting work for the book. Much appreciation goes to the peer reviewers who include Jeronda T. Burley, Coppin State University, Kathleen Boland, Cedar Crest College, Catherine A. Macomber, Saginaw Valley State University, and Yoshie Sano, Washington State University–Vancouver. Without this team of kind and generous experts, this book project would not be possible.

This book integrates materials from my many years of teaching social work research and statistics in graduate and undergraduate social work programs. It also draws much from my experience as a practitioner as well as a researcher and program evaluator for various government and nonprofit agencies. Through all of them, I have come to sincerely recognize a known fact: we can learn a lot from our service recipients, students, and practitioners. They are the experts. Knowledge building is essential for our profession, and it is a cumulative process toward which we all have something to contribute. I hope this book will serve as a catalyst to prepare and inspire students to become competent research-practitioners who will continue to find ways to better serve the people and the community in need.

1

INTRODUCTION TO SOCIAL RESEARCH METHODS AND STATISTICS

INTRODUCTION

Being a competent social worker requires one to acquire and develop proficiency in professional knowledge, attitude, and skills. Among these are social research and social statistics. Social work research and statistics are required content areas for both undergraduate and graduate social work programs (Council on Social Work Education [CSWE], 2015, Competency 4). While there are many social work students who enjoy and are dedicated to using research and statistics, others perceive these tools as dread and difficult subjects. Given this notorious reputation, these students probably would not take these courses if they are not required courses. One of the main challenges in teaching research and statistics to social work students is assisting them in overcoming their misconceptions and "mathematical anxiety." Many are uncertain about their ability to handle the statistics, which is also erroneously equated as research. Critical thinking skills are essential for the profession; however, logical thinking and mathematical reasoning have been challenging for many social work students.

This book aims to develop students' competency in the application of research and statistics in social work practice and to use social work practice to inform research. This book is a basic research and statistics core textbook for social work undergraduate and graduate students. Using everyday language and examples from the profession, humor, and mapping, as well as students' own intuition, this starter book aims to develop students' competency in the application of research and statistics in social work practice and vice versa (CSWE, 2015, Competency

4: engage in practice-informed research and research-informed practice). This book provides students with a manageable, user-friendly, and practical text that allows them to acquire the conceptual knowledge and practical skills of basic statistics and social research methods effectively. This will, in turn, enhance their ability to become better consumers and producers of research in social work.

The book is written from the research-practitioner perspective. It presents key information intuitively, logically, and in manageable amounts. Students will incrementally develop a sense of mastery and confidence (both emotionally and intellectually) that will lead to understanding and competency.

The expected learning outcomes for students will be to acquire the knowledge and skills in the following areas of research competencies:

1. Mastering the problem formulation,
2. Determining the proper research design,
3. Ensuring ethical and culturally competent studies,
4. Constructing appropriate research instruments,
5. Collecting suitable data,
6. Conducting statistical analysis with necessary technological or computer support,
7. Drawing methodologically sound conclusions, and
8. Preparing research proposals and reports.

The structure of this book follows the basic research process that moves from research questions to research designs, data collection methods, data collection instruments, data analyses (statistics), and reporting and dissemination of findings. This book reminds readers to be cognizant of the need to "begin with the end in mind" and "know where you are going." This will allow readers to stay focused and guide their choice of proper research design and statistical methods based on the intent of the research. This cognitive mapping approach will allow students to unfold the connected branches of research and statistics systematically.

The Brief Visual Map of Research and Statistics for Social Workers (Figure 1.1) provides a schema for the research and statistics process, as well as the outline for this book. Users of this book can refer back to this map to spot and to chart their journey of learning. This whole process starts with the values and knowledge of the profession.

Values represent what we consider to be important and worthy. They are our preferences in our personal and professional lives. Values are about what is right and what is wrong. Value statements and questions often include the word "should." Social work values "service, social justice, dignity and worth of the person, importance

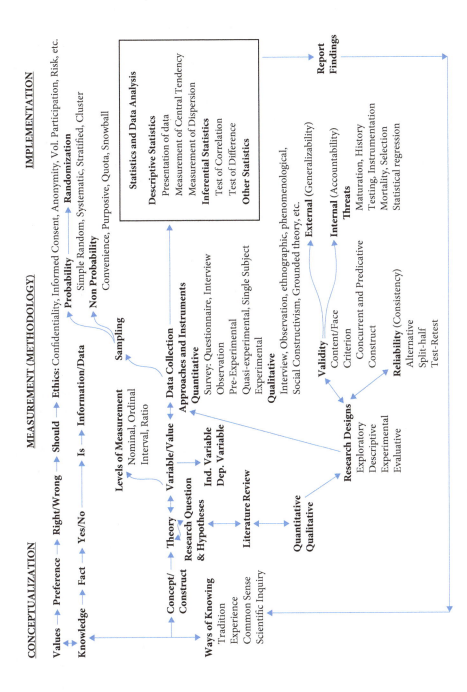

Figure 1.1. A Brief Visual Map of Research and Statistics for Social Work

of human relationship, integrity, and competence" (National Association of Social Workers [NASW], 2017, https://www.socialworkers.org/about/ethics/code-of-ethics/code-of-ethics-english). Ethics is our values in action. It operationalizes the abstract values into principles and standards. Professional organizations, such as the NASW, officially compile and adopt these values and standards, and they become the profession's code of ethics. The code states the mission, values, and standards of the profession. It sets the goals and expectations for its members and for society. It is one of the hallmarks of a profession.

Knowledge is about facts. Knowledge provides information, intelligence, and details of reality. It gives evidence to personal and social experiences on whether they are true or false. It seeks to be indisputable so that one could answer a question about facts with a "yes" or a "no." Factual statements and questions often include the word "is." Is the earth flat? No! Is the earth round? Yes! An exclusive and well-developed body of knowledge is another hallmark of a profession. What do social workers know exclusively that makes them professional? Who is contributing to the knowledge base for the social work profession? What should be included in this knowledge base?

Values and knowledge have a unique reciprocal relationship. Values set the parameter for knowledge, and knowledge helps actualize values. For example, social work believes in promoting social justice. As a result, social workers would advance their knowledge by learning, teaching, and researching human rights, equality, feminist perspectives, community organizing, negotiation, lobbying, and so on. Social workers are not required to learn about aerodynamics or oil portrait painting, for that is not the type of knowledge needed to achieve social justice within the context of social work practice. Values and knowledge are not static; they are evolving. When one changes, the other changes accordingly. The profession's values evolve as they are better informed by new knowledge, and the more refined values set new demands for new knowledge development.

Review the Brief Visual Map of Research and Statistics for Social Work (Figure 1.1) to get a sense of the research process and its associated key concepts.

SOCIAL WORK AND RESEARCH

"What is research? Why is it called research?" When my students ask me this question, I often jokingly tell them, "Because you searched, you found, you lost it, and you had to search again, that's why it is called re-search!" The fact is that research is a process of systematic inquiry and discovery. This process may lead us to discover answers to our questions, but it also may give us clues to many more new or unanswered questions. Research is one of those "the more you know, the more you don't know" marvels. Research is a never-ending process of inquiry for scientific truth.

Research is not a detached, unfamiliar, and unfriendly activity that we seldom do or a course that we take to graduate from social work programs. It is an activity that we do all the time throughout the day. Early in the morning, we turn on the TV, flip through several channels, and get an idea of what the weather and traffic are like. Based on this collective information, we decide what to wear and which route to take. Your best friend informs you that she was just diagnosed with celiac disease. You go on the web (or the library, of course!) and surf as many sites as you can to educate yourself so that you know what questions to ask or what suggestions to make. You need to take a research class. The two professors are Dr. Who and Dr. Hu. Which one should you take? You talk with students who had these professors before; you check them out online; you talk with them directly. Based on these surveys, you have collected a good amount of information to help you make an informed and somewhat confident decision. You may still have some doubts. "Should I just toss a coin and decide Who or Hu?" I hope you get the drift of my examples, and you probably could come up with thousands more. Research, then, is part of our everyday lives, and we all do it continuously. It is part of our everyday reality that we handle intuitively and is not foreign to any of us.

Very often, we use the terms research, social research, and social work research interchangeably. *Research* refers to a process of systematic investigation. It is a process of systematic inquiry about the social world through inductive and deductive reasoning. It uses logical and organized activities to explore, describe, and interpret social phenomena. The purpose is to accumulate dependable and unbiased data about social reality. *Social research* uses various quantitative and qualitative study methods; it is both a science and an art. In human services, research activities help to evaluate and improve professional practice and services for clients, develop a knowledge base for the profession, and ensure the service's accountability to society. When social research methodology is employed by social workers or applied to issues related to social work, it is conveniently called *social work research*.

Sources of Knowledge, Scientific Inquiry, and Social Work Professionalism

So what does research have to do with social work? Social work is a practice profession. Being a profession means that it has its own professional organization (i.e., NASW), code of ethics, altruistic mission autonomy to practice, and specific knowledge base.

These are the criteria similar to those set forth in 1915 by Abraham Flexner who had questioned the professional status of social work.

Commitment to the development of an exclusive knowledge base is one of the characteristics of the established professions and disciplines. Knowledge development activities are often grounded in scientific methodologies. Science expands knowledge through systematic data collection and analysis and involves methodologies that are logical, observable, repeatable, and objective. Logical, scientific knowledge, however, is only one of the sources for knowledge development. Atherton and Klemmack (1982) and Yuen (1999) discuss the four main sources of knowledge: (1) tradition, (2) experience, (3) common sense, and (4) scientific knowledge.

Tradition provides a type of knowledge that is based on custom, recurrence, and routine. It is often rooted in the past or ancient wisdom. It is used as a guide for understanding and navigating the world. "Tradition is customs and beliefs that have been handed down from generation to generation. It is not necessarily logical or rational, but it makes sense to people who practice it" (Yuen, 1999, p. 106). For example, when a child has the symptoms of a cold, his mother may be inclined to feed him a cup of chicken soup; the way she was treated by her parents. In spite of all the modern-day scientific studies that might dispute the medical efficacy of chicken soup, it is still the default choice both by the mother and the child for "treating" a cold. It is also very likely that when the child becomes a father, he will do the same for his child. Having a big turkey for Thanksgiving dinner is just the way it has been. It is not a matter of scientific discovery; it is just a custom—a dear custom that requires no scientific justifications. We have come to know and navigate the world through our traditions that are connected to our customs, cultures, and practices. Tradition and culture have a symbiotic reciprocal relationship in that they shape and form each other. Tradition exists before we do. It is, however, not static; it is an evolving entity that changes continuously.

Experience, although framed by one's tradition, is a subjective and personal account of events. "Experience is the person's firsthand observation. … Experience is unique and sometimes can only be understood by the individuals involved" (Yuen, 1999, p. 106). As a source of knowledge and as the base of our inductive learning (Yuen, Bein, & Lum, 2006), experience helps us establish our very own way of connecting and understanding the world around us. Through our own lens and our own hands, we gain knowledge of the world, reality, and ourselves. It is impossible to learn how to ride a bike by only reading a "how-to" book. It takes experience that includes trials and errors, scratched knees, disappointments, a bruised ego, and, eventually, successful attempts to develop and master the skills. It is about experiencing, practicing, and learning, as well as first-person involvement.

Conceptual and Practical Research and Statistics for Social Workers

Human experience, as we all know very well, can be easily biased. One's perceptions could be affected, among many things, by one's culture, socialization, and personality. Individuals construct their realities through their own experience, yet experience is subjective and has limited ability for generalization and inference. Moreover, Pardeck and Yuen (2001) caution particularly the kind of knowledge that does not result from direct perception but rather from inferences made about those perceptions. Take, for example, adolescent twin sisters are happy to see their dad coming home with their surprise morning treat. They reach in and realize it is a box of delicious donuts. One sister is very pleased that her loving dad has brought her favorite donuts, unhealthy as they may be! The other sister, however, is upset that her inconsiderate and somewhat mean father is teasing her again, for she is on a no-carb diet! Same family tradition, same genetic make-up, and same objective fact, but the father's actions result in different perceptions and different experiences that lead to a different knowledge of the world.

When knowledge is built on tradition and experience, it often blends into what is referred to as common sense. "Common sense is the combination of tradition and experience. Obviously, what is common sense for one person may not be for another person, particularly if the two people have different traditions and experiences" (Yuen, 1999, p. 107). It is contextual. Common sense for certain people with a particular background is not necessarily a shared common sense for another group. It is common sense for Americans that having a big dinner in November with turkey and all the fixings is likely to be their Thanksgiving dinner. It is, however, not at all common sense for a group of new immigrants to the United States. It is common sense for a long-time resident to avoid a certain street during rush hour, but it is not common sense for an out-of-town driver. Common sense is grounded in tradition, experience, conventional wisdom, and, unfortunately, sometimes prejudice.

Again, social work is a practice profession for which practice experience is absolutely essential. It is through the tradition of social work (i.e., respect for human diversity, advocacy for social justice, and accumulated practice wisdom) that social workers can develop their "professional common sense" (Yuen, 1999). This professional common sense allows us to understand our practice environment instinctively, know what to say and what to ask, know how to handle legal responsibilities, know how to handle ethical dilemmas, and alike. This professional common sense is related to what is commonly called "practice wisdom."

Having the tradition, experience, and professional common sense is not enough. Let's imagine a fairly typical neighborhood. A very helpful older lady who has lived in the neighborhood for many years has more tradition, experience, and common sense about life in general and the neighborhood than most of the recent social work graduates from prestigious universities. She knows more than anyone else about what is going on in the neighborhood. Some neighbors jokingly call her the honorary captain of the neighborhood watch committee. If asked, she always has some good advice for anything from how to bake a delicious cake to how to settle an upset stomach or a difficult family dispute. She is the all-around, go-to helper, a very kind, and wise lady who many of the neighbors love and respect. Her help comes from her heart and no one else can replicate it. She is a natural helper, but she is not a professional, a medical doctor, or a social worker. Her activities are based on her personal beliefs and subjective experience. However, her personal beliefs and subjective experience could certainly be further supplemented by objective and systematically proven scientific knowledge. "Scientific knowledge is developed mainly through logical and rational validations. It is not the source of absolute knowledge, but it provides the objective means of knowing in addition to the other more subjective ways of knowing" (Yuen, 1999, p. 107). Teaching and developing this scientifically proven exclusive knowledge is one of the missions of professional education programs. Students go to professional schools to acquire this knowledge.

How do medical doctors know things that only they know, and how do we come to trust their expertise and knowledge? The answer is because of their exclusive research-based knowledge combined with their touch of the art of healing. In this sense, research includes both empirically tested findings and those time-tested practice wisdoms. Medical research findings allow physicians to have a better understanding and proven ways to treat illnesses and to promote health. Similarly, social workers rely on research to improve their practice and contribute to the development of this exclusive knowledge base. This, in turn, undergirds the professional nature of social work. The development of this exclusive knowledge base is an area that social work has long been struggling to establish. It is, however, essential for the development of social work as a profession.

PRACTITIONERS AS RESEARCHERS AND RESEARCHERS AS PRACTITIONERS

Social workers are practitioners as well as thinkers. CSWE (2015) competency on "research-informed practice, practice-informed research" reflects the necessity of integrating practice and research. This is a goal that is critical for the profession, but it is not easily achievable.

It is difficult for practitioners who are busy helping clients and who may not have a good grip on research methods and statistics to engage in research. After all, research is not a reimbursable activity by the funding sources and, therefore, supported by the human service agencies. Moreover, there has not been much of a culture for social workers to evaluate their practice or to become involved in research activities. Research has often been regarded as the competitor of the time and resources used for direct service. Some agencies may have a research and development department that does most of the research. Unfortunately, many of them focus on gathering data for reporting purposes but not for intervention or practice improvement. Conversely, there are researchers in social work who are well versed in research methods and statistics but have no or very limited direct practice experience. For them, social work practice and knowledge development is pretty much an academic and intellectual exercise. The implications and applications of their academic research findings to social work practice are often unclear. At times, it is difficult to tell whether they are in social work or in psychology, sociology, or social policy. With practice approaches that are not supported by research and evidence, and with research activities that have no direct connection and implications to practice, social work activities would essentially become busy work for no justifiable reason and with no clear outcomes.

Social work has not yet adopted the "scientific-professional training model" (Royse, 2011, p. 6) as the field of psychology did following World War II. Doing research is, therefore, more of an afterthought than a regular expectation for many social work students and practitioners. Many are anticipating becoming professional social workers without being scientists who engage in the process of systematic or scientific inquiry (i.e., research). The common debates on whether social work is an art or a field of science always end up with the recognition that it is both. Effective social work combines research with the human elements and the artistic aspects of practice. Boehm (1961) reflected on the rising interest in strengthening the scientific base of social work practice and in establishing more clearly the identity of the social work profession. More than half a century later, Brekke (2012) asserted, "The scientific methodologies and the scientific knowledge relevant to social services have expanded dramatically in the last 30 years" (p. 455). However, "Using the two indicators of the total number of journals and the impact factors of those journals, it would appear that social work's contribution to that expanding scientific knowledge base has been relatively limited" (p. 455). The establishment of the scientific source of knowledge for social work is still very much a work in progress.

The sad reality is that while social work students and practitioners are not afraid of employing critical thinking and engaging in scientific inquiries, they may more likely be intimidated by the mathematics involved in research. Is it true that math and statistics are the roadblock to the development of scientific methodologies for social work? If so, math anxiety among social work students and practitioners is a barrier that needs to be overcome to advance the possibility of integrating research and practice (Lalayants, 2012; Maschi, Wells, Slater, MacMillan, & Ristow, 2013; Morgenshtern, Freymond, Hong, Adamowich, & Duffie, 2015; Pham & Tidd, 2014; Royse & Rompf, 1992). Beyond the possible math anxiety and the inertia to acting, the vast majority of the practicing social workers and social work academics are well aware of the need for this integration. They know that research is a key tool for knowledge development and practice effectiveness for the social work profession. In turn, practice is the source and the end of research. Research and practice share a symbiotic (live together) relationship that is both obligate (interdependent bond, dependent on each other to survive) and mutualistic (reciprocity, beneficial to both parties). This type of relationship is similar to bees and flowers in that they need each other to survive and to benefit each other.

In recent decades, the teaching and use of research and statistics in social work have evolved. It has gone beyond the simple application of general social research methodology to the envelopment of grounded theory and action research, the hailing of single-subject design, the promotion of evidence-based practice and research, the emphasis on program evaluation, and the increasing interest (and split) in qualitative postmodernism research and quantitative statistical approaches, such as structural equation modeling analysis. The teaching and learning of statistics have moved beyond rote memorization of statistics formulas and time-consuming hand calculations to our contemporary ability to process statistics with relevant software on one's laptop computer or tablet and to interpret the enormous analysis outputs. The debate and search for appropriate research methodologies (including statistics) for the profession will continue, but the key issue of promoting the integration of research and practice is an urgent one. "Practice-informed research and research-informed practice" are key for the profession to provide quality services to the community and for the advancement of the profession. It is a charge for every social worker, particularly the front-line social workers (i.e., BSW and MSW). Minimizing math anxiety and promoting research and statistical literacy and competency among everyday social workers will be our major challenges. This book intends to contribute to that effort.

A GENERAL OUTLINE OF THE SOCIAL RESEARCH PROCESS

Table 1.1 lists the general outline of the social research process. It starts with the very important step of deciding the research question and, thus, the appropriate hypothesis. A researcher then draws out the nature and design of the research process.

TABLE 1.1. General Outline of the Social Research Process

1. Research question, ethics, and the elements of research (the purpose, the quest)
   - What do I want to know? Why am I doing this? Why do I care?
   - Is it ethical? Is it feasible? Can it be researched?
   - What has been done, and what do people already know (literature review)?
   - Variables, conceptual and operational definitions

2. Research designs (the framework, the plan)
   - Qualitative and quantitative research designs, inductive and deductive learning
   - Exploratory, descriptive, experimental, and evaluative designs
   - Validity and reliability
   - Causation and correlation
   - Sampling

3. Research/data collection methods (approaches, the work)
   - Survey (questionnaire, interview)
   - Observation
   - Experiment, quasi-experimental study
   - Single-subject study, case study
   - Secondary data, focus group, expert interview, etc.

4. Data collection instruments (the tools)
   - Questionnaire
   - Interview guide
   - Observational guide
   - Field notes and others

5. Data analysis (the "crime scene investigation" [CSI])
   The inquiry:
   - No hypothesis
   - Research hypothesis
   - Null hypothesis: reject versus fail to reject
   - Alternative hypothesis

   The objective and handy mathematical tools—statistics:
   - Categories: parametric, nonparametric
   - Types: presentation of data, descriptive, inferential
   - Some interesting terms:
     o Test of significance: test of association, test of difference
     o Level of significance, confidence level, $p < .10$
     o Degrees of freedom

6. Reporting out (dissemination of findings)

7. New research questions and projects

Specific research and data collection approaches or methods are planned, which include the associated data collection tools used to collect the appropriate information and data. Applying the proper data analysis technologies, including statistics and computer software, such as the Statistical Package for the Social Sciences

(SPSS), the researcher summarizes and applies the study findings to answer the research question.

CONCLUSION

This chapter explained the importance of research and statistics in social work. Social work research and social work practice are two interlocked aspects of the profession. Their reciprocal growth is vital to the future of social work. A schematic map of research and statistics (Figure 1.1) and a general outline of the social research process (Table 1.1) lay out the progression and orientation of how this book approaches research and statistics in social work. Very often, students who study research and statistics find themselves lost in the middle of all the terms, methods, and calculations. It is the intent of these schemas and outlines, as well as tables and figures in the following chapters, to provide learners with useful frameworks that they can use to locate their studies within the contexts of research and statistics in social work. They also highlight readers' progressive competency and learning in different aspects of research and statistics.

PART 1

SOCIAL RESEARCH

2

RESEARCH QUESTION AND LITERATURE REVIEW (THE PURPOSE AND THE QUEST)

QUESTION CONCEPTUALIZATION

Many researchers consider coming up with a good research question as being half the battle for a successful research project. In fact, the process and importance of identifying the right question to ask is itself a valid research question. One has to acknowledge that there is no single right research question; there are only good or appropriate research questions. There is also no single research question that could cover everyone's concerns and interests. A good research question should at least be clear, specific, researchable, feasible, relevant, ethical, and significant to the researcher or society. "What is the correlation between spirituality and help-seeking behaviors among women in a rural community?" is probably a good research question. However, "Is eternal life reserved only for those who are religious?" could be an important question for some people but is not a good researchable question for social scientists.

The quality of the research question affects the merits of the findings. Later in this chapter, in the discussions of various types of hypotheses, examples of research questions are further described. It is, however, important to ask a question that can be tested by the research process. Ask about people's attitudes toward recycling but not determining whether recycling increases one's chance for reincarnation.

In most situations, try not to ask dichotomized questions that force a simple yes-or-no answer. "What contributes to older adults' abilities to stay in their own homes and avoid premature institutionalization?" is better than "Is it generally better for older adults to stay in their own homes?"

Also, try not to ask the obvious questions: "Do homeless people experience more stress?" "Does the absence of one parent have an impact on children?" These questions remind me of other self-evident and even silly questions: "Were you there until you left?" "Were you alone or by yourself?" "How far apart were the cars when they collided?"

There are researchable questions and there are nonresearchable and improbable questions. A listener of the National Public Radio program *Car Talk* program asked a great question that left me wondering, "Do two people who don't know what they are talking about know more or less than one person who doesn't know what he's talking about?" (*Car Talk*, 2014). I believe this is an improbable question best left answered by philosophers.

Sources of Research Questions

Social researchers, ideally, are inquisitive; they are problem solvers, and they are knowledge seekers. Every human experience possesses the potential for investigation—and therefore is a source for research questions. "Have you ever thought about …?" seems to be a good beginning for a wonderful research relationship! Generally, there are three main sources:

1. Professional interest and curiosity
2. Personal experience and concerns
3. Programmatic requirements and evaluation

Researchers may come up with research questions that are merely a result of professional curiosity. Over the course of one's practice, observation of certain unique patterns, trends, or even mysteries may become the basis for a research question. A human service provider may be interested in finding out what contributes to the ability of some of her clients coming from extremely high-risk environments to not only beat the odds but also excel in their lives.

Personal experience and history often inspire research questions. A social worker who has personal experience or knowledge of domestic violence may be very interested in effective helping strategies when working with children from families with a history of violence. A Hispanic social worker may be particularly interested in researching issues related to the Hispanic community.

Reporting or programmatic requirements, although at times unpleasant, could possibly be the key reasons for doing evaluative research, such as needs assessment and program evaluation. The research questions may, therefore, be on the utilization, effectiveness, and efficiency of the program. For example, a homeless advocate has seen many homeless individuals forego overnight shelter because most shelters do not allow them to bring their pets in during their stay. This advocate researcher might have a clear programmatic interest in mind. The researcher may want to first get a better understanding of the service needs and then find ways that could accommodate or resolve this dilemma.

A social work researcher may formulate a general question for his research: What are the family and social adjustment challenges for recently returned veterans? Upon further exploration on this topic, factoring in the issues of feasibility and resources, and considering the most suitable research design, he revises and narrows down his research question. It is now, "What effects does deployment have on spousal relationships among veteran families not living on military bases in Northern California?" or "How do veteran mothers communicate with their children on their post-deployment mental health challenges?" From there, more specific and related "subquestions" could be developed and become the basis for the study's research hypotheses. The selection of a research question is both an evolving process and the results of critical thinking and the reality of the research environment.

Two important questions that I always ask about a social work research question is, "Why do I care as a social worker?" and "What does it mean to our service recipients?" We may wonder why the sky is blue and the ocean is green. The answers are not "just because" but have a lot to do with the science of light and molecules and many other scientific reasons. This type of "wondering aloud" question may be interesting and lead to some important information, but it is not the type of research topic for social workers and students to focus on. Social work research questions need to be of significance to the profession and have implications for our services and service recipients. Why the sky is blue may not be a social work concern, but the effects of a gray, gloomy, and harsh winter on elderly clients who live alone is a social work research question.

Types of Research Questions

A research question sets the course for the research study. How the question is asked or how it is being phrased affects the contents and the nature of the study. The research question lays out the goals of the study, dictates the review of literature, and determines the methodology employed. The three common types of research questions include the following:

1. Description
2. Relationship
3. Causality

Descriptive questions ask "What happened?" "What is the situation?" "What's going on?" "What are people's opinions?" "How would the respondents describe the condition?" They are used to depict the statuses being studied. Surveys and observations are usually involved to portray the state of affairs accurately and adequately. What are the common challenges for caregivers? What do people do when they are being asked for money by panhandlers? How did social workers vote in the last presidential election? How serious is bullying against lesbian, gay, bisexual, transgender (LGBT) youth in a local high school?

Relational questions include both correlational and comparative questions. Correlational questions ask how two or more variables are related. Comparative questions ask how two or more variables are different. They ask, "How are they related?" "How do they influence each other?" "How are they different?" "In what ways?" Does the age of the children in foster care affect their likelihood of being adopted? Does childhood exposure to crime and gang violence increase their chance of being involved in the criminal justice system when they grow up? Do social work students and criminal justice students differ in their ideas about how to address the sex trafficking problem?

Causal questions attempt to address the causes or reasons for certain outcomes. They ask, "Why did this happen?" "What brings about this result?" These questions aim to give answers to what variables cause or affect the outcomes. Does cognitive behavioral therapy bring about the most desirable treatment outcomes for clients experiencing depression? How have community organizing efforts brought about a change in the zoning laws to save this neighborhood from gentrification? To reach the level of answering a causal question, one should have a good description of the situation (descriptive question) and the relationships and differences among related variables (relational question). Causal questions are considered high-level questions that encompass both descriptive and relational questions.

LITERATURE REVIEW: WHAT HAS BEEN DONE AND WHAT DO PEOPLE ALREADY KNOW

"What do you know?" "What should you know?" "What is known?" "What is the current state of knowledge of a subject matter?" These questions are immeasurably easier to address with the advances of information technology over the past 20 years, but they remain crucial to the research enterprise. Reviewing available academic writings, exploring scholarly arguments and research findings, and gaining insights into others' experiences allows us to become educated researchers. This helps us to determine and chart the course of our research projects.

Purpose of the Literature Review

The literature review for a research project is an opportunity for the researcher to develop and to show a genuine understanding of the subject matter and its related issues. This is not a collection of cut-and-pasted information from unverified sources or personal beliefs. It is a well-developed examination of relevant information from credible sources to establish or support the importance and the design of the research project. These sources may include peer-reviewed journal articles, scholarly books, government and other official reports, online databases, and credible journalistic and academic reports.

The purpose of a literature review for a research project is to achieve the following:

1. Identify and demonstrate the current and prior scholarship related to the issues being studied.
2. Describe how they contribute to the understanding of the issues.
3. Delineate how they relate to each other and the issues in terms of similarity, disagreement, distinctiveness, and controversy.
4. Present new ways to interpret and expand prior research.
5. Show areas in which knowledge is lacking—gaps in the literature.
6. Explain the theoretical foundation of the research and the chosen research strategies.
7. Indicate how the review has informed the development and implementation of your research project.
8. Specify how your research is located within the context of the literature reviewed.

A literature review is a chance for researchers to demonstrate how they can integrate information with academic rigor and professional quality into a well-developed narrative that informs the project. It is an integrated narrative, not a running list of annotated bibliographies.

Envisioning the Literature Review—Jigsaw Puzzle and Upside-Down Triangle

"Where do I start?" "How much is enough?" "There is so much (or little) information!" Writing a literature review can be a very confusing process. Here is how a jigsaw puzzle example may be helpful. Doing a puzzle is always a perplexing event. Experienced jigsaw puzzlers look first at the end product (the picture on the front of the box!), sort pieces by their similar characteristics, start building the borders, and fill in the pieces. Writing literature reviews is very similar to putting together a jigsaw puzzle, except that we may not have the completed picture in front of us; we may not even have all of the pieces (the needed information), and we seemingly always question whether our research topic is the one that we really want.

The researcher must first have a general idea of what he wants to achieve (i.e., the likely completed picture and the possible end product). Second, he must set the borders or the parameters. With these completed, the researcher has the boundary and the criteria to decide what information should be included or discarded. Without prior sorting and differentiation, the writer can very likely get lost or overloaded with mountains of information that could impede the writing process. Third, the writer should group all related information together, connect the dots, and draw his conclusion. Essentially, the researcher must imagine what the finished picture is like, set up the framework, identify the main themes, develop the theme or arguments through the grouping of related information, link the arguments, and form the conclusions that support the importance and necessity of the proposed research.

People build their puzzles by putting down one or a few pieces at a time. A researcher should never try to build the whole literature review in his head with complete details of exactly which piece goes where. Many of us have tried that grandiose and noble approach before, but not too many have been successful. So the researcher should start writing—with the end in mind and within the temporary structure—rewriting, regrouping, rethinking, rewriting, rewriting, rewriting, rewriting, and then STOP.

"Stop" because researchers are not going to write the final say on the subject matter for humankind. Their literature reviews are not intended to set the highest standard and save the world from ignorance. When it is good enough to support their claims, it is time to stop and move on to the next part of the project. How does one know whether it is good enough? Certainly, having someone else, perhaps even

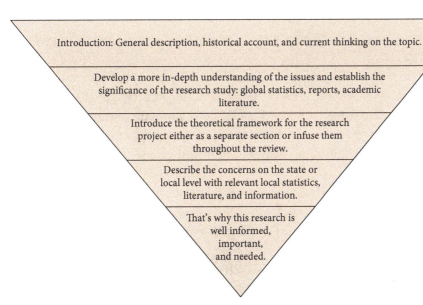

The triangle (read top to bottom) contains:

Introduction: General description, historical account, and current thinking on the topic.

Develop a more in-depth understanding of the issues and establish the significance of the research study: global statistics, reports, academic literature.

Introduce the theoretical framework for the research project either as a separate section or infuse them throughout the review.

Describe the concerns on the state or local level with relevant local statistics, literature, and information.

That's why this research is well informed, important, and needed.

Figure 2.1. The Upside-Down Triangle of Literature Review Conceptualization

experts, review it and give feedback will help. It is also a good idea to set the literature review aside and read it again later to see whether it is comprehensive, has a focus, and is convincing.

Another way to conceptualize the literature review section is by viewing it as an upside-down triangle (see Figure 2.1). It is particularly useful when the researcher is trying to assess or establish a social need that will be studied in the research project. As the literature review gets narrower, the arguments for the needs and concerns of the research project population are demonstrated.

Writing the Literature Review

Depending on the researcher's writing style and the nature of the research, a literature review could be accomplished in different formats using different logics. Many researchers use software programs, such as Endnotes, to assist in the review and writing of the literature review and its references. The following outline provides a general guideline for the development of a literature review.

1. Define the purpose, scope, and boundary of the literature review. Ask "What would be the function of this literature review for this research project?" "Would this research be different if no literature review were complete?"

2. Conduct a literature search by key words, issues and topics, time period, authors, focus, etc.
3. Complete an overview of identified literature. Group or assign them into categories. The categories may include historical accounts, theoretical foundations, methodological considerations, summaries, and distinct and contradictory perspectives.
4. The compiled literature could also be cross-categorized by topics, such as issues, key terms, trends and directions, statistics, authors, viewpoints, and research implications.
5. Review, analyze, and prioritize literature. Take notes and highlight key words and important quotes. Establish links and relevance to the research project.
6. Summarize these reviews and formulate discussions of how they relate to each other and the topics being studied. Point out how they influence the focus, design, and implementation of the research project. Support these discussions with proper references and citations.
7. Identify literature gaps and limitations of the literature review.
8. Conclude how the review relates to the research. Explain how it helps establish the significance of the research and informs the relevance and logic of the research.

Literature Review—Creating a Synthesis

A researcher thoroughly reviewed each of the articles identified for the literature review. He described them one at a time in detail. Each of the reviews was independently written. They were nicely arranged and listed one after the other. Unfortunately, this describes a listed review of extant literature, but it is not necessarily a literature review. It may give the readers an impression of reading a chain of annotated bibliographies.

A literature review should be a synthesis of the literature. It is an integrated summary and discussion of the literature, not a simple listing or reshuffling of the available research. It should be topic—or theme—focused, not individual literature focused. Because it is topic focused, the researcher is very likely to find more than one article addressing that topic. Citing references of several authors who have similar or contradictory views will automatically break up the likelihood of having a chain of annotated bibliographies. The researcher is employing multiple literatures to support or dispute the main argument. A literature review is an essay, a narrative of the current knowledge, including both similar and opposing views. It is an integrated narrative of what the academics, the professionals, and the society know about the topic. It is not a summary with bullet lists. The key words for a quality literature review are synthesis, integration, and critical evaluation.

What to Write When Very Little Has Been Written?

First, search again. Yes, someone somewhere somehow has paid some attention to your topic. It is possible but not likely that you are the first one to set eyes on this important topic. Look again. Ask the question differently. Try different literature search approaches. Use different databases or a different library. Apply different keywords, or simply consult your professor or colleagues. After conducting exhaustive searches, if, in fact, there is very little research available, then you should be excited because you have hit on something potentially neglected by the academics and the professionals. You have a discovery.

When I research a topic that I have found very little literature on, I tend to write out my efforts in the following manner:

"Although ABCD is generally recognized as a serious issue by the public/practitioners/media/academics, it has not attracted much attention from the researchers and scholars in the academic world and in publications. Several internet searches on databases, including Social Science Index (ProQuest), Academic Search Premier (EBSCO), and PsycINFO (EBSCO) using key words such as EFGH, IJKL, and MNOP yield a total of 15 articles published between 1998 and 2018. Among them, only six have direct relevance to the current research. The lack of awareness of this issue and the tendency to only include it under some general and universal discussions further hamper the effort of properly addressing this important issue. The proposed research study attempts to highlight this critical issue and contribute to the body of knowledge regarding how this issue is being understood and addressed. Among the limited published literature, they suggest that …"

In essence, this shows that (a) there is not much yet published on the topic, (b) that I have consulted the databases that seemed relevant (and I am open to learning if I've missed something), and (c) based on what I have found (and have *not* found), I think my study is an important one because it will fill the knowledge gap. Try to avoid saying, "I could not find anything." Describe what you did academically and present the evidence to support your conclusion that this topic really is worth studying given that not much has been written about it.

Literature Review as Qualitative Research

Literature reviews should be presented in an organized and thematic manner and so should the findings of qualitative research using systematic content analysis, grounded theory, Q-sorting, scoping analysis, meta-analysis, etc. The difference between a literature review (narrative) and a qualitative study of the literature is qualitative research's clearly declared and implemented research methodology.

An extensive literature review is essential and necessary for all research projects. When the review is done methodologically with the literature being used as the data, it becomes a qualitative research project. An extensive literature review that has a clear methodology for data sources, data collection, and data analysis could become a research project using systematic review. In this context, the data could be published documents, articles, official reports, pictures, transcripts of interviews, and other structured records. When this statistical approach is used to combine data derived from systematic reviews, it will lead to meta-analysis.

CONCLUSION

What are you interested in studying? What are your questions? Why are they important? What do we know about this topic of interest? How do you build upon this current knowledge to refine your research questions and research methodology? This chapter provided explanations and practical guidelines to identify, formulate, and refine social work–related research questions and methodologies. These become the foundation for the design and implementation of a well-informed and logical research project.

HUMAN DIVERSITY, ETHICAL CONSIDERATIONS, AND PROTECTION OF HUMAN SUBJECTS

HUMAN DIVERSITY AND CULTURAL COMPETENCY IN SOCIAL WORK RESEARCH

Well-developed research approaches and findings equip social workers with respectful ways of "looking into" the lives of people of diverse cultures instead of the more intrusive and not necessarily respectful ways of "looking at" such populations (Gould, 1995; Leigh, 1983). Social workers look into the lives of clients both objectively and from the clients' perspectives. Social workers must develop habits of heart and mind that enable them to approach the world in all its diversity, with respect and openness. Diversity in this context often goes beyond cultural or ethnic diversity. It could include the multiplicities in areas such as individual ability, spirituality, socio-economic conditions, gender, sexual orientation, and life experience.

Human Diversity, Cultural Competency, and Cultural Humility

Yuen (2003) discusses the different extents of learning and commitment to diversity by distinguishing several major terms, including cultural awareness, cultural sensitivity, cultural diversity, cultural pluralism, and multiculturalism:

> The awareness of cultural diversity or human diversity suggests the acknowledgment of the existence of people of

25

Francis K. O. Yuen, Excerpts from "Critical Concerns for Family Health Practice," *Family Health Social Work Practice: A Knowledge and Skills Case Book*, ed. Franis K. O. Yuen, Gregory J. Skibinski, and John T. Pardeck. Copyright © 2003 by Taylor & Francis Group. Reprinted with permission.

different cultures. People who accept cultural diversity do not remain culturally apathetic and are well aware of different cultures. ... Starting at the level of cultural awareness, individuals of different backgrounds who are culturally aware interact in a manner that is sensitive to one another's culture. ... Often, these cultural sensitivity skills can be well performed behaviorally; they are, however, no guarantee of attitude changes. ... Cultural pluralism implies the recognition, the intention, and the practice of working with people of different backgrounds. It involves the advancement from cultural awareness to cultural sensitivity and the development of the ability to effectively interact cross-culturally. Cultural pluralism treats all cultures as equal and valid and asserts that all should be respected. ... Multiculturalism not only recognizes differences and similarities among diverse cultures but also requires a framework of thinking that is inclusive and transcultural. This framework demands the ability to develop beyond cultural sensitivity to the level of cultural competency in interacting with people of various backgrounds. It requires one to think and act not only from the ethnic or cultural specific perspective but also from a multiple and collective perspective that allows one to conceive of common good and understanding among all people. (pp. 22–23)

In recent years, the concept of *cultural humility* has gained much attention, and it is distinctive from the concept of cultural competency. Tervalon and Murray-Garcia (1998) proposed the concept of cultural humility for medical education. "Cultural humility incorporates a lifelong commitment to self-evaluation and self-critique, to redressing the power imbalances in the patient-physician dynamic, and to developing mutually beneficial and nonpaternalistic clinical and advocacy partnerships with communities on behalf of individuals and defined populations" (p. 117). Hook, Davis, Owen, Worthington, and Utsey (2013) conceptualize cultural humility as the "ability to maintain an interpersonal stance that is other-oriented (or open to the other) in relation to aspects of cultural identity that are most important to the [person]" (p. 2). Ortega and Coulborn Faller (2011) advocate for the employment of cultural humility to compliment cultural competence. Social workers are to engage with and be inclusive of clients' cultural expression in service delivery. Tervalon and Murray-Garcia (1998) describe cultural competence as a "body of knowledge" and cultural humility as more of a "suitable goal" (p. 177). Hohman (2013) views cultural humility as an openness to collaboration with and learning from clients. Hohman also raises the question, how do we know we are culturally competent and respectful enough to meet the needs of the individual client?

Effective social work practice and research with diverse populations calls for cultural competency beyond cultural awareness, sensitivity, or cross-cultural communication. It requires the researcher to respect the inherent values and contributions of different cultures in this culturally pluralistic society. Consequently, important cultural competency and cultural humility issues for research and practice may include the following: development of study samples that are representative of the community or population under study, declaration of the limitations and generalizability of the findings to other groups, or being cognizant of the topics and the findings of studies and their implications.

Stereotype, Prejudice, Discrimination, and Oppression

Several key terms—*stereotype, prejudice, discrimination,* and *oppression*—are often used in social work literature. Social work researchers should become mindful of these concepts and their implications for research. Yuen (2003) states the following:

> The term *stereotype* is the oversimplification and overgeneralization of a particular group of individuals based on few characteristics. It is an ill-informed knowledge that may include both positive and negative attributes of the group. For example, a stereotype exists that Asian American students do well in school, excel at math, but do not have the capacity to be good managers. *Prejudice* is a negative attitude that is based on the stereotypical knowledge. This attitude is one's belief that may or may not turn into discriminatory actions. However, when one acts out the prejudice and violates the civil rights or human rights of any individuals, then that is *discrimination.* An employer who has a prejudice against Asian Americans as managers, hurtful as it may seem, simply has a personally held negative attitude. When the employer refuses to hire or to promote any qualified Asian Americans as managers, then discrimination has taken place. When the discriminatory behaviors are being act out in an organized manner at the system wide or societal level, a situation of *oppression* has occurred. The happenings of discrimination and oppression have forced the situation beyond personal virtue and then become legal, social, and civic concerns. (p. 27)

Discrimination involves behaviors that are acquired or learned. Efforts aimed at challenging stereotypes and questioning one's prejudices are the initial step in overcoming discrimination. Part of the difficulty in overcoming discrimination is the denial and ignorance from both sides of the issue. The interactions, if any, between both sides are often defensive, emotionally charged, and political. Social work research could be a tool for addressing the myths, identifying the truth, generating support for the truth, and, hopefully, attaining genuine mutual acceptance and respect.

Social work research contributes to the improvement of appreciation and understanding of diversity in society. It is a tool for social change. Change usually takes place at three different levels: knowledge, attitude, and behaviors. Knowledge is about what one knows; attitude is about what one believes; behavior is about what one does. While knowledge change may bring about attitude and behavioral changes, in practice, this may not always be the case. To a certain extent, each of them could exist independently. For example, it is common knowledge that tobacco use causes many health problems. It is, however, surprising to still discover a few health care providers standing around the back doors of hospitals and medical clinics taking their break and smoking cigarettes. Many of them have expert and in-depth knowledge and experience about the damage caused by tobacco use and the related health problems. They also have a rather negative attitude toward such use. They are, however, behaviorally having trouble quitting smoking in spite of having tried various smoking cessation methods.

ETHICAL CONSIDERATIONS AND PROTECTION OF HUMAN SUBJECTS

Good research should also be ethical research when involving human subjects, particularly vulnerable populations, such as children or other socially identifiable populations. There are several major ethical considerations in developing research questions and their associated research designs. Among the ethical considerations are confidentiality, anonymity, voluntary participation, risks and benefits, and informed consent. In government agencies, universities, research institutions, or established organizations, a system is often in place to safely guide the ethical concerns of research. A main component of such a system is the use of the Human Subjects Review Committee (HSRC) or the Institutional Review Board (IRB). Within these organizations, all research projects are expected to be reviewed and approved before the research process begins.

Social work researchers need to consider the ethical implications and effects of their research activities carefully. The researchers' curiosity does not give them the excuse to tamper with the rights and well-being of their research respondents. Let's consider the following scenarios and see if you can point out some of the ethical concerns:

1. Two social work students disguised themselves as homeless and spent two weeks at a homeless camp for their class project. One of the homeless individuals mentioned that he hated his ex-wife, who lived in their old residence, and wished her dead. He had acquired a gun recently. The students decided to stay silent because they did not want to blow their covers.
2. A new social worker joined several Alcoholics Anonymous groups for a month to observe the dynamics of these groups and to learn about the lives of the people who go to the meetings. He never declared his true identity and intentions to the groups. He wrote up his experience and findings in an article intended for publication in a local newspaper.
3. A school social work intern tried to explore the prevalence of sexual assault among teens. She asked the freshman high school students in the friendship group that she led to complete a one-page survey questionnaire. The survey included a question that asked, "Have you ever been sexually assaulted?"
4. A social work professor wanted to study the experience of depression among college students. He distributed and collected a Depression Assessment Scale as a class assignment from his 30 Introduction to Social Work students. He wanted to make sure he could follow-up with them if they were depressed. He asked the students to put their names down on the questionnaires.
5. A social worker in an assisted nursing care facility was interested in whether older adults who had chronic illnesses considered euthanasia an option. In her daily rounds at the facility, she asked each one of her clients, "Have you thought about assisted suicide?"

Historical and Significant Events in the Protection of Human Subjects

Over the decades, internationally and in the United States, there have been many incidents that involved the improper use of human subjects in research. The principles for the protection of human subjects were finally outlined in the 1978 *Belmont Report* (National Commission for the Protection of Human Subjects of Biomedical and Behavioral Research, 1978). Since 1981, Title 45, Code of Federal Regulations, Part 46: Protection of Human Subjects (45 CFR 46) rules have been applied to all U.S. Department of Health and Human Services (2009)–supported research in the United States.

IMPERIAL JAPANESE AND NAZI GERMANY (WORLD WAR II)

During World War II, the Imperial Japanese Army and doctors conducted "live experiments with dissection, dismemberment, and bacteria inoculation on prisoners of wars" (Kim, 2012, p. 4). They were Chinese, Korean, Mongolians and allied civilians. However, no formal investigation of this atrocity was taken place and immunity was given by the United States to the Japanese military in exchange for protecting information from the Soviet Union (Kim, 2012).

During that time, Nazis were using concentration camp prisoners in various cruel experiments. They were "placing victims in vacuum chambers with low air pressure and a lack of oxygen in order to determine the health effects on pilots at extremely high altitudes" (Kim, 2012, p. 4). "Subjects were immersed for hours in tubs of ice water, fed nothing but salt water for days, and experimented upon with techniques for battlefield medicine" (Kim, 2012, pp. 4–5). In 1947, 23 Nazi doctors and scientists were put on trial in Nuremberg for their unethical treatment of victims in concentration camps. The code that was used to judge the defendants was known as the Nuremberg Code, which highlighted the need for informed consent and the absence of coercion. In 1953, the World Medical Association was tasked with putting the Nuremberg Code into practice, which resulted in the formation of the Declaration of Helsinki in 1964. The Declaration of Helsinki has been revised several times since 1964. It advocates for a systematic and independent approach to address ethical practice in research. This approach has evolved into the establishment and use of IRB in the United States and internationally (Breault, 2006; Kim, 2012).

HAVASUPAI INDIAN DNA STUDY (1990s)

As late as the 1990s, members of the Havasupai Indians in the Grand Canyon gave their DNA samples to researchers from Arizona State University. They wanted to find "genetic clues to the tribe's devastating rate of diabetes. But they learned that their blood samples had been used to study many other things, including mental illness and theories of the tribe's geographical origins that contradict their traditional stories" (Harmon, 2010, para. 2). The Havasupai Tribe filed a lawsuit against the university in 2004. "The lawsuit articulated concerns about lack of informed consent, violation of civil rights through mishandling of blood samples, unapproved use of data, and violation of medical confidentiality" (National Congress of American Indians, n.d., para. 2.). The lawsuit ended in an out-of-court settlement in 2010.

There are many incidents of ethics controversies in research activities that involve human subjects. The Tuskegee Syphilis Study and the Tearoom Trade Study are widely used examples in social work research education.

TUSKEGEE SYPHILIS STUDY (1932–1972)

In 1932, medical workers from the U.S. Public Health Service recruited 600 unsuspecting and poorly educated black males in Tuskegee, Alabama, in Macon County for a government study. In return for their participation, they received free medical checkups, hot meals, and medical treatment for minor illnesses (Science Museum, n.d.). Among them, 399 were diagnosed with latent syphilis and 201 were not infected (Associated Press, 2017). Although penicillin had become a standard treatment for syphilis in 1947, the men who had "bad blood" (a euphemism for syphilis), as they were told, researchers withheld the proper medical treatment. Instead, they were given placebos, such as aspirin or mineral supplements for their "bad blood." The purpose of the study was to find out whether syphilis affected black males differently than white males (Center for Disease Control and Prevention, n.d.; Science Museum, n.d.). This medical study remained a secret from these men and their families for 40 years until it was exposed in the Associated Press's *Washington Star* on July 26, 1972, when the study ended (Associated Press, 2017; Georgetown University, n.d.). During that time, 40 wives had been infected and 19 children were born with congenital syphilis. Only 72 of the original participants were still alive (Science Museum, n.d.) However, it was not until nearly 65 years later, in 1997, that President Bill Clinton apologized for the government's role in the study. The exposure resulted in a $9-million settlement. For living participants at that time, each received $37,500, and heirs of the deceased who did not have a syphilis diagnosis received $5,000. This study contributed to the mistrust of African Americans toward medical trials, which is known as the "Tuskegee effect" (Associated Press, 2017).

TEAROOM TRADE STUDY (1965–1970)

From 1965 to 1968, sociologist Laud Humphreys conducted his ethnographic dissertation study on men who had impersonal sex with men (Humphreys, 1970). He was a doctoral student at Washington University in St. Louis, Missouri. His dissertation was published in 1970. Humphreys wanted to understand the personal motives and public lives of these men who sought anonymous homosexual sex in public restrooms of city parks or along highways. These restrooms were known as "tearooms." He volunteered to be the "watch queen" who warned the men during sexual acts if anyone was approaching. Humphreys passed himself off as a voyeur; he was allowed to observe more than 100 sexual encounters. He disclosed his true identity to some of the men and interviewed them. In other situations, he recorded their car license plate numbers and tracked down where they lived. A year later, he disguised himself as a researcher conducting a public health survey, and he interviewed those men in their homes. In the 1960s, homosexual acts were still considered illegal criminal acts. Humphreys's notes from observing illegal behaviors and interviewing those who committed the acts could, therefore, be subpoenaed. He had put himself and the people he observed in legal jeopardy and personal chaos (DuBois, 2008; SexInfo Online, n.d.). In spite of the serious concerns of informed consent, confidentiality, privacy, risks, and entering research subjects' homes under false pretenses, his study dispelled some of the stereotypes about men who have sex with other men. Humphreys found only 14% of these men identified themselves as gay; 24% as bisexual, happily married, and economically secure; another 24% as singles; and 54% as outwardly heterosexual married men. The Tearoom Trade debates will continue. However, these debates have generated new discussions and findings that could further advance our understanding of ourselves and the disputes of the ethics of research.

CONFIDENTIALITY

Confidentiality is about how to treat data that is collected as classified information that will not be shared with entities that are inessential or indirectly related to the research. Confidentiality denotes researchers' respect of respondents' privacy and of the responses the respondents provide. While they are related topics, privacy is different than confidentiality. Privacy refers to one's rights and freedom to withhold information related to oneself from the public. Confidentiality refers to the trust and understanding that one's private or identifying information will be appropriately secured and not improperly disclosed.

Confidentiality, however, is not an absolute standard. Human service providers need to share work-related information about the service recipients with their supervisors or agencies. Researchers who are mandated reporters are required to report possible abuse and neglect. Documentation and workers' knowledge of certain issues acquired through their research activities may be subject to being subpoenaed by the court. On the other hand, confidentiality is not always relevant to all research projects involving humans. For example, it may not apply to the observation of people's public behaviors in public places.

Section 301(d) of the Public Health Service Act, 42 U.S.C. §241(d), clearly states the requirements of confidentiality in research:

> The Secretary [of the Department of Health and Human Services] may authorize persons engaged in biomedical, behavioral, clinical, or other research (including research on mental health, and on the use and effect of alcohol and other psychoactive drugs) to protect the privacy of individuals who are the subject of such research by withholding from all persons not connected with the conduct of such research the names or other identifying characteristics of such individuals. Persons so authorized to protect the privacy of such individuals may not be compelled in any Federal, State, or local civil, criminal, administrative, legislative, or other proceedings to identify such individuals. (Research and Investigations Generally, 2011)

In addition to respecting the privacy of the respondents and minimizing unnecessary mishandling of data, researchers should be careful in deciding what information they want to collect. A simple rule is to ask only for information related to the research. (This topic is further elaborated later on in this book under Table of Specifications in Chapter 9: Data Collection Instruments and Development.) If the age or marital status of the respondent is a variable that is not essential or relevant to the study, then it should not be included. If it is being asked just because the researcher thinks it may be interesting to know, then, it is not an appropriate question. The researcher's personal curiosity is not a sufficient reason for the possible invasion of a respondent's privacy.

ANONYMITY

Anonymity refers to the secrecy and protection of the identity of respondents. The most common form of anonymity is when researchers have no information about the identities of the respondents. Certain research methods, such as using large-scale surveys with no respondents' names or minimal respondent information, could make identifying the respondents almost impossible. An agency providing researchers with copies of service records and documents that have identifying information blacked out or eliminated is another way to secure anonymity.

Another form of anonymity is within the data and the findings. Even though researchers or users know who the respondents are, they cannot tell who provided what information. In many research situations, respondents are captive audiences or have prior contacts with the researchers. For example, a teacher should know that the course evaluation data are only coming from the students enrolled in a particular class. She, however, cannot tell which students gave which comments because there are no or very few personal identifiers included.

There are situations in which names or other identifying information is necessary for the study. For example, researchers of a follow-up study need to know who the respondents are to collect additional data from the same respondents. An agency may also wish to trace back to respondents if victimization or the safety of respondents is at stake. Usually, a third party, such as the agency administration or supervisors, would serve as a buffer or a clearinghouse. This third party will provide the needed study data to the researchers with no identifying information or with pseudonyms, which could simply be the assigned numbers. In the meantime, it keeps a list of the respondents and their information, including the pseudonyms, in a location where the researchers have no access. The list is, however, available for the third party to use in case tracing back is warranted.

VOLUNTARY PARTICIPATION

Participation in a research project, including program evaluation, should be voluntary. Potential respondents are free to participate without being concerned about any real or implied threat or inappropriate reward. Perhaps college students are asked to participate in a research project conducted by the course instructor before the course grade is assigned. Although they are told that participation is voluntary, they may be concerned that nonparticipation will affect their grades. That is because the instructor is taking notes on who participates and who does not. In another class, the instructor gives extra points to students who participate. It is clear that students are under undue influence and are not voluntary participants in this instructor's study. It is also very likely that these instructors' data collection approaches will be questioned by the university's HSRC or IRB.

Researchers certainly could promote and encourage participation by engaging in proper activities, such as emphasizing the importance of the research. They could also provide symbolic incentives to show their appreciation of respondents' participation. Some researchers attach a small gift certificate (e.g., a gift card to a coffee shop or a lotto ticket!) with the questionnaire; others may make a small donation to a charity for everyone who completes the study.

Voluntary participation is emphasized to potential respondents during the initial involvement in the study. It should be maintained after the study has begun. Participants are free to withdraw from the study or refuse to participate during any portion of the study at any time, even after they have agreed to participate. Participants should be free of any fear that they will be penalized or lose a benefit for their discontinuation in the study.

RISKS AND BENEFITS

Research activities aim to generate results that can benefit the respondents, the general population, and society. There is a possibility that respondents may face different levels of risk (e.g., from experiencing discomfort to retraumatization) because of their participation. The expectation is that the benefits are proportionate to or outweigh the risks that may be generated. Researchers should consider several major types of risks:

1. physical (e.g., bodily harms),
2. economic or financial (e.g., money, employment),
3. psychological (e.g., trauma, fears, sadness), or
4. social (e.g., social standing, embarrassment, stigma).

The degree of risk could range from exempt, to minimal, or to significant. Ideally, the research does not carry any risks, and if it does, the risks should be minimal and reasonable in relation to the benefits.

Exempt studies include research that does not involve vulnerable populations or is not considered "research" according to federal regulations. This may include studies in educational settings, evaluation of service, or demonstration projects; secondary or existing data collection and analysis; and others. *Minimal risk* means that the probability and magnitude of harm or discomfort anticipated in the research are not greater in and of themselves than those ordinarily encountered in daily life or during the performance of routine physical or psychological examinations or tests (U.S. Department of Health and Human Services, 1991, 45 CFR 46.102(i)). Studies that involve more than minimal risks require more thorough and extensive reviews by the relevant IRBs/HSRCs.

Precautions should be taken to minimize risks and provide appropriate coverage or remedy. The careful selection of study subjects, provision of resources or services should the need arise, proper monitoring, and the use of trained personnel to carry out the research activities are some of the approaches that should be considered. Consultation with experts and the use of the IRB further enhance the proper assessment and management of the risks and benefits.

INFORMED CONSENT, ASSENT

Informed consent includes two very distinct elements: informed and consent. Being *informed* means the participants are fully educated and have good knowledge of what they agree to do. *Consent* is their voluntary decision of agreeing to participate. Potential participants could be fully informed and decide not to consent to participate. Some might consent to participate. However, if they are not fully informed beforehand, the legitimacy of their consent is questionable.

Pedroni and Pimple (2001) discuss two notions of informed consent: moral sense and socio-legal sense. Under the moral sense, informed consent transforms the person from merely being a subject in a study to being a competent and autonomous decision maker who is engaged in a cooperative activity. The socio-legal sense refers to the person who legally and socially agrees to the terms and is willing to participate in the study.

As a written document, the informed consent form includes certain common elements. Many organizations have standard templates. They usually include the following main items:

1. Purpose of the study. Describe the intent of the study and identify who the researchers are.
2. General design and research procedures. Describe the overall design of the research. Explain who the study subjects are and how many are participating, how subjects will be recruited and sampled, what data collection instruments will be used, and how the data will be collected and analyzed.

3. Risks and benefits. Describe and explain the potential levels of risk (i.e., physical, psychological, social, and economic) involved. What are the benefits of the study? What resources or assistance is available for participants should the need arise?
4. Compensation and incentive. Make clear whether there will be compensation or incentive, if any, for participation. Describe what the incentives are (i.e., payment, token gift) and the terms.
5. Voluntary participation and withdrawal. Reiterate the voluntary nature of the participation and the right to withdraw at any time.
6. Confidentiality and anonymity. Explain how confidentiality will be protected and how anonymity, if any, will be achieved.
7. Resources in the community. Provide information on relevant services in the community, such as counseling or therapy, should it become needed.
8. Contact information. If there are any questions, who should the potential participants contact and at what phone number or at what email address?
9. Printed name and signature. This indicates one's informed understanding and willingness to participate.

Informed consent is documented by the participant signing the consent form. Under specific situations, for regular adults participating in a no-risk or minimum-risk study, the *implied consent* approach could be considered. Participants are informed about all the ethical considerations. Their completion of the questionnaire or other data collection procedure indicates their consent to participate.

SAMPLE CONSENT AND ACCENT FORMS

Three sample consent forms are included in Boxes 3.1, 3.2, and 3.3. Students may want to modify these templates into a consent form that meets their needs. All of them cover the key issues of confidentiality, anonymity (if that is the case), voluntary participation, harm and risk, and indication of informed consent. Affiliated institutions, type of research, and potential respondents are among the factors that may affect how a consent form is constructed. Students may want to consult their university's research office to see if they have specific requirements that need to be followed.

The use of the Family Strong Project Consent Form for Adult Participants (Box 3.1) highlights an important distinction that an agreement to participate in a program activity does not mean an agreement to participate in its program evaluation

BOX 3.1. SAMPLE EVALUATION CONSENT FORM FOR ADULTS

FAMILY STRONG PROJECT
CONSENT FORM FOR ADULT PARTICIPANTS

As a demonstration project, the Family Strong Project will be evaluated by the Big Help Agency. I have been asked to participate in the evaluation activities. I will be asked periodically to complete questionnaires or to be interviewed during and after my participation in the project. I understand the answers that I give will be totally confidential. No one from my family and community will see them. My information will be grouped with others in the final report; I will be given an ID# so that I will not be identified by name in any report. There is no known risk for participating in any of the evaluation activities. My participation in the evaluation is strictly voluntary. I am free to refuse to participate or withdraw at any time without repercussion.

My signature below indicates my complete understanding about the evaluation and my consent to participate in the project evaluation activities.

_____	_____	_____
(Your Signature)	(Printed Name)	(Date)
_____	_____	_____
(Researcher Signature)	(Printed Name)	(Date)

activities. This is particularly true when the program has a separate program evaluation component.

The Children and Youth Assent Form (Box 3.2) is used because the study involves minors who are under age 18. These minors have the right to agree or refuse to participate in research, even though their parents have already been informed and have approved their participation. The researcher may want to make sure that the description and writing suit the minors' reading levels.

The exempt consent form (Box 3.3) is a cover letter informing potential participants of all the human subject considerations. Human subjects–related notations are included in the example. Some exempt consent forms may still require a signature to indicate consent; however, most do not, including using implied consent. The implied consent format is particularly useful for anonymous exempt studies or internet-based surveys. Again, implied consent can only be used for no-risk or minimum-risk studies involving adults.

BOX 3.2. SAMPLE ASSENT FORM FOR CHILDREN AND YOUTH

FAMILY STRONG PROJECT
CHILDREN AND YOUTH ASSENT FORM

As a demonstration project, the Family Strong Project will be evaluated by the Big Help Agency. I have been asked to give the evaluator my impressions of the program from time to time. I understand my answers will be kept private and confidential. No one from my family and community will see them. They will be grouped with others in the final report. I will be given an ID# so that I cannot be identified. My participation is voluntary, and I can say no to participating or stop at any time. My parent/guardian has been informed about my participation and will be given a copy of this form to keep.

My signature below indicates my understanding and agreement to take part in the evaluation.

_____   _____   _____
(Your Signature)   (Printed Name)   (Date)

_____   _____   _____
(Researcher Signature)   (Printed Name)   (Date)

BOX 3.3. CONSENT FORM (COVER LETTER) FOR AN EXEMPT RESEARCH (USING IMPLIED CONSENT)

SOCIAL WORK PRACTICE PREFERENCES STUDY (TITLE OF STUDY)
CONSENT FORM

You are invited to participate in this research study about social work students' practice preferences (STUDY DESCRIPTION). My name is Saymy Namo (YOUR NAME). I am a graduate student in the School of Social Work at (THIS GREAT UNIVERSITY). You have been selected as a possible participant for this study because you are a graduate social work student (PARTICIPANT SELECTION REASONS, OPTIONAL).

The purpose of this research is to gain a better understanding of social work students' professional interests (PURPOSE). The data you provide will offer much-needed information for our local NASW Job Placement program. This research has been approved by the University

Human Subjects Review Committee as an exempt study. If you decide to participate, you will be asked to complete a survey questionnaire (PROCEDURES). It will take about 10 minutes to complete (DURATION).

Your participation in this research is voluntary. Even after you agree to participate, you may skip answering any of the questions or discontinue your participation at any time (VOLUNTARY PARTICIPATION). This is an anonymous study, no personal identifier will be used, and information collected will only be reported in an aggregated form (ANONYMITY). Any information that is obtained in connection with this study and that can be identified with you will remain confidential and will be disclosed only with your permission (CONFIDENTIALITY). The data obtained will be destroyed one year after the study is completed (RECORD KEEPING).

There are no known risks associated with your participation in this study (RISK). However, if your participation causes any discomfort or emotional distress, please contact Student Counseling Services at 123-456-7890 or County Mental Health Service 321-654-0987.

By completing and submitting the questionnaire, you have indicated that you understand the information provided above and consent to participate (IMPLIED CONSENT).

If you have any questions about your participation in this research project please contact me, Sam Iam, at Myemail@swrk.com or my advising professor, Dr. SmellAs Sweet at Ssweet@swrk.com.

Thank you for your consideration.

ONLINE- OR INTERNET-BASED INFORMED CONSENT

Online- or web-based data collection presents different challenges and advantages for recruiting research participants and obtaining consent. There are many ways that potential research participants could be involved in a research project through the internet. It ranges from a simple survey through email or common social media, such as Facebook or Snapchat, to more formal survey websites, such as the SurveyMonkey. Potential participants could be better informed about the research through the incorporation of social media technologies, such as videos, podcasts, interactive websites, and embedded comments and explanations during the recruitment.

It is also convenient that participation could take place almost anywhere in the world through a simple electronic device, such as a smartphone. Participants could be riding public transit, having dinner at a restaurant, or relaxing at home. They may feel less pressure to participate, more in control, and less anxious. New technologies allow participants to provide electronic consent through the use of a password, electronic signature, or other authentication and compliance systems. Internet-based survey research could also be conducted anonymously. Researchers could use implied consent for the return of the completed questionnaires without collecting any identifiers. All online survey programs, such as SurveyMonkey (https://help.surveymonkey.com/articles/en_US/kb/How-do-I-make-surveys-anonymous) or SoGoSurvey (https://www.sogosurvey.com/help/how-to-create-anonymous-survey/) also provide the anonymous survey setting. The setup will detach identifiers from the responses, and the researchers will not be able to identify the respondents based on information such as IP addresses, email addresses, or date and time of responses. Along with the use of technology, there can be ongoing concerns about confidentiality, information security, encryption, and other cyber risks. Many institutions such as University of California Berkeley (2016) have put out specific guidelines on internet-based research.

CONCLUSION

Respecting human and cultural diversity, as well as promoting the well-being of the target populations, are the cores principles of the profession. Legal regulations and the NASW code of ethics provide guidelines for social work research and practice. They safeguard the health and welfare of the people involved. Key considerations involving human subjects, such as voluntary participation, informed consent, risks and benefits, confidentiality, and anonymity, were discussed in this chapter. Culturally competent practice and ethically affirming considerations set the foundation for a productive, fair, and respectful research study.

4

CONCEPTUALIZATION AND MEASUREMENT (TERMS OF ENDEARMENT)

The Brief Visual Map of Research and Statistics for Social Workers (Figure 1.1) in Chapter 1 describes the reciprocal relationship between values and knowledge and the research process that follows. Values set the parameter for the pursuit of knowledge and in turn knowledge actualizes and influences the state of the values. People used to believe we were the center of the universe and that the sun circled the earth. New knowledge has allowed us to realize that the earth is only a planet in our solar system circling the sun. We also learned that there is much for us to explore to understand our place in this universe better. This chapter describes how basic ideas are being conceptualized and evolved into variables and theories with various characteristics. It clarifies how these concepts and variables are being measured in valid and reliable ways. Types, threats, bias, and errors related to validity and reliability are further explained. The definitions of these key concepts and how they are logically connected are provided.

CONCEPT, CONSTRUCT, VARIABLES, VALUES, AND THEORY

Both concept and construct are abstract representations of objects, ideas, events, conditions, situations, experiences, or instances. Concept and construct form the variables for research studies. Together, they are the building blocks for theories.

Concept

Humans have the unique ability of abstract thinking. It allows people to communicate, to learn, to differentiate, and to problem solve. A fundamental unit of this abstract thinking is a simple and basic concept. A concept is a general idea or notion of something that we observe, conceive, or experience directly or indirectly. It is a generalized summary of our many observations and experiences. It is a meaningful collection and categorization of the common characteristics of the observations. This may include something tangible, such as a chair, car, height, or income. This may also include something more abstract, such as aggressiveness or depression. Based on the many visual and physical aspects of an object and its functions, we may classify the object as a table, a chair, or a rock. Similarly, based on our experience of observing a sufficient number of people and their moods, behaviors, sleep patterns, cognitive abilities, and physical appearances, we may conceptualize and express those clusters of conditions as depression. Concepts help us to distinguish our many life experiences.

Construct

A concept is an abstract that it is difficult to measure. However, a construct is an associate of a concept that can be measured. A construct is a speculative definition of a concept, and it is purposefully created to be measured and studied. As construct is a concept or aspects of the concept that is being systematically studied. There are instances in which concepts are merely agreed-upon phenomena, such as intelligence, enthusiasm, oppression, self-efficacy, or independence. Although they are ideas that cannot be directly measured, each of them possesses certain qualities or aspects that could be assessed. By bringing all or most of these qualities together, a construct can be created and measured. For example, intelligence could be measured in many ways. An IQ score is one such measure, but it does not sufficiently represent the complexity of human intelligence. The concept of intelligence has, therefore, continued to be a construct for studies. In many casual discussions, it is uncommon for the terms "concept" and "construct" to be used interchangeably. Furthermore, this idea of the construct is related to the notion of construct validity, which will be discussed later in this book.

Variable and Value

When a construct is put into operation or is being studied, it becomes a variable. A variable is a construct or certain characteristics of the construct being measured. Dudley (2011) states, "A variable is defined as a concept that has two additional properties. First, it varies, or changes. Second, it is measurable" (pp. 77–78). Similarly, Rubin and Babbie (2017) assert, "A concept is a variable if it (1) comprises more than one attributes, or value, and thus is capable of varying, and (2) is chosen for investigation in a research study" (p. 165). In achieving the intent of research, a variable is to be manipulated, controlled, changed, or studied. When researchers assess the relationship between early childhood trauma and the stability of relationship as adults, both the trauma and the stability are the variables to be studied.

A variable could be further operationalized by its specific features, qualities, or attributes. These attributes are the values of the variables. Values could be presented in many different ways. Age is a variable that could have values of old or young, different age ranges, or actual ages. Similarly, the variable of college students could have values of freshmen, sophomore, junior, or senior.

Theory

When related variables come together and speak to a certain meaning, it becomes a theory. One may believe that by having a positive role model and a supportive environment, any child could become successful in life and school. This becomes one's theory of changing or improving the lives of young people. This preliminary theory is a proposition or a working hypothesis. If this preliminary theory were to be put to the test, its properties, strengths, and weakness would need to be identified. These analyses and findings would become the foundation for further refinements and re-refinements that, in the end, may become an established and tested theory. A tested theory is, therefore, supported and validated by quantitative and qualitative evidence.

In summary, a concept is the basic unit of a phenomenon or theory. Each concept could become a construct and then a variable. A variable is a factor or an entity that has varying characteristics, qualities, or quantities. Those specific and varying characteristics are the attributes or values of the variable. A social work student is a variable. His or her values could be characterized in various ways. The student could be in the BSW or MSW program. The student could be in the MSW program with a specialization in mental health, macro-practice, or disability. Conversely, the student could be of a certain age. The list could go on and on. Table 4.1 provides an example of the relationships.

TABLE 4.1. Concept, Construct, Variable, Values, and Theory

CONCEPT	CONSTRUCT	VARIABLE	VALUE	THEORY
Fear	Frightful emotion	Sense of danger	Acute sense of danger Normal sense of danger Free of the sense of danger	Having a supportive relationship could minimize ones' sense of fear
Support	Substantive affirmation	Level of encouragement	Supportive Not supportive	

MEASUREMENT, CONCEPTUAL DEFINITION, AND OPERATIONAL DEFINITIONS

Charles walked home in the cold from a long day at work. He was tired and hungry. He asked his partner if he could get something good to eat. His partner asked what he meant by "good" and "how good was good?" Charles said, "Good means food that is delicious. More specifically, it is appetizing food that could be ready very soon. It will be particularly good if it hits the spot!" He partner made him a bowl of microwaved mac and cheese, Charles's favorite comfort food, and he was happy. "Delicious food" is a conceptual definition of "good." "Quickly ready and hitting the spot mac and cheese" is the operational definition of "good."

In our daily conversations, we often ask, "What do you mean by that?" "Can you give some examples?" "How do I know this is really what we are talking about?" We want to clarify and specify so that we can fully understand the conversation and respond properly. In social research, researchers go through the same process of clearly defining the concepts involved in the research. Only with these clear definitions of concepts (conceptual definition and operational definition), how they relate to each other (independent and dependent variable), and how they can be understood or studied (levels of measurement) can the research process begin.

A variable is a construct that has characteristics (e.g., values, attributes). It can be defined, and some may have patterns that could be changing and can be measured. Measurement is the systematic process of assigning symbols or numbers to properties of variables according to specific rules. It also consists of how these symbols and numbers are to be collected and analyzed. Among the first steps in this process is to define the variable at two different levels: conceptual definition and operational definition. (See Table 4.2.)

Conceptual and Practical Research and Statistics for Social Workers

TABLE 4.2. Concept, Conceptual Definition, and Operational Definition

CONCEPT/CONSTRUCT	CONCEPTUAL/FORMAL DEFINITION	OPERATIONAL/CONCRETE DEFINITION
Self-esteem	Sense of self-worth and self-appraisal	The respondent's scale on the ABC Self-Esteem Scale
Individual with developmental disability (DD)	DD is a severe, long-term disability that can affect cognitive ability, physical functioning, or both. These disabilities appear before age 22 and are likely to be lifelong. DD encompasses intellectual disability but also includes physical disabilities (US Department of Health and Human Services, https://report.nih.gov/nihfactsheets/ViewFactSheet.aspx?csid=100)	Individuals who have a formal diagnosis of DD and are currently receiving services at the Ability Center
Authenticity	Truthfulness of intentions	The respondent's self-reported degree of authenticity

The conceptual definition of a variable is often the general, abstract, theoretical, or formal description of the variable. It is also called a formal definition. It offers a clear and unambiguous way of describing the concept and communicating the meaning of the concept. The written definitions that we find in a dictionary are typically conceptual definitions. "MSW students are individuals who are enrolled in an educational program and pursuing a graduate degree in social work."

The operational definition, however, specifies what concrete procedures must be performed to arrive at the recognition of the concept in measurement terms. It delineates all the specific and concrete features of a particular concept so that it can be measured. It is a definition that can be touched, felt, or seen. It is also a called concrete definition. "MSW students are individuals in this great university who are in the MSW program and are officially enrolled this semester in Professor De Finition's research methods class."

A word of caution: do not use the term to define itself. To define the term "poor," researchers should avoid stating "it is a state of being poor" or "people in poor conditions." Formally or conceptually, it could be defined as "not having sufficient resources or lower than average quality." Operationally, it could be the living conditions of students who receive free lunch at school, families that are enrolled in the Supplemental Nutrition Assistance Program (SNAP), or families with an annual income lower than $20,000.

INDEPENDENT VARIABLES, DEPENDENT VARIABLES, AND CONFOUNDING VARIABLES

The many variables included in a theory, a research study, or a service project are related to each other. Their relationships are the foundations and the outcomes of the research activities. Their relationships catch our attention and initiate our research. We want to get a better understanding of the relationships and probably discover some new ones. Depending on their relationships and functions, variables have many names. The two basic ones are the independent variable and dependent variable.

The independent variable is the self-governing and unchanging variable that has an effect or causes changes in other variables. It is the instigator, the troublemaker. If this is a case of "the devil made me do it," then the devil is the independent variable. However, an independent variable is not that evil. It is only the source or generator of change. In social work practice, it is the intervention, treatment, or program activities. Does hospice care minimize the need for bereavement care among caregivers? Hospice care is the independent variable that may have an effect on the need for bereavement care. When ketchup makes your french fries taste better, it is still ketchup, nothing has changed. Do we all know that ketchup makes everything taste better?!

The dependent variable is the one that is changed and is affected or responds to the independent variable. In social work practice, it is the expected changes, the outcomes, or simply the results. Does a psychosocial education diversion program for arrested sex workers decrease the recidivism rate more than a jail sentence would? Does more militarized police bring about a safer neighborhood? In these examples, the recidivism rate and the safety of the neighborhood are the dependent variables. They are influenced or affected by the independent variables (e.g., the diversion program and more militarized police). By the way, the taste of french fries is the dependent variable of the independent variable of ketchup!

For those of you who like formulas, the dependent variable (X) is a function (f) of the independent variable (Y). The formula to express this relationship is $X = f(Y)$. In English, the dependent variable is the product of the independent variable.

The confounding variable is an extraneous variable that enters into the equation and affects the outcomes of the dependent variable. Its effect may be misrepresented as the effect of the independent variable and may lead us to the wrong conclusion. The murder rate and the sale of ice cream is a classic example. When the murder rate goes up, the sale of ice cream goes up. Is it because murder makes people eat more ice cream or does eating ice cream make people commit murder? Of course, none of these are true. The real culprit or the confounding variable is the weather. When the weather is cold, everyone stays home; the town is a bit quieter, and not too many people eat ice cream when the temperature is cold. When the weather is hot, more people are out socializing, and there are likely more contacts, more conflicts, and probably more cases of murder.

FOUR LEVELS OF MEASUREMENT

When a service provider believes the relationship with a trusted adult could contribute to the improvement of targeted children's self-confidence, mentoring will likely be included in the program design. In this program, mentoring is the independent variable, which is expected to improve the child's self-confidence level, the dependent variable. Based on the characteristics of these attributes, these variables could be categorized into four levels of measurement: *nominal, ordinal, interval, and ratio*. The level of measurement of a variable dictates the type of statistics that can be used for analysis.

Nominal

A nominal variable is a categorical variable that has discrete values. The etymology for the word "nominal" is the Latin word "name." Different names refer to different people or objects. These values are mutually exclusive in that being in one category means not belonging to another category. At the same time, they are also inclusive in that each value includes all cases in its class. First graders and second graders are two complete sets of students. "First graders" is what all "first graders" are, and "first graders" cannot be "second graders" at the same time.

Variables such as gender, place of birth, social security number, school attended, political party affiliation, or specialization in social work are examples of nominal variables. Nominal variables can have two or more categories, and those that have only two categories are called dichotomous variables, such as the "yes" or "no" answer.

Frequency distribution, counts, or percentages are common statistics used to describe and summarize these variables. A nominal variable is the most basic type of variable. In fact, by nature, all variables have the properties of nominal variables.

Ordinal

An ordinal variable is a ranking variable that has values with a particular inherent order, and the differences among its values are not constant (i.e., equal or the same). An ordinal-level measurement represents the indexing of a set of attributes that each has an incrementally different position in the series. The first-place finish is higher than the second place, which is higher than the third place. "Take a number and wait for your number to be called!" The following are several more such examples:

- For level of education, being a high school student means one has more education than a grade school student.
- For shirt sizes, a large-size shirt is bigger than a medium-size one, which is bigger than a small-size shirt. However, the differences among sizes are not necessarily the same.
- The difference in the amount of soda between a large-size drink and a medium-size drink does not necessarily equal the difference between a super-size drink and a large-size one.
- Similarly, the distances between adjacent values of "very helpful," "helpful," "neutral," "not helpful," and "not very helpful" are not equal.

All ordinal variables are also nominal variables, but not all nominal variables are ordinal variables. "The good, the bad, and the ugly" is a nominal level measurement representing different types. However, in a toddler's words, "the good, the gooder, and the bestest" express the ranking values of "goodness." Statistically, ordinal variables, in addition to frequency distribution and percentage, could be summarized by median, mode, and ranking.

Interval

An interval variable has values that have a meaningful distance (i.e., constant or equal) between its adjacent values. It is similar to an ordinal variable, except the distance (interval) among values is the same. An interval variable can be measured by its numerical values along a continuum.

Johnny is 13 years old; Jeannie is 9; James is 2. The unit that is used to measure their age differences is the number of years. The distance between 2 years is 365 days. Age is an interval variable. When one says "Johnny is the oldest; Jeanie is the middle; James is the youngest" or "Johnny is an adolescent; Jeanie is a child; James is a toddler," their ages are being described at the ordinal level. The unit of measurement for this variable is positional designation. Conversely, the names "Johnny, Jeanie, and James" are nominal measures or titles of three different children.

Often, researchers assign numbers to represent categories. For example 1 = large-size shirt, 2 = medium-size shirt, and 3 = small-size short. These numbers only represent the categories; they do not upgrade the values to the interval level. If the researchers use A, B, and C instead of 1, 2, and 3, do you think the researchers can find an average of A, B, and C?

Today's average temperature is 75°F, which is 10° warmer than yesterday's 65° average. While a 10° difference between 75 and 65 is the same difference as that between 65 and 55 or between 85 and 75, the key is the equal distance between the adjunct units of measure—1.°F Temperature is, therefore, an interval measure.

Interval-level variables have the *arbitrary zero*, which is artificially or subjectively created. Daniel Gabriel Fahrenheit set the stable temperature of an equal mix of ice, water, and salt as the zero degree (0°F) for his temperature scale. Anders Celsius set the freezing point of water as the zero degree (0°C) for his temperature scale. As a result, 0°C is the same temperature as 32°F, and 0°F is −17.78°C. A measurement scale could set its own point of reference (e.g., point zero) subjectively based on its own unique needs and conditions. A social worker claims that he is so poor that he has zero dollars in his checking account. However, he fails to acknowledge that he is the one who decides how much money is left in his checking account. He is the one who creates the artificial zero.

Values of interval-level variables have the quantitative or numeric quality that would allow them to be used for more advanced and complex calculations. Statistics at this level go beyond simple descriptive statistics and extends into inferential statistics for prediction and generalization.

Ratio

A ratio variable is an interval-level variable that has a *natural zero* (*absolute zero*). A person's age, number of participants, or miles traveled are examples of ratio-level variables. It is possible to have an absolute zero number of participants, zero miles of travel, and zero hours for one's productivity.

The existence of the natural zero allows these values to be calculated for their ratio—a meaningful fraction. Someone who is 40 years old is exactly twice the age of a 20-year-old. A program that has 90 participants has three times more people than another program with only 30 participants. A social worker who traveled 200 miles daily to see her clients put in four times more mileage than her colleague who only traveled 50 miles daily. A ratio allows a simple and effective way to summarize and present information.

Many of you might have heard this question before: "If today's temperature is 20° and tomorrow will be twice as cold, what temperature will that be?" A temperature of 60° is not twice as hot as 30°, because temperature (Fahrenheit and Celsius) is only an interval variable, not a ratio. So, is there an absolute zero temperature? Scientists have figured out that it would be 0 K, −459.67°F, or −273.15°C—a temperature that is physically impossible to reach. Can you imagine what happens when there is an absence of temperature?

INTERVAL/RATIO

In human services, it is not uncommon for researchers and program evaluators to group interval and ratio levels into one category for general statistical analysis. The distinction between ratio and interval data is great and important for natural scientists, but the distinction is insignificant for a lot of social science research. As a result, many social scientists consider the levels of measurement as nominal, ordinal, and interval/ratio.

Different levels of measurement have different properties that allow the researchers to apply various statistics for analysis. Table 4.3 summarizes the appropriate statistics for the four levels of measurement.

TABLE 4.3. **Statistics and Levels of Measurement**

STATISTICS	NOMINAL	ORDINAL	INTERVAL	RATIO
Frequency, percentage, mode, presentation of data	Yes	Yes	Yes	Yes
Median, ranking, descriptive statistics	No	Yes	Yes	Yes
Addition, subtraction, mean, descriptive, inferential, and other advanced statistics	No	No	Yes	Yes
Ratio, fraction	No	No	No	Yes

Ranking the Variables

Inherently, there is a ranking among these different levels of measurement. The potential for statistical analysis is limited for nominal-level data, but the sky is the limit for ratio and interval-level variables. Researchers should use the highest allowable level of measurement for data analysis. However, there are times when lowering the level of measurement may create a better data set for analysis. About 50 people of all age groups have provided their real ages for a study. The age distribution may be too spread out; therefore, the researchers regroup them into the categories of older adult, adult, and youth. As a result, the data for age have been changed from being at the ratio level to the ordinal or nominal level. These regroupings allow the researchers to better manage the data and be able to make comparisons across different age groups. Table 4.4 shows examples of how a variable could be transformed into different levels of measurement. Box 4.1 provides a quick summary of the properties of variables.

TABLE 4.4. Examples of Levels of Measurement for Variables

VARIABLE	NOMINAL	ORDINAL	INTERVAL/RATIO
Age	Young age, old age	Young, adult, old or 21–40, 41–60, 60+	# years old
Sex/gender	Male, female, nonbinary, transgender	Not applicable	Not applicable
Teens' tobacco use	Yes/no	Not at all, few, often, …	Frequency per week
MSW students	Yes/no	First year, second year	# months in MSW program
Self-esteem	Yes/no	Low/medium/high	Self-esteem score
Tendency toward violence	Yes/no	Low/medium/high	# of reported violence incidences
Disability	Types of disability	Level of functioning	Ability/functioning score
Developmental Disabilities (DD)	Diagnosed/Not Diagnosed	Mild, moderate, severe	DD assessment score

BOX 4.1. ABOUT VARIABLES

WHAT IS A VARIABLE?

A variable is a construct that has characteristics (e.g., values, attributes). It can be defined, and some may have patterns that could be changing and can be measured.

FORMAL AND OPERATIONAL DEFINITION

This is the common understanding of what the variable or concept is (formal definition—the definition that you find in the dictionary). In the research process, to ensure that the variable is accurately and appropriately measured and applied to a study, it has to be very specifically and concretely defined (operational definition).

QUANTITATIVE AND QUALITATIVE VARIABLES

A variable can be qualitative or quantitative in nature.

LEVELS OF MEASUREMENT

Quantitative and qualitative variables can be deliberated/measured at different levels:

QUALITATIVE	QUANTITATIVE
Categorical variable—Nominal, Ordinal	Nominal, Ordinal, Interval/Ratio

"What's in a name? That which we call a rose by any other name would smell as sweet" Romeo and Juliet (II, ii, 1–2). Other names for independent variable, dependent variable, or whatever!

INDEPENDENT VARIABLE	DEPENDENT VARIABLE
In experimental designs (from pre-experimental to true experimental designs)	
Cause	Effect
Presence first	Presence second
Manipulated variable	Measured variable
Explanatory variable	Outcome variable
Predictor variable	Predicted variable
In nonexperimental designs (survey, observation, etc.)	
Predictor variable, grouping variable	Criterion variable, outcome variable

WHAT KINDS OF VARIABLES ARE THEY?

What is the average year of practice for child welfare workers?	Year: Outcome variable
What percentage of child welfare workers are male?	Gender: Explanatory variable Percentage: Outcome variable
Do male or female workers stay longer?	Gender: Predictor variable, grouping variable Year: Criterion variable, outcome variable
Does quality supervision make child welfare workers stay longer?	Quality of supervision: independent variable, predictor variable Year: Dependent variable, outcome variable

VALIDITY AND RELIABILITY

A driver's license is a valid identification to prove one's age, but it is not so for one's level of education. A rubber-band ruler probably is not the most reliable tool to measure one's height because it will give varying results. *Validity* questions the appropriateness of the measure in producing the results, and *reliability* questions whether the measure will produce consistent results. In other words, validity is whether it measures what it is supposed to measure, and reliability is how well it measures. Validity and reliability are two important measurement concepts in social research. Research activities that fail to achieve appropriate validity and reliability merely amount to busywork that produces defective results and lack credibility.

VALIDITY

A grandma from Mexico who is also a great cook comments that food from this one taqueria in town is very "authentic." Her comments certainly carry more weight and respect (more valid) than comments from someone who only has Mexican food from the chain taco joints. This grandma has a genuine understanding of the explicit and implicit criteria that should be used to make the affirmation with authority. As many would likely point out, this authenticity assertion is dependent on the definition of "*authentic*" as well as how it is compared against another well-known local taqueria. Validity refers to whether the measurement measures what it intends to measure. A simple bathroom scale is intended to measure one's weight but not one's height. Validity reflects the confidence in the truthfulness and the strength of the measurement and the conclusion. It begs the question: "Is it an appropriate measure? Is it the real thing? How real?" These are good questions that can be answered by further understanding the concept of validity. Here are several major types of validity:

1. Face validity
2. Content validity
3. Criterion validity: concurrent validity and predictive validity
4. Construct validity

Face Validity

Face validity refers to whether the measure appears to measure what it intends to measure. It asks questions, such as, "Does it look right?" "On the surface, does it reflect the intended concept?" "Does it appear reasonable and capable of achieving its intent?" Face validity is the most basic and elementary type of validity. It only has limited strength and rigor, partly because it relies heavily on the subjective perspectives and the selection of the "authority" who makes the judgment.

Take this example: A new staff member has just finished writing her case report for an initial assessment of a client. Before submitting the report, she shows it to a more experienced coworker. She asks the coworker to look over the report quickly to see if it looks all right! The words "quickly" and "looked all right" are the tip-offs here. She wants to know if the report appears to be adequate. In another example, it seems to be appropriate to conclude that a handshake between two people when they meet is an indication of politeness and respect rather than an invitation for confrontation and argument. If it smells good, looks good, and sounds good, it probably is good! On the other hand, isn't it?

Content Validity

Content validity is whether a measure has the appropriate substances and compositions to assess the many aspects of a construct. Haynes, Richard, and Kubany (1995) described content validity as whether the assessment measures the most relevant and representative elements of the construct. Face validity asks, "Does it looks right?" Content validity asks, "Does it have the appropriate and correct substances?" "Does it have the right stuff?" Content validity is often the measure of the operation definition of a construct. Someone's height (construct) can be measured by inches or centimeters. Weight can be measured by pounds or kilograms. These measurement procedures are rather straightforward and content valid (Content validity, n.d.). However, some constructs are more difficult or complicated to measure. Constructs such as depression, success, or anger may have many dimensions that need a more complexed procedure to reflect the contents of the construct appropriately. An assessment will have low content validity if it does not adequately represent the various relevant aspects of a concept or variable.

Some researchers consider face validity as the simplest form of content validity. Similar to face validity, content validity relies on the input from experts and their experience. It is more rigorous than face validity in that it aims to measure specific constructs and could be theory based. A test paper on economic theories does not have the face validity to be used to assess college students' learning in a social work human behaviors and social environments (HBSE) class. The economic theories test paper also does not reflect the content being taught in the HBSE class. A valid test paper for the HBSE class should reflect developmental theories and other knowledge included in the HBSE class and its intended learning outcomes.

According to the U.S. Department of Housing and Urban Development, a chronically homeless "individual is defined to mean a homeless individual with a disability who lives either in a place not meant for human habitation, a safe haven, or in an emergency shelter, or in an institutional care facility" (2015). A measure (e.g., an assessment form) that uses this definition to assess if someone is chronically homeless would include individuals who have a disability, live on the street, or in a nighttime shelter, as well as those who couch surf or live in their cars.

Reviews of literature and other relevant studies are some of the most important steps in establishing the content validity of a study. They provide a knowledge-based foundation and framework for conceptualization and the development of the measurement. A thorough literature review gives credibility to the measurement and the study.

Criterion Validity: Concurrent Validity and Predictive Validity

Criterion validity is also known as concrete validity. Criterion validity refers to how well the results of a measure correlate to established criteria or standards in the real world. It is also about the measure's ability to predict the outcomes for another related measure. Criterion validity is similar to but different than content validity. Content validity is concerned with the appropriate composition of the elements and the operationalization of the construct. These contents are the standards or the criteria for establishing such a construct. Criterion validity goes further; it is concerned with the performance of these contents, including the ability to make predictions. Criterion validity includes concurrent validity and predictive validity.

CONCURRENT VALIDITY

Concurrent validity is how well one measure performs in comparison to or in correlation with another valid measure. If a new anxiety test can assess the degree of anxiety as accurately as that of a proven but older anxiety test, then the new one is said to have achieved a good concurrent validity. You know you have become a good cook when you are able to fix a Thanksgiving meal almost as great as that of your mother's! Another example is when social work students' self-report of doing all the assigned readings is significantly correlated to their grades for the class. The degree of completion of reading is correlated to the external criteria or markers for performance, which is the course grade. In this case, measuring one's competition of readings is as good a measure as one's grade point average (GPA).

PREDICTIVE VALIDITY

Predictive validity refers to how one measure is able to predict the outcomes for another related measure. "Head Start children who performed well in their language tests are believed to have better academic performance in kindergarten" is an example of predictive validity. Another example is the ongoing debate among students and professors in graduate schools on whether the Graduate Record Examinations (GRE) really can predict one's success in graduate studies. Social work program admissions faculty could find some answers to this question by analyzing students' GRE scores (one measure) and their final GPA scores in the MSW program (another related measure).

Construct Validity

Construct validity shows the extent to which a measure reflects or assesses a construct, (i.e., the abstract underlying concept or idea, such as depression or intelligence). This is the mother of all validity because it encompasses all the other types of validity. It is concerned with whether a measure appraises a theoretical construct as it is hypothesized to assess. If self-esteem is theorized to consist of self-worth and self-image, then the measure of self-esteem has to reflect the traits of both self-worth and self-image. Self-pity may be a related concept but is not one of the aspects of self-esteem. A measure that assesses self-pity, therefore, does not have the construct validity for measuring the construct of self-esteem. There is a lack of agreement between the theoretical concept and the assessment measure.

How Validity Is Measured

Face and content validity can be established by subjective expert opinions and the use of literature reviews. For criterion and construct validities, advanced statistics such as correlational and factor analyses are involved. While some social work research involves the testing of criterion or construct validity, most undergraduate and graduate research only involves face, content, and criterion validities. Table 4.5 and Box 4.2 provide a summary of various types of validity and validity in action.

TABLE 4.5. Validity and Its Questions

TYPES OF VALIDITY		QUESTIONS ASKED
Face Validity		Does it look okay to you?
Content Validity		Does it have the right stuff?
Criterion Validity	Concurrent	How does it compare to an existing measure or current standards? Does it stand up to the standard?
	Predictive	How well does it make a projection? It is a good forecaster?
Construct Validity		How well does it relate to the underlying theoretical concept? Does the study measure the ideas or elements that the researcher claims to measure?

BOX 4.2. A VALIDITY LOVE STORY

As a young woman in college, Jean met many people, including some interesting and eligible young men. Although she was not active in the dating scene, quite a few fine young men appeared to be the right type (face validity) for her. They were serious, smart, gentle, and churchgoing. Jim stood out from the crowd. His views on life and everything else were very comparable to those of Jean. They also appeared to be rather complementary to each other. They had similar political views, moral values, and ideas about family and career. They seemed to have the right qualities that each wanted for a life partner (content validity). They were considered a good match by their friends. Jim had the qualities that Jean wanted and reminded Jean of her wonderful old boyfriend (concurrent validity), but Jim was even better.

Jean invited Jim home for Thanksgiving to meet her parents. Her parents gave their approval of Jim. They agreed with Jean that Jim had good qualities and would be a good husband and parent (predictive validity). Not long afterward, they got married. Jean and Jim recently celebrated their 50th wedding anniversary. They believe they are lucky to have found their soul mates. They made the right choice and picked the person who had the true and genuine qualities (construct validity) they were looking for in a life partner.

INTERNAL AND EXTERNAL VALIDITY

Validity can be divided into internal and external validity. *Internal validity* is the consideration of whether the independent variables are responsible for the results obtained. *External validity* concerns the generalizability of the study or to what extent the results of this study could be applied to other similar situations, populations, or time.

Internal Validity and Threats to Internal Validity

Internal validity questions whether the variables involved in the study bring about the results, or if there is something else (i.e., threats, alternative causes, alternative explanations, or confounding variables) that affect or threaten the results. Using various articulated research designs, researchers are to limit the effects of these threats to internal validity. This will allow them to examine the real relationships they want to study. The following are several of the common threats to internal validity:

1. *History.* Refers to outside events that affect the results of the study. The bad economy decreases the number of jobs in the market as well as the success rate of a job placement program. Low job placement is the result of the poor economy, not the quality of the program. High prices for cigarettes decrease the number of cigarettes purchased. The numbers for tobacco-related illness are lowered, not because high-priced cigarettes are safer but because people are consuming less tobacco. History here does not refer to past events but to events that happen during the study.

2. *Maturation.* Refers to the natural changes of the participants that take place during the study. This is particularly true when the study is a longitudinal or lengthy study. People get tired after a while and children grow up. All these things may have an effect on their participation in the study. Secret revealed: children who went to boarding schools came home looking different—they have grown!

3. *Testing.* The implementation and the interaction of the testing arrangements or the measures used may affect the results of the study. When tested too frequently or when the posttest is too close to the pretest, this arrangement can affect the performance of the participants. They may become tired of the frequent testing, or they may still remember the test questions and answers from the recently completed first test.

4. *Instrumental decay/instrumentation.* Deterioration of the data collection instrument. Over time, the spring on a scale may become less responsive, the prints of a repeatedly used test paper may become blurry, and even the test administrator may become tired. In a qualitative study, when the interviewers become tired or distracted, the instrumental decay occurs.

5. *Regression to the mean/statistical regression.* During repeated measures, people tend to move toward the mean score, the center. If a study selects participants based on their extreme scores, it is possible that subsequent testing will produce scores that are more average than extreme. Students who are selected based on their low pretest scores to participate in an intensive tutoring program tend to

have a greater gain in performance during the posttest than students whose test scores were average during the pretest. Part of the reason for the gain may be due to the tutoring, and part of it is due to the regression to the mean. On the other hand, researchers should look out for a "time of exception" (e.g., the bad hair day!). Data collection that takes place during that exceptional time may be skewed. However, over time, people do act normally (i.e., toward the mean). People may slow down only for a short time if they see the highway patrol parked on the side of the highway. They are likely to go back to their old driving habits after the highway patrol cannot be seen from the rear mirror.

6. *Selection.* Preexisting differences between study subjects may interact with the independent variable and affect the outcomes of the study. A social media survey can only reach those who use social media. Randomization (i.e., selecting participants by chance only) may be able to minimize this initial selection problem, but randomization is not always feasible. The use of participants who self-selected into an experimental or control group may, by itself, make the two groups not comparable from the start. A convenience sample may only include a homogeneous group of respondents. It is the researchers' responsibility to be cognizant of the recruitment, inclusion, and exclusion of their study participants.

7. *Experimental attrition/mortality.* Study subjects, for whatever reason, may drop out or decide to discontinue their participation in the study. Although this is referred to as mortality, it is not about participants dying; it is about their leaving the study. The loss of study subjects between measures may lead to inflated or inaccurate study results. While oversampling is one of the ways to minimize this threat, running a well-planned research study effectively is often a better option.

External Validity

External validity is the ability to generalize findings from one study to another target population, setting, or time. Externally validity is also called population validity, ecological validity, and historical validity. It is about the inference and applicability of findings from a specific study to a population beyond the sample. For example, several study findings have found that public announcements on TV and mailings of printed materials are effective in promoting the general population's participation in a census study in urban cities, but these findings may not be true for certain cultural minority groups or rural populations. An experimental study finds that religious leaders are among the best spokespersons to promote participation in the census among Hispanics in Sacramento, California. A subsequent Boston study of Hispanics confirms the Sacramento study findings and its external validity.

RELIABILITY

Reliability is the consistency and repeatability of a measure (Trochim, 2006a). To what extent, do the results of the same measure at different observations/testing vary, including all the random and systematic errors that may exist? "Reliability is a ratio or fraction ... the correlation between two observations of the same measure is an estimate of reliability" (Trochim, 2006b).

A reliable measure is consistent such that it will produce the same or very similar results over repeated procedures. A reliable automobile will take you to work every day without much trouble, but it may encounter different traffic or weather conditions. A reliable employee will produce the same quality work day after day and assignment after assignment, usually in somewhat different situations. Reliability is an important concept for social science research. If a test or assessment is not reliable, it is not valid. If it is not valid, then why bother? Why waste the time? Would you like to use a rubber-band yardstick to measure someone's height? How about using a suicidal risk assessment tool that has a variation of +/−5 points on a 10-point scale?

Types of Reliability

Reliability is a concept that could be estimated methodologically and statistically (reliability coefficient). The following are several of the common types of reliability:

1. *Inter-rater reliability.* The measurement is more reliable if two or more raters make the same observation or rates the same observation. This is established by the percent of agreement or the correlation of the scores or findings between two or more independent raters or observers. This helps eliminate personal bias or random errors. Cohen's kappa could also be used to estimate this reliability.
2. *Test–re-test reliability.* The correlation of two administrations of the same measure to the same people over time. Theoretically, the two scores should be

very close to each other. When a mother tactfully asks her older boy on two different occasions whether he ate his brother's cookies, she is checking for the reliability of his answer. In practice, many factors may affect the likelihood of having similar outcomes. A simple correlation analysis could be used to test this reliability.

3. *Internal consistency reliability*. Refers to a correlation among related variables in a measure. It assesses whether related items from a questionnaire or test truly measure the same construct. Do the items connect or hang together nicely, and are they able to measure the same thing? Also, do any of them contradict each other and, therefore, make measuring the same construct not possible? A questionnaire on post-traumatic distress disorder (PTSD) may have 10 items covering two major domains. How well do these 10 items and the two domains correlate to each other to allow them to truly assess PTSD is a question of internal consistency reliability. Cronbach's alpha is a commonly used statistic to do this type of estimation.

4. *Split-half reliability*. This is, in fact, one type of internal consistency reliability. A measure (items 1 to 10) is applied to a group of people. This measure is also randomly divided into two equivalent sets of items (say, items 1, 3, 5, 7, 9 and items 2, 4, 6, 8, 10). The scores for the two equivalent sets are calculated, and the correlation of the two scores is the estimate of the reliability of the measure. To achieve this reliability, many items need to be developed. Often, it is not feasible. The Spearman–Brown formula could estimate this reliability.

5. *Parallel forms reliability*. In a parallel forms situation, when a large pool of items has been tested and established, researchers can extract items from the pool to form alternative but equivalent forms. It is often seen in open examinations that use different but equivalent examination papers. Errors in the assignment of items to construct equivalent forms is a challenge. Parallel forms are similar to split-half. In parallel forms, different (but equivalent) measures are given to different respondents. For split-half, the same measure is given to all respondents, and the split of their responses only happens afterward. Pearson's correlation could be used to estimate this form of reliability.

The following (Box 4.3) is my response to an experienced LCSW colleague who was developing a tool to measure the service needs of clients. This may help you better understand what reliability and validity are and how they are measured.

BOX 4.3. A Q&A ON RELIABILITY AND VALIDITY

Q: The thing I'm wondering about though is how do I measure whether or not this tool is valid and meaningful … how would I determine if the assessment tool is accurate in its assessments? For instance, if the patient receives a total score of 23, which puts him in the "severe" … needs category, how do I prove that he really does have "severe" … needs? I'm struggling to figure out how we would measure something that is less concrete.

A: As to whether your items indeed consistently measure what you intend to measure, that is a question of reliability (does the measure produce consistent results and how closely the items are related to each other and contribute to the measured outcomes) and validity (does it measure what it intends to measure).

The measurement of reliability could be easily achieved by doing a Cronbach's alpha. Cronbach's alpha could also help improve the quality and accuracy of the assessment.

There are three main types of validity.

Content validity (including face validity). Content validity is about the adequacy and appropriateness of the items (indicators) used. Face validity is simply asking, "Does it look right?" Both are based on expert opinions and literature review. Because you have done both, I believe your scale has satisfied this requirement.

Criterion validity (concurrent validity and predictive validity). You can compare the results of your scale to another established and validated scale. Concurrent validity allows you to see if yours is as good as the established one. Predictive validity allows you to see how accurate your scale can project the outcomes. Can a high score on your scale accurately predict high needs? Different correlational statistics could be used to test the validity.

Construct validity asks if the measurement does measure the very essence of the construct that it intends to measure. Does this self-esteem scale measure self-esteem but not self-image? Statistically, there is no one test that can tell you that the assessment tool has the established validity. It is an ongoing and cumulative process. Commonly, we use convergent/discriminant regression analysis and factor analysis to test the construct validity.

As to how severe is severe, that is a question of operational definition and predictive validity. Based on the purposes and needs of your study, you could use your experience, practice wisdom, and current literature to determine which level is severe and which is not. This is both a research and a practice consideration.

Because you have already developed the scale, now is the time to put it to the test. That means putting it into practice and collecting data. Establishing a scale for practice requires the test to be meaningful (have utility) to the clients and the workers to improve the quality of the service. It does not always require advanced statistical backing. However, if you want to validate the tool and make it a "standardized" tool that could be adopted by practitioners and academics alike, you need the research and statistical analyses for the development of a scale. It will then be a long-term and more advanced project and will be a good topic for your doctoral dissertation study.

THE RELATIONSHIP BETWEEN VALIDITY AND RELIABILITY, ACCURACY, AND PRECISION

Validity and reliability are two related but different concepts. Researchers always hope to develop studies that accurately measure what they want to measure (validity) and produce consistent or precise results over repeated procedures (reliability). Validity is about accuracy, and reliability is about precision. *Accuracy* refers to whether a measure hits the target and measures the right construct. *Precision* refers to producing the exact or very close hits time after time, even though they may be right on or far off the target. Similar to playing darts, hitting the bull's-eye means accuracy, and repeatedly hitting the bull's-eye or consistently missing it to the left in the same general area is precision. Foua jokingly tells her beloved brother Ming that he is precise but not accurate; he is consistently wrong! Ming somehow manages to meticulously miss the target every time he tries! (See Table 4.6.)

It is possible to have a measure that has low validity but high reliability. A common example is the bathroom scale. A defective bathroom scale could consistently and precisely (reliability) indicate someone's weight as 100 pounds but fail to accurately (validity) tell the person's real weight of 150 pounds. Certainly, there are measures that have low validity and low reliability, although not much credible information

TABLE 4.6. Accurately Valid and Precisely Reliable

VALIDITY	RELIABILITY
Accuracy	Precision
Hit the right target	Hit the same spot
Correctness	Dependability

- For a test to be valid, it must be reliable. Therefore, a valid test is always reliable. (A birth certificate is a valid form of proof of one's birthday, and it is always reliable because it gives the same date.)
- However, a test could be reliable but not necessarily valid. (A test that yields a highly stable and dependable result that children love eating broccoli is not a valid test for children's intelligence.)

would be produced. It is, however, not likely to have a highly valid measure with low reliability. Measures low in reliability are very unlikely to produce valid measures. It is difficult to believe a person's words are valid if that person has been telling inconsistent tales. As stated in the previous section, if a test or assessment is not reliable, it is, therefore, not valid. If it is not valid, then why bother? Why waste your time?

MEASUREMENT ERRORS AND BIAS

Classical measurement theory suggests that any measurement is made up of two parts: true score and error (Boslaugh, 2017; Trochim, 2006c). It is expressed in the following formula, where X is the measurement or observation, T is the true score, and E is the error.

$$X = T + E$$

When a bathroom scale reading is 122 pounds (X) for a person who is really only 120 pounds (T), there is an error of 2 pounds (E). So what causes the error? It may be the inaccuracy of the scale, time of the day, or just arbitrary fluctuations. In reality, researchers may never know what the true value is or the exact value of the error. Researchers try to maximize the true value and minimize the error. The person may do that by taking many measures and using the average as the best possible true value. The person may also try to minimize the variances or the errors, such as the possible glitch of the scales or the person misread the displayed values (Boslaugh, 2017).

Technically, there are two types of errors: random and systematic. In everyday reality, we learn to live with random errors and avoid systematic errors. Trochim (2006c) expressed that in the following formula, where X is the measurement or observation, T is the true score, Er is the random error, and Es is the systematic error.

$$X = T + Er + Es$$

Random Error

A random error is an error that happens because of chance. Things happen! A researcher may happen to interview someone who has had a very bad day and is not in the mood for much talking. A group of third graders might respond to a math test rather homogeneously and with an average score of 20. Two weeks later, their responses to the same test will be all over the map but magically with an average score of 20. Why? First, chance or random. Second, they are third graders! Random error has no particular pattern, cannot be repeated, and tends to cancel itself out; it is, therefore, also considered as noise (Boslaugh, 2017; Trochim, 2006c). Random errors do not favor any results, and the errors average out to zero.

Systematic Error

Systematic error is often human made. Loud music next door, miscalibration of the measuring tool, incorrect use of the tool, or use of a worn-out tool are all examples and causes for systematic error. It is not because of chance; it is more consistent; it has a pattern that can be repeated and observed; it has a cause and, therefore, can be corrected (Boslaugh, 2017; Trochim, 2006c). The same third graders from the previous example were taking the second test while the school band was practicing next door and the drama club was having an ice-cream celebration across the hallway. Students test scores would likely be lower than when they took the test at a less chaotic time. "Unlike random error, systematic errors tend to be consistently either positive or negative—because of this, systematic error is sometimes considered to be a *bias* in measurement" (Trochim, 2006c). Researchers also refer to this as "artifacts and bias."

Bias (Sampling and Measurement)

Bias is the systematic error that makes the collected data regularly deviate from the true value in the population. Unlike random error that does not give any results an edge, bias tends to favor one over the other by overstating or understating. There are many types of bias that happen throughout the research process; the main ones are sampling bias and measurement bias.

Sampling bias (or selection bias) is getting nonrepresentative or overrepresentative samples for the study. For example, a convenient sample is very likely to be inadequate in representing the population. A study on the role of government in helping vulnerable populations will likely get some distinct results from a group of conveniently recruited social work students. Their perspectives are not going to be representative of the perspectives of all college students. A professor asking students who are always present in class why some students skip her class is not going to get answers that represent those who skip class. A researcher wants to know how members of his church feel about feminism; he mails his questionnaire using the men's group membership mailing list. He probably will not get data that represent the church community. Similarly, an online survey via a social media platform will leave out those who do not use social media.

Sampling bias is different from sampling error. Sampling bias is about the distorted sample caused by the flawed research design or sampling method. Sampling error is a natural and arbitrary variation. Researchers could increase the sample size to minimize the effect of sampling error. However, increasing the size of the sample does not fix the bias problem; it maximizes the distortion instead!

Measurement bias could include experimenter bias, procedure bias, and participant bias (see Table 4.7). The researchers may have particular political, philosophical, or academic preferences. These inclinations may unintentionally affect how the research is framed, how questions are asked or omitted, and how study results are presented. The data collection procedures may be prejudiced or defective. The researcher may be using leading or lopsided questions, or he or she may be omitting questions. The participants may be reading or interpreting the questions incorrectly. They may fall into the *social desirability* trap by giving answers that please the researchers or their moral obligations rather than giving the real answer. A field instructor asks his social work interns at a group supervision meeting how they like his expensive custom-made suit will most likely get a lot of complimentary responses. Researchers could minimize the measurement bias by calibrating the whole research process. This will include the research design, the data collection tool, the data collection process, the collector, and the analysis and reporting. Researchers should maintain a neutral and objective stance throughout the process.

TABLE 4.7. Measurement Errors and Bias

Measurement (X) = True Value (T) + Random Error (Er) + Systematic Error (Es) "(Bias)"
Reported Test Score = My True Test Score + Random Fluctuation (Luck) + Other Factors(I Was Tired)

RANDOM ERROR	SYSTEMATIC ERROR
• Error happens because of chance	• Error is human made
• No particular pattern, cannot be repeated, and tend to cancel themselves out	• Consistent, has a pattern, can be repeated, observed, and corrected
• Do not favor any results	• Favor one over the others
• Noise	• Artifact, bias
	• Measurement bias
	• Sampling bias

~ Researchers should try to maximize the true value and minimize the error. ~

CONCLUSION

This chapter described the evolution of a simple concept into a construct and then a variable with values and a theory that speculates. Measuring a concept accurately requires paying attention to the concerns of validity and reliability and their associated issues, such as types, threats, bias, and errors. After a clear understanding of these key concepts, researchers can proceed to formulating the appropriate research designs for their studies.

5 QUALITATIVE RESEARCH AND QUANTITATIVE RESEARCH (YIN AND YANG)

A s you begin to consider how to approach your research, you might be overwhelmed by the number of choices at your disposal in terms of how the research could be carried out. The following chapters will attempt to demystify and examine how qualitative, quantitative, and mixed-methods research can be used to accomplish your goals by way of different research designs.

There are many research designs that could be used to determine answers to the research questions. A research design is the general plan and structure for the form of study used in achieving its intended purpose. Researchers' creativity is the limit when it comes to strategizing their systematic inquiries. The inductive and deductive approaches are the two fundamental methods of reasoning. Associated with them are the quantitative and qualitative, as well as the research pragmatic methodologies. Grounded in the social work worldviews and informed by the qualitative, quantitative, and pragmatic methodologies, researchers could employ various research designs, including exploratory, descriptive, experimental, evaluative, and mixed methods, for their studies. Figure 5.1, Conceptualizing Research Design, summarizes the relationships among these various elements.

INDUCTIVE AND DEDUCTIVE LEARNING

Inductive reasoning moves from specific to general, whereas deductive reasoning moves from general to specific. They represent two distinct ways to learn about our social world. In reality, we use both reasoning approaches throughout our research projects and our daily lives. Together,

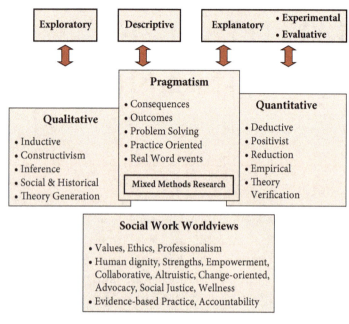

| Exploratory | Descriptive | Explanatory | • Experimental |
| | | | • Evaluative |

Pragmatism
- Consequences
- Outcomes
- Problem Solving
- Practice Oriented
- Real Word events

Mixed Methods Research

Qualitative
- Inductive
- Constructivism
- Inference
- Social & Historical
- Theory Generation

Quantitative
- Deductive
- Positivist
- Reduction
- Empirical
- Theory Verification

Social Work Worldviews
- Values, Ethics, Professionalism
- Human dignity, Strengths, Empowerment, Collaborative, Altruistic, Change-oriented, Advocacy, Social Justice, Wellness
- Evidence-based Practice, Accountability

Figure 5.1. Conceptualizing Research Design

they form a circle of learning that continues to evolve and advance. Yuen, Bein, and Lum (2006) explain the differences between inductive and deductive approaches to learning in the following discussions.

Arguments can be presented deductively or inductively. Moore (1998) explains the difference between deductive and inductive arguments. She cites the old example of deductive reasoning: "All men are mortal. Socrates is a man. Therefore, Socrates is mortal" (p. 5). A conclusion is drawn from the general premises. From a general truth, a conclusion for a specific situation is being drawn. The premises, in fact, contain more information than the conclusion, and the conclusion follows from the premises. In this situation, no matter how much more information is available on Socrates, he is still mortal, and the conclusion still stands. Deductive reasoning provides a more precise and confident assertion than inductive reasoning.

In an inductive argument example, individually specific situations are used to make the generalization. "Socrates was mortal. Sappho was mortal. Cleopatra was mortal. Therefore, all people are mortal" (Moore, 1998, p. 6). The premises of three people's situations become the evidence and the basis for the conclusion that applies to all people. In this case, the conclusion bears more information than the premises. The conclusion could be altered as new information arises and is incorporated.

The inductive conclusion is more of the nature of probability, correlation, or contributory than that of a causal determination of deductive reasoning. On the other hand, inductive reasoning captures the unique conditions of each case and provides a wealth of information for the learning of variation and diversity.

Inductively, people can learn about situations and make generalizations through analogy and inductive generalization. Moore (1998) explains that learning through analogy involves the use of similar situations to comprehend a new or little-known situation. Using information from a member of a set to make a generalization to all members of that set is an inductive generalization.

Conceptual and Practical Research and Statistics for Social Workers

Inductive and deductive approaches represent two ways to learn about our social world. Inductively, a social work researcher could study the effects of childhood sexual abuse by conducting case studies on each of her clients who experienced child sexual abuse. From the findings of each of these individual cases, she may be able to produce some conclusions that might be generalized or applied to the general population. Deductively, the social worker may conduct a statewide study and collect information from 10,000 eligible respondents to produce an important assessment of service utilization or identifying unmet needs. The differences and the integration of the two approaches provide complementary avenues to further our understanding and knowledge of our social world.

QUALITATIVE RESEARCH, QUANTITATIVE RESEARCH, MIXED-METHODS RESEARCH

It is not difficult to find material related to the great debate between quantitative research and qualitative research. Trochim (2006) stated, "The heart of the quantitative-qualitative debate is philosophical, not methodological" (para. 21). Researchers have taken on a variety of positions on this debate. Some believe the two research methods cannot be mixed because of their epistemological differences. Increasingly, researchers deem they could be used alternatively in conjunction with each other and believe mixed approaches should be promoted. The choice of which approach to use is very much dictated by the intent of the study, feasibility and readiness, resources, and training, as well as the researcher's preference.

There are clear differences between the quantitative and qualitative methods. These differences highlight the distinctiveness of the two methods as well as how complementary they are to each other. They are the yin and yang of inquiry. In the famous Italian master Raphael's painting *The School of Athens*, Plato is pointing his finger toward heaven while his student Aristotle is placing his hand in front of him toward the world.

Plato was an idealist. He was more interested in theory, forms, epistemology, ideas, virtue, arts, and justice. He believed in the heavenly dominion where great reality exists. The "being" is immobile and eternal; it is the "form" of "what a thing really is." He examined the nature of the soul. We may call Plato someone who would be more supportive of the qualitative method.

Aristotle was a realist. He was interested in metaphysics, sciences, reasoning, logic, and ethics. He was more practical than theoretical. He examined substances or matters through means such as observation and deduction. We may call Aristotle someone who would be more supportive of the quantitative method.

Aristotle was a student of Plato, and Plato was a student of another great philosopher, Socrates. They are teachers and students, but they all are different in their thinking. These influential philosophers had tremendous effects on the arts, sciences, politics, and philosophy in the Western world. They also set the foundation for how we inquire and search for the truth. Norvelle (2017) provided a one-sentence summary of these three philosophers: "Socrates sought definitions, Plato sought the Forms, Aristotle sought matter and form" (para. 12). Besides their differences, "the main similarity between Socrates, Plato and Aristotle was their dissatisfaction with society. Socrates sought to fix the world through the Socratic method, Plato had his theory of Forms and Ideas and Aristotle used logic and science" (TEDEd, n.d.). Aristotle claimed that philosophy begins in wonder. It is quite clear that, like these great philosophers, we researchers also start our quests in wonder.

Quantitative Research

Quantitative research is a social research method that uses deductive approaches to examine and infer the relationships among variables through statistical manipulation of numerical data. This is the commonly used research method for scientific studies. Quantitative methods allow researchers to use objective measures to collect numerical data from a large or specific sample. The nature of scientific studies gives their results greater objectivity in examining the relationships and making generalizations.

What is science? "Science is a systematic and logical approach to discovering how things in the universe work. It is also the body of knowledge accumulated through the discoveries about all the things in the universe" (Bradford, Aug 4, 2017, para 1). What is a scientific approach to a study? Scientific studies are *logical, objective, observable, measurable, repeatable, and could be hypothesized*. A teacher tells her class that if she or anyone drops the white chalk onto the hard floor, the chalk will break into pieces (logical, measurable, and hypothesized). She drops the chalk, and as the class watches (observable), the chalk breaks into pieces. If any student still does not believe in her assertion, the teacher could do it again. She does several droppings, and they all yield similar results (repeatable, measurable, and objective). If for whatever reason one piece of chalk does not break, then a new scientific inquiry has just been identified!

Among the functions of scientific study is to *study*, *predict*, and *control*. Public health officials study the characteristics and trends of influenza and predict which types will become active and prevalent. They then attempt to control their effects on the human population by cultivating a proper vaccine for the public to prevent an outbreak. Similarly, social workers understand (study) the connection between bullying and suicidal thoughts among lesbian, gay, bisexual, transgender, queer, or questioning (LGBTQ) high school youth. They incorporate suicide prevention training into their LGBTQ youth groups and develop peer support networks in schools. These activities aim to prevent (control) the anticipated (predict) negative behaviors and promote well-being among students.

Quantitative methods are deductive in nature. They gather large amounts of information from the general population through structured data collection approaches and instruments. The numeric data are then analyzed to arrive at findings that are applicable to individual subsets of the population. The findings also have the capacity to make generalizations to other populations, settings, or time periods. When a study of 5,000 hospice caregivers, who themselves are older adults, found that the majority of them have experienced burnout and depression, the finding was very likely to be applicable to most of the hospice caregivers in the United States as well as the ones in the local community.

Quantitative methods employ research designs that range from exploratory design to descriptive design and experimental design. Research may include the manipulation of variables and the research procedures to test the effects and relationships of variables. In some situations, quantitative research could render the ability to test the causal relationships in addition to the regular descriptive correlational relationship. Quantitative methods use a wide range of data collection approaches. It may just be a basic questionnaire survey, a simple pre-/post-assessment, or a controlled experiment of the effects of an intervention. Because the data are numbers, they can be analyzed and summarized using statistical methods and presentations. The investigation can be done with precision and the ability to replicate and make inferences.

QUALITATIVE RESEARCH

Qualitative research is a social research method that aims to achieve an in-depth understanding of a phenomenon through discovery, clarification, and interpretation with qualitative data. It uses subjective descriptions of the qualities of the phenomenon as the data to disclose and explore the phenomenon and its meanings. Qualitative research methods allow the researchers to learn more about a topic in the natural environment. Qualitative research starts with a general question and ends with better informed questions, hypotheses, or theory. It is particularly useful when little is known about the topic or the topic is of a sensitive nature. How does the Hispanic migrant farmworker community (or Russian-speaking evangelical Christian community or any other specific groups) in the United States handle alleged child sexual abuse reporting with possible human immunodeficiency virus (HIV)/acquired immune deficiency syndrome (AIDS) transmission?

Qualitative research methods are inductive in nature in that they start with and focus on the specifics and may eventually move on to some limited generalization. In other words, these methods focus more on the significance of the data to the people affected than on making generalizations of other people or settings. Qualitative research is more concerned about parents who are in distress because there is no food on the table for their children tonight than on how many parents in the United States are facing the same heartbreaking challenge. Qualitative research usually involves a smaller sample.

Qualitative methods use a variety of data collection approaches. They range from observations and interviews, to questionnaire surveys (open ended), focus groups, content analysis, and so on. Qualitative methods gather data that are in the form of words, symbols, pictures, stories, narratives, objects, or behaviors. They are perspectives from the respondents in their own words, based on their own experience, with their own interpretations, and through their own behaviors. Data are usually collected in a natural and less controlled environment with or without predetermined questions or data collection tools. The researchers may have interview guides or observation checklists to follow but are also looking for occurrences that are unscripted and spontaneous. It is organic and more process oriented than outcome oriented. The researchers are frequently also part of the data collection tools. Qualitative methods involve subjectivity both from the respondents and from the researchers.

There are several specific qualitative research methods that are common to social research and social work research. They include the ethnographic approach, phenomenological approach, constructionist approach, and grounded theory approach. Descriptions of these approaches and how they relate to the range of research methods are provided in the Baseball, Quantitative Research, and Qualitative Research section.

TABLE 5.1. Comparison of Quantitative and Qualitative Research

QUANTITATIVE	QUALITATIVE
A pre- and post-study of the effectiveness of a parenting program for teens A cross-state study of the correlation between mentoring program outcomes and the continuation of funding for a federal gang intervention program	The challenges of serving the poor: A case study of a local nonprofit agency Perspectives on program evaluation: Interviews of program officers Does it really matter? An observational study of doing peer counseling by volunteer workers
1. Measure, explain, and predict differences and relationships	1. Discover, describe, interpret, and clarify
2. Exploratory, descriptive, and explanatory studies	2. Exploratory and descriptive studies
3. Research question, testing hypothesis and theory	3. Research question, generating hypothesis and theory
4. More objective and outcome oriented	4. More subjective and process oriented
5. Deductive reasoning	5. Inductive reasoning
6. Analysis based on numbers and statistics. Logical and context-free	6. Analysis based on narrative, words, concepts, pictures, objects. Dialectic and contextual
7. Researcher conducts the research but does not become part of the research	7. Researcher is part of the research process. Researcher is the data collection tool
8. Controlled experimental settings with predetermined research design	8. Natural or less-controlled settings with suitable research design continues to unfold
9. Greater ability for generalization, explanation, and prediction	9. Limited ability for generalization. In-depth understanding of uniqueness and pattern
10. Use instruments such as tests, measures, and questionnaires	10. Use instruments such as documents, observations, and interviews
11. Larger sample	11. Smaller sample

Mixed-Methods Research Introduction

Mixed-methods research is not a simple mix or inclusion of both quantitative and qualitative methods. It is an integrated and coordinated use of both methods and the associated data collection and analysis technologies. It is used to gain a much better and comprehensive understanding of the complex phenomenon under study. The mixed-methods approach is consistent with social work practice and orientations. This method will be discussed in more detail in the latter part of this chapter.

BASEBALL, QUANTITATIVE RESEARCH, AND QUALITATIVE RESEARCH

In 1957, Hadley Cantril of Princeton University concluded his article titled "Perception and Interpersonal Relations" with this story:

> The story concerns three baseball umpires who were discussing the problems of their profession. The first umpire said, "Some's balls and some's strikes and I calls 'em as they is." The second umpire said, "Some's balls and some's strikes and I calls 'em as I sees 'em." While the third umpire said, "Some's balls and some's strikes but they ain't nothin' till I calls 'em." (p. 126)

Borrowing from and expanding on Cantril's baseball story, the following is an to attempt to capture the different research approaches and their underlying theoretical frameworks. These approaches range from quantitative study to qualitative ethnographic, phenomenological, constructionist, and grounded theory approaches.

"Some's balls and some's strikes and I calls 'em as they is."

Quantitative research. An empirical study that assumes there are objective, common, independent characteristics that could be standardized and assessed. One simply is what one is (essentialist, positivist). According to the objectively established and commonly agreed-upon rules and standards, this is a ball, and that is a strike. It is what it is. It is either inside the strike zone or it is outside the strike zone. It is clear-cut and factual. Deductively, the nature and relationship of variables are examined. The pitcher, the batter, the field, and the wind, as well as many other factors all come into play to produce the result. Theories and hypotheses are tested systematically, and often quantitatively, with the help of statistical analysis. These experimental and *scientific methods* are logical, measurable, repeatable, and observable in that they could reach findings with a certain degree of confidence. Quantitative research could also be used to test for difference, correlation, and causation among variables.

"Some's balls and some's strikes and I call 'em as I see 'em."

Ethnographic research. Ethnographic study uses participation, interviewing, and observation in natural environments to learn about people's experience, interactions, behaviors, belief systems, and perceptions of their reality. The word ethnography could literally mean the process of describing or representing the people and the culture. Anthropologists often use this approach and refer to it as "fieldwork," where they engage themselves with the people being studied to learn about the people's reality through their own lens. In our social world, there are independent and objective realities that exist, but what they are as realities are subject to people's experiences and beliefs. Ethnographic research deals with the issues of perceptions, which are related to culture, social environment, and experience. It is a descriptive account of the social and cultural lives of a social situation, such as a community, an organization, or a social group. Is it a ball or is it a strike? The umpire sees each play individually, but what the umpire sees is affected by many factors interacting with the umpire when the observation is made. Based on what is being seen and the rules of the game, the umpire makes the call. The players, the coaches, or the spectators may have very different perceptions or interpretations of the rules for which they may vehemently disagree.

What do people know? How do they arrive at that understanding? What do they do? How do they live? The student life in a high school, the organizational culture of an agency, and the environment and reality in a nursing home or in a family are some examples. "A week in the life of a runaway teen in Skid Row, Los Angeles." "How do female students in a middle school conceptualize the support and encouragement for them to study math and science?" *Simplistically speaking, it is the study of the common sense or the collective understanding of a subject.*

Phenomenological research. "Phenomenological research aims to capture subjective, 'insider' meanings and what the lived experience feels like for individuals. More specifically, phenomenologists explore the 'lifeworld'—the world as directly and subjectively experienced in everyday life" (Finlay, 2009, p. 475). It is a study of phenomena that people perceive in the social world, the essence of their experience, and the *meaning making of their lived experience.* A lived experience is more than an experience; it is an interactive experience that people live through and process. A person's experience of being a woman in the United States is not the same as a person's subjective consciousness of living and relating as a woman in the United States. This lived experience is authentic, subjective, and personal. It is not an account of general social rules, normative expectations, theories, or statistical deduction.

Phenomenological studies are similar to and different from ethnographic studies. Ethnographic studies focus on the community's common understanding and its social norms. Phenomenological studies focus on how people experience things and what the experience means to them. Ethnographic studies describe how people in the United States celebrate Thanksgiving and its social significance. Phenomenological studies explore the meaning of Thanksgiving for a Native American living on a reservation or a refugee living in New York City. Phenomenological studies use interviews and other qualitative approaches to identify, understand, and explain people's experiences as they see them. "What does it mean to be a refugee in the United States?" "How could an abused spouse return to her family and be a wife and a mother again?" "What role does religious belief play when one is facing a life-changing health challenge?" "What is life, and what is hope as a foster child?" *Simplistically speaking, it is the study of the lifeworld, people's life stories according to the people.*

"Some's balls and some's strikes but they ain't nothin' till I calls 'em."

Popik (2015) cited Sydney Harris's assertion in the August 23, 1965, Augusta, Georgia, *Chronicle* when he stated, "What is called a 'strike' or a 'ball' in baseball depends not on the absolute 'truth' of each pitch, but on the decision of the umpire. In a real sense, each pitch is 'nothing' until the umpire calls it."

Social constructivist research. Meaning, knowledge, and consciousness are human constructions and are socially constructed. There are multiple realities. The researchers employ interviews and observation to understand these realities. Research subjects are to assist the researchers in constructing these realities. The very attempt to measure a variable is itself constructing such a variable. The reality of being a ball or a strike is constructed and called by the umpire. One man's trash is another man's treasure. This may be an old dirty rag that is not worth a penny to you, but it is my cherished security blanket that helped me through my tumultuous childhood. Reality is built by individuals through their social worldview to seek out its meaning in their consciousness. Social construct research studies how a phenomenon or an object of consciousness develops within our social context. "The researcher's intent is to make sense of (or interpret) the meanings others have about the world" (Creswell,

2009, p. 8). *"How does a good day come about for a hospice client who lives alone and has no visitors?"*

Social constructivists challenge the notions of "reality" and "meaning." What is real? Do they mean anything? Does what we conjure in our heads have meaning? LaBar (2011) pointed out that moral philosophers often question morals. They wonder if morals that happen inside our heads are real. There is a fundamental challenge for social constructivists: "If nothing is real, how do they know that what they construct is real?" All of these will continue to be topics for philosophers to ponder.

> "Tell me one last thing," said Harry. "Is this real? Or has this been happen-ing inside my head?" Dumbledore beamed at him, and his voice sounded loud and strong … "Of course it is happening inside your head, Harry, but why on earth should that mean that it is not real?" (Rowling, 2007, p. 723)

Social constructionism or social constructivism? These are the "two main branches of constructive theory. These branches are similar in that both perspectives hold firmly to the postmodern idea that knowledge and reality is subjective" (Sommers-Flanagan & Sommers-Flanagan, 2012, p. 369). The authors distinguished the two approaches as "constructivists focus on what's happening within the minds or brains of individuals; social constructionists focus on what's happening between people as they join together to create realities" (p. 370). Constructivism is internal, a personal cognition construction and schema. Constructionism is interactional and external, the process and result of one's involvement in the interaction and, therefore, the construction of reality with others. Philosophers and academics continue to debate the distinct nature and differences between these two approaches. For the purpose of this book, and for general discussions, they are commonly lumped together as a social constructivist approach.

Now, a supplementary quote added by the author of this book: "Based on what I observed over time, this is how this game is played and called!"

A group of people who had no prior knowledge of or experience with baseball was invited to attend a game. They were left by themselves at the home plate box. They had no idea of the rules of the game. They saw players hitting the ball and running around the diamond. They also saw players miss hitting the ball several times in a roll and returning to their teams in frustration. They realized when players were able to progress through the diamond and return to where they started, some people would celebrate, and the score on the scoreboard would change. They hypothesized that this must be a good thing and might be the purpose of the game. It took them several innings (they wondered why it was called an inning not an outing?) to hypothesize and figure out what was going on in the field. Step by step through observation, coding, categorizing, and comparing, they reached sufficient conclusions on their emerging and incremental hypotheses of the game. The ball and the strike are different, but they are only the basics of the game. There are players, coaches, umpires, and fans. More importantly, there are multitudes of emotions, team efforts, strategies, athleticism, and sportsmanship. After many hours, the game finally ended (thank goodness for some, not enough for others!), and they believed they had a good idea (a theory) of how the game was played and called.

Grounded theory research. Sociologists Barney Glaser and Anselm Strauss proposed grounded theory in their seminal 1967 book, *The Discovery of Grounded Theory: Strategies for Qualitative Research*. According to the Grounded Theory Institute, the official site of Dr. Barney Glaser, grounded theory is an inductive methodology, a general method, and not only a qualitative method.

> It is the systematic generation of theory from systematic research. It is a set of rigorous research procedures leading to the emergence of conceptual categories. These concepts/categories are related to each other as a theoretical explanation of the action(s) that continually resolves the main concern of the participants in a substantive area. Grounded Theory can be used with either qualitative or quantitative data. (Grounded Theory Institute, 2014)

Grounded in the data collected, sufficient observations, interviewing, note-taking, coding, sorting (constant comparison), and writing, a hypothesis emerges. After relevant data saturate the hypothesis, the researcher moves on to another appropriate hypothesis. In the end, properties and categories are identified, and a theory (argument) or new area of study is developed. The purpose of research is theory building and the identification of its interrelated concepts.

Grounded theory research is a discovery process using open coding to study "the core category [that] is the concept to which all other concepts related" (Scott, 2009). Over the years, grounded theory research has evolved into different variations or types. Sbaraini, Carter, Evans, and Blinkhorn (2011) summarized and displayed the common and fundamental components of grounded theory in a table. Table 5.2 is an excerpt of their table.

TABLE 5.2. Fundamental Components of a Grounded Theory Study

COMPONENT	STAGE	DESCRIPTION
Openness	Throughout the study	Grounded theory methodology emphasises inductive analysis … moves from the particular to the general: it develops new theories or hypotheses from many observations. Grounded theory … studies tend to take a very open approach to the process being studied. The emphasis … may evolve as it becomes apparent to the researchers what is important to the study participants.
Analyzing immediately	Analysis and data collection	In a grounded theory study, analysis must commence as soon as possible, and continue in parallel with data collection, to allow *theoretical sampling* (see below).
Coding and comparing	Analysis	Data analysis relies on *coding*—a process of breaking data down into much smaller components and labelling those components—and *comparing*—comparing data with data, case with case, event with event, code with code, to understand and explain variation in the data. *Codes* are eventually combined and related to one another—at this stage they are more abstract and are referred to as *categories* or *concepts*.
Memo-writing (sometimes also drawing diagrams)	Analysis	The analyst writes many memos throughout the project. Memos can be about events, cases, categories, or relationships between categories. Memos are used to stimulate and record the analysts' developing thinking, including the *comparisons* made (see above).
Theoretical sampling	Sampling and data collection	A theoretical sample is informed by *coding, comparison and memo-writing*. Theoretical sampling is designed to serve the developing *theory*. Analysis raises questions, suggests relationships, highlights gaps in the existing data set and reveals what the researchers do not yet know. By carefully selecting *participants* and by modifying the *questions* asked in data collection, the researchers fill gaps, clarify uncertainties, test their interpretations, and build their emerging theory.
Theoretical saturation	Sampling, data collection and analysis	Qualitative researchers generally seek to reach "saturation" in their studies. Often this is interpreted as meaning that the researchers are hearing nothing new from participants. In a grounded theory study, theoretical saturation is sought.
Production of a substantive theory	Analysis and interpretation	The results of a grounded theory study are expressed as a substantive theory, that is, as a set of concepts that are related to one another in a cohesive whole. As in most science, this theory is considered to be fallible, dependent on context and never completely final.

Source: "How to Do a Grounded Theory Study: A Worked Example of a Study of Dental Practices," by A. Sbaraini, S. Carter, R. Evans, and A. Blinkhorn, 2011, *BMC Medical Research Methodology, 11*, p. 128. https://doi.org/10.1186/1471-2288-11-128.

A social worker may be interested in the dynamics among medical staff who serve elderly clients in the operating room. He gained access to a large number of such operations and observed the interactions among medical staff. He employed the grounded theory approach to document and develop his theory on the interpersonal dynamics among medical staff and their implications for services to the elderly. Gerontologists Bradly Fisher and Constance Peterson conducted a similar observation and interview study. They reported their findings in their (1993) article, "She Won't Be Dancing Much Anyway: A Study of Surgeons, Surgical Nurses, and Elderly Patients." They found many surgeons saw themselves as the captain of the ship, the nurses were not to question their authority, and the well-being of the elderly patients at times was compromised. They found many medical staff members were caring professionals and concluded that surgeons could be positive role models. They recommended specialized training on serving elderly patients.

Have you ever wondered what the experience of being a client waiting at a county welfare office is like? A social worker could spend time in the lobby conducting grounded theory research on the interaction between county staff and the welfare applicants and recipients. Are the staff members professional, helpful, respectful, or are they bureaucratic and impersonal? Are the clients anxious, confused, demanding, or reserved? How exactly does the public welfare system function in this office? What are the spoken and unspoken rules? How do they play out? Who is in there? What do they mean to the people who are involved? What do they call this process? For the researchers, what codes, hypotheses, and theories would be generated by such a study?

CONCLUSION

This chapter described the different research methodologies as they relate to inductive and deductive reasoning, as well as the qualitative and quantitative approaches to inquiry. Building upon this understanding, the following chapter will discuss the major research designs that are commonly used. These chapters reflect the logical progression of the research process from conceptualization to design and implementation.

Credits

Img. 5.1: Rafael, "Escola de Atenas," 1509.
Table 5.2: Alexandra Sbaraini, et al., "How to Do a Grounded Theory Study: A Worked Example of a Study of Dental Practices," *BMC Medical Research Methodology*, vol. 11, pp. 128. Copyright © 2011 by Springer Nature (CC BY 2.0).

6 RESEARCH DESIGNS

As described in the previous chapter, a research design is the general plan and structure for the form of study used in achieving its intended research purpose. A research design could be categorized by whether it is a qualitative or quantitative method of study. By nature, qualitative approaches use inductive reasoning and quantitative approaches use deductive reasoning. There are advantages and disadvantages in the use of quantitative or qualitative research approaches. A researcher needs to learn the appropriate use of both approaches as well as the increasingly used mixed-methods approaches to carry out the research tasks effectively. Research designs could also be presented in terms of their functions and structure as **exploratory, descriptive, experimental, or evaluative**, plus the steadily more accepted mixed methods (see Figure 5.1, Conceptualizing Research Design). These different designs will be discussed in this chapter.

RESEARCH HYPOTHESIS AND ASSUMPTION

Both hypothesis and assumption are concepts that become working theories used to explain a phenomenon. They are, however, different within the context of social research. Research efforts are tied to hypothesis, not assumption. A hypothesis is a proposition that is formulated by the researcher to explain a phenomenon or phenomena. It is a working theory, an argument, which needs to be tested and verified. An assumption is similar to a hypothesis except it is not intended to be tested. It is a proven working theory in the mind of the person who makes the assumption. A hypothesis is a setup to find the answer, an assumption already has the answer.

A third-grade teacher heard someone behind her talking as she wrote on the board. She turned around and immediately asked Johnny why he was talking in class although she did not see who was talking or recognize the voice. It was her assumption. Alternatively, based on her knowledge of the class, she had an educated hunch that Johnny or someone in that traditionally garrulous corner was doing the talking. She hypothesized that it was one of them, but she needed to investigate to determine the truth. One of the social work practice principles is being "nonjudgmental," which demands that social workers competently assess and learn before they formulate their opinions and make their determinations.

A research hypothesis is an informed hunch or an educated guess. Using a very simplistic way to conceptualize that, one could say a hypothesis is a statement form of a research question. The research hypothesis for the research question, "Does participating in this parenting class increase parents' abilities to use positive parenting skills?" could be as follows: "Participating in this parenting class increases parents' positive parenting skills." A hypothesis describes the relationship between variables and provides grounds for empirical verification. Alternative hypotheses can be derived from a single research question; therefore a hypothesis is more than a statement form of the research question.

FOUR MAJOR TYPES OF RESEARCH DESIGNS AND MIXED-METHODS DESIGNS

There are four major types of research designs: *exploratory, descriptive, experimental, and evaluative* (Atherton & Klemmack, 1982; Grinnell & Unrau, 2008; Royse, 2008; Yuen & Terao, 2003). Often, experimental and evaluative designs are collectively called *explanatory* design. Each is used for its ability to meet different purposes. Oftentimes, a mix of different designs is used to meet the particular needs of the study. A program evaluation may involve the use of exploratory study design, descriptive study design, experimental design, or a combination of them.

Exploratory Designs

Exploratory studies help programs gain familiarity and develop a better understanding of a given question or situation. They also help the researcher to formulate more refined questions for future studies. Exploratory studies could involve an extensive literature review, an observation, or a survey with a questionnaire or interviews. They may be carried out in the form of a needs assessment survey, a case study, a review of the experience of selected examples, or interviews with individuals with unique or different viewpoints.

For example, a community social worker has become aware that the lack of affordable housing in the community is a concern, and her agency is interested in starting a new service program addressing this concern. What should she do? Where should she start? A good way to start is for her to educate herself on this issue by studying the current literature. Reviews of professional documents and academic literature allow her to incorporate established knowledge to approach this issue. Local statistics, community reports, and news reporting provide her with an understanding from the perspective of the local community. She may also want to seek input through interviews, focus group discussions, or town hall meetings from knowledgeable individuals, (i.e., local residents or people who are affected).

Incidentally, another local agency has just completed an exploratory community needs assessment study. The study results indicated that the targeted populations, although they contribute greatly to the local economy, are priced out of the housing market both in ownership and in rentals. Many of them are not aware of their options and the ways to access support services to obtain stable housing. The agency staff members also found that the city is not in compliance with the affordable housing benchmark set from a prior legal settlement.

Based on these findings, this social worker designs a multilevel service and advocacy program. Informational workshops, personal coaches, and case managers are used to increase access and success in obtaining affordable housing. Intensive advocacy and legal activities are developed to ensure compliance from the city. These exploratory studies help identify the focus and the entry points for services and their development. Affordable housing in this community is a complicated issue, and many questions remain unanswered, awaiting further study.

In research, exploratory studies do not necessarily have research hypotheses. Instead, they help generate more sophisticated or precise research questions and hypotheses for further study. An exploratory study allows the researcher and service provider to define and further elaborate on a general belief or suspicion with more refined questions. The aforementioned social worker may think affordable housing is a concern, but it is just hearsay until it is better defined by her exploratory studies. The results of her exploratory studies enable her to develop interventions and generate hypotheses for further studies on the relationships among affordable housing, community education, and advocacy.

A social work student is trying to decide which section of social work research and statistics courses he is going to take. There are five sections, and all are taught by different instructors he does not know. He certainly would try to talk to students who had these instructors before to get their opinions. He probably would go online to check out other students' reviews, even though they tend to either love the instructors or dislike them for whatever reason. Similarly, if he is planning to take a vacation to Hawaii and is not sure which island to go to, this student will do the same kind of checking. Surveying and getting a better understanding of the situation, separating facts from fictions, and asking more pointed questions are all exploratory research activities. After completing the checking, the student is able to ask more specific questions: "Is this instructor a hard grader?" "Is this instructor good at connecting research to practice?" "Where in Hawaii should I stay that would allow me to get inexpensive but good food and is close to the beach?!"

Exploratory studies employ both quantitative and qualitative research approaches. They usually have a smaller sample size. Dudley (2012) comments that exploratory studies are often cross-sectional studies that collect data at a point in time. They are not designed to have representative samples to which findings could be generalized to the larger population. Examples of questions for exploratory studies could include the following: "Is bullying a concern among parents in this elementary school?" "What has been done in this agency to address the high turnover of social workers?" "How do social workers work with clients who refuse to speak?"

Descriptive Designs

Descriptive studies provide in-depth information about a situation, its variables, or its characteristics. They also illustrate the relationships between two or more variables. A descriptive study is more specific in its scope and focus than an exploratory study. Atherton and Klemmack's (1982) differentiated a descriptive study from an exploratory study in the following ways:

1. Attempts to secure a more representative sample and may involve comparison groups
2. Uses more precise data-gathering methods
3. Provides clearer and more specific information on what is being studied

There is no exact cutoff line to separate a descriptive study from an exploratory study. It is, therefore, a matter of the depth and the focus of the study, (e.g., extent of the relationship between identified variables). A high school senior engaged in an exploratory study when he went on an on-campus tour and orientation to learn more about the prospective university. After the tour, he was able to ask precise questions about scholarship opportunities for a particular major from a counselor. He also asked current students from that university about their learning experiences and the job market, particularly in regard to his potential major. He was doing a descriptive study by examining the specific relationships between variables (i.e., enrollment and scholarship, job market and major).

Similarly, when a new community worker enters a community, he needs to talk to many people to explore and learn about the community. However, an experienced community worker not only gives the new worker a general introduction to the community but also accurately describes the unique dynamics and relationships among the key elements existing in the community. A long-time resident could tell a newcomer which part of the community is safe, which part is unsafe, and exactly why. They are able to describe the interplay and unique relationships among variables.

The service provider who completed an exploratory study on affordable housing learned that there is a relationship between the number of hospitality and retail industries in the community and the demand for affordable housing. The exact nature of the relationship, therefore, is the target of her descriptive study. Through a survey of hospitality and retail industry workers and employers, she learned that there is a positive relationship between the two—more hospitality and retail jobs means more demand for affordable housing. Reviews of the local statistics also revealed that as the community attracts more businesses and becomes more affluent, the amount of affordable housing decreased, although more workers are needed to staff these businesses. She was able to describe more precisely the correlations through her descriptive studies. As a result, she was able to refine her service program to better address the identified situations.

Descriptive studies illustrate identified variables, their characteristics, and how they relate to or correlate with one another. A descriptive study could be a survey with a questionnaire or interviews, an observational study, a documentary study, or other quantitative and qualitative data collection approaches. Similar to all research activities, descriptive research designs need to pay attention to validity and reliability issues that were discussed earlier in this book.

HYPOTHESIS FOR DESCRIPTIVE DESIGNS

A descriptive study could include research hypotheses. Hypotheses in descriptive research could take many forms (Atherton & Klemmack, 1982):

1. X has certain characteristics
   a. "Parents who neglect their children were themselves neglected."
   b. "Youth substance abusers often have a history of tobacco and alcohol use in their early teens."
2. X occurs more frequently than Y in a given population
   a. "Low income occurs more frequently than the lack of formal education in parents who neglect their children."
   b. "Hard work contributes more than luck in the success of one's education."
3. X is associated with Y in some important way
   a. "The greater the parental deprivation, the greater number of abusive incidents with their children."
   b. "Participants who attended more than 90% of the sessions have a significantly higher rate of success."

Human service providers will find exploratory and descriptive designs to be the most commonly used designs for their practice-based research or evaluation projects. The ease of these designs also allows them to be used by providers with various levels of training and preparation. A very common type of descriptive study often used by social workers is a survey.

Experimental Designs

Experimental studies, also known as explanatory studies, examine changes in the dependent variable (Y) based on the manipulation of the independent variable (X). An experimental study is designed to assess causality or correlation among variables to the extent possible. Later in this book, the concepts of causality and correlation will be discussed further. Experimental designs often involve the comparison between groups (e.g., clients received intervention vs. clients did not receive intervention) or different subsets within a group (e.g., male vs. female). However, experimental study can also be conducted with one group or one participant (e.g., effect of sleep on a group of social work students' academic performance).

Experimental studies are useful in assessing the effects of a given program model (i.e., independent variable) by comparing the difference in outcomes (i.e., dependent variable) between a group of people receiving intervention (i.e., experimental group) or services and those who did not receive the intervention (i.e., control group). The group that receives the intervention or services is called the *experimental group*, and the one that does not is called the *control group*.

HYPOTHESIS FOR EXPERIMENTAL DESIGNS

Experimental designs involve the use of research hypotheses. The following are a few common forms of hypotheses (Atherton & Klemmack, 1982):

1. Contributory: X increases (or decreases) the likelihood of Y but is only one of a number of factors.
    a. "Hard work increases the likelihood of getting good grades."
    b. "Consistent family support contributes to the decrease of relapse among program participants who are in recovery."
2. Contingent: A condition may have a causative influence when X increases the likelihood of Y under certain circumstances in certain contingencies.
    a. "Job placement services will decrease the number of people who are on welfare when the economy is doing well."
    b. "Ex-foster care youth will more likely be successful in achieving independent living if they are paired up with mentors for at least two years after emancipation."
3. Alternative: Either X or Z increases the likelihood of Y.
    a. "Changes in either parents' or their children's behaviors will lead to fewer child abuse incidents."
    b. "Improvement in either the instructor or the students' level of involvement will increase the educational outcomes of this class."

TYPES OF EXPERIMENTAL DESIGNS

Experimental designs include a variety of research designs that involve the manipulation of the independent variables, timing, dosage, and sampling. Based on the level of rigor, sampling, and randomization, they could be categorized into the following designs:

A. Preexperimental designs
B. Quasi-experimental designs
C. Single-subject design/single-case study
D. True experimental designs

Technically, preexperimental designs, as the name implies, do not possess all the characteristics of true experimental designs. True experimental designs use experimental and control groups and involve sampling and randomization (i.e., random assignment and random sampling of participants). Preexperimental designs do not attempt to control threats to internal validity and have very limited ability to make generalizations. Different true experimental designs have different capacities for controlling the threats to validity and reliability. Quasi-experimental designs have some abilities to control the threats; however, unlike true experimental designs, they do not use randomization.
Diagrams for each of the designs are included next.

X – Administration of the independent variable (intervention/activity)
O – Observation and measurement of the dependent variable (outcome/change)
R – Randomization—that is, random sampling or random assignment (participants are chosen/assigned by chance)

A. Preexperimental Designs
(No randomization)

CROSS-SECTIONAL SURVEY
This is one of the most commonly used designs used by social workers. It is a point-in-time, across-the-board study of the target population. It could be a simple show of hands in a parenting class of how many of the participating families are dual-income families. It could also be a large-scale multifaceted community needs assessment survey or a citywide homeless point-in-time count. It does not have an intervention, just a simple targeted (e.g., female social work students' perspective on abortion) or sweeping (e.g., the whole class's opinion on canceling the last examination!) study of the population.

O   (O – cross-sectional measurement)

ONE-SHOT CASE STUDY/ONE-GROUP POSTTEST ONLY

This is often used as an assessment of the effect (O) of an intervention (X). It is to assess possible changes that may be related to the intervention. Compton and Galaway (1984) asserted that clients come to social workers for assistance when their life situations have overwhelmed them. It is not uncommon for social workers to not have the luxury of thoroughly assessing clients and setting baselines before the implementation of interventions that may range from basic psychosocial education to crisis intervention. That makes it ever-more important for social workers to demonstrate the effectiveness of their interventions. Has the suicide intervention been effective in helping an unemployed single dad void a suicide attempt and seek ongoing professional support? Have the dating violence workshops been successful in preparing teens to develop a proper understanding and skills for respectful relationships? What happened to the participants 6 months after they graduated from the Women's Empowerment Job Readiness Program? Has the rape crisis hotline been effective in providing callers with immediate emotional support? Also, who would forget those feel-good evaluations after training workshops: "Would you rate this workshop very good or excellent!?"

$$X \quad O \quad (X - \text{intervention}, O - \text{performance at post-test})$$

ONE-GROUP PRETEST-POSTTEST

This design is similar to the posttest-only design except for the presence of a pretest. Commonly, this is being referred to as the pre- and posttest. The pretest provides a baseline for comparison with the posttest to assess the change. While this change can be measured, whether it is due to the intervention or the threats to internal validity is questionable. During an intake assessment, the social worker administered a standardized anxiety test to confirm and assess the severity of her client's anxiety disorder. After 8 weeks of intensive treatment, she gave the client the same anxiety test again to find out to what extent the treatment goal had been achieved. In an older adults service center, a field instructor realized that her young social work intern appeared to be intimidated by her older male clients and did not know how to present herself professionally and effectively. During supervision, she provided the intern training on assertiveness and sense of self in professional settings. She observed the intern during subsequent meetings with her older male clients and concluded that the intern had shown confidence and competency without signs of feeling Intimidated.

$$O_1 \quad X \quad O_2 \quad (O_1 - \text{pretest result}, X - \text{intervention}, O_2 - \text{posttest result})$$

STATIC GROUP COMPARISON/POSTTEST ONLY WITH NONEQUIVALENT GROUPS

This design includes a control group that does not receive the intervention. This will allow the researcher to compare the outcomes between two groups. This is an improvement over the one-group posttest-only design for its ability to control threats, such as history, and the capacity to weigh against a comparison group. However, because the two groups were not randomly set up to be equivalent, whether the intervention or something else causes the differences between them after the intervention is always inconclusive. One group of foster children was matched with Court Appointed Special Advocate (CASA) volunteers. Another group of foster youth was not set up to receive services from CASA. After the children left the foster care system a year later, students were assessed on their readiness for the world outside of foster care. They found children who received CASA services doing better than those who did not. While it is reasonable to claim that CASA services made a difference, the claim will have many limitations, including failing to address the threats to internal validity. For example, it is not clear if the two groups were different to begin with and, therefore, their outcomes were already different.

X   O   (experimental group – receives intervention)
     O   (control group – does not receive intervention)

B. Quasi-Experimental Designs
(Without randomization, multiple measures of change)

Quasi-experimental designs or *time-series designs* are located between preexperimental and true experimental designs. Quasi-experimental designs have multiple points of measure and, therefore, are different from the preexperimental designs. This provides the designs with more useful data and addresses some of the threats to internal validity, such as history and regression to the mean. Quasi-experimental designs are not true experimental designs because they do not use randomization to recruit or assign participants. Campbell and Stanley's 1963 book *Experimental and Quasi-Experimental Designs for Research* is the classic text for quasi-experimental designs.

Trends and patterns of performance are usually observed before and after the intervention. Changes in the trends and patterns may indicate that the intervention could have contributed to the difference (Lammers & Badia, 2005). This, however, is not a strong assertion because so many other factors may have contributed to the change. If the difference is consistently detected over time or over different groups, then the argument on the effect of the independent variable will be strengthened.

BASIC TIME-SERIES/LONGITUDINAL STUDY

When enacting an intervention that may require time to see its full effect or its regimen requires regular monitoring, a longitudinal study design will be very useful. A social worker may want to find out the long-term effect of his drug abuse treatment program beyond its normal 30 days free of relapse standard. Setting up multiple check-ins after the 30-days-free relapse period allows him to monitor and observe factors that may enhance or hinder a client's progress. A longitudinal study is able to capture changes that otherwise would be affected by the threat of regression to the mean because, over time, people tend to behave like they normally do. In fact, this design is often included in research texts as a stand-alone research design. It has also been listed under preexperimental cross-sectional studies as well as under quasi-experimental, time-series studies. No matter how it is classified, it includes repeated measures and has the capacity to identify trends and changes over time.

$$X \quad O_1 \quad O_2 \quad O_3 \quad O_n$$

INTERRUPTED TIME-SERIES DESIGN

Several measures (pretest) are made before the implementation of the intervention and then followed by several more measures (posttest) after the intervention. The researcher needs to have a sufficient number of measures to establish the trend and pattern of the condition. The time between measures should also be comparable. Multiple measures before and after the introduction of the independent variable (intervention) allow the researcher to acquire a more reliable and stable observation of the condition. The post intervention observations permit the researcher to measure the incremental and overall changes.

A school social worker implemented four 1-hour sessions of an anti-bullying and healthy relationship training to all fifth graders in a school. Along with the school-teachers and yard duty volunteers, they observed how the fifth graders interacted in the playground during recesses, as well as before and after school, using a standardized data collection form. They derived a schedule that included two different designed observations on Monday, Wednesday, and Friday for week 1, as well as Tuesday and Thursday for week 2. The anti-bullying training was offered the following week. They

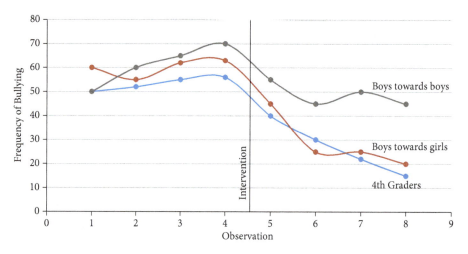

Figure 6.1. Quasi-Experimental Design—Anti-Bullying Program for Fifth Graders

used the same data collection form and observation schedule to record students' performance after the implementation of the training.

$$O_1 \qquad O_2 \qquad O_3 \qquad O_4 \qquad X \qquad O_5 \qquad O_6 \qquad O_7 \qquad O_8$$

During the pretest, they observed that there was a general "acceptance" of bullying among students, particularly verbal bullying by boys toward girls, as well as fourth graders at the latter part of the school day. Posttest observations revealed a noticeable decrease in verbal bullying toward fourth graders and girls. Bullying between boys was still common, but the language used was less abusive (Figure 6.1).

One of the advantages of using the quasi-experimental design is the ability to display changes and results graphically on a chart. This form of data and results presentation could be versatile in reporting and showing outcomes to the administration, the funders, the clients, and the general public.

NONEQUIVALENT COMPARISON GROUP PRETEST–POSTTEST

This quasi-experimental design includes both an experimental group and a control group to test the effects of the intervention. Because no randomization is used, the two comparison groups are probably not equivalent groups. Researchers could use natural groups with similar characteristics as the control groups for the comparison. A third-grade class that receives anti-bullying training could use another third-grade class in the same school as the control group. An Alcoholics Anonymous (AA) group

Conceptual and Practical Research and Statistics for Social Workers

on the east side of the city could use another AA group in the area for comparison. The idea is to match as many of the key characteristics as possible for the two groups. Researchers not only have to avoid comparing oranges to apples, but they should also avoid comparing good oranges to bad oranges (unless that is the intent!) The pretest in this design could also be used to judge the compatibility between the two groups. Going back to the third graders and the anti-bullying training, the pretest equips the social worker with the baselines for comparison with the posttest results. Changes in students' knowledge, attitudes, and behaviors regarding bullying as the result of the training can be measured by comparing the control group's posttest results with the pretest results. Comparison between the experimental group posttest results with the control group posttest results allows the social worker to assess the different results between receiving and not receiving the training.

$$O_1 \quad X \quad O_2$$
$$O_1 \quad\quad O_2$$

MULTIPLE TIME-SERIES DESIGN

The inclusion of a control group and an experimental group increases the rigor of the design and gives the study findings a higher explanatory power. From the earlier example, the social worker who conducted the anti-bullying training was responsible for two different elementary schools in the same neighborhood. The social worker was able to use the fifth graders from another school as the control group. She compared the differences between the two groups after the training. To make sure students at the second school were not denied service, after the research and training were completed at the first school, the social worker replicated the training at the second school.

$$O_1 \quad O_2 \quad O_3 \quad O_4 \quad X \quad O_5 \quad O_6 \quad O_7 \quad O_8$$
$$O_1 \quad O_2 \quad O_3 \quad O_4 \quad\quad O_5 \quad O_6 \quad O_7 \quad O_8$$

C. Single-Subject Designs/Single-System Designs

While quasi-experimental designs are used to assess changes and outcomes for a group of subjects, the single-subject designs are used to evaluate changes for a single subject. "*Time series analysis* is characterized by repeated measurements of the dependent variable over time with an introduction of the independent variable at a particular point in time. Trends or patterns of behaviors are observed both before and after introduction of the independent variable" (Lammers & Badia, 2005, pp. 14–26). A parallel definition for the single-subject design could, therefore, be the following: *Single-subject design* is characterized by the repeated measurement of the dependent variable or variables through the applications and nonapplications of the independent variable for a single subject.

With repeated measures, a quasi-experimental design is used to assess the effect of the introduction of a mentoring program, the independent variable, for a group of single teen mothers. With the use of repeated measures, the trends and patterns of change are identified. Similarly, a single-subject design is used to assess the effects and outcomes of a mentoring program for an individual single teen mother with the manipulation of the implementation of the mentoring program—the independent variable. Both approaches could be conducted by the practitioners who have a direct connection with the subjects and could use the results to inform practice. They are not outside researchers who may not have direct contact and understanding of the clients involved.

Single-subject designs are useful for social workers for many reasons. Clients don't come in a bundle, presorted with similar needs and characteristics, and they can wait until social workers are ready to perform group studies. They come individually with unique needs and require differential and often immediate interventions. The effectiveness of interventions differs from person to person; social workers need to evaluate their services and can use timely input to modify their services and measure results. Single-subject designs allow these interventions to happen without delay or other research-related limitations. They are also user-friendly and can use line graphs to show progress and results. Single-subject designs are often used in social work for program evaluation.

Single-subject designs often start with achieving a *baseline (A)*, which will be used to make comparisons with the subsequent data. The baseline is the phase in which no intervention is applied. Through repeated observations and measurements, when a *stable trend or pattern is obtained*, the baseline is established. An *intervention (B)*, the independent variable, or *additional intervention (C, D,* etc.) can then be applied or withdrawn. Their effects on the dependent variable will be assessed. Both the dependent and independent variables need to be quantifiable so that they can be measured.

Researchers should look for a stable baseline through multiple observations or measurements. The baseline reflects a steady pattern of the usual performance when no intervention is applied. Researchers should avoid patterns that are not yet clearly established or already show a trend of natural progression, even without the

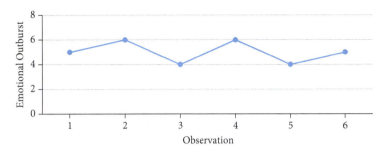

Figure 6.2. Baseline With a Steady Pattern

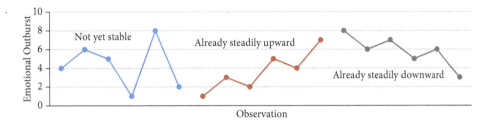

Figure 6.3. Unsuitable Baselines

intervention. That means the pattern of the behavior being observed is still changing or has already been changing in spite of not having the intervention. Figures 6.2 and 6.3 are examples of a baseline with a stable pattern and baselines that are unsuitable, respectively.

A-B DESIGN

A social worker, Nancy, is a member of a treatment team at an eating disorder clinic. As a clinical case manager, Nancy's responsibilities include monitoring clients' medication compliance, providing individual psychotherapy, and running a support group. She wants to make sure she is serving her clients well and that her services are effective. One of her clients, Jill, had trouble complying with her prescribed medication schedule. She observed Jill over a period of 5 days and established a baseline (A) that Jill had been consistently missing four or five of her scheduled medications. After meeting with Jill, Nancy implemented an incentive program that aimed to improve medication compliance (B). Soon after the intervention, Nancy noticed that Jill's compliancy had steadily improved to full compliance. Nancy is using the A-B design (Figure 6.4) that includes one baseline and one treatment phase. The A-B design is a simple "no treatment" and then "provision of treatment" approach. It appears the

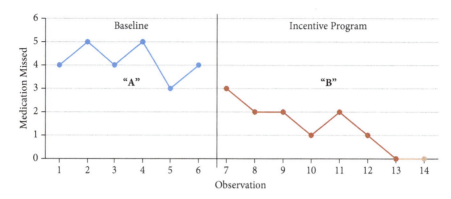

Figure 6.4. **A-B Design**

incentive program has been producing positive change. It is straightforward, but it also has very little control over threats to internal validity, such as history, instrumentation, regression to the mean, and selection. It is not possible for Nancy to claim conclusively that the incentive program (independent variable) is the reason for the change in Jill's medication compliance (dependent variables).

A-B-A DESIGN AND A-B-A-B DESIGN

The A-B-A design (Figure 6.5) is also known as the reverse design. The intervention is withheld or discontinued after its effects have been observed. The discontinuation returns the intervention phase to the nontreatment phase. Nancy stops the incentive program to see if Jill's compliancy will (a) continue or (b) return back to the baseline phase. It is possible that Jill will return to being noncompliant. It is also possible that

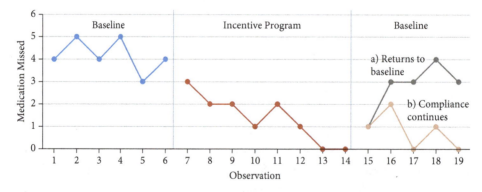

Figure 6.5. **A-B-A Design**

Conceptual and Practical Research and Statistics for Social Workers

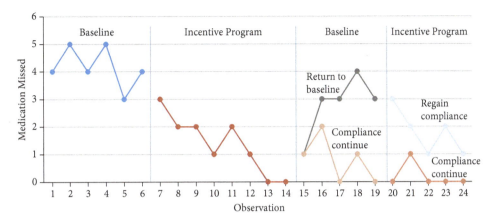

Figure 6.6. A-B-A-B Design

the intervention will have a lasting effect, and Jill will continue to comply and never return to the baseline.

The return to the baseline may not necessarily mean the intervention is not effective; after all, improvements have been seen in the B phase. It possibly means that the intervention may not have had enough time to develop solid impact; the dosage may need to be adjusted; there are other factors that need to be considered. The nonreturn to the baseline condition would certainly be good news and a sign that the intervention possibly has both short-term and long-term effects.

Rightfully, some may question the ethics of withholding treatment and reversing the client's condition and improvement. There are several ways to address this concern. One is to take advantage of the natural occurrence that provides a break from the implementation of the intervention. For example, Nancy could use the long winter holiday break when the clinic is closed as a natural "A" phase for Jill. Another alternative is to use the A-B-A-B design (Figure 6.6).

The A-B-A-B design is an extension of the A-B-A design with the return of the intervention after the second "A" phase. The regaining of improvement in the second "B" phase after the advance was lost during the second "A" phase may be a validation of the positive effect of the intervention.

A-B-C-D DESIGN (SUCCESSIVE INTERVENTION DESIGN)

There are many variations of the single-subject design. For example, the A-B-C-D (Figure 6.7) design is used to assess the introduction of three interventions. Social worker Nancy wanted to see if the combination of interventions (independent

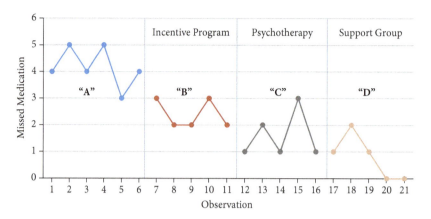

Figure 6.7. A-B-C-D Design

variables), including the incentive program (B), along with psychotherapy (C) and peer support group (D), will increase Jill's medication compliance (dependent variable). Nancy first implements the A-B design. After a period of several measures to gauge the effectiveness of the incentive program (B), she added weekly psychotherapy (C) to the schedule and followed up with including Jill in a peer-support group (D).

This A-B-C-D design is able to show the progressive improvement of the dependent variable with the consecutive use of several interventions. It is, however, unclear which intervention was responsible for the change and what the likely effects of the interactions among these interventions will be. To address these concerns, researchers may consider withholding certain interventions to single out their specific effects. They may, therefore, use designs such as A-B-A-C-D, A-B-C-A-D, A-B-A-C-A-D, or the like. However, if the overall outcome for the client is more important than the rigor of research, then the cumulative effect of the A-B-C-D design results should suffice.

B-A-B DESIGN

Social workers often do not have the luxury of obtaining a baseline with no service provided. Clients may arrive in crisis or the situation is so severe that it demands immediate actions. In other situations, service and professional constraints may limit the likelihood of getting the baseline established. The B-A-B design (Figure 6.8) provides the intervention first and establishes the baseline later. Nancy learned that for the last month, Jill had not taken her medication and had had several incidents of binge eating. Upon seeing Jill, Nancy immediately intervened and coordinated with Jill's care team to stabilize her physical and mental health conditions. Nancy realized

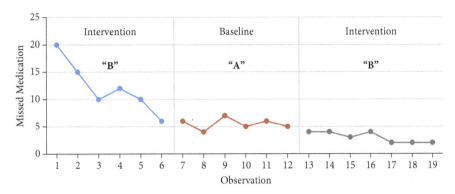

Figure 6.8. B-A-B Design

that Jill's relapse was probably instigated by other challenges that Jill was experiencing in her relationship with her significant others. After Jill's condition was sufficiently under control and in consultation with her care team, Nancy decided to withdraw the intensive treatment. That would allow her an opportunity to test the effect of the intensive treatment and time to establish a baseline. During this baseline phase, Jill's compliancy was stable but still needed improvement. Nancy reintroduced the planned intervention.

D. True Experimental Designs

True experimental designs are different than the other research designs in that they involve random sampling or random assignment in their acquisition of study participants. Simple random sampling (random selection or choice) means the researcher is to select participants out of the population or a pool of potential participants (sampling frame) by chance or probability. Random assignment means allotting potential participants into the experimental and control groups by equal chances. Both random sampling and random assignment involve the use of probability sampling. The random selection allows the research findings to have a greater capacity to be generalized to other individuals or population, while the random assignment allows the research to make generalizations within the sampling frame. Trochim (2001) asserted, "Random selection is related to sampling. Therefore it is most closely related to the *external validity* (or generalizability) of your results ... random assignment is most related to *internal validity* ... [that] treatment groups are similar to each other (equivalent) prior to the treatment" (p. 196). The topic of sampling, including probability and nonprobability sampling types and methods, will be discussed further in the following chapter.

Yegidis, Weinbach, and Myers (2018, p. 111) listed three requirements for an experimental design:

1. The independent variable or variables are introduced or manipulated by the researcher.
2. There are one or more control groups that are not exposed to the independent variable.
3. Research participants are randomly assigned to experimental and control groups.

Through random assignment, controlled use of the independent variables, and availability of experimental and control groups, the researcher is able to exercise the maximum control for the **threats of internal validity** (Rubin & Babbie, 2015; see

TABLE 6.1. Research Design and Threats to Internal Validity

RESEARCH DESIGNS	THREATS TO INTERNAL VALIDITY
Preexperimental Design	
Cross-sectional survey O	History, maturation, selection, mortality
One shot-case study X O	History, maturation, selection, mortality
One-group pretest-posttest O_1 X O_2	History, maturation, testing, instrumentation, statistical regression
Static group comparison X O O	Selection, mortality
Quasi-Experimental Designs	
Basic time-series/longitudinal study X O_1 O_2 O_3 O_n	History, maturation, selection, mortality
Interrupted time-series design $O_1 O_2 O_3 O_4$ X $O_5 O_6 O_7 O_8$	History, maturation, testing, instrumentation
True Experimental Designs	
Pretest-posttest, control group design R O_{E1} X O_{E2} R O_{C1} O_{C2}	All threats controlled
Posttest-only control-group design R X O R O	All threats controlled

Conceptual and Practical Research and Statistics for Social Workers

TABLE 6.2. **Comparing Experimental Designs**

R – Random sampling or random assignment (participants are chosen/assigned equally by chance)

X – Administration of the independent variable (intervention, activity, treatment)

O – Observation of the measurement of the dependent variable (output, outcome, change)

A. PREEXPERIMENTAL DESIGNS	B. QUASI-EXPERIMENTAL DESIGNS	C. SINGLE-SUBJECT DESIGNS	D. TRUE EXPERIMENTAL DESIGNS
Cross-sectional survey O One-shot case study X O	Basic time-series/longitudinal X O_1 O_2 O_3 O_4	• A-B • A-B-A • A-B-A-B • A-B-C-D, B-A-B	Cross-sectional survey R X O
One-group pretest-posttest O_1 X O_2	Interrupted time series O_1 O_2 O_3 O_4 X O_5 O_6 O_7 O_8 Non-equivalent comparison group pretest-posttest O_1 X O_2 O_1 O_2	A (baseline phase), B (intervention phase/first intervention), C (second Intervention), D (third intervention)	One-group pretest-posttest R O_1 X O_2 Pretest-posttest control group R O_1 X O_2 R O_1 O_2
Static group comparison X O O	Multiple time series O_1 O_2 O_3 O_4 X O_5 O_6 O_7 O_8 O_1 O_2 O_3 O_4 O_5 O_6 O_7 O_8		Posttest-only control group R X O R O

discussions in Chapter 4). Table 6.1 lists how such threats can be related to specific experimental designs. In addition, experimental designs allow for the use of statistical procedures to analyze and describe the results, as well as make inferences. There are many variations of the experimental design ranging from simple to complex and advanced. Examples of the common designs that are often useful for social workers are listed in Table 6.2.

CROSS-SECTIONAL SURVEY/ONE-GROUP, POSTTEST-ONLY DESIGN

R   X   O

This is similar to the one-shot case study for the preexperimental designs except it involves a random selection or assignment of participants. A child welfare social worker, Nogn Yee, was preparing for her youths who are about to age out of the system. She had found this newly developed Successful Life Skills (SLS) curriculum. She thought it was a very well-developed and culturally competent program for her youths. Out of all the eligible youth in her caseload, she randomly selected (R) 10 to participate in the SLS program (X). After the completion of the program, she then assessed how much the youth had learned from the SLS and to what extent they attained the goals of the training (O). The results of her posttest were very positive. She, however, did not have the confidence to make the claim that the SLS was responsible for the positive changes. The posttest-only design has many limitations and is subject to all the threats to internal validity. It does not have a pretest and a comparison group and is affected by all the extraneous factors or confounding variables.

ONE-GROUP, PRETEST-POSTTEST DESIGN

$$R \quad O_1 \quad X \quad O_2$$

This is essentially a classic pre- and posttest or before-and-after study. With some planning, social worker Amanda was able to conduct a pretest (O_1) of the youth she had randomly selected (R) prior to their participation in the SLS training (X). Amanda was mindful of an ethical concern of denial of service to the youth who were not selected. It happened that this whole group of youth was scheduled to receive the life skills training within the subsequent 12 months. Immediate participation was not required. Also, because of limited resources, the agency could only offer one training at a time. Amanda arranged for the nonselected youth to participate in the next SLS training. After the training, a posttest (O_2) was conducted. With the information collected from the pretest and the posttest, Amanda was able to compare the changes. She could make the claim that the changes assessed took place between the pretest and the posttest, which was during the SLS program. She, however, still could not confidently claim that the changes were related or caused by the SLS program. She also understood that many of the internal threats and external factors or confounding variables were not controlled and could affect the outcomes of the posttest.

PRETEST-POSTTEST CONTROL GROUP DESIGN

$$R \quad O_{E1} \quad X \quad O_{E2} \quad \text{(Experimental group)}$$
$$R \quad O_{C1} \quad \quad O_{C2} \quad \text{(Control group)}$$

This classical experimental design addresses many of the threats to internal validity and the influences of confounding variables. Amanda was able to use random assignment (R) to draw up an experimental group and a control group. Because of the random assignment, the two groups were equivalent groups that were statistically comparable to each other. Both received a pretest (O_1) and then a posttest (O_2). The experimental group participated in the SLS while the control group did not. Again, Amanda addressed the ethical considerations as she did for the one-group, pretest-posttest design. In fact, the way she provided SLS for the control group after the posttest formulated a new research design:

$$R \quad O_{E1} \quad X \quad O_{E2} \qquad O_{E3} \quad \text{(Experimental group)}$$
$$R \quad O_{C1} \qquad\quad O_{C2} \quad X \quad O_{C3} \quad \text{(Control group)}$$

The research design provides opportunities for various analyses. The researcher can test the changes over time, the effect of the independent variable, the effect of the absence of the independent variable, the effect regarding the timing of the intervention, and many others. The following are examples of such comparisons.

a. Comparisons between O_1 and O_2 (and O_3 if it is included) for the experimental group and the control group to assess the differences or changes in the group with and without the intervention. They are in effect time-series, before-and-after comparisons.

b. Comparisons between O_{E2} and O_{C2}, as well as between O_{E3} and O_{C3} to assess the differences concerning having the intervention (independent variable) and the absence of the intervention.

POSTTEST-ONLY, CONTROL-GROUP DESIGN

$$R \quad X \quad O$$
$$R \qquad\quad O$$

This design can be used when the inclusion of a pretest may have an undesirable effect on the posttest or in situations where the pretest is not available. The researcher could still use random assignment to set up the experimental and control groups for comparison. The difference in the outcome between the two groups is expected to be related to the involvement of the intervention.

From Preexperimental to Quasi-Experimental, Single-Subject, and Ture Experimental Designs, there are many ways to carry out experimental research studies. Table 6.2 below summarizes and compares these various types of experimental designs.

Experimental designs have been the hallmark for research studies that have academic rigor and prestige. With their ability to control the effects of cofounding variables, minimize variability of the testing conditions, use randomization, and understanding of independent and dependent variables, experimental research studies serve the need of identifying causal relationships. This is very true for pure research projects in the sciences and medicine and has brought about many breakthroughs that have improved the well-being of humankind and the world. However, how likely is it that the social sciences are able to employ experimental designs? Trochim (2006) gave a personal guess that "randomized experiments are probably appropriate in no more than 10% of the social research studies that attempt to assess causal relationship" (para. 12). He further argued that there are many technical, logistical, and ethical limitations in conducting experiments in social research. "The bottom line here is that experimental design is intrusive and difficult to carry out in most real world context" (para. 11). Social workers may or may not agree with this assertion. However, the reality is that just because it is an experiment does not mean it is better than other research designs. They all serve particular purposes, and social workers should be proficient in various research designs, including experimental designs, to better serve the needs of their clients.

EVALUATIVE DESIGNS

An evaluative research design involves the use of exploratory, descriptive, and experimental designs. It is the application of various research designs to study issues such as program performance, accountability, challenges, and improvement. It asks important questions: "Did the program achieve the goals it set out to achieve?" "How effective and efficient is the program?" "Should it be continued?" "Is it cost-effective?" "What changes are needed?"

Many terms are used to describe the various types of evaluative research designs: process evaluation, outcome evaluation, progress evaluation, implementation evaluation, formative evaluation, and summative evaluation. A few of them are basically the same; they are named differently for their unique contexts and purposes of application. Most importantly, researchers distinguish two key forms of evaluative research: formative and summative evaluations.

Formative and Summative Evaluations

Formative evaluations monitor the progress of the program and study, (i.e., whether it is on course). Some characterize formative evaluations as taking the

Conceptual and Practical Research and Statistics for Social Workers

temperature of the program. They are usually done while the program is being formulated or in progress. They generate information that could help validate, develop, and improve the program. Examples of a formative evaluation include needs assessment, process evaluation, case conference, case study, and implementation evaluation.

Summative evaluations assess the results of the program. The focus could be on the extent of goal attainment, challenges and successes, effectiveness and efficiency, as well as expected and unexpected outcomes. At the end, the merits of the program are examined. Examples of summative evaluation include cost analysis, outcome valuation, impact evaluation, and goal-attainment assessment.

Yuen and Terao (2003) used the flight of a commercial jetliner as an example to explain program evaluation and highlight its importance. A huge Boeing 747 was parked at the gate of an airport. Its front wheels rested on a small square box painted on the ground underneath the plane. With a detailed flight plan in hand, the pilots took the plane into the air and hours later landed at another airport several thousand miles away. The pilots parked the plane by the gate, and, again, its front wheels rested on another small square box painted on the ground.

The passengers happily deplaned, but they did not know that the plane was "off course" most of the time. Many factors, such as traffic, weather, and ground conditions, made following the preset flight plan exactly impossible. It was the pilots' competence and consistent adjustments, guided by the well-developed flight plan, that made the trip successful.

These pilots' professional performance is, in fact, not that different from what we do every day while driving on the road. With the destination in mind, we determine the route and get on the road. We consistently evaluate the road conditions and adjust our driving accordingly. This ongoing monitoring and use of new information to assist our trip is an example of formative evaluation. Whether you arrive at your destination safely and on time just like those happily deplaned passengers is the summative evaluation.

Robert Stake, an evaluation theorist and researcher, is credited for the famous metaphor, "When the cook tastes the soup, that's formative; when the guests taste the soup, that's summative" (Miller, King, Mark, & Caracelli, 2016, p. 287). Formative evaluation provides information to the practitioners and participants, summative evaluation reports to the stakeholders, including the funders, organizations, clients, and community. We engage in evaluation, both formative and summative, in our everyday life. Details of conducting evaluative research (e.g., program evaluation)

BOX 6.1. A SCHOOL SOCIAL WORK EVALUATIVE RESEARCH EXAMPLE

An evaluative research design (e.g., a program evaluation plan), may involve the use of exploratory study design, descriptive study design, and experimental design, collecting both quantitative and qualitative data. The following is an example of an evaluative study with mixed designs.

A school-based service program conducted a general needs assessment (*exploratory study*) and learned that the target students might benefit from intensive one-on-one tutoring in math and reading to improve their academic performance and sense of self-confidence. They did several surveys (*descriptive study*) using questionnaires, observations, academic testing, and existing data to assess the intended change, as well as the relationship between students' academic performance and self-confidence. The social worker monitored the progress of the program and sought help from teachers who completed the monthly performance checklist for their students (*formative evaluation*). Biweekly program meetings with tutors and regular family contacts (*formative evaluation*) gave further information for program improvement. The end-of-the-semester student survey and focus group meetings with teachers and parents provided an overall assessment of the effects and outcomes of the program (*summative evaluation*).

In the same school, a social work intern wanted to apply a better monitored and more focused assessment to a group of participants in the semester-long, anti-bullying program. She was interested in studying the likely effects of the intervention and the changes in attitudes and behaviors related to bullying throughout the semester. She measured these students' attitudes and behaviors weekly for a month before they were enrolled in the program. She then used repeated measures every 4 weeks during the semester to track the changes in the targeted measures as well as the collective trends and patterns (quasi-experimental study preexperimental study).

A group of students with emotional difficulties was identified by their teachers and parents. They were referred to the social worker and his graduate social work intern for counseling. With their parents' consent, in addition to individual counseling, the students were randomly assigned to participate in a controlled study (*experimental study*). The experimental group would participate in an added 4-week, peer-support group. During that time, the control group only received individual counseling. This was set up to find out if the peer-support group further improved students' capacities in emotional regulations. The control group participated in the peer-support program after the experimental group concluded its support group.

Findings from these studies helped the school social work services to design and deliver interventions that are more effective and evidence based. They also influenced student services to be more accountable to the funding sources, the schools, the parents, and the students. The valuable findings helped the program prepare better grant proposals to continue the financial support for those needed services.

will be discussed in Chapter 10, Needs Assessment, Program Planning, and Program Evaluation (What and What Happens).

MIXED-METHODS DESIGNS

Mixed-methods designs have become well received in recent decades as an addition to the quantitative and qualitative research paradigms. Authors in research evaluation, education, psychology, and health sciences have been instrumental in promoting and advancing the use of mixed research methods. Some of the noted publications on this methodology include Greene, Caracelli, and Graham (1989), Creswell and Plano Clark (2007), and Tashakkori and Teddlie (2003). Social work has also been active in the use and discussion of mixed-methods research. In August 2004, the National Institutes of Health held a 4-day workshop titled the Design and Conduct of Qualitative and Mixed-Methods Research in Social Work and Other Health Professions. Many social work authors, such as Padgett (2009) and Townsend, Floersch, and Findlinig (2009) discussed the role of mixed-methods research in social work related to research and knowledge development. In the last decade, the number of mixed-methods research–related social work books, articles, and studies has been on the rise. Are mixed-methods research and social work a good fit? Haight and Bidwell (2016) asserted that mixed-methods research is well suited to social work. It is consistent with the profession's ethics, legacy, pragmatism, practice principles, and research orientations.

What is mixed-methods research? Johnson, Onwuegbuzie, and Turner (2007), after methodically reviewing and comparing 19 different definitions of mixed methods research, offered the following general definition.

> Mixed methods research is the type of research in which a researcher or team of researchers combines elements of qualitative and quantitative research approaches (e.g., use of qualitative and quantitative viewpoints, data collection, analysis, inference techniques) for the broad purposes of breadth and depth of understanding and corroboration. (p. 123)

Haight and Bidwell (2016) indicated that "the mixing of qualitative and quantitative research components is *planned* to address the research question(s) of interest, and *flexible* to respond to new information and understanding that emerges as the study unfolds" (p. 2). They emphasized that it is not just a mix of quantitative and

TABLE 6.3. Comparisons Among Quantitative, Qualitative, and Mixed Methods

	QUANTITATIVE TRADITION	QUALITATIVE TRADITIONS	BOTH (MIXED) TRADITIONS
Philosophical underpinnings	Positivism/post-positivism	Constructivism	Pragmatism
Logic	Deductive logic	Inductive logic	Both deductive and inductive
Questioning	Research questions address quanta	Research questions address qualia	Employ logical arguments
Data	Data are represented numerically	Data are represented textually or pictorially	Data are represented both numerically and textually/pictorially
Emphasis	Emphasize the objective	Emphasize the subjective	Are empirical: based on deliberate, careful observations
Methodological emphasis	Sampling, measuring, calculating, abstract-ing	Interpretation, thematization, contextualization, and exemplification	Incorporate safe-guards to minimize biases and strength inferences
Social inquirer	Scientist	Interpreter	Employ interpretation and are concerned with broader implica-tions of empirical findings View knowl-edge and theory as provisional
Associated terms	Survey research, probability sampling, experimental and quasi-experimental designs, descriptive and inferential statistics	Grounded theory, ethnography, case studies, purposive sampling, categorical versus contextualizing strategies, trustworthi-ness, credibility	Concurrent (parallel) and sequential mixed designs, triangulation, data conversion, inference quality

qualitative components. They are, in fact, "*integrated* to provide a better understanding of the phenomenon under study" (p. 2).

In what manner does mixed-methods research relate to quantitative research and qualitative research? Combining information excerpted from Angell and Townsend's (2011) workshop on mixed-methods studies at the Society for Social Work and Research's annual meeting and a comparison table from Haight and Bidwell (2016, p. 5), Table 6.3 lists the differences among quantitative, qualitative, and mixed-methods research.

Haight and Bidwell (2016) used the spectrum of colors to represent the continuum of the three paradigms. Qualitative methods are the yellow color on one end of the spectrum; quantitative methods are the blue color on the other end; mixed methods are the equally proportioned green color in the middle. They believe that mixed-methods research could help social work practice and policy to have an improved understanding of complex phenomena. It could also prepare the profession to find new and creative ways to approach persistent social problems.

Angell and Townsend (2011) described quantitative and qualitative components as strands. The way these strands interface forms different mixed-methods research designs. The interface could be the level of interaction, priority of the strands, timing and point of interface, and their research stance. Creswell and Plano (2011) and Creswell (2014) described the three basic mixed-methods designs.

1. Convergent parallel-quantitative and qualitative strands are conducted separately. They merge at the point of interpretation to give a more complete understanding of the data.
2. Explanatory sequential-quantitative stands are first collected and then contextualized with the qualitative data. Researchers are using qualitative data to make sense of quantitative data.

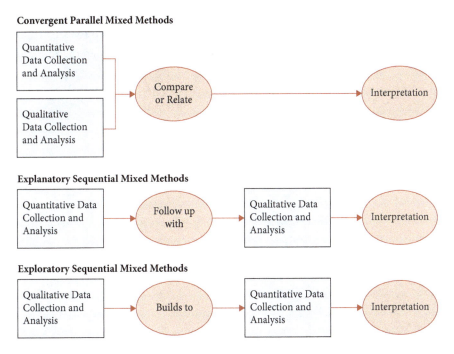

Figure 6.9. Three Basic Mixed-Methods Designs

3. Exploratory sequential-qualitative data are first collected and then validated by quantitative data. Researchers are using qualitative data to develop more refined and focused research questions and approaches.

These three basic approaches are depicted in Figure 6.9 (Creswell, 2014, p. 220). Mixed-methods research has evolved into a new force in social research and has its own specialty journal as well as books and followers from different disciplines. The discussions will continue regarding the use and development of mixed-methods research design.

CONCLUSION

This chapter explained the various research designs. They include an exploratory design that aims to seek better understanding, a descriptive design that studies the relationship between variables, an experimental design that examines correlation and causation, and an evaluative design that assesses outcomes and performances. Experimental designs include several major subcategories: preexperimental, quasi-experimental, single-subject, and true experimental designs. Mixed-methods research designs add versatility to the traditional designs. A common characteristic of research projects is the use of samples. The next chapter will explore the important topic of sampling. Different sampling approaches and their related issues will be discussed.

7 SAMPLING (HOUSE OF REPRESENTATIVES)

Who and what are the data sources for social work research? Many social workers' research projects involve people such as the general public, service recipients, social work students, other human service professionals, or social workers themselves. They may also include nonhuman subjects, such as academic and professional literature, social policies, or other artifacts. Researchers may or may not have direct contact with or access to the potential data sources. They may not readily know where or how to find the data sources. *Sampling* is about locating and recruiting those data sources that will provide the much-needed information for research projects. It is a process of selecting study subjects. This chapter explores both the nonprobability and probability sampling approaches, as well as sampling bias and errors.

NONPROBABILITY SAMPLING AND PROBABILITY SAMPLING

When the population is accessible and small enough that all could be included in the study, sampling is not needed. However, there are situations where the population is too large, not accessible, or unknown, whereby sampling procedures may be needed. Sampling may or may not employ probability theory and statistical methods to draw a *sample* (i.e., a representation, a subset, or a specimen) from the whole (i.e., population or class) for the study. The *population* is the target group the researcher is interested in studying. It could be a rather huge group, such as male college students in the state. Because of resources, cost, feasibility, and other reasons, the population may be unreachable or too large to census. The researcher may wish to consider a more feasible and accessible group of the population, such as male students at a local college. This accessible population is called the *sampling frame*. Out of this sampling frame, samples who become study subjects will be drawn. Sampling could be categorized into **nonprobability sampling and probability sampling**. Based on the purpose and nature of the study, researchers choose which sampling method is to be used.

Nonprobability sampling selects its sample by methods involving subjective judgment and not by equal chances. The odds of someone being selected into the sample are not equal and cannot be statistically calculated. When a nonprobability sampling method is used, the results from studying the selected sample are snapshots of the population and will have limited ability for generalization.

Probability sampling selects its sample by methods that offer everyone an equal chance to be chosen. The odds are theoretically the same for everyone and could be calculated. The odds for anyone who has one of the 100 raffle tickets sold to win the grand prize is 1 out of 100. When a probability sampling method is used, the results from the sample will have the ability to make generalizations or predictions to the population.

In her class of 20 students, the professor declares she will pick 10% of the students (i.e., two students) to receive an automatic "A" for the class. Would you want to be one of the two lucky students? Would you worry about the professor conveniently picking her favorite students and leaving you empty-handed? Would you prefer her to give everyone an equal chance to be selected? If you are thinking about these questions, then you are thinking about probability and nonprobability sampling.

RANDOM SAMPLING AND RANDOM ASSIGNMENT

Probability sampling includes both random sampling (random selection) and random assignment. *Random sampling* refers to the units being randomly selected (i.e., each has an equal chance of being chosen and becoming a study subject). Drawing a name from a hat or picking the short straw are everyday examples of random sampling. *Random assignment* refers to the systematic and chance-based process of assigning the study subjects to different groups (i.e., the control group or the experimental group, group A or group B). Because random sampling encompasses the selection of subjects from the population, it is, therefore, more related to the concerns of the study's external validity (i.e., generalization to the population). Random assignment, however, is more concerned about issues related to internal validity (i.e., are two groups equivalent to the point that they can be compared?). Random sampling and random assignment are key features for experimental research design. It is through them that a researcher can have confidence in claiming findings to be more trust-worthy and valid. Table 7.1 lists the common sampling strategies for both probability sampling and nonprobability sampling.

TABLE 7.1. Common Sampling Strategies

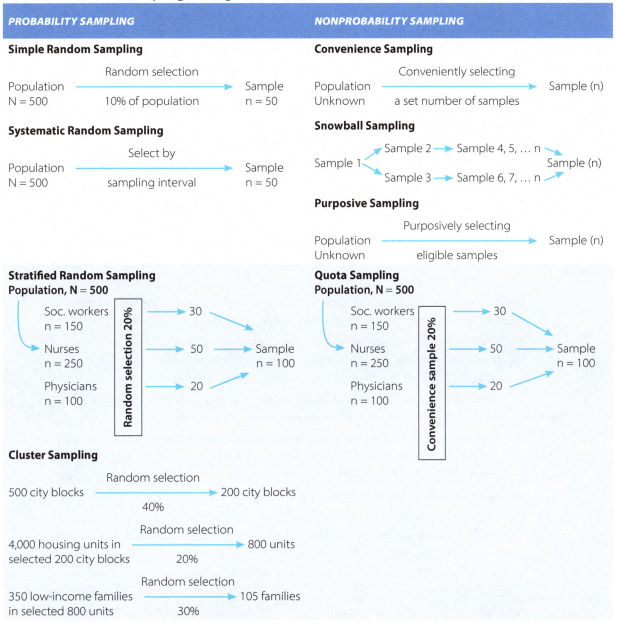

PROBABILITY SAMPLING	NONPROBABILITY SAMPLING
Simple Random Sampling	**Convenience Sampling**
Systematic Random Sampling	**Snowball Sampling**
Stratified Random Sampling Population, N = 500	**Quota Sampling** Population, N = 500
Cluster Sampling	

PROBABILITY SAMPLING (RANDOM SAMPLING)

Random sampling with or without replacement is sampling in which each case in the population has the same chance to be selected. If there are 10 students in a class and the teacher wants to select three randomly to participate in a school-wide survey, she writes each student's name on a separate piece of paper and places them in a container. She mixes them up and draws names out one at a time. Each student should have an equal 10% (i.e., 1 out of 10) chance to be selected.

To ensure that everyone has the same 1/10 chance, any of the names picked are to be returned to the container. There is a possibility that a student may be selected twice. If so, that student's opinion will be counted twice as if they are from two separate respondents. This is an example of *random sampling with replacement*. The values of the samples or observations are considered *independent*. Because of the replacement, each is being drawn from the same original population. The result of the first draw does not affect what the second draw will be. The covariance between two draws is zero. A *covariance* is a measure of how two values change together.

In another situation, the teacher is to give out prizes. Again, she puts names in a container and starts drawing names. However, she does not want the same students to get more than one prize. Therefore, she sets aside the names that are already drawn. This is a case of *random sampling without replacement*. Because there is no replacement, each of the drawings is from a slightly different or new population. The chance for the first student drawn in her class is 1/10, the next student is 1/9, and the next one is 1/8. Each sample or observation changes the probability of the other. The results of the first draw effects what the subsequent ones will be. They are, therefore, considered *dependent*, and the covariance between them is not zero.

The differences in these two approaches are of great interest to mathematicians. They are, however, not that significant to professionals who are mainly users of statistics. "In general, if the finite population is extremely large relative to *n,* then sampling without replacement is, for all intents and purposes, equivalent to sampling with replacement" (Panik, 2005, p. 301). In human services, because of small populations and other limitations, random sampling without replacement is more feasible and is more commonly used.

Simple random sampling is the basic form of random sampling. Study subjects from the population are selected entirely by chance. If a researcher decides to draw 20% of the population as the sample for her study in a housing complex, she could randomly pick 20 names from the list of the 100 residents. Besides drawing names from the hat, selection of random samples could be achieved by using a random

Conceptual and Practical Research and Statistics for Social Workers

number table or by using a computer program to generate the random numbers. People who buy lottery tickets know there is an option for the ticketing machine to pick their, hopefully, winning ticket numbers!

Systematic random sampling is a simpler and less expensive way to draw a random sample than the simple random sampling method. It is the selection of samples from a population or sampling frame with a sampling interval. Once the sample size is determined, it will be used to divide the population and come up with the sampling interval. Starting with the randomly selected first element, additional elements will be selected at the increment of the sampling interval. For example, 120 client files are organized numerically from 001 to 120. The researcher wants to randomly select 20 of them for the study. The population is 120, and the sample size is 20; therefore, the sampling interval is 6 (i.e., $120 \div 20 = 6$). The researcher also randomly selects a starting point number, say, four. As a result, the 20 samples will be 004, 010, 016, 022 … 106, 112, and 118. If the randomly selected starting point number is 15, then the samples will be 015, 021, 027 … 111, 117, 003, and 009. This is a very useful random sampling method, particularly when the population is already organized in some existing order. Client files, roster of participants, phone books, student seating charts, raffle ticket numbers, waiting lists, or even items from a gigantic restaurant menu are all sources for systematic random sampling.

Stratified random sampling draws samples that are representative of the different strata of the population. A stratum is a segment or category that shares a common characteristic (e.g., male and female or instructors, students, and parents). A random sampling method is then used to draw a sufficient number of samples from each of the strata. If a researcher wants to know the effectiveness of the program, including all parties involved, he may want to make sure that he will have sufficient representations from the three strata: 10 administrators, 30 staff, and 100 clients. He may determine to use the stratified random sampling method to draw 20% from each of the strata to form the sample for his study: 2 administrators, 6 staff, and 20 clients. This approach has the advantage of ensuring equitable participation from all segments of the population. This is particularly important and suitable for a heterogeneous group.

Cluster random sampling is used to draw samples from natural groupings or existing structures, such as the county, city blocks, or schools. The population is divided into clusters. Samples of these clusters are randomly selected. Further sampling from these clusters would then be conducted as demanded by the study. For example, a community organizer could use cluster random sampling to develop a useful sample for her single-parents needs assessment. A random sample of 15% of all the clusters of the community is drawn by using city blocks, zip codes, or catchment areas. If this community has 200 city blocks, then 30 (15% of 200) of the randomly selected blocks will be identified. Single-parent households within these identified 30 city blocks will then be randomly selected to become potential study subjects.

The social worker has many options for reaching her desired number of samples—for example, 60 single parents. She could randomly draw samples from the 30 identified city blocks until the number reaches the target sample size of 60. However, if she decides to survey 25% of these households, she could do so by randomly selecting 25% of the single-parent households in the identified 30 city blocks. Cluster sampling is less precise than simple random sampling. It is, however, more feasible and suitable for heterogeneous populations. It is used by researchers, particularly in less accessible or organized areas, for surveying the effects, such as natural disasters, poverty, or damages caused by war.

NONPROBABILITY SAMPLING (NONRANDOM SAMPLING)

Nonrandom sampling selects samples not on the basis of probability but on choice and judgment. The sample is biased, not representative of the population or the sampling frame, and has limited ability to make generalizations. It is, however, a useful approach for gathering samples for exploratory and descriptive studies. It is also often employed for case selection for qualitative studies. If a researcher is merely interested in the efficacy of a program for its participants and not in the intention of making generalizations to other programs, then nonrandom sampling is the appropriate and less expensive choice.

Convenience sampling is the use of accessible and readily available study subjects. They could be the current service recipients, coworkers, or whoever happens to be present at the time of data collection. It may be a wonderful idea to study the efficacy of cognitive behavioral therapy for female clients who are victims of domestic violence. Achieving a statewide random sample or gaining cooperation from other agencies may keep this study from ever happening. A study of eligible clients from the researcher and her colleagues' current caseloads may be a reasonable, feasible, and practical alternative. Study results may not be generalized to agencies elsewhere in the United States, but they have much implication for the researcher's agency. The results could also be used for comparison with other similar studies.

Snowball sampling is developed through referral. It is particularly useful for studying hard-to-reach subjects. In a study of AIDS in the early 1980s, stigma and taboo made reaching individuals with AIDS very difficult. The researcher would complete a case interview with a person with AIDS and then ask the respondent to make a recommendation for additional potential respondents. Similarly, the study of home remedy or folk medicine in the South among African Americans could have only been done by the referrals from the initial respondents. As the name implies, gathering respondents is just like starting with a small snowball that gets bigger as it begins to roll out.

Purposive sampling selects samples that have the particular characteristics sought by the study. A community service provider may be more interested in studying the effects of unemployment on grandparents who are raising grandchildren. Therefore, only such grandparents in the community will be selected for the study. Purposive sampling has a set of clear inclusion and exclusion criteria to determine whether someone is to be included or not. A study of the effect of multiple placements on the well-being of foster children may purposively target former foster youths who had at least 10 placements. Qualitative studies often use purposive sampling, seeking to reach respondents who have the characteristics and rich information about the subject matter (e.g., key informants or experts).

Quota sampling is the nonrandom equivalent of stratified random sampling. A set of quotas is established for each of the strata or categories. Through convenience, snowball, purposive, or any of the nonrandom methods, study subjects in each stratum are recruited until the quota is filled. A study of the effectiveness of the "cold turkey" approach to quitting smoking may require a sufficient number of individuals from groups that are "successful," "failed," and "still trying" to get a comprehensive picture of the issue. A quota sampling for this program effectiveness study could use the convenient sampling method to fill the slots of 2 administrators, 6 staff, and 20 clients.

Nonprobability sampling methods are not mutually exclusive. Researchers could use a convenient sampling method to fill the quota for the quota sampling. They could also use a convenient sampling approach, along with the snowball approach to complete a purposive sample.

SAMPLING BIAS AND SAMPLING ERRORS

When samples are drawn from the population, the samples could be somewhat different than the population. Sampling biases and sampling errors are two of the reasons that contribute to the difference. Sampling bias and sampling errors are about the sampling procedures, not the samples. Sampling biases are organized differences that are made intentionally or unintentionally. Sampling errors are differences that naturally occur.

Sampling biases are systematic mistakes made during the sampling process. A biased sample would not have the expected ability to represent the sampling frame or the population. They could be the overrepresentation or underrepresentation of the population. There are several major sampling biases: (1) self-selection bias, (2) under-coverage bias, and (3) survivorship bias (Lane, n.d.).

Self-selection bias happens when certain respondents are more likely to participate or be included than the others. If the NASW is conducting a national survey of social workers' views on current social policies affecting children, it is likely that more social workers who are involved with children, youth, and families will respond than social workers in other specializations. With the increased use of social media to conduct online surveys or opinion polls, only individuals who have an online presence will be included. Also, only those who have an opinion and bother to share will likely participate. It is similar to telephone surveys in the old days that excluded people who did not have a phone and were more likely to be the poor. In addition, there are potential respondents who choose not to respond (*nonresponse bias*). They may be individuals who just don't want to participate, who truly have no opinions, or who are still undecided.

Under-coverage bias means a certain subset of the population is not adequately represented in the sample. The opinions of the poor in the telephone survey example mentioned earlier were not sufficiently covered by the study. A parent survey of their children's afterschool activities between when they get home and before dinnertime is likely to undercount the experience of many low-income families. These families are more likely to have both parents working in multiple jobs and, at times, the students may also be working. Stratified or quota sampling methods would ensure the proper representation of the major segments of the population.

Survivorship bias is the tendency to focus on those who continue or survive than those who discontinue or drop out. End-of-the-program evaluations are more likely only getting responses from those who completed the program and not those who already left the program. A study on former foster youth on essential coping skills and mental preparedness while aging out of the system is more than likely to include former foster youth who "survived" the system. If engineers only study bridges that were not damaged by a strong earthquake and not those that collapsed, they would miss the important lessons about why some bridges failed—a failure analysis.

Sampling errors are the estimated difference of parameters, such as characteristics or statistics, between the drawn samples and the population. The sampling error is unknown for nonprobability sampling. However, the sampling errors can be estimated when it is a random sampling or random assignment. It is the price researchers pay when they have the honor of using probability sampling. Researchers, however, could attempt to minimize sampling errors. Two terms are associated with sampling errors: *confidence level* and *margin of error*. For many polling reports, we often hear these terms.

Level of confidence or confident interval is a term that will be further discussed later in this book. Essentially, it is how much confidence the researchers have about their findings. A 95% level of confidence means the researchers believe the statistical outcome is 95% accurate, and 5% of the time, the statistics may be inaccurate because of chance and other reasons. The researchers have 95% confidence that a hamburger joint has the most delicious hamburgers. It is expected that if you visit the place, 95% of the time, you will say the place has some delicious burgers. And 5% of the time, you find the burgers are no good. Remember, you are one of the samples or samplers! Your friends also go there, and they all have similar experiences. In other words, the samples possess or reflect the characteristics or parameters (i.e., good burger) of the population. If a poll says it has a level of confidence of 95%, that means if they repeat the polling again and again, 95% of the time, they will get similar results.

Margin of error (margin of sampling error) is the percentage point difference or uncertainty between the sample values and the population values. In general, the larger the sample size, the smaller the margin of error. "Margin of sampling error is always expressed in percentage points, not as a percentage—for example, three percentage points and not 3%" (American Association for Public Opinion Research, n.d.). Researchers selected a national random sample of 1,000 respondents to study their support of having free childcare and education for all children under the age of 5. Their results showed this idea received 65% support from the respondents with a margin of error of three percentage points in either direction. That means one would expect between 62% (65% – 3%) and 68% (65% + 3%) of the population supported the idea. The study findings further indicated the level of confidence was 95% with a margin of error of plus or minus three percentage points. That would mean if the study were to be conducted 100 times, 95 of those times, they would have results that were within plus or minus three percentage points of the population values. In other words, 95% of the time, they would get the results of support between 62% and 68%. Saying it in yet another way, the study findings would be within three percentage points of the population values 95% of the time.

SAMPLE SIZE: HOW MANY ARE NEEDED

The decision on sample size could be affected by the number of responses desired and the size requirements of the statistical analyses selected. For example, the average mailed questionnaire survey has a response rate of 20% to 30%. A researcher who wants to have 30 usable responses may need 100 to 150 potential respondents (samples). Dudley (2011) suggested that probability samples need larger numbers than nonprobability samples. Probability samples intend to represent the greater population; therefore, the larger the samples, the more likely they represent the population. The general rule for determining the sample size is to try to obtain as large a sample as the research can afford. However, nonprobability sampling is limited by the biases it inherits. Because a nonrandom sample is intrinsically biased, more cases may merely mean more biases rather than more representation. It may be a better idea to draw two nonrandom samples or use random assignment to create two samples for the results to be compared and contrasted.

The sample size also depends on the nature of the study, the research questions, and the statistics used. For a study that works with a heterogeneous population, a larger sample will be needed to capture the diversity within the population. For exploratory and descriptive studies, the purpose of the research questions is to get a better understanding of the topic being studied. Researchers are not interested in making generalizations to the greater population. In fact, oftentimes, the population is unknown or inaccessible, and many of the studies are agency-based studies that are intended for program improvement for the agency only. For these reasons, the demand for a larger sample size is not necessary. Statistically, for example, a chi-square analysis is desirable to have at least five cases for each of the cells in the table to avoid misleading statistics. A two-by-two contingency table will, therefore, minimally require 20 cases, while the chance of having a cell with less than five cases is very likely. It is recommended to have at least 50 cases when using the Chi-square statistic. In the statistics sections of the book, parametric and nonparametric statistics will be introduced. To use the more powerful parametric statistics, researchers are advised to have at least 30 cases, particularly when nonrandom sampling is used. In case studies, it is not the size of the samples but the quality of the samples that is of more importance. For qualitative studies, such as ethnographic or phenomenal studies, a small sample of 10 people may be sufficient and does not mean it is less desirable than a big number. Based on statistical principles, statisticians have particular methods to calculate a desirable sample size for random sampling. The calculation of sample size is beyond the scope of this book.

CONCLUSION

Probability and nonprobability samplings offer many ways for researchers to access their data sources. The sampling methods that they choose affect the quality of their studies and their ability to make statistical generalizations. Once the researchers confirm where they can find the data for their research, the next question is how they will gather the data. The next chapter will explain various data collection methods.

8 DATA COLLECTION METHODS

The concept of "beginning with the end in mind" is key to the research process. The research questions dictate the research design and its associated data collection methods and data collection tools. Commonly used data collection methods by social workers are survey, observation, testing and assessment, case study, secondary and existing data, and experiment. This chapter will discuss each of these data collection methods and their associated data collection tools.

SURVEY

The survey is probably the most popular and commonly used data collection method that social workers have access to. A survey is a data collection method, gathering information from a sample of people with a specific set of questions in a systematic fashion. It includes both the questionnaire survey and interview survey.

1. Questionnaire survey
   a. Telephone survey
   b. Self-administered paper and pencil survey (in person or mailed)
   c. Self-administered online survey

2. Interview survey (face-to-face survey)
   a. Individual interview
   b. Group interview

It is common to walk into an office, such as a medical clinic, a government office, or a business establishment, and be asked to sign in or complete a form to indicate the purpose of your visit. Even when making a phone call to these places, one will have to answer a lot of triage questions from the automated system before reaching someone who may or may not be the person you want to speak to! It is not that different in social work practice. Clients come to the reception desk and are greeted and questioned by the receptionist before being directed to the right office. Upon seeing the client, the social worker will complete an intake form or conduct an intake interview. In universities, there is always an end-of-the-semester course evaluation. All of these are just different examples of a survey.

Survey research is a useful tool to gather a large amount of information from individuals. This may be factual information, such as demographic data or service utilization records, as well as historic, current, or future statistics. The information could also be something more abstract, such as someone's attitudes, feelings, beliefs, or nonobservable behaviors. Social service agencies could use surveys for clinical, administrative, and research purposes. They could range from client assessments and triage, service monitoring, community needs assessment, program evaluation, understanding social problems, to scientific research projects. Some surveys are large-scale community or general surveys, such as census or epidemiology surveys, while some are small-scale descriptive surveys, such as the effect of not having a major grocery store in a neighborhood district.

Survey research could be used for both qualitative and quantitative research. Questionnaire surveys employ closed-ended and open-ended questions to gather data for qualitative research and quantitative research purposes. Interview surveys are mostly for qualitative research and use open-ended questions to gather qualitative data. *Closed-ended* questions are questions with a fixed choice of answers for respondents to make their selection. *Open-ended* questions allow space for respondents to provide their narrative answers. Table 8.1 provides comparisons between open-ended and closed-ended questions.

Questionnaire surveys and interview surveys are two valuable survey approaches, each with its own unique qualities and purposes. Based on the goals and the environments of the research projects, researchers could decide which one is better suited for their use. It is not unusual for researchers to employ both questionnaires and interviews in their survey research. Table 8.2 compares the major differences, advantages, and disadvantages of these two survey approaches.

TABLE 8.1. Open-Ended and Closed-Ended Questions

OPEN-ENDED QUESTIONS	CLOSED-ENDED QUESTIONS
Respondents provide narrative or free-form answers that they choose.	Respondents provide fixed-choice answers preselected by the researchers.
They are not limited and could be opinions, stories, listings, recollection, personal insights, or others.	They are limited by the researchers' answer selections or the ways that the questions are framed.
Researchers intend to elicit respondents' personal perspectives and elaborations.	Researchers intend to elicit respondents' reactions to a particular set of answers.
Answers are unrestricted.	Answers tend to be yes/no or multiple choice.
Your answer: _____	Yes, No A, B, C, D All of the above
Discover unexpected, surprised, or un-anticipated answers or findings	Collect limited responses to test against a hypothesis or expand a specific understanding
Questions start with: How, What, When, Where, Who, etc.	Questions could start with any interrogative pronouns. Open-ended questions that start with "did" or the verb "to be" tend to elicit closed-ended answers.
How did you do that? What happened when you …? Where would one seek support for …? What are your opinions on …?	Did you do that? How difficult was it for you? To what extent do you agree with this statement?
Asking for more: What else would you like to add? Are there things we failed to discuss? How would you summarize your thoughts on …?	Asking for more (with open-ended questions): Please specify: _____ Additional comments: _____

QUESTIONNAIRE SURVEY

Questionnaire surveys, like all the other research activities, start with having a clear research question. It could be an elementary and exploratory one, such as, "What do people know about homelessness in this city?" It could also be a more descriptive, such as, "Do income and education correlate with the perception of homelessness in this city?" Again, beginning with the end in mind provides direction for the design and delivery of the research project. Depending on the purpose of the study, researchers could use probability or nonprobability sampling methods to draw up the sample

TABLE 8.2. Comparison of Questionnaire and Interview

	QUESTIONNAIRE SURVEY	INTERVIEW SURVEY
Description	A series of purposefully written and structured questions or statements intended for the respondents to provide answers regarding the research topics	A series of purposefully written questions asked by the interviewer in a planned conversation with the interviewees for their answers regarding the research topics
Tool	Questionnaire	Interview guide
Form	Written	Oral
Administration	Self-administration	Interviewer
Type of questions	Mostly closed ended and predetermined	Mostly open ended and could be modified
Nature of questions and information provided	What respondents do and think, more factual and objective	What interviewees think and do, more analytical and subjective
Order of questions	Structured	Structured or varies
Respondents reached and time used	Larger number in a shorter time	Smaller number and time-consuming
Cost (time and money)	Less cost for more data	More cost for lesser data
Convenience	Fewer scheduling challenges and participate at one's convenience	More scheduling challenges and less convenient
Geographic accessibility	Less limited	More limited
Literacy and comprehension	Respondents need to be able to read and write	Respondents could give oral responses and seek clarifications at their level and in their language
Anonymity	High	None
Who answers the questions	Unknown. Little control	In-person verification
In-depth information	As in-depth as the questionnaire could collect	More in-depth. Interviewer could record observation or prompt for additional information
Truthfulness of responses	Unknown. No control	More merits
Response rate	Varies, low	Varies, low
Readiness for data analysis	Precoded, open-ended answers are more ready for quantitative data entry and statistical analysis	Less ready. Qualitative data need to be transcribed for qualitative analysis
Challenges	Social desirability	Social desirability, interviewer effect

for the survey. The nature and the quality of the sample affects the representativeness and adequacy of the survey results.

The advantages of using questionnaire surveys are their ability to reach a large number of respondents at once and their cost- and time effectiveness. Most questionnaire surveys only require self-administration and employ many closed-ended questions that are ready for statistical data analysis. They can reach respondents with little geographic limitations and allow them to respond at their convenience and anonymously. Questionnaire surveys can be delivered through many venues. The basic one is the paper-and-pencil survey administered in person to individuals and groups. It can be a mailed questionnaire, a telephone survey in which the questionnaire is completed over the phone, or an increasingly common online survey.

Questionnaire surveys have large nonresponse rates in general, and special considerations need to be included to increase the *response rate*. Bumgardner, Montague, and Weidenbeck (2017) described an average 31.6% response rate for surveys of the forest products industry. The National Research Center (2016), a national research firm, recounted a 20%–30% response rate for their citizen surveys conducted by mail and web. SurveryGizmo (2015), an online survey platform, reported an average 30%–40% response rate for internal surveys and 10%–15% for external surveys. There are many factors that researchers can consider to increase the response rates of their surveys.

Ways to Increase the Response Rate

1. *Improve the quality of the questionnaire.* It is frustrating to fill out a questionnaire that seems to be aimless, disorganized, confused, contradictory, convoluting, poorly laid out, and full of grammatical errors. Respondents' choices for this type of questionnaire are either not responding or toying with the researchers with inferior or irrelevant responses. Besides, researchers should pay attention to the physical appearance, layout, and design of the questionnaire. Respondents are more likely to respond to questionnaires that are easy to read and navigate, have a clear and logical layout design, and, in general, are pleasing to the respondents.
2. *Clear goals and benefits of the survey.* Respondents want to know why they are spending their time and effort completing the survey. It should be something that they feel strongly about or something that interests them. Develop the buy-in from the get-go. This speaks to the importance of the cover letter or introductory starting page of the questionnaire.

3. *Length of survey.* Completing a questionnaire is likely something that people do in between tasks. It is supposed to be done quickly; it is not a term paper or client report that one would set aside time to complete. The longer the survey and the longer it takes to complete, the less likely it will be completed. Try to limit the survey to two printed pages or less.

4. *Format of answers.* Closed-ended questions are easier and more convenient to answer. However, good open-ended questions will demand that respondents think analytically and carefully. Researchers could get quality responses from both formats.

5. *Brand recognition.* Respondents want to know their information is being used by a trusted entity. They are more likely to respond to a university or recognized organization affiliated survey than a survey from a stranger with unknown affiliation. Likewise, try to distribute the questionnaire through a reputable and respected medium.

6. *Incentive.* Researchers could offer incentives whether or not the completed questionnaire is returned. A small coffee shop gift certificate, a lotto ticket, or a brand-new United States two-dollar bill could be included with the mailed questionnaire. It is a costly investment with no guarantee, although research has shown incentives increase participation. Nonetheless, potential respondents may feel guilty for taking your prepaid incentives without participating and end up deciding to respond. Another way is to provide promised incentives. This may include a raffle, lottery, or monitory payment. An alternative is to give a small donation to a local charity for every completed questionnaire returned. Researchers could give the respondents a small list of local charity groups that respondents could designate for their "contribution."

7. *Timing.* Market research results show that different days of the week are better for sending out email surveys. Commonly, weekend days are not the best days. Generally, Monday or Tuesday mornings are preferred, allowing respondents the whole work week to decide to respond. Understand the activity or professional cycles of your respondents. Try not to catch them during the high seasons or busiest days of the month.

8. *Reminders and self-addressed envelopes.* Researchers may want to send out one or two friendly reminders 7 to 14 days after the initial invitation. People are busy; polite reminders are useful and usually appreciated. Self-addressed stamped envelopes also make returning the completed questionnaire easier and more likely.

Cover Letter and Questionnaire

A key component of a survey is the data collection tool (i.e., questionnaire). A questionnaire usually includes a cover letter (Box 8.1). The cover letter is more than an invitation for the respondents to be your partner. It also details the essential *ethical concerns* involving human subjects, including the following:

1. Voluntary participation
2. Risks and benefits
3. Anonymity
4. Confidentiality
5. IRB approval
6. Consent to participate

BOX 8.1. SAMPLE CONSENT COVER LETTER

Dear Participant,

My name is <insert your name>. I am a social work graduate student at the Great State University. I am writing to invite you to participate in my thesis research project titled <insert your study title>. The purpose of the study is to <insert study purpose>. This study has been approved as an exempt study by the Great University Institutional Review Board.

The following questionnaire will take approximately 10 minutes to complete. Your participation in this study is completely voluntary. You may decline to participate, refuse to answer any or all of the questions, or withdraw at any time. This is an anonymous study; please do not include your name. All information collected will remain confidential. There are no known risks to participate beyond those encountered in everyday life. The potential benefits of the study include <insert the benefits>.

If you choose to participate, please return the completed questionnaire <to the sealed collection box in the back of the room or other instructions for returning>. If you have any questions, please contact me by email, myname@gsu.edu, or through my research advisor, Dr. Ed Wising, at edwising@gsu.edu.

Your return of the completed questionnaire indicates your consent to participate in this study. (For the online survey: By clicking the "Submit" bottom at the end of the completed questionnaire, you indicate your consent to participate in this study.)

Thank you for your willingness to assist me in my educational undertakings.

Sincerely,
Student's Name

The letter should also include the following information:

1. The institution/person who is conducting the study
2. The purpose of the study
3. How long it takes to complete
4. How to return the completed questionnaire
5. Deadlines
6. Contact information

Many have discussed the procedures for the development of a quality questionnaire. The main contents of a questionnaire include (1) basic demographic items and (2) items that gather the needed information to achieve the goal of the survey. The details of how to develop data collection instruments, including a questionnaire, will be discussed in the next chapter.

INTERVIEW SURVEY

Interviews are another way to collect data for survey research. They can be done in person, over the phone, or via computer audio- and video-conferencing technology. Usually, the interviewer will conduct the interview with interviewees individually. In some situations, an interviewer will conduct an interview with a group of interviewees. Focus group interviews are one type of such group interview.

Interviews involve direct contact between the researchers and the participants. This approach can provide more in-depth and personal qualitative data for the research questions. However, interviews can be demanding and costly. Many researchers have suggested the use of interviews, along with other methods, such as questionnaires, to increase the sample size and to address the challenges of measurement errors and threats to internal validity.

Types of Interviews

Based on the research questions or the types of information needed, researchers can decide which types of interviews are the most suitable. The interviews can be conducted or structured in the following formats:

1. Unstructured interviews
2. Semistructured interviews

3. Structured interviews
4. Group interviews

Unstructured interviews (unstandardized interviews, informal interviews, discovery interviews) are more like general conversations. Interviewers interact with the interviewees and use the dynamic of the moments to guide the conversations. Interviewers have a general idea of what to talk about, but it is only a guideline or, by all means, a reflection of the goal of the interview. This general guideline is called an *interview schedule*, which provides a broad agenda and time line for the interview. The main idea is to allow the interviewees to speak freely about what they have in mind instead of what the interviewers have prepared. These types of interviews have the flexibility and originality of the information. However, the lack of structure and lines of inquiry may make data analysis difficult and findings questionable. This can be a very useful exploratory approach, along with observations to assist researchers in gaining familiarity with a topic or formulating and refining a better research question. Imagine during a college campus visit that you wander around the student center, talk to students and faculty, check out places, and ask questions about anything that comes to mind. At the end of the day, you get a better idea of what the campus is like, and you will have specific questions that you want to follow up on.

Semistructured interviews (nonscheduled, standardized interview) employ an *interview guide* that aids every interviewer in asking the same set of questions methodically. However, how those questions are being phrased, in what order, and in what manner are not issues that are predetermined or restricted. If appropriate, interviewers can probe supplementary questions, seek clarifications, and differentiate which questions will be emphasized. This approach to interviewing provides a more consistent set of responses that are within particular parameters. The semistructure makes data analysis more manageable. Different interviewers with different interviewing styles and different emphasis still pose challenges to the research process. Anyone who has gone through a job interview will probably remember facing an interview panel that asked all kinds of questions. Some of the panel members were rather harsh, while others were more helpful, and there was also one who had an unlimited number of questions. In front of them, there was a set of standardized questions (i.e., interview guide) that they all had to follow somewhat.

Structured interviews enable interviewers to use the predetermined interview guide to ask identical questions to all interviewees in the same order, same wording, and same manner. This approach is more like a question-and-answer session than a conversation. Questions on the interview guide are carefully crafted and expected to be presented exactly as they are written. Some of these questions have a predetermined range of expected answers and are even precoded to facilitate quicker note-taking. Effectively, the interview guide is the same as a questionnaire, except the interviewers, instead of the interviewee/respondent, checks the answer boxes. The interviewers may have a rating scale or a rubric to help document the answers. Probing questions are still employed to get to the deeper questions or to achieve an accurate understanding of the answers. Many job interviews employ the structured interview approach to ensure that all grounds are covered in the questioning and fairness of the hiring process. In-take assessments for certain programs, such as a substance abuse treatment program, may have specific requirements that a structured interview will be used to ensure eligibility is properly established and needed information is collected for treatment planning. Structured interviews provide somewhat standardized answers that can make data analysis easier.

Group interviews (focus groups) are used in situations where researchers want to gather information from a group of individuals who are similar or dissimilar in their perspectives. A group interview involves a congregation of two or more individuals. The interviewers can take advantage of the group dynamics to conduct their group interviews. The focus group is a specific form of group interview, which normally has about 10 to 12 participants. The focus group is a rather specific group interview. It behaves more like a panel of jurors. Participants are intentionally included because of the purpose of the study and the participants' qualifications (e.g., purposive sampling). The format for focus groups is mostly a highly structured group, but they can also be unstructured to meet the needs of the study. Highly structured focus groups have a moderator or facilitator (interviewer) and a panel of individuals representing different beliefs or opinions. A carefully designed *focus group discussion guide* is used to direct the discussions. The guide can include a network of interrelated questions as well as different short case scenarios or snippets. The monitor is expected to attentively engage in guiding the discussion while an observer, who also serves as the recorder, watches the interactions during the discussion. The recording is further supported by audio and video recordings. Focus groups usually last for 60 to 90 minutes. This approach is commonly used for market research or political campaign efforts. It is also frequently used by demographers and social researchers. The U.S. Census Bureau routinely uses focus groups to gain input from the diverse populations or to test out new forms or categories. For example, how do ethic minority groups interpret or differentiate the terms of race, ethnicity, and origin? Should people be allowed to check more than one category? How can we develop categories that capture the diversity of the populations in the United States?

An older adult service needs an assessment focus group. This author conducted a questionnaire survey to assess the service needs and barriers for an older adult community. Based on the questionnaire survey findings, a composite figure was constructed and used in a focus group meeting with a selected group of 12 residents. Focus group members were greeted and welcome to the focus group meeting. They were asked to sit around a big conference table. The meeting facilitator explained the purpose and format of the meeting, thanked the group members for their participation, and emphasized that all responses are valid and valued. The facilitator distributed the composite figure handout (Box 8.2), allowed time for members to read it, and observed members' reactions. The facilitator proceeded to pose questions listed in the focus group discussion questions guide (Box 8.3) sequentially but organically. An assistant sat on the side of the room to record the discussion in writing. The meeting was also recorded by a recorder sitting in the middle of the meeting table.

Conducting Interviews

A lot of preparation needs to take place to get ready for conducting interviews. Certainly, refining the research questions and setting up the research design and methodology are among the first. Developing an interview schedule and interview guide, if needed, will help in setting the focus on gathering the appropriate information that gives answers to the research questions. Recruiting the respondents (interviewees) can be done by using various sampling methods. They can be chosen using randomized samples or purposefully recruited interviewees who represent the target population or someone who is an expert in the topic being studied. A *pilot study* is a mock exercise of the interview process with people who are similar to the actual interviewees; this will help identify challenges and refine the interview questions and the interview process. This pilot study is an important step that, unfortunately, is often overlooked when researchers are in a time crunch to roll out their studies.

Using social work practice skills, interviewers start the interviews with a skillful mix of rapport building and logistic clarifications. Again, the interviewees are more than subjects for the study, they are the partners. The purpose of the study, the format of the interview, the anticipated time used, and all the human subjects' concerns should be made clear.

Interviewers should keep in mind the reasons why the interview method is being used. While both the interviewers and the interviewees have equal footing, interviewing is supposedly a *respondent-lead process*. Interviewers are there to pose questions, collect data, listen, observe, and manage the interviews. How much the

BOX 8.2. MRS. TURNER—A COMPOSITE RESIDENT

JOURNEY FAMILY SERVICES: HOME FOREVER PROJECT— A COMPOSITE SUNSHINE PARK RESIDENT

My name is Edith Turner, and I am a 73-year-old widow living in Sunshine Park. In general, I am happy with my condition, although I am not in very good health. I have no major disabilities. Most of the time, I do not have any difficulty in completing daily chores. If I need any medical attention, I rely on Medicare or my HMO. My home is paid off, and I have moderate monthly expenses. I enjoy meeting with friends and family, but that does not happen too often. I know I have been blessed because many of my friends in the neighborhood are not doing as well as I am financially or physically. They do not want to let other people know about their problems. That may be why they refuse to participate in any activities. The lack of money, health, family, friends, and independence are the usual things that we deal with every day. As to the people who have moved in within the last 10 years, I don't know many of them. I, however, know they are struggling like my friends.

If I need help with something, I feel comfortable asking for assistance or speaking up for myself. I can either ask a friend or know how to contact someone who can lend a hand. The things I seem to need the most assistance with are home repairs for problems such as plumbing and appliance malfunction. It costs so much to get a simple problem fixed, and you never know whom you can trust to avoid being ripped off! Of course, there are always problems with getting to medical appointments, knowing my medications (there are a lot of them!), and having someone guide me through the medical and service bureaucracy and explain to me my options. I could drive my old car, but I much prefer not to do that. If I need to take the bus, I know where the stops are, although they are not close. I could use a ride to the grocery store or to run some errands, but I do not want to trouble people. They always refuse to take my money for gas. If for some reason I could no longer take care of myself, I know there are assisted living communities nearby. However, I really don't know much about this assisted living thing. All I know is that they are expensive, and I am afraid that I could not afford the cost. I really don't have many options. I want to stay in my own home as long as I can. I wish our neighbors could come together more often and socialize.

Source: Yuen, Terao, & Schmidt (2009). *Effective Grant Writing and Program Evaluation* (pp. 176–179). Hoboken, NJ: Wiley.

interviewees want to disclose is controlled by the interviewees and is positively correlated to the sense of partnership and rapport with the interviewers. Similar to social work practice, clients don't necessarily remember what the social worker told them, but they remember how they were treated. The interview process should be an

BOX 8.3. FOCUS GROUP DISCUSSION QUESTIONS AND GUIDE

FOCUS GROUP DISCUSSION QUESTIONS AND GUIDE

1. Please meet Edith Turner. In your opinion, how much does Mrs. Turner represent the characteristics of older adult residents of Sunshine Park? What are your immediate comments about this description?
2. What else is important but not being captured in this description?
3. Some have claimed that "driving/transportation," "information about alternatives to living at home," "home repair assistance," and "lack of social connections" are the four main areas of concern for older adults in Sunshine Park. Do you agree? Should anything else be added to this list?
4. Is transportation or your ability to drive a concern to you? Do you agree that older adults' driving is a concern?
5. If so, please list three possible solutions that could address those concerns.
6. Is a lack of information about alternatives to living in your own home a concern for you?
7. If so, please list three possible solutions that could address those needs.
8. Is getting home repair assistance a concern for you?
9. If so, please list three possible solutions that could address those needs.
10. Is a lack of social connection a concern for you?
11. If so, please list three possible solutions that could address those concerns.
12. If Journey Family Service were to organize activities to serve residents in Sunshine Park, would you be interested in participating in any of the following proposed activities? (Provide participants the one-page Proposed Activities Checklist.)
13. Specifically, the possibility of an intergenerational mentoring program is being explored. Would you be interested in learning more about that?

Source: Yuen, Terao, & Schmidt (2009). *Effective Grant Writing and Program Evaluation* (pp. 176–179). Hoboken, NJ: Wiley.

empowering experience that makes it clear that interviewees' expertise and insights are being respected, not exploited.

Like questionnaire surveys, interview surveys experience the challenge of *social desirability bias*. Respondents or interviewees do have concerns about how others are viewing them, including the researchers, as well as themselves. There is a human tendency to keep our self-identity or self-image intact. There is also the need for social approval. As a result, respondents may not respond truthfully to make themselves more likable or acceptable to the researchers and themselves. Interviewers should try and build rapport and trust with the interviewees. Also, emphasize the fact that all answers are valid and that there are no right or wrong answers. Start the interview with less sensitive or personal questions to develop a sense of comfort and commitment. Save the more sensitive questions for the latter part of the interview. Researchers should allow interviewees enough time to answer questions fully and explain themselves to eliminate the fear of being misunderstood or judged. The social work principle of being "nonjudgmental" is crucial here. Furthermore, researchers can use different questions to probe the same concept or behavior for cross-validation. *Interviewer effects* are another challenge in interviews. This refers to the variances caused by the personal backgrounds of the interviewers and how they are being perceived by the interviewees. This may be due to the interviewers' presence, age, gender, appearance, demeanor and mannerism, language and cultural capacities, training, social status, and others. Again, social work practice skills in handling transference and countertransference are rather useful here.

Asking questions and more. The interview schedule and interview guide are crucial for asking the appropriate questions. They form the base, the framework, and the direction for what questions are asked and how they are asked. Box 8.4 lists the major kinds of questions and important considerations when interviewing participants (Kvale, 1996; Open University, 2013; Mcniff, 2017).

Steps for conducting interviews. There are a lot of dos and don'ts when conducting interviews. However, doing interviews is more than complying with some mechanical guidelines. It is an art in itself. It takes practice, experience, and critical thinking to perfect the art of interviewing. Until one becomes an expert interviewer, Box 8.5 offers a list of key steps for conducting interviews.

OBSERVATIONS

Among the famous Yogi Berra sayings is, "You can observe a lot by watching." Yes, indeed. Watching is seeing and paying attention to what is being presented; observing is perceiving, absorbing, and griping beyond what is being presented. Surveys involve people telling researchers their thoughts, feelings, and behaviors through questionnaires or interviews. Observations involve researchers gathering information about people's actions, which are supposedly inspired by their thoughts, emotional expressions, and, therefore, behaviors and practices through direct visual and audio experience. Observation is more than physically watching; it is perceptually observing, and

BOX 8.4. IMPORTANT CONSIDERATIONS WHEN ASKING QUESTIONS

1. Introducing question: Introduce the topic. "Can you tell me about …?" "What do you think about …?"

2. Probing and specifying questions: Looking for more, locating evidence, seeking clarification. "What happened after that?" "So, how did you handle that?" "Could you tell me more about …?"

3. Follow-up questions: Elaborating from the initial answers. "What do you mean when you say …?" "Wow, tell me more …" "Do you mean …?"

4. Structuring questions, transitional question: Moving the interview forward. "Moving on …" "That's interesting. As to the topic of …?"

5. Ask open-ended questions: "How did it start?" "What happened?" "Tell me what you think."

6. Encourage storytelling: "Tell me what happened next." "What did you see?"

7. Acknowledge emotion: "That was upsetting for you, wasn't it? So, what did you do?" "It must be chaotic! What went through your mind at that point?" Paraphrase interviewees' comments to acknowledge and to seek further understanding. "What you are saying is …?"

8. Purposive use of silence and sighs: The sound of silence is loud. Use pauses and sighs to show interest and to encourage more details.

9. Listening to the unspoken and reading between the lines. Watch out for information that is being left out, minimized, or reframed. Read between the lines for information that cannot be stated explicitly. Some is whispered, and some is told not with words but with the body.

10. Be familiar with the questions to ask related questions and to move back and forth freely. Assist interviewees with staying focused and avoiding wandering off topic.

11. Pay attention to the moment while planning for the next step. Stay with and acknowledge the interviewees' thoughts and emotions in that moment. Planning for the next question is important but not ignoring the gold mine that is right in front of you is a waste of opportunity.

12. Avoid leading (and misleading!) questions: "Being a patriotic, God-loving, red-blooded American, do you think we should …?" "Being led by a group of experts, was it a rather good training?" Instead, "How did you feel about the training?"

13. Avoid interrogation: It is the challenge of asking "why?" Questions that start with why sound like blaming and interrogating. Not, "Why did you do that?" Use, "Could you walk me through your decision-making process?"

14. Avoid interrupting interviewees or completing their sentences. This is different from paraphrasing, summarizing, or staying focused.

BOX 8.5. STEPS FOR CONDUCTING INTERVIEWS

1. Refining the research question
2. Setting up the research design
3. Developing an interview schedule and interview guide
4. Pilot testing of the protocol
5. Making a plan for the logistics to set up the interviews
6. Selecting, sampling, and recruiting respondents (interviewees)
7. Interviewing interviewees, using and developing interviewing skills
8. Recording data collected
9. Organizing data collected
10. Analyzing data collected
11. Reporting out

it is a demanding mental process. This may be what Yogi Berra observed when he said, "Baseball is ninety percent mental; the other half is physical."

Observational research methods are essentially a nonexperimental qualitative research. They are interested in actual behaviors in the natural environment. These observations can help researchers to get a better description of the subject matter, help develop better questions, or generate a hypothesis. Go to a 24-hour Walmart at midnight regularly for two months to observe who shops at that hour and how do they pay for their purchases. Based on your observations, formulate your research hypothesis. Are they mostly people who just got off work? Are they mostly adults? Do they have children with them? Do they mostly pay by credit cards, checks, cash, or SNAP Electronic Benefits Transfer cards? What are the realities of living for the midnight shoppers? Do they reflect the economic structure of the community?

There is no control group or independent variable in observation research. The observation in observational research methods is not the same as the observation in an experiment, which means measurements of attributes. Observing how children resolve peer conflicts on a school playground is observational research. Observing how children resolve different staged peer-conflict scenarios presented by the re-searchers is a measurement used in experimental research. However, increasingly, research scholars are including and expanding observation in experiments as part of observational research and calling it *controlled observation*.

There are many ways to categorize the different types of observation. Commonly, there is **unstructured observation and structured observation**. In unstructured observations, researchers participate in the subjects' natural environments and watch the everyday events unfold as they happen. Researchers take notes and prepare the narrative summary of when events have been observed. In structured observation, researchers have a more developed agenda, have identified areas that are chosen to be observed, and use specific data collection tools to record the observation.

Another way to conceptualize observational methods is by basing the methods on the roles that the researchers (observers) play in data collection.

1. Participant observation
2. Nonparticipant observation (unobtrusive or nonreactive)
   a. Hidden observation
   b. Disguised observation
   c. One-way mirrors
   d. Physical traces
3. Other observational methods
   a. The critical-incident technique
   b. The use of judges

Participant Observation

This is a typical unstructured observation. Researchers are participants in the community or target population that they observe. They become another person in the crowd, and they experience the insider information and knowledge. Participant observation could be covert or overt.

In *covert observations*, the observers' research activities are not disclosed, and their identities are concealed. Subjects are not aware of being observed. This type of observation could obtain genuine and authentic information. This is particularly useful for behaviors that otherwise might not be studied. The controversial Tearoom Trade observation that was discussed in Chapter 3 is an example of a covert observation. A social worker who wants to understand how people feel about applying for welfare can spend time in the waiting room of a welfare office or even attempt to file an application. A long layover at an airport usually is not a pleasant experience; however, many travelers take on the opportunity to find a front-row seat to watch people and to kill time. Convert observations have many advantages and many ethical concerns that need to be addressed. No one wants to be secretly watched. Covert observations may violate the trust and respect between the researchers and the people being observed. It may also pose a danger to the personal safety of the researchers.

In *overt observations*, people are informed about the identities of the researchers and the research activities that they do. The researchers would get permission from the people to conduct the observation. This declaration oftentimes provides more opportunities for observations and opens more doors for insightful understanding. Anthropologist Margaret Mead did fieldwork and lived among natives of Samoa and Papua New Guinea to study gender roles, attitude toward sex, and youth in the 1920s. Several decades ago, this author had a graduate student from South Africa who wanted to study African American Christian churches in the South. Two weeks after her arrival, she went to a predominantly black church close to the university and attended many of their services, seriously taking notes but not making contact with anyone in the church. It did not take more than two weeks for a tall white young woman to stand out from the crowd and attract the attention and suspicion of the church members and pastor. After a phone call from the pastor to me and after holding a joint meeting, the graduate student was formally invited, introduced, and welcomed by the congregation to be a member. The lesson to me is respect, transparence, and partnership.

Do people act differently if they know they are being watched? Yes, we do. However, remember, the concept of regression to the mean, one of the threats to internal validity. Over time, people tend to act out their normal selves. A social work intern may act very cautiously when the field instructor is in the same room watching. However, over time, she will act the way she normally acts. Try another example. Do you slow down to the speed limit when you realize a highway patrol car is parked on the side of the highway ahead of you? You would likely slow down, pass the highway patrol, and maintain the speed limit a little bit longer, just like all the other cars. However, as soon as you realize more and more cars are passing you by, you recognize that it is "safe" and find yourself back at your "normal" speed!

In both covert and overt observations, the observers become participants and part of the community, gaining insightful observations that are not obtainable by an outsider. Imagine the difference in experience between spending a month living with a local family in a foreign country versus being a tourist in an organized tour group for a month in the same country. Interviewing is also often included in observational research to add information about participants' personal and primary accounts, enriching the data collected through observations.

The following are steps that are involved in conducting participant observation:

1. Identifying and refining the research question
2. Gaining entry into the target population, seeking permission if needed
3. Developing rapport with target population

4. Getting involved with target population
5. Note-taking, recording, and summarizing
6. In-depth interviewing
7. Analyzing data
8. Writing the report

Nonparticipant Observations

Nonparticipant observations involve many approaches. However, they share the characteristics of covert observation in that those under study are not aware of being observed. Also, these are *unobtrusive measures* in that the researchers strive to not interfere or encroach on the public and the social context. The researchers do not participate or interact with the target population to avoid changing the natural behaviors and social processes. The researchers are watching from the outside. They have limited interaction with the target population. While they remain passive, they are actively in control of the interaction (Atherton & Klemmack, 1982).

Hidden observation takes place when researchers are out of sight from the main stage and take on an inconspicuous position to observe the targeted behaviors. It is not about researchers hiding behind bushes or trash cans. The researchers can still be in the public setting and be seen in plain sight, except that the subjects are not aware of being observed. From the classic *Candid Camera* TV show to today's surveillance and cellphone cameras everywhere, we all have been watched.

Disguised observation does not require the researcher to wear a fake mustache or a masquerade mask. It involves a certain degree of deception, and the merits and ethical challenges for this approach have been an ongoing debate. It could be as simple as being a mystery shopper to compare prices to the classic "ten days in a mad house" (Bly, 1887). Nellie Bly, a young journalist, pretended to be mentally ill and got herself committed to the Women's Lunatic Asylum on Blackwell's Island. Her brave reporting brought public attention to the brutality and neglect experienced by the patients, which resulted in major changes to the mental institutes in New York.

One-way mirrors have been wildly used in clinical practice and in clinical training for many disciplines. Social workers are familiar with the use of one-way mirrors to observe children during play therapy and other activities. Experienced clinicians may sit with less experienced clinicians or trainees to observe another clinician in action. This provides immediate opportunities for direct observations as the process unfolds. Researchers can use one-way mirrors to observe and gather data without intruding on the occurrence being observed. Some clinical and research activities intentionally set up a process for someone to record the event and the discussions behind one-way mirrors to allow the clinicians or researchers in the room to concentrate and focus on their tasks. This is a commonly used approach for formal focus group meetings.

Physical trace is the use of physical evidence or products to learn about people's behaviors, attitudes, and preferences. These may include gang graffiti in different parts of the city or graffiti in public restrooms verse those in the university, the extent of the wear of magazines in the waiting room, or the number of students in the checkout record of a required reading reserved in the library. *Garbology* is a particular observational approach, using physical traces by examining people's waste, trash, and refuse to study their lifestyles, preferences, habits, and wellbeing. Ask janitors in the office and prepare to be surprised how much they know about everyone's families, work habits, productivity, lunch preferences, and every minor and significant tidbit. It is modern-day archaeology!

OTHER OBSERVATIONAL METHODS

Critical Incident Analysis or Critical Incident Technique

Critical incident analysis is an observational approach that describes and studies routine or significant events and activities that lead to positive or negative outcomes. Colonel John Flanagan's work during World War II for the U.S. Army Air Corps, which studied effective and ineffective work behaviors, first described this approach in 1954. According to Flanagan, "The critical incident technique consists of a set of procedures for collecting direct observations of human behavior in such a way as to facilitate their potential usefulness in solving practical problems and developing broad psychological principles" (1954, p. 327). Many researchers have also suggested that English sociologist and mathematician Sir Francis Galton laid the foundation of this approach in his study on positive eugenics. Galton coined the term "eugenics," which means "well-born" (University of Virginia, n.d.). Critical incident analysis has evolved over the years into many forms and has been used by various disciplines for research, training, system design, investigation, and many other purposes. However, at its core, it deals with our everyday living in our regular environment. It describes what and how we perform in particular situations that contribute to memorable, clear, or serious outcomes.

Different authors have different interpretations of the term "critical" and apply critical incident analysis differently (Spencer-Oatey, 2013). Critical incident analysis involves both the critical incidents and the critical analysis. *Critical incidents* are significant or transformative events that have substantial effects that make us stop, raise questions, and review our thinking, values, attitudes, and behaviors. They are incidents that we do well or do poorly. Some incidents are problematic, difficult, in crisis, an emergency, demanding, or unusual. Some of them are circumstances that we are effective, successful, impressive, innovative, and creative in. Critical analysis involves thoughtful subjective reflections and objective examination of the incident to identify crucial factors and to seek deeper understandings and competencies. It is the practice of personal and professional reflections and critical thinking about one's performance beyond the routine expectations.

While all of these sound serious, critical incident analysis can also be used for minor or routine incidents. After all, "critical" or "significant" is being defined by the people who are involved. Think about your own health needs. At what point do you decide that your headache is beyond over-the-counter drugs, and you have to make an appointment to see a doctor? At what point do drug addicts decide to seek treatment? Is it always when they hit bottom? If so, where is the bottom? Similarly, at what point have family members had enough and decide that Uncle Dmitri needs to get professional mental health services? Having a caring family is just not enough. Critical incident analysis could be a study of the "straw that broke the camel's back," the turning point, and the making of the turning point. What made you decide to buy one car instead of the other one? Is it because its horn sounds louder and not because it has a better reliability record?

The procedure for conducting the analysis includes the following:

1. Define the problem or area of investigation
2. Determine the data collection approach—field notes, personal or service records, standardized forms, survey form, etc.
3. Data collection approach
4. Data analysis-qualitative analysis and quantitative analysis of individual and group processes
5. Report out

At a youth center, a youth suddenly approached Emily, the new social worker, and told her that she had been living on the streets for the last 3 weeks, and she was hungry and scared. What should Emily do? She rushed to recall her agency protocols, her old textbooks, her social work training, and she scrambled to find the youth temporary housing for the night and made sure she was safe and had access to food. Did Emily serve her properly? What else could Emily have done?

Did she miss anything? An experienced social worker looked at Emily with a grin on her face and seemed to be telling her, "Get used to it and learn to handle it quickly because it happens all the time!" The youth came back the next day and asked to see Emily again. She told Emily she could not sleep much in the shelter because she had been contemplating whether she could trust her enough to tell her the reason she was homeless. Emily spent the next 2 hours listening to the youth's horrific personal history. Emily handled the girl's situation professionally and set up an intervention plan that met the youth's immediate and long-term needs. Emily felt good about what she had accomplished but still had some uncertainty, and she was also exhausted. Emily asked to discuss her performance in supervision with her supervisor.

The new social worker, Emily, sat down with her supervisor and talked about her own reflections on how she handled the situation with the homeless youth. The supervisor listened carefully, provided support, and worked with Emily to review the incident. The supervisor could ask Emily a variety of questions to help develop a deeper understanding of the incident.

1. "What happened? What did you write down in your recording?"
2. "What were your client's concerns?" "What brought the client to you?" "What made your client decide to seek services?"
3. "What were your concerns?" "Could you further elaborate on your concerns?"
4. "What did you and your client decide to do?"
5. "Were there dilemmas?" "Were they resolved? How?"
6. "At what point was the decision made about what to do?"
7. "How did the decision turn out in reality?"
8. "How did you and the client feel about the outcomes?"
9. "What made it work? What made it fail?"
10. "What are the takeaways of key factors that contributed to the incident and outcomes?"
11. "Would you handle this incident differently?" "How?"

Critical incident analysis is used for research purposes, and increasingly it has been used as a tool to promote critical reflection in social work practice and development (Fook & Askeland, 2007; Lister & Crip, 2007). As a research tool, critical incident analysis involves framing research questions from practice with actual events, real actors, and factual outcomes. It is evident-based qualitative research that can inform the profession regarding best practices as well as failure analysis.

Use of Judges

Among the things that we can do when we try to make the most informed decision is to consult an expert. To make a better decision, we consult a collection of experts or knowledgeable people we trust. The involvement of judges or referees is a fact of life for all people of all ages, particularly in situations of competition or section. These range from toddler coloring contests, children's choir competitions, college admissions, job applications and promotions, eligibility determination, grant proposal applications, academic publication reviews, medical diagnosis determination, to the choices of long-term care facilities!

Researchers can employ a group of trained observers or experts to make focused observations individually and formulate decisions collectively. Competitive sports, such as figure skating, springboarding, or platform diving use panels of judges to observe and grade each performance. These judges are experts who follow the same deliberately defined criteria and have the technical and critical eyes that can detect the clear and subtle differences that differentiate the performances of the competitors. In the 2002 Winter Olympics, it was not the figure skating judges' expertise but the judges and officials' conduct that was called into question. The scandal of judges trading votes ended with awarding two sets of gold medals and a change in the scoring system. This change involved using the "trimmed mean" procedure that eliminates the highest and the lowest scores and then the mean of the remaining seven is calculated. Also, the judges' names were not posted with their scores. This anonymity is supposed to give a degree of secrecy and shield judges from outside pressure and retribution. Unfortunately, the possible fault of the new system was exposed in a 2014 Winter Olympics controversy in women's figure skating. Many were surprised by the size of the gaps between the judges' scores and cast doubt on the judging and the judges. The anonymity made the fact-finding difficult. The Winter Olympics examples show the challenges of using judges who may come with many human liabilities and issues of trustworthiness.

Judges can be used in social work research for assessing the progress of a case, the learning of skills and competency by clients and social workers, and in program evaluation. In case conferences, the progress of a case is presented. It is being assessed by a panel of professionals of different disciplines to judge the progress and to ensure a more holistic coverage. A social worker has applied dialectical behavior therapy over the last 2 months with a client who has a dual diagnosis of mental health and drug abuse issues. He is meeting with a panel made up of a senior social worker, a psychiatrist, and a psychologist to assess his work, approve his treatment plan, and make recommendations. Direct observations of the trainees' (who could be a service recipient or a social worker) competency in performing certain tasks by several experienced individuals will provide evidence of their degree of mastery and need for further training. Two senior social workers may sit in a couple of the groups led by a junior social worker to observe the trainees' group work skills, particularly in conflict management and group dynamic development. Similar observations can be made by program evaluators to provide direct evidence for both formative and summative evaluations.

Advantages and Disadvantages of Observational Research

The observational methods offer direct and real-life information that can raise questions or give answers to research questions. It also has many limitations that challenge the utility of this approach. While it certainly can be a stand-alone research approach, it is also a method that complements other research methods and provides a more comprehensive understanding of the problem under study. Table 8.3 displays the advantages and disadvantages of the observational research method.

TESTING AND ASSESSMENT

Testing and assessment, along with evaluation, are common terms used in education, psychology, and human services. Their meanings can be slightly different depending on the professional context that they are used. Testing is a measurement of the worth and value (e.g., presence, quality, quantity) of a certain construct or variable. Tests or examinations in the classrooms involve the use of testing tools (e.g., test paper, multiple choice, situational test, debate) to find out students' retention and application of the material taught. Psychological testing is the use of norm-referenced or standardized tools to measure the individuals' personality traits, capacities, behaviors, and other constructs. Students having trouble in school may be tested to explore whether they have attention problems, and a client who refuses to come out of his room could be tested for mental health challenges, such as depression. Assessment is a process of systematic data collection to help make the determination of the state of the constructs or questions being studied. It consists of many *components*, including the results of the testing. Other components can include clinical interviews, observations, and rubrics, as well as analyzing records. The purpose of the assessment is to reach a determination (i.e., diagnosis) that can be used as the foundation for planning, intervention, and improvement. Social workers are familiar with doing psychosocial assessments that may include testing, interviewing, and observing to help develop

TABLE 8.3. Advantages and Disadvantages of Observational Research Methods

ADVANTAGES	DISADVANTAGES
Record what people do in real time instead of asking people to recall or self-report what they do	Subject to chance. Observers may pick the wrong day, time, location, or focus for the observation
Eliminate recall errors	Observers' biases and errors
Offer accurate descriptions of real-world behaviors that can help generate more fitting hypotheses	Observers' skills, conditions (e.g., fatigue), and personal beliefs and preferences affect the quality of the observation
Size up public behaviors and situations to generate a more complete picture that the people who are involved may not be aware of or comprehend	Observers' presence and involvement may affect how people act
Able to capture individual behaviors and group outcomes	Time-consuming. May limit how much can be observed
Able to capture nonverbal behaviors	Not able to capture people's thinking and feeling
Less cost for more accurate information	The cost is in direct proportion to the scale of the observation and could get costly
Compliment other research approaches. Use in tandem to formulate a more comprehensive research	Observational method alone may not be sufficient to compile strong research
Actual and real-time data increase the validity of the overall research	Ethical considerations: privacy, trust, and partnership
Provide deeper and more insightful information	Replication not possible

intervention plans for service recipients. Evaluation is a process of collecting data to gauge the progress and attainment of certain constructs or variables against the preset goals or criteria. Social workers conduct evaluations of their services to individuals, groups, communities, programs, and organizations. In summary, testing is about judging; assessment is about appraising, diagnosing, determining, and planning; and evaluation is about concluding and goal achieving.

Standardized Test

A *standardized test* is a set of items that are to be administered to test takers and scored in a consistent manner so that the results can be compared. Standardized tests are used in almost every aspect of our lives. Students need to take examinations for the classes in which they are enrolled, prospective drivers need to take the paper and road tests to get their driver's licenses, federal worker hopefuls need to take the civil service examination, and social workers need to take the licensing examination to get their state licenses. Impaired drivers who decide to risk seriously endangering themselves and others by driving while intoxicated will face the standardized field sobriety test when they get pulled over by the police. Many grade school and high school students take some type of standardized test to assess their academic performance. In California, the California Standardized Testing and Reporting program is used to measure the performance of students from grade 3 to 11. In the United States, the No Child Left Behind Act of 2002 and the Common Core Initiative in 2010 have both raised controversies regarding the use of standardized tests to assess students' and schools' performances.

The *pros and cons* of using standardized tests, particularly in education, have always been a topic of heated debate. Nonetheless, standardized tests offer common standards to measure against. They are objective, structured, have clear guidelines, and make it possible for comparison using analytical tools, such as statistics. The statistical data also allow us to make specific analysis and comparisons across different demographic variables, such as gender, ethnicity, neighborhoods, and socioeconomic backgrounds. On the other hand, standardized tests are often criticized for being limited by the predetermined scope, lack of flexibility, unfair to lower socioeconomic or marginalized individuals, stressful for testers, and, most importantly, their political implications. Standardized tests have created sort of a grading system for students and schools regarding how well or bad they do. However, many factors contribute to the lower ranking in standardized tests, and these factors need to be taken into consideration and studied further.

Norm-referenced tests are standardized tests that have been "normed" to allow comparing test takers' performances against those of a larger group of similar test takers or a hypothetical average test taker. Rodriguez (1997) defined "norms are statistics that describe the test performance of a well-defined population" (para 1). Norm could also be understood as "a statistics describing the location of a distribution" or "the magnitude of a vector" (Norm, 2017). Whereas a vector is "a quality ... that has size and direction" (Vector, 2017). Norm-referenced tests are usually multiple-choice tests that produce scores as a percentile rank. Statistically, the scores are ranked on a normal curve. The California Achievement Test, the SAT and ACT for college-admissions applications, and the GRE for graduate schools applications are just a few of those norm-referenced tests. The SAT test has scores ranged from 400 to 1600. A high school senior who received an SAT score of 1010 would be ranked at the 50th percentile among the nationally representative sample (all U.S. students, regardless of if they took the SAT) and 36th percentile among SAT users (students in the 2017 graduating class who took the SAT) (College Board, 2017). This SAT score of 1010 means the student performed better than 50% of the national sample and 36% of those who took the SAT in 2017.

Criterion-referenced tests are another type of standardized tests. They mostly use the multiple-choice format and possibly some written short answers. Criterion-referenced tests are not always administered in the standardized manner. They measure test takers' performance against the established standards or fixed criteria. The results are presented in percentage of correct answers (e.g., 90%) or categories (Pass/Fail). Criterion-reference tests are used to measure a degree of understanding, mastery of, or proficiency. In other words, they test how much the test takers have reached the benchmarks. Most tests used to satisfy the No Child Left Behind Act and the Common Core are criterion-referenced tests (Norm-Referenced Test, 2015). The Association of Social Work Board (ASWB) social work licensing exams are pass/fall exams. They also take into account local requirements and statistically use the "equating mean" to adjust each exam based on the difficulty levels of the items. Test takers need to have a certain number of correct answers to reach a pass point. "Generally, pass points range from 93–106 correct of the 150 scored questions" (ASWB, 2017, para. 3). In their most simplistic form, a course final exam or a post-training quiz are criterion-reference tests used to assess students or participants' learning and proficiency. If test takers achieve a certain cutoff score, they are considered proficient. The question here is how the cutoff score is being set. If a teacher lowers the passing grade from 80% to 70%, certainly more students will pass the class.

Norm-referenced tests assess how one does in comparison to the norms of other test takers. They rank or sort test takers on a curve. Criterion-referenced tests assess how one does in comparison to the set standards. They categorize test takers and describe their performance. Both are testing assessments but measure something different. Theoretically, in education, we could see a report that says, "In Tesla High School, based on the standardized State Achievement Test, 80% of the tenth grade students ranked above the 75th percentile of the state norm. However, only 60% of them were proficient according to the state curriculum standards and merely 30% of them passed the Tesla High School benchmark for excellence."

Social workers are not heavily involved in the development and implementation of standardized testing and assessment. However, social workers are frequent users of standardized tests and their results. It is particularly true when social workers are part of the interdisciplinary team in settings such as schools, mental health clinics, or hospitals.

It is important for social workers to understand the function and nature of standardized testing to become a valued member of the team and to advocate for the clients.

Program-Developed Tests

Many agencies or programs that provide specialized service to unique populations may find the standardized tests helpful but not particularly useful for their purposes. Agencies and programs may develop specialized tools that will aid them in their testing and assessment. A local LGBTQ service center may develop tools that tailor to their specific situations and challenges. A homeless service agency may develop tools that take into consideration of the local ordinances, housing conditions, and demographics of the local homeless populations.

The creation and use of these program-developed tests are guided by the purposes of the agencies and the goals of the programs. Their development is the same as those for research data collection tools, which will be further explained in the next chapter. Locally developed testing and assessment tools are mostly criterion-referenced tests. They are intended to categorize data to inform program assessment, planning, and evaluation.

THE CASE STUDY

The case study is an in-depth and extensive study of one (N = 1) individual, group, community, organization, or event. It is traditionally and mostly a qualitative study using observation and interview data collection approaches to gain the deeper understanding of the happenings as they present to the study subject. Increasingly, researchers have applied quantitative and mixed-methods approaches to conducting case studies. Some have also conducted case studies that involve multiple cases at once, such as the multiple-case studies design that explores the differences between and within cases. This book will focus on single case studies. Cases studies can be atheoretical in that they do not follow any theory and are only used to provide more vivid descriptions and to generate better-refined hypotheses for future research. They can be theory based in that they explore the fitness between theories and real cases.

What makes a case worthy of a case study? There are cases so unique that they warrant detailed documentation and exploration. There are cases so rare that they can open our eyes to new dimensions. There are also cases so typical or representative that they can serve as models for references. Everyone has a story to tell, but there are notable stories that are worth telling. A day in the life of a homeless elderly, an

LGBTQ youth who is considering coming out, a single parent who has to stretch every dollar, and a veteran who has PTSD and is screaming on the inside are all meaningful and suitable cases for the case study.

Social workers are trained to develop a professional understanding of the lives, strengths, and challenges of service recipients and, therefore, should be well prepared in conducting the case study. Developing rapport and mutual respect with an objective and nonjudgmental stance and acceptance through the purposeful expression of feelings and controlled emotional involvement that affirms individuality and self-determination while honoring a person's privacy are the guiding principles for social work practice. These are also the principles for conducting case studies.

Case studies follow the common research process by employing the following steps:

1. *Select areas of concern and formulate specific research questions.* Are you interested in homeless issues or agency mismanagement issues? If it is homelessness, what are your research questions? Are they more exploratory or descriptive in nature? Are you interested in any of the following? Exploring, understanding, or assessing these families' situations; examining the process and outcomes of the services that they have received; or developing an in-depth insight into their lives, their perspectives, and possible recommendations for improvement?

2. *Specify the target population and narrow down possible data sources and recruitment strategies.* Would it be homeless people in general or homeless families with children? If it is homeless families with children, who are the likely families, and how do you approach and recruit them? What are the inclusion and exclusion criteria? How many of them do you plan to have for your study?

3. *Decide on the data collection approaches.* Do you plan to do interviews, observations, or use secondary data? Do you plan to use multiple approaches to collect the data needed? Which approaches are the most respectful, appropriate, efficient, or effective ways to collect the data? How do you plan to implement your data collection?

4. *Data analysis and discussions.* How do you plan to analyze the qualitative data? How do you plan to analyze the quantitative data? What do those findings mean?

5. *Report writing, findings dissemination, and putting findings into action.* How do you plan to report and present your findings? Who would be interested in your findings, and how would they be informed? What are your findings' implications for practice?

Case studies are interested in what the results mean to the cases being studied and are not meant to be used for generalization. A case study tells the unique story of the case and can be used as an example for others but not used as a standard or benchmark. Each case is different in and of itself. Each is situated in different environments and affected by different sociocultural and other factors. Understanding the unique situations of each case study can help researchers to ask better questions and pinpoint areas of focus for more in-depth research. A case study of a failed case management effort gives social workers a lesson for what to do, what not to do, what to watch for, and how to improve. It does not make predictions or tell social workers the causes of all other failed or successful cases. However, when sufficient case studies are conducted, together they provide a rich collection of carefully studied practice knowledge. This could become a foundation for the development of practice guidelines, evaluation of performances, and ways for improvement.

Case studies can be further accomplished by using other qualitative research designs, such as quasi-experimental designs, single-subject designs, or preexperimental designs. Interviews and observations are the main data collection approaches. The analysis of the data from case studies is dependent on the data collection methods that are used. While quantitative studies can provide the structures or skeletons for our understanding of the issues, the qualitative case studies can provide the rich contents or the "meat" to the structure. They add the human dimensions to the overall understanding.

SECONDARY DATA ANALYSIS

Primary data are firsthand data originated and collected (or to be collected) directly by researchers explicitly for the purpose of attaining the goals of the research project. They are the raw data collected through research studies' original data collection approaches such as questionnaire surveys, interviews, observations, or case studies. *Secondary data* are secondhand data already collected by other researchers for other research projects intending to achieve the goals of those research projects. These existing data are repurposed to address the questions of the current research project. These may be data from government statistics, such as U.S. census data and vital statistics; government reports, large-scale or longitudinal study databases; available literature in books, articles, and websites; organization service statistics, reports, and case studies; and previous or ongoing research data and findings.

The following are examples of locations where one can find quality databases for secondary data studies:

- World Health Organization Global Health Observatory Data Repository http://apps.who.int/gho/data/?theme=main

- U.S. Federal Open Data https://www.data.gov/
- U.S. Census Bureau https://www.census.gov/
- U.S. Substance Abuse and Mental Health Services Administration https://www.samhsa.gov/data/
- Inter-university Consortium for Political and Social Research https://www.icpsr.umich.edu/icpsrweb/
- Adverse Childhood Experiences https://www.cdc.gov/violenceprevention/acestudy/index.html
- Child Welfare Information Gateway https://www.childwelfare.gov/
- Early Childhood Longitudinal Study https://nces.ed.gov/ecls/
- General Social Survey http://gss.norc.org/get-the-data
- Head Start Family and Child Experience Survey https://www.acf.hhs.gov/opre/research/project/head-start-family-and-child-experiences-survey-faces
- National Longitudinal Study of Adolescent to Adult Health http://www.icpsr.umich.edu/icpsrweb/DSDR/studies/21600
- National Longitudinal Survey https://www.nlsinfo.org/
- National Survey of Family Growth https://www.cdc.gov/nchs/nsfg/index.htm
- State, county, and city databases
- The World Wide Web
- University libraries: Social Work Abstract, Social Services Abstracts, Sociological Abstracts, and search engines, such as EBSCO, Medline, and PsycINFO.

There are many advantages and disadvantages of using secondary data (see Table 8.4). Researchers need to weigh the pros and cons and decide how best the secondary data, if they are used, can serve their research efforts. Other considerations will include whether the data are available, relevant, and rigorous enough to be used for current studies.

A graduate thesis student of this author sought to study families who had experienced adoption dissolution with children from the foster care system (Masten, 2015). We used the Center for Disease Control and Prevention 2007 National Survey of Adoptive Parents https://www.cdc.gov/nchs/slaits/nsap.htm. The study phone-interviewed 2,089 adoption families. Among them, 766 families had adopted children out of foster care in the United States, and 19 of them indicated they had considered or taken steps toward dissolution of the adoption. A random sample of another 19 families out of the 747 families that had not considered dissolution were used as a comparison group. Factors related to whether the dissolution was

TABLE 8.4. Advantages and Disadvantages of Secondary Data Studies

ADVANTAGES	DISADVANTAGES
• *Time and cost-effective.* Data are readily available and collected, save time and resources.	• *Data may not be appropriate or meet the specific needs of the current study.* A large-scale survey on sex trafficking may not have the appropriate data for a local study on sex workers, although some of them were trafficked.
• *Data may come from a large sample size, including a great number of variables.* The data would cover a large range of interests, and the findings are likely to have greater external validity.	• *Data may not be in the format that the current research uses.* Secondary data collected respondents' age by categories or age groups. Unfortunately, current research needs the actual age to test one of the key hypotheses.
• *Data could possibly be easily accessible either in a database, printed formats, or online.* Literature is often in a published format; databases are mostly in electronic formats or available online.	• *Data may have validity and reliability concerns.* The use of a subset of data or a subset of items from a large study poses a range of validity and reliability concerns.
• *Data can already be in refined condition.* Data will normally be cleaned and organized to be used for the original studies. They may already be in usable formats.	• *Data may have availability and accessibility problems.* They are available and accessible when the owners of the original data decide to make it so. Availability and accessibility are as methodological as they are political. Researchers do not necessarily have the rights or opportunities to acquire the data. In other words, researchers do not have control of the research data.
• *Longitudinal study data afford the opportunities for historical comparisons as well as trend and pattern analyses.* The U.S. Census shows the changing U.S. population, and the longitudinal adolescent health study shows how adolescent health has changed and how it has not changed.	
• *Large databases can be paired down by using random sampling.* The researcher can use random sampling methods to draw a more manageable set of data for analysis that has the potential for generalization to a larger population.	• *Data may be of poor quality.* Just because they are published or available does not mean they are of good quality.
• *Large databases can be purposefully sorted to meet current research needs or to acquire a sufficient number of unique cases.* See adoption dissolution example below.	• *Data may be outdated.* If you are not interested in historical data, the usefulness of old data may be limited.
• *Able to study sensitive topics.* Large-scale general studies on or including sensitive topics provide a better degree of anonymity for data collection. Human subjects–related concerns will be challenging if they were done in a small-scale project or in a small community.	• *Time lag and social change.* Normative expectations or definition of terms a decade or two ago were not the same as they are today. Similar to the data, the nature and the contents of previous studies could be outdated.

Conceptual and Practical Research and Statistics for Social Workers

considered were examined between these two groups of families. This is an example of the use of secondary data for some hard-to-find data. Many dissolutions were not reported because the children were adopted and no longer tracked by the foster care system, or the children had turned 18 years old and become adults. Even with the scale of a national study, only 19 cases were located. Certainly, this study would not find enough cases if only local or state statistics were used. This, in fact, speaks to the advantages to using secondary data to study this topic. This study also used random sampling to compare post-adoption experiences between the dissolution group and the nondissolution group.

Secondary data studies have been a common research method; however, "there is a lack of literature to define a specific process" (Johnston, 2014, p. 620). In being consistent with the basic research process, secondary studies could be conducted following these steps:

1. **Defining the research questions.** Again, beginning with the end in mind, researchers should be clear about what they want to study. It could be simply seeking a deeper description or understanding of the subject matter or testing against an established theory or hypothesis. The research questions set the aim for the research.

2. **Identifying potential and relevant sources of data or databases.** The research questions help decide the scope and the focus of the identification. Consult subject experts or review relevant research to identify possible data sources, including the typical large databases. Again, the data sources could be government reports; peer-reviewed journal articles and books; published statistics; research reports; case studies; databases for large-scale, cross-sectional or longitudinal studies; and online information.

3. **Evaluate the data source or databases:**
   a. Become familiar with the data source, the original study, and the databases. What were the purposes of the original study? Who were the target populations? When was the study conducted and by whom? What was the design? What were the data collection tools and procedures? How were data analyzed and reported? What is the current format of the data? What is the structure of the databases, and how were they aggregated and disaggregated?
   b. Are they relevant to your current or intended study? How were the variables constructed and defined? Are they applicable to your study?
   c. Are they readily available? Are they in public domains? Is copyright a concern?

    d. Are the data useable and credible? Are the data in good and complete shape for reuse? Have the data and authors established the needed creditability and been recognized in the academic and professional arenas and through dissemination or publication in refereed journals?

4. **Transferring and preparing secondary data for analysis:**
    a. Download the data sets to be used for the current study.
    b. Prepare a new data form to transfer the needed segments from the original data set. For human subjects concerns, some organizations may assign a staff member to transfer their service record data to the new data form for the current research. The organizations can eliminate identifiers, private information, and information that is not related to the current research.
    c. Clean up, recode, or reformat the collected data into the format used by the current research. Original data may be in Excel format, but the researchers are planning to do the analysis using SPSS.

5. **Create new variables.** Researchers may need to create new variables to aggregate or disaggregate data from the original data set. Data collected over time may need to be normalized to form a common variable. Income was grouped into seven categories 10 years ago; it was grouped into six categories 5 years ago and then four categories 2 years ago. The researchers may need to regroup or normalize them all into a new set of categories for the current research. In other situations, researchers may employ data from different sources, each source using different categorizations for the same variable, which may necessitate the need to normalize the data.

6. **Conducting data analysis.** Guided by the research questions and the nature of the data, secondary analysis can involve both quantitative and qualitative methods. Cheng and Phillips (2014) discussed the "research question-driven" and "data-driven" approaches (p. 373). The research question-driven approach aims to analyze the data to give answers to the research questions and hypotheses. However, when the data set is insufficient to address the research questions, researchers can go over the data set and "decide what kind of questions can be answered by the available data. In practice, the two approaches are often used jointly" (p. 373).

7. **Report writing.** The research process is not complete until the findings are organized, presented, and disseminated.

TABLE 8.5. Data Collection Methods for Program Evaluation

Pre-/Post-Standardized Tests

Characteristics: Preexisting tests with a large group of respondents. Tests are administered at two points in time (i.e., the beginning and end of activities).

Advantages: They offer a rigorous, readymade context for documenting improvement. They are widely accepted as credible evidence if appropriate for the activity. They may allow for comparisons across programs or settings.

Constraints: The tests may not be designed to measure the outcomes the program expects. They lose validity if changes in content, administration, or context occur.

Pre-/Post-Program-Based Tests

Characteristics: An alternative to standardized tests. Service programs can create such tests to document specific knowledge or performance. The program can decide how often these tests are administered (e.g., the beginning, quarterly, and end of activities).

Advantages: The tests are widely accepted as credible evidence of accomplishments if they are directly related to the services provided. They must be administered to respondents both before their participation (a "pretest") and upon the conclusion of their participation (a "posttest").

Constraints: It is difficult to verify the degree to which the responses to test questions are an accurate representation of changes in knowledge or skills because of the program. They may not show changes in a consistent manner.

Logs or Tally Sheets

Characteristics: A log documents a participant's attendance or achievement, such as "acquisition of skills." It is especially appropriate for programs where it is difficult to identify exactly what will be learned at any point in time.

Advantages: Logs are performance based. They accommodate a range of starting and ending points and are easy to complete.

Constraints: Data are unreliable and invalid if observation/recording is not systematic. Logs should include specific questions or categories directly tied to the results and indicators to prompt the user.

Rubrics

Characteristics: Rubrics provide a detailed scale that can be used to measure performance. Rubrics are used either with other records, such as portfolios or written work, or with direct performance, such as conversation.

Advantages: Rubrics can be used to measure a variety of abilities and behaviors. When well constructed, they are relatively easy to administer.

Constraints: Developing a good rubric takes time. Off-the-shelf rubrics may be useful, but you need to match the rubric to the services you provide. The people administering the rubric must be thoroughly trained in its use.

Performance Ratings

PERFORMANCE

Characteristics: Set of questions regarding the manner in which service participants carry out activities that they are trained to perform. The focus is on issues, such as attitude and ability to carry out specific tasks.

Advantages: Data collection can be integrated with regularly scheduled meetings with the supervisor or accomplished through a supervisor questionnaire.

Constraints: Rating for performance standards must be explicit and consistent. The rating process must be short and focused. Supervisors are unlikely to be able to assess the persistence of any traits observed outside the service site.

Interviews

INTERVIEW

Characteristics: Data are collected orally. The interviewer asks clearly defined, systematic questions. Usually, questions are predetermined and limited to a specific topic. Sometimes there are additional questions asked to elicit a more detailed response.

Advantages: The data demonstrate specific examples of the observed outcome of national service programs. Interviews allow for flexibility.

Constraints: The interviewer must be skilled in the process of interviewing and conduct the interviews in a systematic manner to ensure unbiased results.

Surveys

Characteristics: The data are collected in a written format. Each respondent provides data on a set of clearly defined questions.

Advantages: The data can be collected efficiently on paper, by mail, and online. Data collected can be in qualitative or quantitative format. They can be used for a variety of research purposes.

Constraints: It is difficult to balance specific and general questions and ensure that larger or unexpected issues are not missed. Survey instruments must be completed consistently to avoid biased results.

Focus Groups

Characteristics: A moderator guides a group discussion involving six to 10 individuals representing specific stakeholders.

Advantages: Focus groups provide specific, pertinent data. Group interaction can produce more information than individual interviews.

Constraints: A specific set of skills is required of the focus group moderator. Data are difficult to summarize succinctly.

Plugging in Secondary (Existing) Data

Characteristics: Other sources have collected the existing data, often statistical in nature. This may range from student GPAs to neighborhood crime statistics.

Advantages: It is often perceived as being more reliable and less subject to bias than other kinds of data. It can be less burdensome than other methods and prevents duplicating data collection.

Constraints: The secondary data may not be appropriate, available, or accessible. Researchers need to evaluate these data's validity, reliability, and overall quality.

Source: Modified from Aguirre Division, JBS International, Inc. (2006). CNCS National Service training material Yuen, F., Terao, K., & Schmidt, A. (2009). *Effective Grant Writing and Program Evaluation* (pp. 62–63). Hoboken, NJ: Wiley.

EXPERIMENTS

In the prior chapter, details of various experimental designs were discussed. Experiments, particularly, true experimental designs, aim to test hypotheses and to generate clear evidence of relationships between independent and dependent variables. Experimental designs involve systematic data collection approaches that can exclude alternative explanations, minimize variability, and increase confidence in investigating the causal and correlational relationships. Randomization (sampling) is often used to create comparison groups. Independent variables (treatments, stimuli) are methodically and differentially introduced to produce outcomes on the dependent variables that are to be measured. Carefully developed and tested data collection methods, such as the use of questionnaires, observation, and testing scales, are employed to gather to output data for statistical analysis. The rigorous process of the experimental designs allows the researchers to infer and make generalizations of the study findings. Detailed information on the development of data collection instruments will be discussed in the following chapter.

Common Data Collection Approaches for Program Evaluation

The use of data collection approaches, like research designs, is only limited by the creativity of the researchers. Examples of some of the data collection approaches for program evaluation that are commonly used by social work students and practitioners are summarized in Table 8.5.

CONCLUSION

There are many ways to collect relevant data for research projects. Surveys include the questionnaire survey and interview survey, which can gather qualitative and quantitative data. An observation can be carried out in the form of participants, nonparticipants, and experts. Standardized and program-developed tests are often used for assessment and evaluation. Case studies, secondary data analysis, and formal experiments are additional ways to collect different data for different purposes. All of these data collection methods require unique data collection instruments to record and document the data. The next chapter will focus on the construction and development of these data collection tools.

Credits

9 DATA COLLECTION INSTRUMENTS AND DEVELOPMENT (THE TOOLS)

I nstruments are the tools—such as forms or electronic systems—used to collect and document the information that is aggregated and analyzed for the purpose of the research project. Different research designs and research purposes require different data collection instruments. The choice of the data collection tool is determined by the purpose of the research. This is important. Consider the wisdom of the saying "When all you have is a hammer, everything looks like a nail!" Using the best and most appropriate tools will positively affect the quality of the data collected. In turn, the quality of data will boost the overall quality of the research. "Garbage in, garbage out" (GIGO) applies to social research. The data collection tool is key to whether the data will be valuable or just garbage.

CHECKLIST, INDEX, AND SCALE— PROGRAM-GENERATED AND STANDARDIZED MEASURES

Clarifications for a few commonly used terms will be helpful in our discussion of data collection instrument development. They are checklist, index, and scale. They form the basis for the data collection instruments.

Checklist

A checklist is merely a to-do list or a check-off list. Many of us have a to-do list for the day to make sure we are on task. Unfortunately, for a few of us, we forgot where we put the list but found it at the end of the day, and it became the failed-to-do list! Another common example is our grocery shopping list. Checklists are essentially a list of items that are expected to be checked off. When the last item is checked, the list is done. The items listed represent things to do, not how important they are. MSW students need to take certain courses to graduate. The list of such required courses is also a checklist. Similarly, some will have a bucket list of things that they want to do before they die. Social workers in a childcare center loading children onto a school bus will check and double-check the list of children's names to make sure everyone is on the bus for the field trip. Foster care social workers may use a foster home safety checklist when conducting home studies.

Everything on the checklist is just individual items that need to be included, attended to, or require action. It is a nominal level measure of a variable (e.g., things to do, grocery, student roster); all items on the schedule are of equal importance. The following is a hypothetical and oversimplified Household Appliance Checklist for a home study. Whether the house does or does not have a certain appliance determines if the item is checked or not checked.

Household Appliance Checklist: (Nominal)

- Stove
- Refrigerator
- Mixer
- Blender
- Disposal
- Toaster

Index

An index is a sum of the counts or composite measure of a variable. In its basic form, it is a summary measure of yes/no answers that serve as an indicator of the condition of a variable. In the following hypothetical Household Appliance Index example, the total number of appliances is the index. Family B has more appliances than Families A and C. Family B appears to be "better equipped." However, if Family B is not available and you were the foster care social worker, would you place a foster child in Family A, which has more appliances than Family C? Why and why not? Many would choose Family C over Family A because Family C has a refrigerator, but Family A does not. For the safety or suitability of having a child in the home, refrigeration is much more important than having a disposal or a blender. A basic index is essentially a checklist with a sum score that shows if one has more or less than the other. It is an ordinal measure of a variable. It does not consider the importance or significance of the items included.

Household Appliance Index (Ordinal)

	FAMILY A	FAMILY B	FAMILY C
Stove	X	X	X
Refrigerator		X	X
Mixer		X	
Blender	X	X	
Disposal	X		
Toaster	X	X	X
Total	**4**	**5**	**3**

In another example, two clients showed up for assistance at a domestic violence intervention center. A social worker used the agency-developed Spousal Relationship Index to assess their situations. They both received the same score. You are the director of the agency, and your staff members have been overwhelmed with requests, and you only have room to serve one client at this point. Which client is more in need of service?

Spousal Relationship Index (Ordinal)

HOW MANY TIMES DID YOUR SPOUSE	FREQ. (f) CLIENT A	FREQ. (f) CLIENT B
1. Push you or shove you	9	4
2. Shout at you	3	2
3. Hit you with an opened hand	1	7
4. Make fun of you in front of someone else	4	5
5. Punch you with a closed fist	5	4
Total	**22**	**22**

As shown in the two examples, a basic index provides a summary of the variable. It gives equal weight (i.e., importance, significance) to each of the items. More sophisticated indexes take into consideration the different "weights." For example, the Dow Jones Industrial Average (DIJA) is an index of stocks. It is "a price-weighted average of 30 actively traded blue-chip stocks, primarily industrial stocks that trade on the New York Stock Exchange" (Nasdaq, n.d.). The Consumer Price Index (CPI) "is a measure of the average change over time in the prices paid by urban consumers for a market basket of consumer goods and service" (Bureau of Labor Statistics, 2017). DIJA is based on the 30 large stocks, and CPI includes 73 components. Items are put together to form the index without worrying about their item intercorrelations.

Scale

A scale is a "measurement instruments that are collections of items combined into a composite score and intended to reveal levels of theoretical variables not readily observable by direct means" (DeVellis, 2017, p. 15). A scale is similar to a sophisticated index in its function as a summary measure. But unlike the index, the development and selection of items for a scale requires careful evaluation of the item intercorrelation to the intended construct. There are many types of scales, and many different procedures are involved in their development. A detailed discussion of scale development is beyond the scope of this book; however, we will continue to use the spousal relationship example from earlier to show one method of scale development.

A researcher was interested in developing a more precise and useful scale that could measure and distinguish the severity of spousal abuse. She wanted to develop the Spousal Relationship Scale (interval level measure) based on the Spousal Relationship Index (ordinal level measure). This process is called instrumentation. She recruited 200 volunteers representing various backgrounds and asked them to rate the five spousal relationship items. Volunteers rated the severity of each of the actions (items) on a measure between 1 (not at all serious, not a problem) and 11 (extremely serious). The median scores for all the volunteers' ratings (value assigned–v) for each of the items were calculated and used as the "weight" or "value" for the item in the scale. The following is an abridged example using only nine volunteers' ratings on five items.

Values Assigned (v) by Nine Volunteer Respondents, Arranged by Ascending Order, and the Median Scores

QUESTION	v	v	v	v	v	v	v	v	v	MEDIAN
1. Push	5	5	6	7	7	8	8	9	10	7
2. Shout	2	2	3	3	4	4	5	6	7	4
3. Hit	7	8	9	9	9	10	10	10	11	9
4. Make fun	1	3	4	5	6	6	6	7	8	6
5. Punch	10	10	10	10	11	11	11	11	11	11

The researcher decided the score for the draft Spousal Relationship Scale will be the sum of the weight multiplied by the frequency of the incidence of each item.

$$\text{Score} = v1\,(f1) + v2\,(f2) + v3\,(f3) + v4\,(f4) + v5\,(f5)$$

* v = value: 1—Not at all serious, not a problem … 11—Extremely seriousness
* f = frequency: Number of incidents

She worked with several domestic abuse service agencies to test out the utility of this draft tool and collect a large pool of data. Using advanced statistics, she calculated the psychometric properties of the draft scale. The intercorrelation among the items supported the inclusion of all five original items. In other words, the five selected items are interconnected in relation to (or measuring) the same construct in a significant manner. At the end, she proposed this new five-item Spousal Relationship Scale for use in the assessment.

The social worker applied this new scale to assess Client A's and Client B's situations and was able to calculate the spousal relationship scores for both clients. Although both clients had 22 incidents, the severity of the incidents was different. The weighted composite scores were able to tell that Client B (score = 173) was more in need of immediate service than Client A (score = 158).

Scores for Client A and Client B

ITEMS	CLIENT A			CLIENT B		
	VALUE	FREQ.	SUBSCORE	VALUE	FREQ.	SUBSCORE
Push	7	9	63	7	4	28
Shout	4	3	12	4	2	8
Hit	9	1	9	9	7	63
Make fun	6	5	30	6	5	30
Punch	11	4	44	11	4	44
Total Score			**158**			**173**

A scale may not be a scale but may be a scale. One of the reasons for the inclusion of this simplified scale development example here is to show that a quality psychometric scale is a product of a complicated and technical process. Merely assigning numeric values to loosely put together questions that are not interrelated and adding up the total or calculating the average does not meet the standard of being a scale. However, social work practitioners should bear in mind that in everyday research discussion and usage, scale are often used interchangeably with index and other terms. Scales mean different things in different research contexts. For example, *measurement scales or scales of measurement* mean different levels of measurement: nominal level data (yes, no), ordinal data (ranking), interval, and ratio (numeric values). The definition of scale in a general sense, as expected, is less restricted. Some research projects may not require highly established or normed scales to achieve their goals. Their purposes are more practical than academic, and resources are limited. In those situations, a program-developed data collection tool that has a respectable quality may be considered a scale. It is the social workers' responsibility to gain the academic and professional understanding of the current trends and usage in social research to be smart consumers and producers of research.

TYPES OF SCALES

Scales have different names, such as inventories, tests, schedules, and composites. No matter what they are called, scales include intercorrelated items that measure the common construct and can be represented by a numeric value. Scales can be at the ordinal or the interval/ratio level of measurement. The common scales that we encounter in social research are the Likert scales, the Thurstone scales, the Guttman scales, and the semantic scales. All of them are unidimensional scales.

Unidimensional means measuring one common construct (e.g., students' ability in social statistics and not in Spanish, woodwork, or leadership) or a construct that has one dimension (e.g., height, weight, age, attitude, performance). Unidimensional constructs can be represented by a numeric value or a single number line. As one would suspect, many social constructs are multidimensional and are not concrete constructs, such as life expectancy or number of children in a room. Narrowing down a complex social or psychological construct into a single measurable construct requires a clear definition of the terms, methodical selection of items, and many other rigorous scale development steps.

Likert Scale

The Likert scale is the most commonly used scale in social research, particularly in surveys. It is a rating scale measuring the degree of intensity of one's attitude, opinion, or emotion. The 5-point format is the most common one, but it could also be a 7-point format or 11-point format. The Likert scale is named after Rensis Likert, who developed the scale in 1932. Next, are some of the response formats:

Strongly agree	Agree	Neither agree nor disagree	Disagree	Strongly disagree	Don't know
Strongly approve	Approve	A bit of both (about 50/50)	Disapprove	Strongly disapprove	
Always	Often	Sometimes	Seldom	Never	

Note that the "don't know" is placed at the end. It is an odd response. "Don't know" does not necessarily fit into the agreement and disagreement continuum. It is a lack of opinion or lack of knowledge. Mixing it in the analysis may distort the findings. Numeric values are assigned to each of the responses (e.g., strongly agree = 1, agree = 2) for statistical analysis. There is an ongoing debate of whether the Likert scale should be treated as an ordinal level scale or an interval level scale.

Thurstone Scale

Louis Thurstone developed the Thurstone scale in 1932. He proposed three different ways to develop this unidimensional scale: the method of equal appearing intervals, the method of successive intervals, and the method of paired comparison. We will briefly describe the equal appearing intervals method here (Stephanie, 2016; Trochim, 2006; University of California, Davis, n.d.(a)).

1. Researchers first develop a large number of items that represent a wide range of attitudes toward a particular topic, say, abortion.
2. They gather a large group of judges (about 100) and ask them to rate (from 1— less favorable to 6—neutral, and 11—extremely favorable.) This process is similar to the Spousal Relationship Scale example.
3. The respondents are asked to rate how unfavorable (negative), neutral, or favorable (positive) the statement is toward the topic of abortion, not whether they personally agree or disagree with the statement.
4. Researchers use the items "median (M)" and "interquartile range (IQR)" scores (the difference between Q1-25th percentile and Q3-75th percentile) to select items that have the higher agreement (homogeneity) and least variability (smaller IQR) (included).
5. Items that have a large variability of rating or considered confusing to the respondents would be eliminated (not included).

6. The average (mean score, $\bar{x}$) of the numeric ratings received for individual items becomes the score for that item.

ITEMS (VALUES)	M	Q1	Q3	IQR	RESULT	$\bar{x}$
As a woman, abortion will never happen to me	2	2	3.5	1.5	Include	2
Abortion is immoral	1	1	2	1.0	Include	1
Abortion encourages promiscuity	1	1	3	2.0	Include	2
Abortion is a human rights issue	9	9	11	2.0	Include	10
Abortion is a safe medical procedure	6	6	9	3.0	Include	7
The availability of abortion clinics contributes to the increase of abortion	3	2	5.5	3.5	Include	4
It is unethical for medical doctors to perform abortion	4	3	7	4.0	Not Include	4
Abstinence and responsible contraception are better alternatives	2	1	10	9.0	Not include	5
Our society is too permissive to deviant behaviors like abortion	3	1	5.5	4.5	Not include	4
Women are responsible for having the need for an abortion	2	2	9	7.0	Not include	3
Women who have had an abortion can still live a normal and productive life	8	10	11	1.0	Include	9
Abortion is a woman's health issue	9	9	11	2.0	Include	10

7. Researchers then put out the final items for the scale (usually 15 to 20 items).
8. They add the choices of agree and disagree at the front of each item to allow respondents to indicate whether they agree or disagree.

A THURSTONE SCALE ITEM (VALUE—NOT SHOWN TO RESPONDENTS)		
☐ Agree	☐ Disagree	1. As a woman, abortion will never happen to me (2)
☐ Agree	☐ Disagree	2. Abortion is immoral (1)
☐ Agree	☐ Disagree	3. Abortion encourages promiscuity (2)
☐ Agree	☐ Disagree	4. Abortion is a human rights issue (10)
☐ Agree	☐ Disagree	5. The availability of abortion clinics contributes to the increase of abortion (4)
☐ Agree	☐ Disagree	6. Abortion is a safe medical procedure (7)
☐ Agree	☐ Disagree	7. Women who have had an abortion can still live a normal and productive life (9)
☐ Agree	☐ Disagree	8. Abortion is a woman's health issue (10)

9. Based on the respondents' choices of items that they agree with (not the items that they disagree with) and their associated values, the researchers calculate the

Conceptual and Practical Research and Statistics for Social Workers

average scores that reflect the respondents' level of agreement or attitude toward the construct being studied. The higher the scores, the more favorable attitudes are represented.

10. If the respondent indicates agreement on #4, #6, #7, and #8. Then the respondent's score would be $(10 + 7 + 9 + 10)/4 = 9$. The respondent is supportive of the issue of abortion.

Guttman Scaling

The Guttman scaling was developed by Louis Guttman in the 1940s to measure the positive and negative attitudes toward a particular construct. It is also called a cumulative scale that represents an increasing unidimensional hierarchical agreement. Guttman scales are intuitive and have been widely used in public opinion studies. The Guttman scale is similar to a Thurstone scale in that it asks for agreement and disagreement toward a list of items. Through statistical analyses, final items will be selected and each will also have its own associated scale value. The researchers use the responses alone or with the associated scale values to calculate the results. Guttman scales are cumulative in that items are increasingly intensive or extreme. Respondents will agree with the items up to a certain point, and then they stop. If a person stops at item #3, that means the person agrees with items #1 and #2 but not #4 and #5. The following is an example of a Guttman scale on caregiving of one's elderly mother-in-law:

Please check all the statements with which you agree:
- ☐   I will call or go to visit her weekly
- ☐   I will bring her meals every other day
- ☐   I will prepare her meals and attain household chores daily
- ☐   I will take care of her personal hygiene, including bathing and other household chores daily
- ☐   I will move her to live with me

Obviously, caregiving is not a simple linear list of tasks. How would you rate someone who will pay for a full-time, live-in home health-care worker? Does it mean this person is more or less caring than the one who is willing to bath the care recipient? The challenge is that it is difficult to achieve a perfect cumulative scale, and Guttman scales are less popular than some other simpler scales.

Semantic Scales

The semantic scales or semantic differential scales are used to measure dichotomized constructs. The sematic scale was developed in the 1950s, and it is somewhat similar to the Likert scale in that it measures responses on opposing stands. Respondents can give their answers along the continuum of two polar adjectives or terms indicating where they stand by a slash, a number, or a pick.

"The semantic differential is a scale used for measuring the *meaning* of things and concepts. There are two aspects of meaning: denotative and connotative. The semantic differential measures *connotative* meaning" (University of California, Davis, n.d.(b), para. 1). Denotative is the direct meaning or indication of the term, such as names of universities or cities. Connotative refers to the suggestive or associated meaning of the term, such as the Alabama Crimson Tide! The denotative meaning of the term "horse" means the animal that we refer to as a horse. The connotative meaning, however, conjures up the image (i.e., emotion and feeling) of hardworking, loyal, power, and dependable.

The first example shows a variety of response options for a semantic differential scale. The second one shows how the scale can be scored and the results presented graphically.

How would you describe the quality of our county's services to people with disabilities?

Not enough	1, 2, 3, 4, 5, 6, 7, 8, 9, 10, 11	Enough
Slow	1 2 3 4 5	Fast
Inadequate	Very much, Somewhat, Neither, Somewhat, Very much	Adequate
Unacceptable	_____:_____:_____:_____:_____:_____:_____	Acceptable
Very poor	1-----------------------------11	Outstanding

How would you feel about social services for individuals who are poor and HIV+?

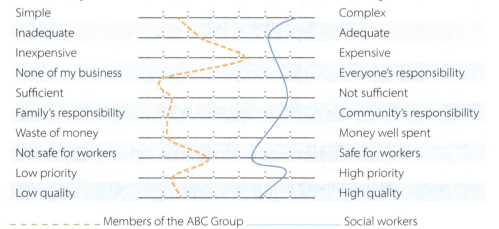

Simple	Complex
Inadequate	Adequate
Inexpensive	Expensive
None of my business	Everyone's responsibility
Sufficient	Not sufficient
Family's responsibility	Community's responsibility
Waste of money	Money well spent
Not safe for workers	Safe for workers
Low priority	High priority
Low quality	High quality

– – – – – – – Members of the ABC Group _____ Social workers

Conceptual and Practical Research and Statistics for Social Workers

In this example, two groups of respondents are asked to respond on a seven-point measure for the items on this semantic scale. They are the local social workers and members of an active community group called ABC. Researchers can analyze and report their responses in numbers or through a graphic presentation. Statistically, the researchers can calculate the mean score for each of the items for analysis. Scores for both groups on each of the items can be compared and further dissected. Graphically, the researchers can plot the groups' mean scores for the items onto the scale for an effective visual presentation.

COMMON DATA COLLECTION INSTRUMENTS AND WHICH ONE TO USE

Common Types of Instruments

Instruments are tools that researchers use to collect the intended data. The quality of the instruments affects the quality of data collected, and, therefore, the quality of the findings and the research. GIGO is a common saying that vividly describes the relationship between the input and the output. Among the common types of instruments for data collection are pre-post surveys, post-only surveys, retrospective surveys, observation rating forms, observation checklists, transfer data forms, phone interview protocols, in-person interview protocols, and focus group protocols. These instrument types are described next.

> **Pre-post survey questionnaire.** Generally used when information is needed prior to participating in a service activity or receiving the intervention (independent variable), the presurvey (baseline data), then again collecting the same information after receiving the independent variable, the postsurvey.

> **Post-only survey questionnaire.** Generally used when existing data is available as baseline data; therefore, information is collected only after the intervention, the post-only survey.

> **Post-only retrospective survey questionnaire.** These types of surveys can be used when baseline data are not available. The surveys ask respondents retrospectively to rate the level of change that occurred since receiving

services; this is called a retrospective survey. Here is an example of a question and a choice of responses: "To what extent have the participants increased their sense of self-efficacy since participating in the support group? Not at all, made little progress, made progress, made substantial progress."

Observation rating form. Observing attitudes or behavior of the study subjects is generally done over time. An observation rating form asks the data source, usually the researcher or a person who has regular contact with the study subjects to rate attitude or behavior changes. Generally, observation rating forms operate similar to post-only retrospective surveys; baseline data may not be necessary because the questions are crafted in a manner that indicates rating the level of change that occurred since the beginning.

Observation guide. Observation guide documents the study subjects' behaviors and performances (benchmarks) in the form of completion, frequency, duration, and intensity. Pre-checklist observations can be made before the intervention and then again afterward to determine changes. The rubric is a useful tool for observation.

Transfer data form. For existing secondary data studies, this form is needed so information can be transferred from secure records to the researcher for analysis. The setup of the form is guided by the purpose of the current research and the pertinent human subjects' concerns. A study on the adaptive behaviors of caregivers for hospice patients, based on the agency's client records from the last 10 years, requires such a form to transfer the needed data while protecting the privacy and confidentiality of the patients and caregivers.

Phone interview protocol/guide. Generally, phone interviews are short, 15 to 20 minutes maximum. A phone interview protocol instrument is needed to serve two functions. First, it provides a guide for how the questions should be asked; secondly, it allows the interviewer to document the responses quickly and accurately. Generally, the questions are predetermined, focusing on specific issues and looking for specific responses (e.g., how has the city's affordable housing shortage affected you financially?).

In-person interview protocol/guide. As with the phone interview protocol, the in-person interview protocol acts as a guide for what questions will be asked of an individual. However, because an in-person interview is conducted face-to-face, it is usually longer (e.g., 30 minutes to an hour). Depending on the type of interviews employed, the questions may not need to be as focused, allowing the participant flexibility in responding (e.g., please describe how the affordable housing shortage affects your quality of life in this city?).

Focus group protocol, discussion guide. A focus group protocol is used when interviewing a small group of people. The advantage of this data collection method is that it allows the researcher to collect rich qualitative data, information generated by the interaction between individuals in the group. A focus group protocol acts as a guide for what questions to ask; however, these questions are used to generate discussion. The group is allowed to expand the discussion beyond the questions.

Choice of Instruments

Where does one begin when identifying or developing an instrument? The type of instrument will depend on the information needed to meet the purpose of the research. Therefore, reviewing the purpose of the study and anticipated results in the research proposal will help determine the type of information needed, as well as where or who will provide the information. Table 9.1 provides questions to consider when choosing an instrument. This table is particularly geared toward program evaluation.

TABLE 9.1. Questions to Ask When Determining the Type of Instrument to Use

DO YOU NEED TO ...	THEN CONSIDER USING ...
document the number of people served or the number of times service was delivered?	a participation roster or a service activity log.
get information from existing records?	a data documentation/transfer form.
know whether something (an idea, opinion, or behavior) exists or not?	a checklist or an index.
assess knowledge, behavior, or skills?	a test, observation instrument (e.g., rubric), or a survey.
learn about attitudes, feelings, and emotions?	a test or a survey.
get a rating, such as quality or satisfaction?	a survey.
get details about something?	open-ended questions or interviews.
be able to ask follow-up questions?	an in-person format such as an interview protocol, phone survey protocol, or focus group protocol.

Existing Instruments

Data collection instruments can be obtained by identifying an existing instrument that will collect the data needed or by developing an instrument to fit the data collection needs. There are advantages and disadvantages to each of these approaches.

A large number of instruments are available to the public that were developed for other research studies. There are also many commercial instruments available that measure a variety of community and educational service areas. These instruments can be found online and in printed publications. However, finding an existing instrument that will collect the data you want can be a challenge. If you can find one, consider the advantages and disadvantages of using an existing instrument.

Advantages
- Do not need to develop an instrument
- Instrument, in many cases, has been tested for validity and reliability
- May provide instructions on how to analyze the data or a data aggregation

Disadvantages
- May require "buying" the instrument and/or its services
- May require training before one can administer the instrument
- May have copyright issues

Researchers searching for an instrument need to make sure they are thorough in their review processes. They may feel that they have found an appropriate instrument because the title of the instrument reflects the services they are providing or describes similar outcomes the program has identified. However, researchers should review the instrument in detail and consider the following cautions:

- Does the instrument measure what you want to measure?
- What degree of burden will be placed on the researchers and the program staff or respondents in administering the instrument?
- Will you, the researcher, know how to aggregate and analyze the data after the data is collected?

In some cases, the researcher may find an instrument that will collect the data needed to measure the variables for the study if modifications or revisions are made to the instrument. For example, questions may need to be added or deleted; the wording of the questions may need to be simplified; the formatting and/or layout design may need to be altered. Modifying or revising existing instruments is a common practice; however, a few potential problems need to be considered before doing so.

- Does the instrument have a copyright?
- Will revising the instrument affect the validity or reliability?
- Will modifications affect the analysis plan?

Research Developed Instruments

Oftentimes, it is more effective if researchers design their own data collection tools. The key point to keep in mind is to make sure the instruments collect the relevant data in an appropriate manner and with the desirable quality that will achieve the purpose of the research. Again, GIGO! Many social work students are surprised to find that choosing a suitable research question and crafting useful and well-designed instruments is not that easy, yet each task is crucial to the success of their research projects. No matter if the instrument is a questionnaire, interview protocol, observation guide, or data transfer form, they all follow the logic of gathering pertinent information on variables related to the purpose of the research. One way to ensure the instrument collects the information needed to measure the anticipated results is to create a table that matches the needed information with the questions in the instrument. That table is called a table of specifications.

TABLE OF SPECIFICATIONS

The table of specifications is a simple table with several columns that helps organize the thinking and logic of the design of the instrument. There are no fixed rules of how many columns are needed. This is only a working document for the researchers when developing the instrument. A very basic table will have two columns. The first column is about the domains or components that are to be studied. Within it are the variables to be studied. The second column is about the items or questions that will collect the needed information. It is also a good idea to add a third column about planned analysis. The intended analysis may affect how the questions are asked and what levels of measurement data are needed. The following is a basic framework of a table of specifications. Table 9.2 shows the contents for a job training outcome study.

TABLE 9.2. Table of Specifications for a Job Training Outcome Study

DOMAINS/COMPONENTS/ VARIABLES/INFORMATION (WHAT IS THE INFORMATION YOU NEED?)	ITEMS/QUESTIONS (WHICH QUESTIONS COLLECT THIS INFORMATION?)	ANALYSIS (WHAT DATA ANALYSIS WILL YOU USE?)
Demographic data	Name of participant	Frequency (f)
	Age	Mean, mode
Basic Personal and Social Skills		
Personal skills	Keep appointment	f, %
	Dress appropriately	f, %
Social skills	Proper manner	Assessment score
	Work well as a team member	Assessment score
	Take leadership	Assessment score
Proficiency in job skills	Training completed	f
	Grade	Grade
Job seeking ability	Resume writing	Assessment score
	Interview skills	Assessment score

For program evaluation (see Chapter 10 for details), the researchers may want to keep in mind the target (or the benchmark of success) for the program. They may want to add a target column to make this possible. The table of specifications also serves as a tool to communicate among researcher partners.

Table 9.3 is a table of specifications for an aging-in-place (AIP) senior program postsurvey questionnaire/interview guide. Table 9.4 is a table of specifications for a foster youth independent living mentoring program pre-/post-questionnaire. Both of these examples show additional details that researchers can include in the table. Table 9.4 also includes more advanced analysis.

Putting the Table of Specifications to Work

After the table of specifications is complete, researchers can extract the items or questions. They are the core contents of the final questionnaire or interview guide. Researchers can rearrange them in the final instrument, based on the needs of the study. Some researchers prefer to start with fewer personal questions and move slowly to more sensitive questions. For that reason, the demographic questions are placed at the end. Some like to group related questions in a cluster; others prefer to scatter them around. The details of developing a questionnaire will be discussed later in this chapter.

During data analysis, the table of specifications will become an analysis guide. It shows how items are to be analyzed and which items should be clustered together to

TABLE 9.3. Table of Specifications for a Postservice Survey Questionnaire for an AIP Senior Program

	TABLE OF SPECIFICATIONS FOR SOCIAL CONNECTEDNESS WITH ANALYSIS METHODS		
VARIABLES/ INFORMATION	**ITEMS/QUESTIONS**	**TARGET**	**ANALYSIS**
	As the result of my participation in AIP in the last 3 months . . .		
Linkage to others (socializing, participation, knowledge of neighbors)	#1. I have come to know at least three new neighbors. ___ Yes, ___ No #2. I have phone numbers of at least two neighbors I recently met. ___ Yes, ___ No #3. I feel more comfortable greeting and chatting with my neighbors. ___ Agree, ___ Disagree #4. I have visited one of my neighbors for the first time. ___ Yes, ___ No	Meet at least three new neighbors and get two additional phone numbers. Accomplish three of the four results.	*f*, %
Knowledge of resources	#11. If I need assistance, I know I could call on my neighbors without feeling putting a burden on them. ___ True, ___ Not true #12. I learn more about how and where to get help for my social security benefit. ___ Agree, ___ Disagree #13. I store the emergency safety kit that I received from Emergency Training in a proper place in the house. ___ Yes, ___ No #14. I have the Community and Emergency Service Contact Information Sheet posted/stored close to my phone. ___ Yes, ___ No	Seventy-five percent participate in emergency training. Sixty-five percent know where and how to seek assistance. Thirty percent would seek help if needed.	*f*, %
Social Involvement	#5. I signed up to be visited by a senior companion volunteer. ___ Yes, ___ No #6. I have become more active in clubhouse activities. ___ Strongly Agree, ___ Agree, ___ Disagree, ___ Strongly Disagree #7. I am out of my house meeting people more than before. ___ Strongly Agree, ___ Agree, ___ Disagree, ___ Strongly Disagree #8. I have been or plan to go to one of the neighborhood parties. ___ Strongly Agree, ___ Agree, ___ Disagree, ___ Strongly Disagree #9. All these activities have disturbed the quiet and calm life that I enjoy. ___ Strongly Agree, ___ Agree, ___ Disagree, ___ Strongly Disagree #10. I would rather be left alone for the time being. ___ Strongly Agree, ___ Agree, ___ Disagree, ___ Strongly Disagree	Fifty-five percent would give at least three positive responses to items 5–8. No more than 5% would respond positively for items 9 and 10 and their desires would be honored.	*f*, %, descriptive statistics
Demographics	#15. Gender: ___ Male, ___ Female #16. Age: ___ 60–69, ___ 70–79, ___ 80 and above #17. County of residence: _____		*f*, %

Basic considerations:

- Is this tool culturally competent?
- Will seniors need assistance to complete the questionnaire? If needed, this could become an interview guide.

TABLE 9.4. Table of Specifications for a Foster Youth Independent Living Mentoring Program Pre/Post Questionnaire

WHAT IS THE INFORMATION YOU NEED? (FOCUS)	WHICH QUESTION(S) COLLECT THIS INFORMATION (CONTENTS AND INDICATORS?)	(TARGETS)	WHAT DATA ANALYSIS METHOD(S) WILL YOU USE?
Demographic data	# 1 (name), #2 (gender), #3 (age), #4 (class level), #5 (living condition)	Match at least 25 target youth with mentors.	Frequency count
Self-confidence level	#16, #17, #18, #19, #20 (self-confidence items) #21 (self-confidence composite score Pre-mentoring). #22 (self-confidence composite score Post-mentoring).	Forty percent of the youth who spent at least 100 hours with their mentors will show a significant improvement in their self-confidence score in at least three of the four items.	Frequency count Percentage distribution Comparison of pre/post score, t-test
Proficiency of independent living skills	Pre/post Scores for #6, #7, #8, #9, #10 – living skills assessment checklist	Ninety percent of the participating youth will demonstrate mastery of all five of the identified living skills on the checklist.	Frequency count Percentage distribution
Advanced Analyses			
Case management and counseling	#11, #12, #13 (frequency, hours, and outcomes of counseling) #14, 15 (frequency and outcomes of case management)	Sixty percent of the youth will remain active in receiving counseling and case management. Thirty percent will achieve intervention goals.	Frequency count Percentage distribution
Examination of correlations (intervention outcomes)	Self-confidence and independent living skills Case management and independent living skills Counseling and independent living skills		Test of correlation (i.e., X^2, Rho, Pearson's r)

Important considerations:

- Is this instrument appropriate to age, reading level, culture, and other concerns?
- Is this instrument being formulated and implemented in a least burdensome and most efficient manner?

provide answers to certain domains. This table also helps visualize the data analysis process and keeps the research on track to attain its intended purpose.

SURVEY INSTRUMENTS (QUESTIONNAIRE AND INTERVIEW GUIDE) DEVELOPMENT

Survey methods are most commonly used by social workers. Survey instruments include questionnaires and interview guides. They are very much alike, and the differences lie in how they are being used. Respondents respond to the questionnaire on their own, while interviewers record the interviewees' responses. The questions involved are the same but are different in their delivery. Many have experienced the frustration of answering a questionnaire that is confusing and could be better developed. Let's try out this one, which was used for a post-workshop evaluation:

QUESTIONNAIRE

1. Name:

2. Birthday:

3. Phone number:

4. Spouse's phone number:

5. How often do you attend workshops?
   _____1–5, _____ 5–8, _____ 8–14.

6. How did you like this or any workshop?
   _____ Yes, _____ No

7. Why didn't you like this workshop?

8. People should be able to do what they want to do.
   _____ Strongly agree, _____ Agree, _____ Somehow agree, _____ Disagree

9   Highest level of education
   _____ Grade school, _____ 11th grade, _____ High school

Do you see any problems with this questionnaire? I am sure you do. Here are some of the problems:

1. Format issues: Title of questionnaire and direction are missing
2. Ethical/privacy issues: Name, birthday, and spouse's phone number, are they needed?

3. Item 5: Clarity—which and what workshop? Overlapping—1–5 and then 5–8. Also 1–5 of what?
4. Item 6: Be specific—this or any?
5. Item 7: Leading question and sounds accusatory—Why didn't you?
6. Item 8: Skewed answer—3 positives (agree), 1 negative (disagree).
7. Item 9: Poor answer choices—Grade school? What grade? Why 11th? High school graduate or attended high school? What if someone has a college degree?
8. Other questions:
    a. Does this questionnaire measure what it intends to measure—participant's satisfaction with the workshop? The problem is that even the purpose is not clear.
    b. Should some of the items be eliminated?
    c. Are you able to construct one much better than this one? I am sure you can!

Steps for Developing Questionnaires and Interview Guides

The development of a questionnaire or an interview guide includes the basic steps listed in Box 9.1. It is a careful and intentional process that is guided by the purpose of the research and the arts of inquiry. It certainly is not just a bunch of random steps and questions that came up during our morning drive to work or something that sounds like a good idea while we are having dinner!

There are other concerns that need to be attended to for designing a quality survey tool. The following Questionnaire Development Checklist (Box 9.2) could be used as a guideline and a check-off sheet. The Ready to Read Survey (Figure 9.1) is an example that highlights the items from the checklist.

Box 9.3, Asking Effective Outcome and Impact Questions belongs to both this chapter on instrument development and Chapter 10, which focuses on needs assessment and program evaluation. Because it is a guide to developing outcome and impact questions for questionnaire and interview surveys, it is included here. Some of the terms, such as needs and outcomes, are to be introduced in Chapter 10. Readers may wish to consider both Chapters 9 and 10 when using Box 9.3.

OBSERVATIONAL GUIDE DEVELOPMENT

As discussed in Chapter 6, there are many ways to conduct observational research. In observational studies, like interviews, the researchers are the tools. Therefore,

BOX 9.1. STEPS FOR QUESTIONNAIRE AND INTERVIEW GUIDE DEVELOPMENT

1. Determine the purpose and objectives of the proposed questionnaire and interview guide.
2. Review current literature, establish content validity.
3. Review existing questionnaires and interview guides.
4. Develop the table of specifications.
5. Use table of specifications to organize and develop items.
6. Develop directions for administration and examples of how to complete questions.
7. Sequence the questions. Flow from noncontroversial or interesting to sensitive or personal.
8. Prepare a cover sheet, consent form, and other ethical and instructional attachments.
9. Format the questionnaire. Fonts, styles, length, color—clean, clear, and pleasant.
10. Establish procedures used for scoring or tallying the instrument.
11. Conduct a preliminary review of the instrument with colleagues.
12. Revise instrument based on reviews.
13. Pilot test the instrument with subjects similar to the potential respondents.
14. Check instrument for reliability and validity.
15. Revise and finalize the instrument.
16. Get Human Subjects Review approval.
17. Use instrument to collect data.

training and preparation are extremely important for any successful observational research projects. The researchers are assisted by their notebooks, cameras, audio recorders, computers, and some standardized data collection tools—observational guides.

A key question is, "What are we observing?" Certainly, this is determined by the purpose of the study. In turn, variables to be studied are identified, operationally defined, and observation strategies and tools are planned. Still, "How exactly are the variables being observed?" Again, it depends on the purpose of the study—the researchers may just be observing to get a deeper understanding or to document how things evolve. The researchers could also be observing specific markers about the variable. Generally, these include the following:

1. *Duration.* The length of time of the continuing presence or absence of the observed phenomenon or behavior. "How long have you been experiencing

BOX 9.2. QUESTIONNAIRE DEVELOPMENT CHECKLIST

1. *Instrument Title.* Is the name of the program stated and the type of service indicated?
2. *Introductory Statement.* What is the purpose of the instrument; how will the data be used; is there a level of confidentiality or anonymity of the information?
3. *Demographics.* Are there questions about the respondents' backgrounds and necessary information that are relevant to the research?
4. *Directions.* Are there directions that describe how to complete the instrument?
5. *Questions.*
   - *Questions.* The questions are short.
   - There are no double-barreled questions.
   - The questions are clear and focused.
   - There are no leading questions.
   - The respondents are capable of answering the questions.
   - The questions are in a language that can be understood.
6. *Format.* Is the instrument pleasant to the eye; does it have enough space between questions; does it use a font type that is clear; does the layout cover the entire page?
7. *Pilot-testing.* Arrange for the pilot test participants and conditions to be as close to the actual administration conditions as possible (e.g., time of day, location, methods, respondents).

the stress?" "How long did the grief last?" Duration is often recorded in some form of time system (e.g., minutes, hours, days, or years). This is called *duration recording.*

2. *Magnitude or intensity.* The strength and potency of the observed behavior. "How severe was the stress?" "How consuming was the grief?" Because magnitude is not always observable, some categorizations will be used to indicate the intensity. For example, nurses cannot directly observe the intensity of pain experienced, so patients are asked to rate it on a scale between 1 and 10. This is called *magnitude recording.*

3. *Frequency.* The rate of occurrence of the observed behavior. "How often has the stress been experienced?" "How many times in a week does the sense of grief arise?" Researchers can use *interval recording* to record how many times the behavior takes place during a set period of time. Alternatively, researchers

1 (Title) ─────────▶ **READY TO READ SURVEY**
Our Tutoring Program   **7** (Pilot)

This is a: ☐ pre-test   ☐ post-test ◀── **6** (Format)

Dear Tutor:

This instrument will help measure school readiness and listening skills for students participating in the Our Tutoring Reading program. All data will remain confidential and results will be reported anonymously. ◀── **2** (Introductory)   **4** (Directions)

Please indicate above if this is a pre- or post-test. The pre-test should be conducted within the first month of the program. The post-test should be conducted after the students have participated in the program for at least seven months.

3 (Demographics)

Your Name: _____ Date: _____

School: _____ Students Name: _____

School Readiness

Directions: Please check ☑ all items that you observe for each student.

5 (Questions)
6 (Format)

1. Before tutoring session begins:

☐ Student is prepared for tutoring session (e.g., read assigned material, completed homework).

☐ Student has materials (e.g., pencils, paper).

☐ Student arrives on time.

2. During tutoring session:

☐ Student follows ground rules.

☐ Student participates in activities (e.g., participates in discussions, completes seatwork, and works cooperatively with other students).

☐ Student asks for assistance when needed.

Listening Skills

Directions: Based on your observations, please check ☑ the items that best describes your perception of this student.

☐ Student pays attention to whoever is speaking.

☐ Student does not interrupt someone speaking.

☐ Student actively listens and tries to answer questions.

☐ Student is able to reiterate clearly what the speaker said.

☐ Student demonstrates the ability of recognizing the main idea of discussions.

4 (Directions)

☐ *If there are any comments you would like to add, please do so at the back of this page. Thank you. Please return the completed form to the Program Manager*

Figure 9.1. **Ready to Read Survey—Use of Questionnaire Development Checklist**

BOX 9.3. ASKING EFFECTIVE OUTCOME AND IMPACT QUESTIONS

QUESTIONS RELATE TO IDENTIFIED NEEDS

Effective outcome and impact questions need to relate to the objective statement identified in your evaluation plan or hypothesis for your research. Specifically, effective outcome and impact questions are designed to assess to what extent your services have met one or more of the following four types of needs that you identified in the evaluation plan or research design.

1. Normative need: below the established social standards (e.g., poverty line).
2. Felt need: individual's unique wish and desire (e.g., isolated seniors want to connect).
3. Expressed need: documented attempts (e.g., waiting list).
4. Comparative need: relatively worse or less desirable (e.g., low-income older adults have more health problems and receive less preventive health care).

DESIGNING OUTCOME AND IMPACT QUESTIONS

Type of questions/items:

1. Open-ended items: Respondents create the responses from their perspectives in regard to your question.
   - What has been your experience in working with students at Johnson elementary school?
   - In your opinion, what are the most noticeable changes in the relationship between you and your colleagues?
   - Please contrast the major emotional responses of people who approach the volunteer staff at the missing children's booth at the state fair.
2. Closed-ended items
   - Categories (e.g., male, female)
   - Checklists (e.g., yes/no or true/false responses)
   - Index (e.g., counts of risk and resiliency factors)
   - Rating scales (e.g., Likert scale; low = 1   2   3   4   5 = high)
   - Multiple choice (e.g., select the best fit)
3. Combination of open and closed-ended questions
4. Others: Top choice list, shopping with a limited budget (zero-sum game), and others

Wording and other considerations:

1. Express only one idea per question (e.g., avoid multiples such as "it was beneficial and cost-effective").
2. Avoid using technical terms/vague terms/slang.
3. Ensure that the meanings of the questions are clear and unambiguous.
4. Avoid leading questions (e.g., avoid asking, "You liked that, didn't you?")
5. Use respectful language.
6. Write them in plain, direct, and simple language with the appropriate reading level.
7. Make sure they appropriately cover all concerned variables.
8. Pay attention to the length and appearance of the instrument to have a positive overall impression.

Constructing outcome and impact questions:

1. Follow the logic of
   - Objectives or hypotheses and their associated variables
2. Organize each question around
   - results (why),
   - indicators (what to look for),
   - measure (instrument), and
   - standard of success (how much change).
3. Aim the questions at the topic:
   - "How well did this program do?"
   - "How much change has the program made?"
   - "So what?"
4. Distinguish and decide on the choice of questions that generate data on how people
   - think and know—*knowledge*
   - feel and prefer—*emotion, attitude, and opinion*
   - do—*behavior*
5. Ask the experts:
   - Consult and pilot test to ensure questions are understandable.
6. Overall impression:
   - Assess whether early questions affect the later ones.
   - Determine the appearance/format of the instrument and the flow of questions.

can use spot-check recording to document random or spontaneous drop-in observations.

An observation guide is used to document these observations. A group of observers can be divided up to do recordings of different markers at the same time during the same observation period. On the other hand, a researcher can record one or two markers in every observation and rotate to different ones at subsequent observations. Box 9.4 is an example of an adapted in-class observation exercise that shows the different basic observation recording methods: duration recording, magnitude recording, spot-check recording, and interval recording. Duration recording documents the length of time of the presence of the behavior. Magnitude recording documents the intensity. Spot-check and interval recording document the frequency.

BOX 9.4. "DO YOU SEE WHAT I SEE?"—AN OBSERVATIONAL EXERCISE

DO YOU SEE WHAT I SEE?

- This 5-minute exercise is designed to facilitate students' learning of different recording methods for observation.
- Break up the class into small groups and form a big circle that everyone in class can see each other.
- Each small group secretly picks a student from any of the other groups as the target/subject for the observation of a behavior: a smile.
- Assign student(s) within the group to do duration recording, magnitude recording, spot-check recording, or interval recording.
- Record observations of the target student's smile for 5 minutes without the target student knowing.
- Each group reports back to the class on the results of its observations.

Subject Name: _____ **Recorder name:** _____
Observation Time period: _____ a.m./p.m. _____ a.m./p.m. *Target behavior to be observed:*
Smile ☺

---

1. Duration Recording

(Time period for observation: _____ a.m./p.m. _____ a.m./p.m.)

DATE	LENGTH OF TIME PER EACH OCCURRENCE (I.E., SECONDS PER EACH SMILE OBSERVED)	ADDITIONAL COMMENTS
	1.	
	2.	
	3.	
	4.	
	5.	
	Total Time:	

2. Magnitude Recording

(1) A very little smile. (2) A little smile (3). A regular smile. (4) A big smile (a grin). (5) A very big smile (a laugh).

TIME, (E.G., 1:01, 1:05)	MAGNITUDE (E.G., 1, 2, 3, 4, OR 5)
1.	
2.	
3.	
4.	
5.	

3. Spot-Check Recording

TIME OF SPOT-CHECK (E.G., 1:02, 1:14)	BEHAVIOR WAS OCCURRING	BEHAVIOR WAS NOT OCCURRING
e.g., 1:02	√	
e.g., 1:14		√
1.		
2.		
3.		
4.		
5.		

4. Interval Recording

Put a check mark √ in the box under the time if the behavior (smile) happens at least once. (If there is more than one smile per time interval, only one check is needed)

E.G., 1:40–1:45 P.M.	__:00–__:05	__:06–__:10	__:11–__:15	__:16–__:20
	√			

PILOT TESTING INSTRUMENTS

The purpose of pilot testing instruments is to determine if the instruments will collect the information needed to respond to the anticipated outcomes. Instruments should be pilot tested whether existing instruments were selected, or instruments were developed. Pilot testing the instruments can address uncertainties, such as whether the questions are clear to the respondents, are the respondents able to complete the instruments, or are the instruments too long or too complicated? Logistic concerns can also be identified. Box 9.5 outlines the steps on how instruments can be pilot tested.

INTEGRATING DATA COLLECTION METHODS AND INSTRUMENTS

So far, we have discussed different research designs, data collection methods, and data collection instruments. This section will use two actual examples to demonstrate how they are being used together. Both of these are real-life examples that were conducted to generate data to promote target populations' well-being. Some of the terms, such as different types of needs and types of results, will be further explained in the next chapter on program evaluation.

Box 9.6 is an example of using different data collection approaches and tools to evaluate a Meals on Wheels and Home Visiting program. The social workers and researchers wanted to know if this program really made a difference in helping the elderly stay in their home and preventing premature institutionalization.

Table 9.5 is a planning guide provided to a county welfare agency for a needs assessment. The agency wanted to gather information to develop a community action plan that aims to promote self-sufficiency. Key questions and a summary of different data collection approaches are presented.

BOX 9.5. STEPS TO PILOT TESTING INSTRUMENTS

1. Find some participants who are similar to the people being surveyed/interviewed. (*Usually, four to five people are sufficient for general pilot test.*)
2. Arrange for the participants to take the survey/interview. Try to make the pilot test conditions match the actual administrative conditions whenever possible.
3. If it's a phone survey, pilot test over the phone; if it's a mail survey, have them fill it out without any assistance, or even mail it to them.
4. If the instrument is written, ask participants to record the time it takes them to complete it.
5. After each participant completes the instrument, set up a time as soon as possible to talk with him/her. Ask the following questions to determine if this instrument will collect the information needed:
6. *For individual items:*
   - Are the directions clear?
   - Do participants understand how to answer each question?
   - Are there any sensitive questions?
   - Are there any questions that don't make sense?
   - Any suggestions for improvement?
7. *Overall:*
   - What do participants think the survey/interview is about?
   - What problems, if any, did participants have in completing the survey or interview?
   - Do participants understand, from the information provided, how their responses will be used?
   - Do participants understand how to return the survey?
   - Are participants interpreting the questions in the way you intended?"
8. Collect the answers and write up the results from the pilot participants.
   - Try to analyze the data and see if they can be analyzed in the manner that you planned.
   - Identify additional data collection, data input, and data analysis concerns.
   - What other academic, methodological, logistic, fiscal, ethical, and social concerns should be further addressed?
9. Share the pilot results with other people who will be using the data. Will this data provide answers to their questions?
10. Modify the survey/interview based on the pilot results you have gathered.

BOX 9.6. MEALS-ON-WHEELS AND HOME-VISITING PROGRAM

MEALS-ON-WHEELS AND HOME-VISITING PROGRAM

1. *Research question.* Does this Meals on Wheels and Home Visiting program increase elderly clients' ability to stay in their own homes?
2. *Data sources.* Elderly clients, family members, service providers, volunteers, and secondary data.
3. Data collection methods:
    - Volunteers will observe the well-being of the elderly by using the Home Safety Checklist (Observation).
    - They will also interview the elderly or the caregivers at the beginning and the end of the program year using the Stay-at-Home Interview Guide (Interview).
    - A sample of the volunteers will be selected to complete a Service Quality and Input Questionnaire in month 6 of the program to identify ways to improve (Questionnaire).
    - Eight representatives from partner agencies and service recipients will participate in a Program Enhancement Focus Group meeting at the end of the program year to evaluate the overall outcome of the program and make suggestions for future directions (Focus group).
4. Instruments and indicators development:
    - Home Safety Checklist (What items indicate the degree or the presence of safety in the home? For example, adequate lighting, fire hazard, food, and medication.)
    - Stay-at-Home Interview Guide (Sample indicators: How many elderly people report that they may need to reside in a nursing home if this program is not available to them. An elder who is not able to cook for himself/herself now has regular visits from his/her caregiver, etc.)
    - Service Quality and Input Questionnaire (What constitutes quality service?)
    - Program Enhancement Focus Group Discussion Guide (Indicator: Overall, what has happened to the targeted elderly because of this program?)

Box 9.6 and Table 9.5 are included as examples to show the connections between research question, research design, data collection methods, and data collection tools. However, they also provide applicable and relevant information for the discussions of needs assessment and program evaluation in the next chapter. Readers may wish to revisit these tables when studying Chapter 10.

TABLE 9.5. Data Collection Approaches and Tools—A Planning Guide for a County Needs Assessment for Self-Sufficiency

Goal: (e.g.,) Conduct a comprehensive needs assessment to inform the development of a community action plan to achieve the goal of self-sufficiency for clients.

Guiding Questions:
1. What do you want to find out? What is self-sufficiency? (Beginning with the end in mind)
2. What is available to you? (Data Sources)
3. What types of data collection approaches will you use? (Methods)
4. What types of tools do you need and how do you develop them? (Instruments: Including Indicators and Targets)

Assess all Four Types of Needs: Normative, Felt, Expressed, and Comparative Needs

	SECONDARY DATA	QUESTIONNAIRE SURVEY	INTERVIEW SURVEY	FOCUS GROUP	OBSERVATION
Examples	• Census Bureau reports • Other community needs assessments	• Needs assessment survey • Satisfaction survey • Pre/post-questionnaire	• Intake interview • Exit interview • Key informant interview	• End-of-the-year program impact focus group • Opinion study	• Home safety check • Classroom behavior observation
Likely Data Source	• Service providers, volunteers, service recipients, samples of recipients, samples of related stakeholders, general public, etc.	• Firsthand information by respondents	• Key informants • Experts, knowledge-able person	• Key informants • Experts, knowledge-able person	• Whatever was present • Behaviors
	• Service records, published reports				
Data Collection Methods	• Decide areas to be studied: children, elderly, basic needs, health and mental health, disability, veterans, employment, etc. • Gather published reports, summarize findings	• Respondents are reached in person, by mail, by phone, or through the internet. • On their own, they respond to the instruments. (questionnaire) in their own words. • Document what respondents put in writing.	• Respondents are reached in person, by mail, by phone, or through the internet. • The interviewer records the responses on the instrument (interview guide). • Document what interviewees say to the interviewer.	• A small group of respondents is recruited and meet through a structured group process in responding to a set of structured questions. • Guided discussions. • Document what participants' express during the group process.	• Evaluator records behaviors observed and documents them on a record form or checklist. • Observe the presence, frequency, duration, and strength of the happening. • Document what people do.

TABLE 9.5. Data Collection Approaches and Tools—A Planning Guide for a County Needs Assessment for Self-Sufficiency (*Continued*)

	SECONDARY DATA	QUESTIONNAIRE SURVEY	INTERVIEW SURVEY	FOCUS GROUP	OBSERVATION
Instruments	• Secondary data and literature reviews grid	• Questionnaire (online, mailed, in-person) • Consider using cluster sampling (random sample) or quota sampling (non-random) to ensure representations. • Use a table of specifications to develop the tool.	• Interview guide (it could be very similar to the survey questionnaire) • Gather qualitative data. • Use a table of specifications to develop the tool.	• Focus group discussion guide • Add substance to the summary of findings from the survey and interviews. • Use a table of specifications to develop the tool.	• Observation Record Form
Use of Data	• Understand and build upon current knowledge. • Use it to guide the development of the survey questionnaire.	• Gather inputs (both quantitative and qualitative) from samples that represent the population.	• Collect qualitative data from knowledgeable interviewees.	• Validate findings and add depth to the data.	• Collect qualitative and quantitative data.
Types of Results Assessed	• Output, intermediate, and outcome	• Output, intermediate, and outcome	• Output, intermediate and outcome	• Intermediate and outcome	• Intermediate and outcome

CONCLUSION

This chapter provided explanations and examples for the development of various data collection tools. The differences between checklist, index, and scales were discussed, and the many types of scale, such as Likert scale and Thurstone scale were described. The table of specifications can be used to develop a focused and organized tool for data collection and analysis. Survey questionnaires, interview guides, and observation guides are the common data collection tools for social work studies. Different research designs (exploratory, descriptive, experimental, and evaluative) demand different data collection approaches and tools. The next chapter will focus on the development and use of the evaluative research design, which includes needs assessment and program evaluation. As described before, the evaluative design employs a combination of methods used for exploratory, descriptive, and experimental research.

Figure Credit

Fig. 9.1: Adapted from Anna Marie Schmidt, Fracis K. O. Yuen, and Kenneth L. Terao, "Ready to Survey - Use of Questionnaire Development Guide," Effective Grant Writing and Program Evaluation for Human Service Professionals, pp. 198. Copyright © 2009 by John Wiley & Sons, Inc.

10

NEEDS ASSESSMENT, PROGRAM PLANNING, AND PROGRAM EVALUATION (WHAT AND WHAT HAPPENS)

In the late 1930s, a young man graduated from high school and decided to make a good living for himself and his future family by becoming a door-to-door salesman, selling Hoover vacuum cleaners out of his used station wagon. He drove up to a farmhouse in the middle of Iowa and knocked on the door. A nice older lady answered. The young man immediately said, "Ma'am, I got this wonderful modern machine that can clean up any dirt in your house. I mean everything." Before she got a chance to say anything, he went to the barn and picked up several buckets of manure from the cows and spread them around the house. He pulled out one of his Hoovers and was about to get into action until the old lady finally got a chance to say something. She said, "Young man, you better get busy because we ain't got no electricity!" Having wonderful ideas or programs is great but whether they are what the people need or whether the people are ready is a different story.

As I often tell my students, "Help is not help until the receiving side considers it help." Here's another example: a mom was busy, hurriedly preparing the big Thanksgiving feast before the relatives arrived. Her five-year-old son Johnny came into the kitchen and said he wanted to be mom's little helper. He loved to help mom make the dough for the apple pie. Normally, the mom would really enjoy doing that and welcome the "help." However, today, she would much prefer Johnny be helpful by staying out of the kitchen. While wishes (needs) and helpfulness (evaluation) are defined by the receiving side, they are not always that obvious to the receivers or the providers.

This chapter examines key elements in needs assessment that set the stage for the program planning and program evaluation.

- What is a **need**?
- The **needs assessment** establishes and describes the compelling problems for a target population in the community and existing or new service plans on addressing those issues.
- **The program planning formula** outlines the key components of a program using a handy equation.
- The **theory of change** (also called program theory), a predecessor to the logic model, makes implicit the linkage between a valid conceptualization of the problem and an appropriate means of remedying the service. It answers the question, "Does the response make sense?"
- By developing a **logic model**, a program obtains a snapshot of how the need, program services, and results are aligned. How are the intended improvements in the social conditions or lives of the beneficiaries to occur and under what circumstances (e.g., resources, activities)? "Does it or will it work?"

NEEDS ASSESSMENT AND PROGRAM EVALUATION IN SOCIAL WORK PRACTICE AND RESEARCH

Social work is a profession that serves people in need. However, what do people need? How do social workers know what the needs are? What services or interventions should be in place to meet the needs? After plenty of money and resources are spent, how do the funding sources and the community know whether these needs have been met and problems have been addressed? Have the programs and services been accountable to the funding sources and to the people? Needs assessments, needs-informed program/service planning, and program/service evaluation are key components of social work practice and research. Let's picture this Good Idea Program for the Shoestring community in Box 10.1.

What does the Shoestring community need? What are the presenting problems, and what are the underlying problems? How can the social workers find out what the community's needs are? Has there been a community needs assessment study done that documents what the community requires? If programs and services have been provided, have their successes and challenges been evaluated? Did they make a difference? If so, what difference did they make? Do you think Box 10.1 in and of itself

BOX 10.1. THE GOOD IDEA PROGRAM

The Big Help Agency plans to seek funding to support its Good Idea Program to improve racial relationships, facilitate economic recovery, and address major needs in the Shoestring community.

Shoestring was once a growing town in the 1950s. Eighty-five percent of the residents were white and the majority of them were employed by the only local industry—Comfort Shoe Factory. Since the closing of the factory in the mid-1970s, the town and its residents have experienced economic hardship. Many residents moved out to the neighboring towns for better employment opportunities. In the late 1970s, gentrification in the Upward City, 30 miles away, forced many African American families to move to Shoestring for affordable housing. African Americans brought new life to the town and opened up many new businesses and economic opportunities. Unfortunately, the growth was hindered by the recession of the early 1980s, and the growth did not last. The expansions of several nearby towns, with the opening of a meat-packing plant in the 1990s, have not benefited Shoestring. In fact, these towns have diverted many economic investments away from Shoestring. Shoestring did not have a bank or a major grocery store until the mid-2010s.

The arrivals of the Korean, Vietnamese, and Mexican immigrants since the mid-1990s have pumped in new energy, as well as conflicts, into this community. Asian immigrants have taken over 60% of the local small businesses. However, according to the residents, they have provided very few employment opportunities for the community. "They only hire their own families." The only obvious growth in the community has been the number of liquor and cigarette stores. Again, Asian immigrants own most of them. Hispanics have also been competing with long-time residents for jobs at all levels. The influx of new immigrant families increases demands on the school system. Unfortunately, the local real estate and retail tax bases are not strong enough to support an increase in the school budget.

Many white residents have felt that they have been displaced, and some, those who could, moved. Asian Americans have also been slowly leaving Shoestring. Residents of all racial backgrounds grumble that they do not feel safe living in the town. Older residents complain, "This is not the town I used to know anymore." They worry about the young people because there is too much violence in the homes and on the streets. Many of the problems are attributed to the increase in alcohol and substance abuse. Almost 30% of the elderly have been victims of crimes. Domestic violence and child abuse cases have been on the rise. Recently, there were four incidents of suspicious burning and destruction of two African American churches, one synagogue, and one gay-friendly church. No one has claimed responsibility for the fires. Local youth problems have intensified because of the increase in ethnic gangs, high dropout rates in schools, and the lack of employment opportunities. Latchkey children and youth are everywhere after school,

BOX 10.1. THE GOOD IDEA PROGRAM (*CONTINUED*)

except at home. Vandalism and other youth problems have become serious concerns. The city has unwisely spent 90% of its budget on law enforcement but violence persists. The city is at the brink of bankruptcy, and essential services to the community have been disappearing.

In the last couple of years, several major political figures dropped by to make speeches and have photo ops with the few "self-proclaimed" ethnic community leaders. So far, there are only empty and broken promises.

You are a social worker with one of the agencies in the community. Recent budget cuts have downsized many of these agencies. High turnover rate, lack of professional staff, and low morale are common among these agencies. The Big Help Agency in the county is to apply for a 5-year $3.5 million community partnership service grant called "The Good Idea Program." Your agency is part of this joint effort. What will your agency do? What current programs and expertise does your agency have in serving this community? What kinds of programs will you propose? What are the needs of the community? What kind of program evaluation will be in place to verify whether the program goals are met?

is a needs assessment report? If not, is it a good starting point for a more detailed or pinpointed needs assessment?

The effectiveness of a program's response to the identified needs within the target community is the core question of needs assessment and program evaluation. Can the services bring about some needed change to the target population? To weigh the question of change because of an intervention assumes that multiple processes, strategies, and structures are in place, all of which precede the evaluation.

WHAT IS A NEED?

Need is different from but related to want. Children at the checkout in the grocery stores whine to have candy because they want it. Parents refuse to buy because they believe the children do not need it. Many have used this common distinction: A need is something we have to have to survive and cannot live without. A want is something we would like to have but is not entirely necessary. We need food and water to survive. We want arts and music, but they are not required for survival. Need and want to have intricate relationships and are not mutually exclusive. Need is fundamental and basic; want adds quality and values. At times, need and want overlap. Would it be enjoyable if you had your favorite food and drinks in a nice environment with beautiful music playing in the background? An elderly woman who lives alone can have her basic nutritional needs met through the Meals on Wheels program; however, her desire is to maintain healthy human connections, so she attends activities and has her meals in the elderly center. Human service providers deal with human needs often more complex than basic physiological needs. Maslow (1943) proposed the hierarchy of human needs that range from the basic physiological needs, safety and security, love, esteem, and to self-actualization. Human needs are complicated and are interwoven with an individual's unique quality and the social environments. It is, therefore, both the target population's and human service providers' responsibility to identify and articulate what the needs are and how they are to be addressed.

Types of Need

Yuen and Terao (2003) explain the definitions of needs discussed by Mayer (1985) and Bradshaw (1997). Needs can be defined as four basic types (Figure 10.1): normative, felt, expressed, and comparative. These needs are not mutually exclusive. Human service providers may want to describe all of them to provide a better account of the needs for the target population.

"Normative need refers to conditions that are below the established social standards" (Yuen & Terao, 2003, pp. 12–13). Distribution of resources, such as funding for school lunches or after-school activities, can be based on the number of students who are living in households below the national poverty line. Health disparity statistics or prevalence of a specific disease in a particular population also serves as an indicator for needs deviating from the norm. The neighborhood's more than average pedestrian-related traffic accidents points to the need for attention to traffic and pedestrian safety in the neighborhood. College students whose GPAs fall below 2.0 are performing below the norm academically. Help needs to be provided to improve their grades.

"Felt need refers to the wants based on the individual's standards" (Yuen & Terao, 2003, p. 13). Bradshaw (1997) also equated it with want. It is a matter of personal or collective preferences and choices. Felt needs are, however, meaningful and distinctive to the people who make the selection. For example, a frail elderly woman prefers to remain in her own home and receive home health services instead of moving into a nursing home. In a severe budget cut year, the school PTA supports the elimination of the school football team to keep the library open because they believe the library is more vital to students' learning.

"Expressed need refers to attempts by the individuals to fulfill their needs" (Yuen & Terao, 2003, p.13). Bradshaw (1997) equated it with the economic concept of demand. The out-of-control youth gang problems in this neighborhood have severely affected every aspect of life in the community. Residents brought the issue to the attention of the city leaders through the mass media and a letter-writing campaign. Several town hall meetings were organized to document complaints and solicit input. A community organizer also conducted a community survey and published a report on his findings. A documented felt need will become an expressed need that is also being referred to as a documented need. Community needs assessment or town hall meeting reports document expressed needs. U.S. Census reports provide a detailed description of a given community and a wealth of information of the documented needs. A simple way to establish expressed need for a human service agency is to use its waiting list. By putting their names on the waiting list, people express their need for such service and, obviously, the supply is less than the demand.

"Comparative need refers to the situation that an individual's condition is relatively worse off or less desirable than that of other people" (Yuen & Terao, 2003, p. 13). Children who live in drug- and gang-infested neighborhoods are more likely to be involved in the criminal justice system when they grow up, reflecting that they are more at risk than children from average neighborhoods. Families without health insurance coverage have more emergency room visits and longer hospital stays than those who have insurance. They are comparatively less healthy and more in need of health services.

TABLE 10.1. Four Types of Need

TYPES	WHAT IT IS	EXAMPLES
Normative Need	Conditions deviate from the norms or social standards	Poverty line, GPA, crime rate, homeless statistics
Felt Need	Wants, personal preferences, and choices	Older adults prefer to stay at home over a nursing home
Expressed Need	Documented attempts to meet demands (recorded felt needs)	Needs assessment, town hall meeting, wait list, diagnosis
Comparative Need	Conditions relative to those of others, likelihood	Neighborhood conditions and youth development, health status, and income

Conceptual and Practical Research and Statistics for Social Workers

NEEDS ASSESSMENT

The "[n]eeds assessment … is a systematic approach to identifying social problems, determining their extent, and accurately defining the target population to be served and the nature of their service needs" (Rossi, Freeman, & Lipsey, 1999, p. 119). As an evaluative study, the needs assessment responds to questions about the need for program services, whether it is to explore a new initiative or to review an existing service to determine its priority and value among, within, and across service areas. This method of gathering and examining information is meant to determine the current status and service needs of a defined population or perhaps a geographic area. In considering a needs assessment, there is an assumption of the existence of a need; the gap between "what is" and "what should be." This gap between the "real" and "ideal" is acknowledged by society as the social condition judged as substandard or unacceptable and deemed worthy of attention. Finally, the need is perceived as "potentially amenable to change," and social programs or interventions are identified as the vehicles to remediate the condition (Reviere, Berkowitz, Carter, & Gergusan, 1996; Rossi, et al., 1999).

Needs Assessment and Program Evaluation

Evaluations use various methods and approaches to address different categories of evaluation questions. The needs assessment tackles one of the most fundamental sets of program evaluation questions—that is, to develop an understanding of the characteristics of a social problem, areas that require remedy, and the targeted population.

Needs assessment and program evaluation share many of the same goals, strategies, and methodologies. Both are important to the decision-making process. Many of the methods, data collection processes and analysis, and reporting strategies are the same. Furthermore, one informs the other; a strong needs assessment sets the framework for thoughtful activities (service, intervention) and structures the program evaluation questions. Likewise, the program evaluation, through the measurement of the effect of an intervention, serves as a catalyst for a needs assessment, specifying the questions that need to be addressed for program expansion and improvement, realignment of services, or the reexamination and update of the earlier defined social problem or condition.

The program evaluation responds to the question, "Did the services meet or change the need?" The evaluation measures the current service—that is, "What happened or changed as a result of the intervention?" The needs assessment identifies the future of what should and could happen. The goal of the needs assessment is to ascertain, "What is the need in the community?" For instance, let's imagine that the needs assessment uncovers high rates of infant illness among Haitian Americans because of limited access to early child health care. Even before the intervention—the infant vaccination program—is implemented, evaluation questions are formulated to respond to the identified need. "Did the vaccination program reduce infant illness among Haitian American families in Miami?"

Purposes of the Needs Assessment

The needs assessment is used by human service providers for program planning and advocacy of program direction, for proposals for funding, and to set the course of the program evaluation of services. Program services require financial decisions and community commitments with limited or diminishing resources, prudent expenditures, and interventions. This is especially the case during economic downturns coupled with increased levels of accountability. The needs assessment can be a powerful tool in the decision-making milieu. The needs assessment can produce information used to prioritize who gets assistance or service, how much assistance to provide, and what service model or strategy will be used. It assists in determining the appropriate service approach for the target population. The needs assessment serves human service organizations interested in planning a new service, expanding existing services or reducing or eliminating services. Further, it can shed light on how an organizational mission is aligned with the needs of the community they currently serve or hope to serve in the future. By uncovering community conditions, the needs assessment can identify gaps in service. A gap analysis presented in a format useful for decision making identifies what does not exist and what is needed. The needs assessment also renders an inventory of resources, complementary services, or competition to providing services.

The needs assessment is critical to the effective design of new programs. The inquiry will inform the program components, including program theory, mission, and practice. It is equally important for an existing program. The needs assessment is the means by which an evaluator or social worker determines if, indeed, there is a need for the program or program expansion. If expansion or continuation is needed, what program services are most appropriate to fulfill that need for the target population? In many circumstances, whether in response to community accountability or funding, an established program mission and implementation may be called into question. It cannot merely assume that a proposed set of services is needed or that the services it provides are well suited to the nature of the need. This is the opportunity to scrutinize assumptions in detail and review the social conditions of the target population and the appropriateness of the service (Rossi et al., 1999, p. 119).

Strategies for Needs Assessment

The needs assessment employs all the basic research methodologies in gathering the necessary information. Fundamentally, the data can be collected through existing data or original data. Oftentimes, both data sources are used to compile a more comprehensive picture of the needs.

EXISTING DATA

- *Current population survey.* The U.S. Census is the primary population survey and can be disaggregated to state and local levels. Like all instruments, it has limitations, such as it undercounts several population groups, including African Americans, Hispanics, and homeless.
- *Social indictors.* Social indicators are often used to describe or project population trends and report statistics on relevant variables and estimate the needs. These regularly occurring measures are called social indicators, and they can be used to estimate the size and distribution of a problem and the status of social conditions. Social indicators are limited in coverage, mainly providing data in the areas of poverty and employment, criminal victimization, and national program participation. The poverty rate, school dropout rate, child abuse reports, and drug use statistics are the common indicators.
- *Agency records.* Agency records tend to be excellent for describing the characteristics of the population. However, they are typically limited with respect to the rate of incidence in the community.

ORIGINAL DATA

Existing data are not always available or, at least, not for the particular locale or target population in question. In this case, original data will need to be collected. The following are common methods used in needs assessment:

- *Key informants (interviews or surveys)* prove to be one of the easiest approaches to obtaining estimates. Key informants are those persons whose position or experience provides them with unique knowledge of the community and perspective on the magnitude of the problem. Included among key informants are community leaders and professionals, current clientele, or, in case of a new program, representatives of those who are being affected. Often grassroots individuals provide as much, if not more, important information as the elected officials, formal leaders, or professionals.

- *Questionnaire and interview survey of communities or target groups* are methods that directly gather information from a large number of respondents in the community. The use of appropriate sampling methods and research design improve the quality of the information when this data collection method is used.
- *Focus groups* bring together selected knowledgeable people for a discussion of a particular topic, supervised by a facilitator. They provide immediate, interactive, and collective information to the service providers.
- *Community forums,* such as town hall meetings and open forums, provide an opportunity for people to come together to express their concerns, seek common ground, and identify solutions.
- *Onsite observations* allow researchers to have an eye witness account of the condition and/or target population, although this is not always easy. They can render rich descriptive information about the nature of the problem and the population.
- *Rates undertreatment* is a documentary study or secondary data analysis on service utilization and the gap between demand and supply of services. Using the waiting list is one of the common methods that can provide such information. This is used to predict and plan for future service usage.

NEEDS AND PROBLEMS STATEMENT

A needs assessment study can generate a large number of data and findings. As a way to summarize the findings and to communicate the identified needs to the community and to the funding sources, a needs statement (or a needs and problems statement) can be formulated. This summary statement becomes the foundation statement that justifies the necessity of a service plan, a grant proposal, or a research project. Box 10.2 is an example of such a statement.

The Evergreen Community Service has experienced 60% annual increases in respite service requests in the last 3 years [expressed need]. A recent community survey found that the majority of the caregivers are overstressed and socially isolated [felt and expressed needs]. Over 70% of them have incomes below the poverty level [normative need]. Research findings have indicated that these caregivers are at higher risk for depression and unintentional elderly neglect [comparative need].

PROGRAM PLANNING FORMULA

With a needs assessment in hand, program planning moves to the next stage. Program planning is a process and a product. As a process, it is a dynamic and evolving course of development. As a product, using a systems theory expression, it represents a whole that is greater than the sum of its parts. A program plan is the result of the active interplay of its many key elements. The key elements and their relationships are represented in a simple program planning formula (Yuen & Terao, 2003).

$$\mathbf{P}^2 = \mathbf{W}^5 \times \mathbf{H}^2 \times \mathbf{E}$$

- P^2 = <u>P</u>rogram <u>P</u>lanning
- W^5 = <u>W</u>hy, <u>W</u>ho/<u>W</u>hom, <u>W</u>hat, <u>W</u>here, <u>W</u>hen
- H^2 = <u>H</u>ow, <u>H</u>ow much
- E = <u>E</u>valuation

The most important W is the **"why,"** the reason and purpose of any plan. As a reason, it can be the motivation and the need for the program. It is the rationale for the plan and the action. As a purpose, it represents the aim of the program. Program planning is a goal-oriented activity. Program planning without the "why" can easily lose its function of being an agent of change and become merely "work." Although the "why" is the anchor of the program, it is not static. It should be dynamic and reflective of the changing demands and evolving conditions. A program that lacks rationale can become confusing and without a goal, causing the people involved to become lost. ***"Beginning with the end in mind"*** is one of the mottos of this book.

"Who" and "whom" are the target population, and the people who carry out the program. A Chinese proverb says, "Know others and know yourself, one hundred battles with one hundred wins." The question of "who the clients (or customers) are" may seem basic but is a very important one that guides the services to meet the unique needs of the population. Understanding the population may include its demographics, strengths and challenges, history, and social backgrounds, as well as its unique connection to the proposed services. The "whom" includes the program staff, volunteers, community resources, and other providers. A program plan should match the needs of the population and the resources required: staff, volunteers, and providers of appropriate qualities and qualifications. Cultural competency is inherent in this consideration. Program activities cannot be effective until they have meaning and value to the service recipients within their cultural context.

"When" is about the schedule and timing; "what" is about the resources and inputs (e.g., equipment and supplies); "where" is about the location, facilities, and accessibility. These are basic logistics for the implementation of the program and the attainment of the program goals.

"When" includes the "life span" of the service program. Many programs are time-limited programs in which services are provided within a certain time frame to achieve the objectives. A clearly delineated time line for the whole project and each of the activities provides the tempo and timetable for the program. "What" concerns having the right tools for the right jobs. It would be difficult to teach social work practice skills on a blackboard without interactive role-playing, or, even better, internships.

"Location, location, location," a familiar motto for success in business, also applies to human services; it is about the "where." Whether the program is appropriately and conveniently located affects its visibility and degree of utilization. Varied and convenient transportation, including public transit, is often a key concern, particularly for low-income participants. To be more client centered and less agency focused, an agency may consider bringing the service to the clients instead of bringing the clients to the agency. The facility used needs to be suitable for program activities. A cooking class will need a kitchen and a basketball team a basketball court. In addition to facilities within the agency, program staff needs to be knowledgeable and resourceful in using other facilities in the community. In addition to physical location (i.e., convenient location, accessibility of the facility for people with disabilities), there is also the cultural aspect and other accessibility. A culturally competent agency can provide a sense of cultural connection and accessibility to its clients. Hiring staff who represent the gender, ethnic, and cultural backgrounds of the target population is one of the many strategies. However, ethnic and background match are no guarantee for desired cultural match.

The following is an example that demonstrates the effect of location and cultural competence on successful program implementation. In the early 1990s, this author developed a reproductive health education program for refugee Cambodian mothers. The impetus of the program came from a group of middle school Cambodian girls approaching their school social worker and indicating confusion about ways to care for their female hygiene needs. They were frustrated that their mothers, who were also new to the United States, could not offer much help that made sense in this country. The girls were learning quickly through their teachers and friends. However, the mothers were stuck in the old practices or those that they used in refugee camps, and mother-daughter conflicts ensured. In the beginning, the program had a difficult time recruiting participants. All the targeted women relied on their husbands to drive them to the agency for the two-hour class. The husbands called it a "female's problems" class. It was a dreaded task for these Cambodian men. A small needs assessment was conducted. A change in using a well-trained Cambodian female staff instead of a medical professional and having the program at the clubhouse of the apartment complex where many of the clients lived, and later on rotating among participants' apartments, boosted the dynamics of the program. Renaming it "Sister to Sister Tea Time" also turned it into something more like an educational group than a class. With those changes, the clients no longer relied on their husbands to access the program. They could simply drop in, bring a friend, and show off their culinary skills by bringing in the goodies for the gathering. They ate, chatted, exchanged tips, and provided support to each other. They also turned to the agency staff for information and assistance. In the end, the class went beyond the topic of reproductive health. It had become a self-help support group for the participants and a gateway for the agency to engage the underserved population. It all started when the program went to the participants with an outstanding and culturally competent staff member to meet clients where they were.

"How" is about the program activities. What program activities or interventions are used to achieve the program objectives? Through what steps will the program objectives be achieved? It concerns the program procedures guided by the program objectives and goals. "How" is the operationalization of the program ideas and beliefs. It plays out what should take place when the program puts its idea to work. It is not about what should be done but what will be done. "How" can be further broken down into strategies, activities, and tasks.

"**How much**" is the fiscal consideration for the program: costs, revenues, and expenses. It is the budget of the program in dollars and cents. Budgeting provides the program planner a means by which to estimate the cost and benefit of the program and to set the parameters for fundraising and expenses. Ideally, program activities drive the budget; in reality, the program budget often drives the program activities.

Evaluation or evaluative research helps the program tell its stories: both challenges and successes. It measures the attainment of the program objectives. It provides ongoing feedback as well as an end-of-program report for program improvement. Evaluations ask key questions regarding what was accomplished, what changed, and what the effects were.

LOGIC MODEL AS A TOOL FOR PLANNING AND EVALUATION

The logic model can help unpack the program and set the stage for the evaluation. Successful grant writing and program planning require an understanding of the "big picture" of the service as well as a thorough articulation of program components.

Wyatt Knowlton and Philips (2009) classify logic models into two types: theory of change and program logic model. Both are representatives of the same logic but differ in appearance, detail, and use. The theory of change is conceptual and tests plausibility, "Does it make sense?" A program logic model is operational and tests feasibility, "Will it work?" "A *theory of change* model is simply a general representation of how you believe change will occur. A *program* logic model details resources, planned activities, and their outputs and outcomes over time that reflect intended results" (Wyatt Knowlton, & Philips, 2009, p. 5).What the logic model and theory of change share are a common theory, research practice, and literature. Where they diverge is in their points of view and the utility of their viewpoints.

Theory of Change

Programs are typically very good at knowing what they are doing, but weaker in articulating why they chose to conduct the activities. The theory of change is a set of assumptions upon which the service model is based; why we think the program will work. It embodies expectations, beliefs, experiences, and conventional wisdom, the concept that underlies the activities and structure of service. It influences ideas about the nature of the problems, the resources needed, the expectations for impact, and how the participants "work"—their behavior motivations and learning styles. These underlying beliefs are validated with research and experience. Theory of change is included in all levels of social work practices. It is also called the "*working hypothesis.*"

Theory of change uses limited information to present an idea or program. It looks at strategies and results. For instance, a program that teaches youth conflict management identifies some strategies, curriculum, and role-play experiences in small groups that will affect results—positive youth relationships at school. The theory of change presents the core rationale for the expanded program logic model, whether explicitly stated or implicitly (part and parcel of the program's services and practices but not articulated or recorded as such).

A Program Logic Model

The logic model is a linear approach to program planning and thinking through what should be achieved and evaluated. It is a planning tool that diagrams how project goals should be achieved. It combines resources (inputs) and service activities to produce specific results (outputs or outcomes) that address the community need identified by the project. The use of logic models began in the 1970s, although they did not become part of the tools used by programs until after the United Way of America published *Measuring Program Outcomes* in 1996 (Wyatt Knowlton & Phillips, 2009), and later, there was another publication of the logic model development guide by the Kellogg Foundation (2001).

The program logic model provides a concise visual representation of activities that are the core services of a program. It can assist a program in thinking about the big picture and can be very helpful in multiyear planning. Logic modeling can be used for the planning and development of the program design, including identifying the results the program intends to achieve (Yuen & Terao, 2003). The logic model is particularly valuable for developing results that are aligned with the activity (i.e., the activity produces the output; the activity and the output produce the outcomes). The *"if, then" logic* displays how each element is related to one another. For example, if an immunization program for children is implemented, then children ages 2 through 6 will be immunized; if children ages 2 through 6 are immunized, then fewer children will catch a communicable disease; if fewer children catch a communicable disease, then the schools and neighborhoods will be healthier places to live. The logic model can also illustrate how the results from 1 year may support the anticipated results for the subsequent year. Ultimately, the logic model can help guide the program in selecting important outputs and outcomes related to its project efforts. They, therefore, become the bases for program evaluation.

Taylor-Powell, Jones, and Henert (2002) note that the logic model is a tool that illuminates and, therefore, strengthens program elements in planning, management, evaluation, and communication.

- *Planning.* The logic model process uncovers shared understandings about program theory of change—what is really happening at the ground level.
- *Program management.* The logic model provides a quick check-in to explain why the intervention is needed and to track program functions and processes.
- *Evaluation.* The logic model allows program stakeholder groups the opportunity to identify what they understand to be the program successes and to set up their own accountability system.
- *Communication.* Through a visual diagram, the logic model communicates to others, and to us, the core of the program service or initiative.

COMPONENTS AND STEPS OF A LOGIC MODEL

With needs clearly identified and having reasonable results in mind, one can develop an effective program plan and its associated evaluation strategies. There are a variety of ways to construct a logic model. The visual displays commonly move from left to right. A basic logic model consisting of six components, as illustrated in Figure 10.1. The continuum of elements begins with the community need and finishes with the outcome.

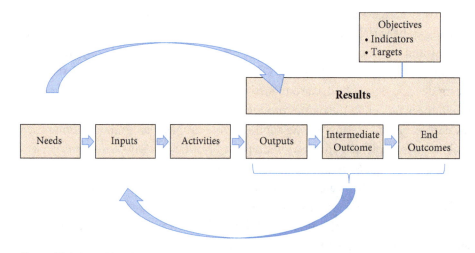

Figure 10.1. **Logic Model**

Conceptual and Practical Research and Statistics for Social Workers

Community needs, or needs for the target population, are the starting point, the first step, of any logical model. Many believe that the second step is input. However, following the "beginning with the end in mind" approach, the second step is the results. For these identified needs, these are the intended results to be achieved. It then goes back to step three, which is the inputs and then followed by the activities. For example, if a person is hungry (need), and he wants to have some food to stop the hunger (result), he will first reach into his pocket to see how much money he has (input) to decide what he can afford. That dictates his activity of deciding what, where, and how he gets his food.

Needs

If there is no presumed need, then there is no reason to conduct a needs assessment, propose a service program, or evaluate the outcomes. Earlier in this chapter, different types of needs, including normative need, felt need, expressed need, and comparative need, were presented. A need and program statement summarizes the identified needs and sets the foundation for planning and evaluation. The need statement should be backed up by a reliable source to establish the compelling nature of the need. The needs are the *"why"* in the program planning formula.

- What is the problem? What is the issue in the target population or community that needs to be changed or improved?
- What are the key factors that contribute to or cause these problems?
- Who is most affected by these problems (individuals, families, specific groups?)
- Which assets within the system are currently being underused?
- What are the barriers to using these individual and community assets fully?
- What opportunities exist to address these contributing factors?
- Which of these opportunities can be addressed with the existing resources?
- What research or study is available that provides evidence of this need?
- What does existing research/experience say about this problem/issue?

Results

After identifying the need, move to the end of the logic model and focus on the results, the output, intermediate outcome, and end outcome. "Ultimately, what do we want to change? During this program year? After 3 years, what change should we expect?"

Results are the accomplishments or changes that occur after a program's services are provided. Results are evidence of the accomplishment of service and change in attitudes, skills, knowledge, and behaviors of the service recipients after receiving service. The results are categorized as outputs, intermediate outcomes, and end outcomes. Some activities generate all three types of result, but most just generate one or two types of results. The results are the *"why" and "evaluation"* in the program planning formula. The following are definitions of each type of result, questions to help identify the type of result, and examples of result statements.

Outputs. Outputs refer to the amount of work or products completed and services delivered by the program. These are the counts, often identified as *"bean counting."* This is about tasks that the program and staff have accomplished. Examples may include the following:

- Number of service recipients served
- Units of counseling provided
- Number of programs organized
- Number of volunteers recruited
- Number of community meetings held

Outputs answer the question, *"Did we do what we set out to do?"* "How much work did we do?" But they do not answer the question, "What changed as a result of our work?"

Intermediate outcomes. Intermediate outcomes are changes or benefits experienced by service recipients that are milestones or indicators of more significant future change. They may include quality indicators, such as transitional accomplishments and client satisfaction. However, intermediate outcomes do not represent the final result the program hopes to achieve. Intermediate outcomes are expected to lead to or support the achievement of end outcomes.

For example, if the final result is to improve parenting skills for "at-risk" parents, then intermediate outcomes might be improved knowledge or attitudes toward parenting and child development. These are likely preconditions for improved parenting skills. Positive results for intermediate outcomes are usually a sign the program is on track to achieving the related end outcomes. Examples of intermediate outcomes may include the following:

- Increased number of youth feeling safe and not pressured to engage in risky behavior.

- Decrease in volunteer attrition by 45%.
- Sixty-five percent of students will complete homework assignments.
- Fifteen more neighborhoods agree to set up drug-free zones.
- Eighty percent of clients achieve 75% of the treatment *goals.*

Intermediate-outcomes answer the question, "What difference did it make?" "How well did we do?" and *"What changed?"*

End outcomes. End outcomes are the positive changes the program ultimately hopes to achieve for its service recipients. These are the changes hoped for in the lives of service recipients that constitute the most important or significant benefits to them. End outcomes are the collective and accumulative results of many activities. They are not often achieved by one single activity; instead, they are the results of many activities over the course of the program. *Women in a particular community being more willing to report sexual assaults and harassment* is likely the result of years of hard work by many advocates through many activities that have made changes in knowledge, attitude, and behaviors. Examples of end outcomes may include the following:

- Parents develop appropriate parenting skills
- More seniors are able to stay at home
- Students demonstrate better in-school behaviors
- Clients receive proper mental health care
- A sense of community developed

End outcomes answer the question, *"So what?"* This shows the significance and relevance of the service outcomes. Table 10.2 shows examples of the different types of results.

TABLE 10.2. Examples of Results

OUTPUTS	INTERMEDIATE OUTCOME(S)	END OUTCOMES
• Three trainings on personal financial planning • Fifty participants	• Increased knowledge and skills in budgeting	• Taking concrete steps toward reducing debt and making a plan for savings
• Design parent education curriculum • Six training sessions provided • One hundred and fifty targeted parents trained	• Parents learn new ways to discipline • Parents increase knowledge of child development	• Parents use improved parenting skills • Reduced rates of child abuse and neglect

Inputs

The inputs are the resources needed to implement the service activities. These are the key resources, or "big picture" resources, needed before a program can begin. Examples of key resources include number of staff, qualification of staff, facilities or buildings, equipment, partnerships with other organizations, and support from the community, as well as funding to operate the program. It is the *what, who/whom, where, when, and how much* in the program planning formula.

- What resources, human and financial, are necessary before the program can begin?
- What resources are currently available to assist in the implementation of the program?
- Does the program have what it takes to get the program off the ground?

Activities/Interventions

Service activities are what will be offered to the recipients to meet the need and to affect change. Service activities address the identified need and, hopefully, achieve the anticipated results, which are the outputs, intermediate outcomes, and end outcomes. The activity statement should describe who does what, when, where, how, and with whom for how long. Obviously, it is the *how, who/whom, what, when, and where* of the program planning formula. When making a plan for activities, social workers may want to consider the following:

- What activities will be implemented to accomplish the strategies proposed?
- What research, theory, or past experience supports the choice of strategies?
- What kind of skills and qualifications will staff need to implement these activities?
- Do the activities consider FIT (Frequency of occurrence, Intensity or strength of the given efforts, Targeted at a specified group of service recipients)?

The following are some examples of activity statements in a logical model. They should provide succinct descriptions of the activities. They should not be one-word descriptions, such as "counseling."

- Fifteen senior volunteers will tutor 45 children one-on-one in reading, 3 times per week for 20 minutes for the semester.

- Three staff members will conduct 15 community workshops on developing neighborhood watch programs.
- By the end of the program year, 400 units of individual mental health sessions will be provided to at least 50 eligible clients.

Table 10.3 is an example of a logical model for a school-based parenting program. In addition to the regular components of a logical model, evaluation instruments, data source, and approaches are also included. This will provide a one-page summary of the thought process of the program design, logics, and evaluation strategies.

PROGRAM EVALUATION

In Chapter 6, the basics of evaluative designs and the formative and summative forms of evaluative designs were discussed. Program evaluation is a particular use of evaluative designs to demonstrate and assess the performances of programs. An evaluative research design involves the use of exploratory, descriptive, and experimental designs, and, therefore, their data collection tools.

Human service providers, including social workers, are committed to service. They much prefer spending their time directly working with clients and programs than gathering information and writing up evaluation reports. What if there is nothing outstanding to show? Is program evaluation a means for the management and funding sources to check to see if the program did something wrong? Besides, the usual workloads are already unbearable, and program evaluation is the last thing on the service providers' mind. To make it worse, it does not generate billable hours or improve "productivity!" These assessments are valid, and they speak to the need to convince both the workers and the management to acknowledge the importance of program evaluation. It is part of the workflow and is not an afterthought. Time should be allocated for program evaluation and not a last-minute task to be completed on a late Friday afternoon before the workers have to run to catch the last train to go home. This author has found that viewing the program evaluation task as *a way of telling the program's stories* has been an accurate and effective way to frame this task. This is just one of our "in-the-trenches" stories.

TABLE 10.3. Logic Model for a Parenting Program

NEEDS (STEP 1)	INPUTS (STEP 3)	ACTIVITIES (STEP 4)	RESULTS (STEP 2)		
			OUTPUTS	INTERMEDIATE OUTCOMES	END OUTCOMES
High dropout rate: severe parent-child conflicts, parents want additional support for children and themselves	Program staff, school district, and teacher support Parenting skills curriculum	Program staff will implement a coordinated dropout prevention program for students, including an 8-week positive parenting class.	Parental skills class taught Hours of training Parent participants	Parents demonstrate positive parenting skills.	Decrease school dropout rate of students whose parents complete parental skills program.
			Instrument/ data source: Class rosters and attendance	*Instrument/ data source: Parent skills assessment survey*	*Instrument/data source: School records, interviews*
					Instrument/data source: School records and parent survey

Conceptual and Practical Research and Statistics for Social Workers

In addition to reporting outcome results to the funding source, there are many other benefits of conducting a program evaluation. Program evaluation can be helpful to accomplish the following:

- Gather information for continuous improvement.
- Collect useful data for management and decision making.
- Assemble information for grant writing to pursue needed funding.
- Assess the effectiveness of the program design.

The Level of Rigor

On one side of evaluation, the design can be highly rigorous and research focused, while on the other side, evaluation can be less formal and conducted internally within the program using an empowerment or participatory evaluation approach. The level of rigor depends on the validity and reliability of the instrument, how the subjects are selected, how the instruments are administered, how the data is aggregated, and how the data analysis is conducted. Many programs employ an external program evaluator to conduct the more rigorous program evaluation. The cost of the evaluation is generally in direct relation to the level of rigor (i.e., the higher the rigor, the higher the cost for an evaluation).

Funders and management expect the majority of program dollars to be used for program implementation, not evaluation. However, they still want to know whether the program services made a difference. A less rigorous evaluation, or a *performance-measurement* process, may be suitable for most proposals. "Performance measurement is the ongoing monitoring and reporting of program accomplishments, particularly progress toward pre-established goals. It is typically conducted by program or agency management" (GAO, 2005, p. 2).

Performance measurement does not measure whether the services caused the change, only whether change occurred. "Performance data do not, by themselves, tell why the outcomes occurred. In other words, they do not reveal the extent to which the program caused the measured results" (Hatry, 1999, p. 5). In spite of the fact that performance measurement does not measure change by causation, measuring change because participants were involved in the program services (i.e., by association) can be very helpful to stakeholders. It ensures program accountability and can help improve services and client outcomes.

This chapter discusses evaluation in terms of measuring change based on participants' association with program services (e.g., performance measurement).

This approach to evaluation will provide the opportunity for program staff to plan, implement, and conduct an evaluation internally with guidance from a *coach* (e.g., professional evaluator or program staff members who are knowledgeable and competent in conducting an internal evaluation)—would that be you? This approach is also cost-effective and can be implemented at various levels of rigor, depending on the resources available.

Outcome-Focused Evaluation

Outcome-focused evaluation is one approach to conducting a simple internal evaluation. This approach measures whether change occurred as a result of participating in services. It measures change based on participants' involvement in the service activity or by association. Outcome-focused evaluation informs funders and other stakeholders that a difference did occur after program services were provided. Programs that developed a logic model prior to implementing program services will have already identified these expected changes or anticipated outcomes. The logic model not only helps to build the program design by aligning the needs to the service activities that address the need but also by aligning the anticipated outputs (i.e., level of effort) and outcomes (the anticipated outcomes as a result of the activities) with the service activities. For the purpose of this chapter, we refer to evaluation as measuring the outcomes and the change that occurred as a result of service recipients participating in the service activities.

Empowerment Evaluation

Empowerment evaluation is the process of having program staff and service recipients participate in the planning, development, implementation, and data analysis for reporting results. In most cases, program staff may need or want a "coach" to assist in this process. In the case where program staff members have evaluation experience, a coach may not be needed.

The purpose of empowerment evaluation is to allow program staff to set their own terms for measuring the effectiveness of their services in a systematic manner. The primary purpose of implementing an empowerment evaluation is to assess the results of their services and use these results for program improvement. One important nugget of empowerment evaluation is that the process of planning for and developing an empowerment evaluation contributes to program improvement almost as much, if not more, than using the results for revising or modifying program services. A key benefit of empowerment evaluation is that program staff self-assess, or self-evaluate, their program services; this eliminates the high cost of hiring an evaluator to evaluate the program, keeping the cost of the evaluation low.

There are challenges to empowerment evaluation as well. The benefit of program staff members being informed because of their involvement in conducting the evaluation also places a burden on them. In addition to implementing program services, they have an added responsibility of assisting in planning for the evaluation, as well as conducting the evaluation (e.g., collecting and analyzing the data).

Outcome-Focused Empowerment Evaluation

Combining the concepts of outcome-focused evaluation and empowerment evaluation allows programs to develop an evaluation that will support the program design, focusing on the anticipated outcomes of program services. Allowing program staff to be part of the evaluation process will help them understand how the evaluation results can be directly linked to the services provided. This connection can help program staff use these results for program improvement.

The logic model process described earlier educates stakeholders on how to identify program services based on needs, and links these services with the anticipated results, both outputs and outcomes. The use of these anticipated outputs and outcomes will ensure that the alignment of what is being evaluated will be directly associated with the service activities and needs. The next steps in constructing an evaluation will be to enhance these outputs and outcomes by identifying indicators, what is to be collected, and the target for success. After these enhancements are established, the type of instruments and the data source, which will determine the methods of data collection, can be identified.

Indicators. Indicators are the information that can be documented to determine whether the program services accomplished what they set out to do. They are the specific, measurable items of information that specify progress toward achieving the result.

Outputs do not have indicators. Generally, outputs are the counts of service recipients served or the number of units being addressed (e.g., number of Americans with Disabilities Act compliance workshops conducted). For a literacy tutoring program, for example, if the program design is to provide one-on-one reading skill tutoring to youth, the outputs can include the number of youth tutored, number of sessions each youth was tutored, and amount of time tutoring was provided. These counts or numbers measure the effort made in the program service delivery. They do not measure change in the participants or change in the units after service activities were provided.

Indicators are needed to measure outcomes. What information can be collected to show that change has occurred? If, for example, the outcomes for the literacy tutoring program are to increase positive attitude toward reading and increase reading skills, what information can be documented to show these changes have occurred? To measure increased positive attitude toward reading, documenting the increased number of books read, the increased amount of time spent in a library, or the increased amount of time reading or browsing through books and other reading material can be the indicators. Indicators that measure increased reading skills can include results of student reading assessments, reading test scores, or teachers' assessment of students in what they have observed over the course of the school year. For example, teachers might be asked to rate the degree to which students increased in their reading skills as a result of the tutoring service after the first half of the school year, and then again at the end of the school year; the choices can be (a) not at all, (b) a little, (c) made progress, or (d) excelled. As these examples demonstrate, identifying indicators for outcomes can be more challenging in such situations because measuring "change," especially change in peoples' attitudes or behavior, can be more difficult.

Targets for success. When conducting an outcome-focused evaluation, target statements for each anticipated outcome might need to be stated to show what the program designers minimally hoped to be achieved. Targets are the level of success the program expects to gain over a particular period of time, often expressed as an integer or percent. For example, if the outcome was, "tutored students will improve their reading skills," the target might be, "60% of the students tutored will improve their phonetics by at least three assessment category levels. Students improving their phonetics by three or more levels will indicate that they have increased their reading ability." Identifying the target for each anticipated outcome can be challenging. Here are a few guidelines to help identify targets.

- Be realistic! You are the best judge of how much change to expect over a given time period as a result of your program's activities. If this is the first time you are collecting data for this measure, usually the target is considered a "guesstimate."
- Consider the amount of service or "dosage" (e.g., once a week for three hours) and length of time (e.g., three months) beneficiaries will receive.
- A target is an anticipated amount of change for services provided. Consider whether each of the anticipated outcomes should include a target. Some don't.

- Targets need to reflect what you hope to see as change, given the level of resources (e.g., staffing, funding, and material). Does the target justify the resources invested? Do not underestimate the target, yet try not to be overly optimistic.
- Service recipients with more challenges may require more resources or dosage of service for change to occur, resulting in a target that is not as high as compared to beneficiaries with fewer challenges (e.g., tutoring youth in literacy who have learned English as a second language versus tutoring youth are who are behind in reading ability). What are the characteristics of the beneficiaries you plan to serve?

From Logic Model to Program Planning and Evaluation Worksheet

A program planning and evaluation worksheet is a working document that can be used as a tool to help in both program planning and developing an evaluation plan. If the logic model is developed, it can play an important role in the development of the worksheet. The components of the logic model can be elaborated and transferred to the program planning and evaluation worksheet. After transferring this information, detailed information can be included in each of the logic model components to complete the program planning and evaluation worksheet. The worksheet enhances the information of each of the anticipated results (i.e., outputs and outcomes) stated in the logic model, including the indicators, data sources, type of instruments, and targets.

Box 10.3 shows a blank Program Planning and Evaluation Worksheet. Box 10.4 shows how the information in a logic model can be transferred to a program planning and evaluation worksheet. This is an example of a School-Based Youth Development Project—Parental Skills Training.

PROGRAM EVALUATION PLAN

A well-developed logic model serves as the basis for program planning and evaluation. It articulates the program's thinking from needs to inputs, activities, and results. It also frames the key program evaluation questions and results for the program planning and evaluation worksheet. This is especially true when key results—outputs, intermediate outcomes, and end outcomes—for core activities have been

BOX 10.3. PROGRAM PLANNING AND EVALUATION WORKSHEET

PROGRAM PLANNING AND EVALUATION WORKSHEET

Program Name:			
Objective Title:		**Activity**	
Activity Start and End Dates:			**Staff:**

1. Identified Needs Describe what identified needs are to be addressed (the why)	
2. Target Populations/Service Recipients Briefly describe the target groups (and the estimated number) your activity will serve.	
3. Activities/Interventions Describe the service or interventions (the what). (Also, include who, what, when, and where.)	
4. Desired Results (Outputs and Outcomes) Explain what results will be achieved because of the described activity (the products and effects). (Number and type of results may vary, e.g., output only, output and intermediate outcomes, two intermediate outcomes, and one end outcome.)	*Output:* *Intermediate Outcome:* *End Outcome:*
5. Method of Measurement Describe the method and the instrument used to assess results (e.g., survey).	
6. Indicators/Benchmarks Describe the concrete and observable evidence used to determine progress toward desired results.	
7. Targets/Standards of Success Define a level of success you hope to achieve. (How good is good enough? At least X% show improvement.)	
8. Resources and Inputs Briefly describe the resources/input needed.	
9. Data Collection, Aggregation, Analysis, and Reporting Describe when and who will be collecting, aggregating, and analyzing the data and how often.	

Objective Statement: Combine #1–7 into a single statement of objective.	***Example:*** *Volunteer tutors will provide one-on-one tutoring to 50 at risk fourth-grade students weekly for 60 minutes for 4 months, resulting in 75% of those who participate regularly demonstrating improved reading ability, as measured by a diagnostic reading test administered prior to and following the program.*

BOX 10.4. LOGIC MODEL TO PROGRAM PLANNING AND EVALUATION WORKSHEET

LOGIC MODEL: SCHOOL-BASED YOUTH DEVELOPMENT PROJECT—PARENTAL SKILLS TRAINING

Logic Model

Needs (Step 1)	Inputs (Step 3)	Activities (Step 4)	Results (Step 2)		
			Outputs	Intermediate Outcomes	End Outcomes
High dropout rate: severe parent-child conflicts, parents want additional support for children and themselves	Program staff School district and teacher support Parenting skills curriculum	Program staff will implement a co-ordinated dropout prevention program for students, including an 8-week positive parenting class	Parental skills taught Hours of training Parent participants *Instrument: class rosters and attendance*	Parents demonstrate positive parenting skills *Instrument: parent skills assessment*	Decrease in student behavior problems in school *Data source: school records*	Decrease school dropout rate of teenage students whose parents completed a parental skills program *Data source: school records, and parent survey*

Program Planning and Evaluation Worksheet

Program Name: School-Based Youth Development Project					
Objective Title: A short, easy to remember name for the objective		Parenting Program	**Activity**	Parental Skills Training	
Activity Start and End Dates:	09/01/2022	05/31/2023	**Staff**	Ed Jucate, MSW, Dee Valarman, BA	

<table>
<tr><td rowspan="7">Program Planning / Program Evaluation</td><td>1. Identified Needs
Describe what identified needs are to be addressed (the why).</td><td>One in five students in this school dropped out last year (Ridgeway School District Annual Report) and many are involved with the criminal justice or child welfare system. Parents have indicated that they need help to support their children through high school (Survey of Ridgeway Parents, conducted by the school district and the Successful Parenting Project).</td></tr>
<tr><td>2. Target Populations/Service Recipients
Briefly describe the target groups and the estimated number served your activity will serve.</td><td>Fifty current students and their parents who are referred by the child welfare judge, teachers, social workers, or self-referred.</td></tr>
<tr><td>3. Activities/Interventions
Describe the service or interventions (the what). (Also, include who, when, and where.)</td><td>Program staff will implement a dropout prevention program, including an 8-week class for parents. The class activities will prepare parents with the skills they need to support their children and keep them in school and out of trouble.</td></tr>
<tr><td rowspan="2">4. Desired Results (Outputs and Outcomes)
Explain what results will be achieved because of the described activity (the products and effects). (Number and type of results may vary, e.g., output only, output and intermediate outcomes, two intermediate outcomes, and one end outcome)</td><td>Output: Twenty parents enrolled and 75% completed the training.

Intermediate Outcome: Among the parents completed the course, at least 60% of them will demonstrate effective parenting skills as measured by the assessment form. Their children will also be at least 10% lower in reported behavioral problems according to the school records.</td></tr>
<tr><td>End Outcome: Twelve percent lower dropout rate compared to students of parents who are on a waiting list (if available) for the program or previous dropout rate according to the school record and parent survey.</td></tr>
<tr><td>5. Method of Measurement
Describe the method/instrument used to assess results.</td><td>Roster, attendance record, school records, parenting skills assessment form, survey questionnaire</td></tr>
<tr><td>6. Indicators/Benchmarks
Describe the concrete and observable evidence used to determine progress toward desired results.</td><td>Dropout statistics, attendance, student behaviors report, and responses on the survey questionnaire.</td></tr>
<tr><td></td><td>7. Targets/Standards of Success
Define a level of success expected. (How good is good enough?)</td><td>Twenty enrolled, 75% completed, 60% demonstrate skills, and 12% lower drop out.</td></tr>
<tr><td></td><td>8. Resources and Inputs
Briefly describe the resources/input needed.</td><td>Program staff, school district staff and teacher support, parent support, parenting skills curriculum</td></tr>
<tr><td></td><td>9. Data Collection, Aggregation, Analysis, Reporting
Describe when and who will be doing these and how often.</td><td>Program staff and teacher, before and after training.</td></tr>
<tr><td colspan="2">Objective Statement:
Combine #1–7 into a single statement of objective.</td><td>Example: Among the parents of the 50 identified students, 20 of them will enroll in the parenting program and 75% will complete the program. It will lead to an increase in parenting skills and the decrease in student behavioral problems and dropout rate.</td></tr>
</table>

identified. The evaluation plan will incorporate the logic model, the program planning, and evaluation worksheets, and add further detail necessary for clarity and implementation.

An evaluation plan is a written document that describes the purpose, approaches, and strategies/steps of the program evaluation. It is essentially a program evaluative research proposal. There is no one format or template for developing an evaluation plan. The plan can be a basic summary (one page) to a very detailed description (20–30 pages) of the proposed evaluation. Some funding sources or agency management might ask for a basic summary of how the proposed program services will be evaluated, while in other cases, especially if the funding is substantial, the funder may require a higher rigor evaluation and request that a detailed evaluation plan be included in the grant application proposal. There is no one design for developing an evaluation plan. *For a simple one, the program planning and evaluation worksheet itself may be all that is needed.*

Do we need to evaluate everything? No. An evaluation is to tell the major stories of the program. It is not a play-by-play announcement for the program; it should focus on responding to the program goals and objectives. Like telling stories of your recent vacation, only the exciting, memorable, worthwhile happenings, and lessons learned, not every single detail of everything. There is a difference between telling a good story and dumping a large set of data in a verbose and rambling manner.

When do we need to develop an evaluation plan? It should start prior to the beginning of the program. The development of an evaluation plan is an integral part of the whole program planning process. From the very beginning, with the help of developing an evaluation plan, the program can stay focused and be attentive to gathering stories of successes and challenges.

Should the evaluation plan dictate the program plan? No in most cases. It is important to have a *"program-driven evaluation"* but not an *"evaluation-driven program."* The program evaluation's purpose is to tell the story of the program, which is to serve the needs of the service recipients. The program is not there to serve the needs of evaluation or the evaluator. This author has witnessed some service programs hire external evaluators who had impressive credentials and wanted to implement sophisticated evaluations that had potentials for academic publications. It is a great idea to publish evaluative research findings. However, it is not a good idea for the programs and the service recipients to divert their already limited resources to goals that are not directly benefiting the service recipients. Program evaluation and program planning have reciprocal relationships in that they affect each other. In the end, programs that directly serve the clients should be the lead.

BOX 10.5. STEPS IN DEVELOPING A PROGRAM EVALUATION PLAN

1. Beginning with the end in mind. What are the goals of the program and the purpose of the evaluation?
2. What does the funding source or management want to know? Give the customer what he or she wants.
3. Follow the logic model.
4. What does the evaluation want to know? What are the goals and objectives for the evaluation tasks?
5. What does it mean to the service recipients and the community? Going beyond.
6. Identify the results (output, intermediate outcome, end outcome). See the following for example:
   - Fifty clients served
   - Forty-five clients remained in the program after 4 sessions, and 30 (60% of the 50 clients) completed the program
   - Among those who completed the program, 21 (70% of 30) of them showed improvement.
7. Identify the result's indicators:
   - Clients count
   - Success or improvement as evidenced by achieving at least half of treatment goals set at assessment
8. Identify the result's targets (Often, a faction of the results aimed):
   - Forty clients served
   - Thirty-five clients remained after 4 sessions, 25 completed the program
   - Fifteen (60%) of the 25 completed demonstrated improvement
9. Develop the data collection approaches (e.g., documentation, client survey) and instruments (client's treatment plan, progress notes, attendance records, and survey questionnaire)
10. Identify the data sources, time line, and personnel
11. Tie the whole thing together as follows:
    - Writing up a narrative
    - Completing the Program Planning and Evaluation Worksheet
    - Doing both
12. Be prepared to rewrite it several more times.

EVALUATION PLAN FOR A BENEFITS OUTREACH AND ENROLLMENT PROJECT

Objectives of the Evaluation Tasks are to coordinate key process data for service improvement and reporting and to assess the outcomes and impacts of the proposed program. This evaluation will employ an outcome focused empowerment approach and be guided by the program's goals and logic model. **Process evaluation:** The evaluator will document the program's planning, development, and implementation processes. This will include collecting formative information on program development activities, participants and partners' recruitment and training, program usage, participants' information, community linkage, and the attainment of stated output objectives. **Outcome evaluation:** The evaluator will use both quantitative and qualitative approaches to assess the attainment of outcome objectives, changes resulted, and their potential impacts. Major evaluation questions may include the following: Has a new community collaborative system been developed and deployed? To what extent has it achieved the desirable qualities (feasible, practical, integrated, efficient, and effective). Is it sustainable? Does it reduce the burden on the underserved residents? In the end, is it a system that has positive effects and better serves the target population? **Implementation:** The evaluator will work with the advisory committee and other stakeholders to refine the program-driven evaluation plan with appropriate data collection strategies, including the utilization of existing electronic technology. Regular meetings, consultation, and midterm and final reports will be used to solicit input, develop buy-in, ensure cultural competency, monitor progress, and disseminate findings. A program evaluation worksheet will be used as a means to present and organize evaluation tasks among various data sources and stakeholders. All evaluation activities and materials will be kept confidential as required by the Federal regulations (42 CFR Part 2).

PROGRAM PLANNING AND EVALUATION WORKSHEET

Program Name: *Evaluation Plan for a Benefits Outreach and Enrollment Project*

Objective Title:	Develop and deploy a new coordinated system	Activity	Test out a new approach to outreach of potential clients	
Activity Start and End Dates:	November/This Year	October/Next Year	Staff:	Al Rich and Berne Fit

1. Identified Needs	A region with higher than average unemployment and underserved eligible recipients dispersed near many small rural communities with multibarriers to accessing, enrolling in, and receiving eligible benefits and services.
2. Target Populations/ Service Recipients	Eligible recipients in four California rural counties of A, B, C, and D.
3. Activities/ Interventions	Develop, field test and deploy a new system for recipient focused social service and income maintenance enrollment coordination using existing structure and information technologies. Pilot tested in A County and will extend to another three counties later.
4. Desired Results (Outputs and Outcomes)	*Output: (Tasks to be accomplished. Does the program do what it set out to do?)* 1. Completion of tasks: Program design development (before month 2), implementation with field testing (before month 10), and deployment (before month 12) 2. Partners in place: Steering committee established and evaluator hired. 3. Program coordination: Monthly steering committee meeting and operational partners monthly meeting. *Intermediate outcome: (What change? How well?)* 1. A coordinated rural network of diverse community access points to reach the underserved established 2. A coordinated comprehensive system to assess and enroll recipients in multiple services accomplished 3. A comprehensive recipient centric technological infrastructure with shared client database developed 4. The implementation of the new system will increase the enrollment of at least 300 (20%) more of eligible clients 5. The implementation of the new system will increase the delivery of services to at least 300 (20%) more of eligible clients 6. The new system will achieve its intended characteristics, e.g., feasible, practical, integrated, efficient, and effective

	End outcome: (So what?) 1. A more accessible and effective system for client outreach and enrollment is established to bring needed service to more eligible clients 2. This new system with lessons learned in a county and with proper refinements will be deployed to improve the well-being of the eligible clients in B, C and D counties
5. Method of Measurement	**Documentations (ongoing):** 1. Current service data will be used to serve as the baseline for comparison 2. Standardized service logs or checklist will be used at various access points to document services provided and client flow (i.e., number of clients served and trends) 3. Memorandum of Understandings, agreements, or other correspondence such as support letters will be used to document cooperation among agencies 4. Reports from subcontractors upon work completion 5. Meeting minutes, agendas, and dates to document operational group and steering committee meetings, as well as successes and challenges encountered **Survey (at month 9):** 1. *Clients.* A simple questionnaire survey will be used for a set of randomly selected clients to find out the effectiveness, usefulness, and degree of burden of the new system 2. *Service providers.* A quota sample of providers will be anonymously surveyed through a questionnaire to identify program successes and challenges **Focus group meeting (at month 11):** 1. A focus group meeting will be organized, including steering committee members to gather comments, reflections, lessons learned, and recommendations
6. Indicators/ Benchmarks	1. A coordinated rural network of diverse community access points becomes functional in month 4 2. A coordinated comprehensive system to assess and enroll recipients in multiple services in use in month 4 3. A comprehensive recipient centric technological infrastructure with shared client database developed in month 3 4. Number of clients served/reached increased by 300 (20%) as indicated by service logs and other records 5. Program surveys and focus group reflect the attainment of the program goals and qualities and recommendations for improvements 6. System in place and ready for field test in month 8 7. System in place and ready for deployment to additional counties in month 10

Conceptual and Practical Research and Statistics for Social Workers

7. **Targets/ Standards of Success**	1. A coordinated rural network of diverse community access points becomes functional no later than month 6 2. A coordinated comprehensive system to assess and enroll recipients in multiple services in use no later than month 6 3. A comprehensive recipient centric technological infrastructure with shared client database developed no later than month 4 4. Number of clients served/reached increased by 70% of the original estimate 5. Program surveys and focus group meeting reflect the attainment of 70% of the desirable program goals and more than half of the intended qualities and recommendations for improvements 6. System in place and ready for field test in month 10 7. System in place and ready for deployment to additional counties in month 12
8. **Resources and Inputs**	1. Grant funding support, cooperation from the four counties, support from other stakeholders, staff involvement, and clients' participation 2. In-service training on program design, program intents, and program evaluation may be needed 3. A graduate social work intern with interest in program evaluation and macro practice to assist the program evaluation tasks
9. **Data Collection, Aggregation, Analysis, & Reporting**	1. Ongoing data will be collected monthly and other tasks will be collected as scheduled 2. Program data are to be recorded or entered, as much as they are possible, in electronic format 3. Quantitative data will be recorded or input using Excel or SPSS program for analysis 4. Qualitative data will be recorded in Microsoft Word files 5. A midterm progress report will be produced in month 6 6. All program data collection tasks will be completed in month 11, and a final report will be completed in month 12
Objective Statement:	*This one-year rural collaborative is focusing on retooling currently fragmented outreach and enrollment efforts into a more coordinated, efficient, and effective recipient-centric, county-wide system. It will design, develop, and deploy a new system for recipient focused social services and income maintenance enrollment coordination that provides underserved recipients with access to multiple benefits. The program is to be developed as a pilot project in A County by operational partners: the nonprofit B–C community resources, and the A County public agency of CalWorks. The project will start at A County and be expanded to B, C, and D Counties.*

BOX 10.7. SAMPLE PROGRAM EVALUATION PLAN FOR A COURT DIVERSION PROGRAM

EVALUATION PLAN FOR RESTART COURT DIVERSION PROGRAM AT COSH

RESTART Program Goals

Goal 1: Reduce recidivism rate among program participants as indicated by no rearrest or citation for at least 6 months.

Goal 2: Increase participants' personal resilience via positive behavioral change and perspective shift.

Goal 3: Promote participants' psychosocial well-being through the initiation or attainment of key measures such as stable housing, personal safety, interpersonal connections, and health and mental health wellness.

Objectives of the Evaluation Tasks

The objectives of this evaluation are to coordinate key process data for the implementation of RESTART and to assess the outcomes and impacts of the RESTART program. The RESTART program is a court diversion program offered by Community Opposes Sexual Harm (COSH) in Big City, California. The evaluation plan is guided by the program's goals and is delineated through its *logic model* and the associated *Program Planning and Evaluation Worksheet* (Yuen, Terao, & Schmidt, 2009) (See below). **Process Evaluation:** The evaluation will document the program's planning, development, and implementation processes. This will include collecting formative information on program development activities, recruitment and training, usage (level of participation), participants' information, community linkage, and the attainment of stated output objectives. **Outcome Evaluation:** The evaluation will use both quantitative and qualitative approaches to assess the attainment of results, changes resulted, and their potential impacts. Major evaluation questions that guide this evaluation include the following:

For the Court

1. How effective is the RESTART program as a diversion program? (Goal 1)

For the Participants

2. What are the outcomes of their participation?-What related knowledge, skills, and attitude changes have taken place (Goals 2 and 3)?
3. Has this program enhanced participants' capacity in personal resilience and making positive changes (Goals 2 and 3)?

For RESTART and COSH

4. How have the program activities been implemented? What activities have been accomplished and with what level of participation? Who are involved? What are the challenges and successes (Goals 2 and 3)?

5. Does the RESTART program have positive effects and serve the target population better (Goals 2 and 3)?

Implementation

The evaluation team will work with the COSH program staff to implement this goal-driven evaluation plan with appropriate data collection strategies. This evaluation will employ a collaborative approach. Regular meetings and consultation will be used to solicit input, develop buy-in, ensure cultural competency, and monitor progress. Evaluation findings will be disseminated via reports and presentations to entities, such as the agency's board of directors and sponsors. A program planning and evaluation worksheet will be used as a mean to present and organize evaluation tasks among various data sources and stakeholders. All evaluation activities and materials will be kept confidential as required by the Federal Regulations (42 CFR Part 2).

I. University Evaluation Team

The evaluation team will be led by Dr. F. Neuy, ABC University social work professor, and be assisted by two second-year master of social work (MSW) students, Thelma Juan and Louise To.

II. Reviews of Literature, Reports, and Statistics

Based on the inputs from the agency staff, a comprehensive and systematic review of relevant literature, statistics, reports, and records of best practice will be developed. This review will take place during the summer of this year. RESTART staff will collect or facilitate the access and gathering of local data for this review. The following four main questions guide the basic development of this review of the current literature:

- What is sex trafficking? How does it relate to prostitution or commercial sexually exploited survivors?
- What are the historic and current knowledge of prostitution in Big City?
- What are the community's capacities in providing treatment, intervention, and prevention services (e.g., substance abuse treatment and counseling services) to the target population?
- What is a diversion program? Is it effective? How has it been used and what have been the outcomes, particularly in relation to commercial sexually exploited survivors? How did the RESTART program come to existence?

III. Respondents and Sampling Plan

It is expected a total of 60 women will participate in RESTART in this program year. They all have been given the option by the Superior Court to attend RESTART as an alternative sentencing. The evaluation plan for this project attempts to access all program participants between June, this year and May, next year. Because it will reach the population, no sampling procedure is needed. Inclusion criteria involve a valid court order and the willingness to participate.

IV. Data Collection Tools

1. Pre- and Post-Diversion Program Training Survey Questionnaire

A pre- and post-survey of program participants will be conducted to assess the progress of the participants toward their goals. Specifically, it focuses on the following areas of concern:

- Knowledge and attitude toward prostitution
- Personal values, boundaries, experience, and trauma regarding prostitution
- Readiness to address health, mental health, substance abuse, violence and abuse, and wellness
- Capacity to formulate concrete action plans to move forward

A pre-post survey questionnaire will be formulated for the survey. The development of this questionnaire will be based on the input from RESTART staff, previous experience, the pre- /post-questionnaire that is currently in use, systematic literature review, and the objectives of the diversion program. To ensure this survey's appropriateness and cultural competency, its design and implementation will be advised by the agency staff. It is important that this questionnaire has to be respectful, user-friendly, least burdensome and able to collect useful data. It will collect both qualitative and quantitative data. Various answer formats will be used to collect data that will allow content analysis as well as descriptive and inferential statistical analyses. The evaluator will use a **table of specifications** (Yuen, Terao, & Schmidt, 2009) to help organize and develop the questionnaire and to ensure the suitability and relevance of the data collected. This will be translated into Chinese, Korean, and Vietnamese.

2. Individual and Group Observations

Current individual and group observation forms developed by RESTART staff will be further refined into a checklist to improve their efficiency and accuracy for data entry and analysis.

3. Existing Records

Relevant demographic variables, service records, or follow-up results will be collected by the RESTART staff. This information will be extracted, de-identified, and organized in electronic files for data analysis by the evaluation team.

V. Data Collection Procedures

The completion of the paper-survey will be done upon participant's first arrival at the program and upon their completion of the program. If suitable, one-on-one assisted completion of the survey will be provided for individuals who prefer a personal approach to data collection. For the individual and group observations, RESTART staff will conduct and report the observations as scheduled. RESTART staff will extract and organize relevant de-identified existing records in an electronic format to be used by the evaluation.

VI. Data Collection, Analysis, and Reporting Time Line

- For RESTART, all evaluation activities will start as soon as the system is in place, probably starting in June of this year.
- Data analysis will start in June of this year.
- A summary of the major findings will be presented to RESTART in August of next year.

VII. Data Analysis Plan

The RESTART program needs to develop an information management system/database to store evaluation data. The program should update all process data on a regular basis. Descriptive statistics such as single-variable analysis, measurements of central tendency and dispersion (i.e., frequency distribution, percentage, mean, mode, median, minimum, maximum, and range) could be used to present data collected. Outcome data for assessment of changes can be achieved through content analysis of qualitative observations and statistical analysis of quantitative data. These will likely involve inferential statistics such as correlated t-test, analysis of variance (ANOVA), Mann Whitney U test, Pearson's R, Spearman Rho, chi-Square, and possibly multiple regression.

VIII. Human Subjects Review (ISR) and Ethical Practices

All evaluation materials will be kept strictly confidential as required by the Federal Regulations. All forms will use numerical codes for identification. Participation in the program evaluation will be voluntary to the extent that is limited by their court-mandated requirement for participation and no other incentive is given. RESTART staff will inform the participants about the nature of instruments and the approximate length of time for survey completion. The questionnaire aims to evaluate the RESTART program and it will involve topics related to participants' behavioral and perspective shifts. Participants may feel some degree of discomfort but are not greater than those ordinarily encountered in daily life or routine assessment. In addition, they are under care by the RESTART program and referrals to county mental health or other mental health services will be provided. This program evaluation task will complete a Human Subjects Review application and seek approval from ABC University Institution Review Board (IRB). Although this study may involve minimum risk, it will be an Exempt [45CFR46.101(b)(2)] study according to the federal regulations.

RESTART COURT DIVERSION PROGRAM AT COSH—PROGRAM PLANNING AND EVALUATION WORKSHEET

Program Name: *RESTART Court Diversion Program at COSH*

Objective Title:	RESTART Program Evaluation—Master Objective	Activity	Pre-Post-Survey, Observation, and Others
Activity Start and End Dates:	**June of this Year-On-going**	**Staff:**	**Kayla Gonzales, Ho Bon-Yan**

1. Identified Needs	Assess program outcomes and enhance service proficiency to better serve participants
2. Target Populations/ Service Recipients	It is expected a total of 60 women will participate in RESTART between June of this year and May of next year. They all have been given the option by the court to attend RESTART as an alternative sentencing. The evaluation plan for this project attempts to assess all program participants.
3. Activities/Interventions	The approved 8-week (25 Hours) Diversion Program Curriculum.
4. Desired Results (Outputs and Outcomes)	*Output: (What have been completed)* 1. At least 60 women will choose to participate in the RESTART program 2. At least 80% of the participants will complete the RESTART program 3. At least 35 mental health or alcohol and other drugs referrals will be made *Intermediate Outcome: (What change? How well?)* 1. Of those who complete the 25-hour curriculum, 60% will show improvement around problem-solving strategies, self-control, and antisocial behaviors as measured by qualitative and quantitative data 2. Of those who complete the 25-hour curriculum, 60% will take documented steps to reduce harm in their lives, including the reducing or abstaining from prostitution and drug use, obtaining an HIV test, and having safety planning for violence. 3. At least 20 of the referrals will sign up for mental health or AOD treatment *End Outcome: (So what?)* 1. At least 80% of enrolled participants will complete the 25-hour curriculum. Of those that complete, at least 50% will be free from prostitution rearrest for 6 months after completing the program.

5. Method of Measurement	**Documentations (Ongoing):** 1. Current service data will be used to serve as the baseline for comparative analysis 2. Service logs or checklist will be used at various access points to documents service provided and client flow (i.e., number of clients served and trends) **Pre-/Post-Program Survey: (Beginning and end of participation)** 3. Participants will be surveyed at the beginning and at the end of their participation. **Observations: (Every session)** 4. Individual observation 5. Group observation
6. Indicators/Benchmarks	1. Rate of completion of the diversion program by participants 2. Rate of rearrest after completion of program 3. Improvement in the areas of problem-solving strategies, self-control, and antisocial behaviors as indicated by their responses on the survey 4. Improvement in the areas of taking documented steps to reduce harm in their lives, including reducing or abstaining from prostitution and drug use, obtaining an HIV test, and having safety planning for violence as indicated by either their responses on the survey or their communication with staff 5. Findings from individual and group observations
7. Targets/Standards of Success	1. Rate of completion of the diversion program by participants will reach 60% 2. Rate of rearrest after completion of program will not surpass 50% 3. At least 60% graduates will show improvement in the areas of problem-solving strategies, self-control, and antisocial behaviors as indicated by their responses on the survey 4. At least 60% graduates will show improvement in the areas of taking documented steps to reduce harm in their lives, including reducing or abstaining from prostitution and drug use, obtaining an HIV test, and having safety planning for violence as indicated by either their responses on the survey or their communication with staff 5. Survey questionnaire will be in place and ready for field test before May of this year 6. Evaluation plan in place and ready for use in June of this year

8. Resources and Inputs	1. Court referral and mandate 2. Curriculum in place for implementation 3. Research team is formed 4. Human subjects review approval from the university
9. Data Collection, Aggregation, Analysis, and Reporting	1. On-going data will be organized monthly and other data will be collected as scheduled 2. Program data are to be recorded or entered, as much as they are possible, in electronic format 3. Quantitative data will be recorded or input using Excel or SPSS program for analysis 4. Qualitative data will be recorded in Microsoft Word files 5. Program evaluation report completed in August Next Year and will share findings with stake- holders
Objective Statement:	*A total of 60 participants will enroll in the RESTART diversion program between June of this year and May Next Year. At least 60% of them will complete the 25-hour curriculum and will demonstrate increased personal resilience. They will achieve positive behavioral change and perspective shift toward a more "safe and stable" life course. These changes will be evidenced by their actions of attaining stable housing, developing a safety plan, giving attention to personal health and mental health needs including HIV testing and building supportive interpersonal connections. Subsequently, there will be a decrease of recidivism rate that at least 50% of the graduates will be free from prostitu-tion rearrest for 6 months after completing the program.*

Preparing an Evaluation Plan

Different funding sources and management may have their own program evaluation plan format. The outline in Box 10.5 provides one example of the components that might be included when developing an evaluation plan.

Two examples of a program evaluation plan are included next. The first one, Box 10.6 is an evaluation plan for a benefit outreach and enrollment program for a rural county in California. The second one, Box 10.7 is an evaluation plan for a court diversion program as an alternative sentencing for sex workers who have been arrested. Both examples include the evaluation plan narratives and the associated Program Planning and Evaluation Worksheet.

Finally, a one-page tutoring program evaluation plan that employed the various research designs and data collection is presented in Box 10.8. This example shows how a program evaluation employs various research designs and data collections to attain its goals.

BOX 10.8. TUTORING PROGRAM WITH ONE YEAR TO MEASURE RESULTS

I. Exploratory Studies

Program planning and development data:
Use the following "data collection methods" to collect data for a better understanding of the issue and to inform the service program designs that will meet the needs of the target population.

- Needs assessment (town hall meeting, students, teachers, and parents surveys, expert interview)
- Review of successful program design
- Review of current literature

Output and/or intermediate outcome data:
Use the above data collection methods to explore new service locations, service needs, or approaches.

II. Descriptive Studies

After the program is implemented, use various "data collection methods" to collect output, intermediate outcome, and end outcome data that can describe how the program was used and their results.

Output:
Across the board documentation of activities and participation/service utilization.

- Instruments: Program activities record, sign-in and -out form, registration form, etc.

Intermediate outcome:

Using activity-specific data collection methods and instruments to assess the performance of individual program component.

- Pre- and posttest on reading of tutored students in ABC school.
- Comparison between tutored students and comparable nontutored students in ABC school.
- Tutors' assessment of students' performance.

End outcome:

Using end-of-the-year survey, focus group, nominal group, key informants interview, comparison of reading scores, and other methods, the program could detail the utilization and the results of the program including challenges, successes, and ways for improvement.

Other programmatic related data:

Specific relations between variables can also be examined.

- How many hours of tutoring are needed per student to see the initiation of change (the question of dosage)?
- What types of tutoring (one-on-one, group, study hall) work best for the target students on which subject (reading, math)?
- Do parent involvements make a difference?
- What are the key variables or contributing factors for a successful tutoring program?

III. Quasi-Experimental/Longitudinal Case Study of Change Over Time

Intermediate and end outcome:

- Selected number of students who meet the established criteria will be followed and assessed as case studies. These criteria may include active participation in the program, able to establish a stable baseline and to stay with the program, school data available, and willing to be studied.
- They will be assessed for their baseline performance. Then, their changes after the intervention is implemented will be documented over several assessment points to monitor and assess changes.
- These case studies will provide a human face to highlight the possible effects of the intervention.

IV. Experimental Designs

Intermediate and end outcome:

- Use comparison groups to measure the difference in academic achievement.
- Use pre and post test to determine changes.
- Measure students' study skills and other attributes via an established instrument to measure change.

CONCLUSION

Program evaluation is one of the most commonly employed research approaches that we use in human services. This chapter described evaluation approaches that are needs based and outcomes oriented. A logic model can guide the development of the evaluation and its activities. A Program Planning and Evaluation Worksheet can be used to summarize and present the various aspects of the evaluation processes.

Credits

Box 10.3: Adapted from Francis K. O. Yuen, Kenneth L. Terao, and Anna Marie Schmidt, "Program Planning and Evaluation Worksheet Checklist," Effective Grant Writing and Program Evaluation, pp. 109. Copyright © 2009 by John Wiley & Sons, Inc.

Box 10.4: Adapted from Francis K. O. Yuen, Kenneth L. Terao, and Anna Marie Schmidt, "Program Planning and Evaluation Worksheet Checklist," Effective Grant Writing and Program Evaluation, pp. 108. Copyright © 2009 by John Wiley & Sons, Inc.

PART 2

Social Statistics

Descriptive Statistics

11 INTRODUCTION TO DATA ANALYSIS (THE "CSI")

"*Do I really need to know statistics?*" The answer to that is, "You already know it and are using it every day! Certainly, you can know more about it." You may have this belief that "I am not good at numbers!" That is understandable—not all of us like numbers! However, statistics is not just about numbers. Just because you are not good at writing does not mean you are not good at the English language. It is not always about how well you write but how well you express yourself using critical thinking and creativeness. Do you know people who can speak eloquently but cannot handle grammar and punctuation? Proficiency in using statistics is a learnable skill.

The most crucial thing to understand is that "knowing" statistics is not about memorizing statistical formulas but rather knowing what statistics to use and interpreting the computer printouts so that research can make sense to the researchers, practitioners, and communities. After all, some people claim "86.2% of the statistics are made up on the spot." If you do not like that number, they could give you another number! In this and the following chapters, we will try to make statistics concrete, and less confusing. You probably have heard that "Figures do not lie, but liars do figure." If you want to know how to figure or do not want to be figured, knowing statistics is a good first step. Mark Twain made famous the saying, "There are three kinds of lies: lies, damned lies, and statistics." While the origin of this saying is still under debate, it speaks to a core reality—there are different ways of interpreting evidence, and often it must be determined whether there is really evidence at all. It also points out the importance of how statistics should be handled properly as well as the need to understand statistics within the context in which the statistics are derived and applied.

Knowing basic statistics is a learnable task that we all can do. It is a basic life skill and professional skill that we all should possess. CSWE emphasizes that social workers should have the competency of doing "practice informed research and research informed practice" (CSWE, 2015, p. 4). Statistics allows social workers to monitor the effects of services and provide the bases for evidence-based practice. Statistics is one of the key tools in our professional toolbox. It is useful for many tasks but not all tasks.

By now, just at the beginning of the chapter on statistics, how many of you are getting excited about learning statistics? How many are still contemplating? How many are thinking this is not for you? How many really do not care? Does your high school education, family background, SAT score, gender, future aspiration, personal strengths, the professor of the class, the quality of this book, or anything else have anything to do with how you feel about statistics? If you are wondering, then you are all set, ready, and capable of learning and using statistics to find answers to your curiosity. For those who are not wondering, do you wonder why you are not wondering?

CONCEPTUAL STATISTICS

With the proliferation and sophistication of computers and software programs, memorizing formulas and crunching numbers by hand is somewhat obsolete. Yet we may make understanding statistics difficult as we deal too much with the minutia of calculation. Such an approach makes students more apprehensive. What is more important to their understanding is the proper conceptualization of statistics and the appropriate use of practical analysis to generate findings for their study. Conceptual statistics is about understanding statistics by developing a mental map, or a framework of reference, using intuition, following the logic and flow of the materials, and seeking a systematic way to provide answers for the research questions. Do not get hung up on crunching numbers, the computer will assist you with that. Go beyond how it is done; remember why it is done.

Statistics is a mathematical science that helps describe and summarize the features of the data that have been collected. It includes the process of collecting data, organizing data, analyzing data, and interpreting data. Based on the data obtained, one can also make inferences and predictions about the topics being studied. In numbers and logics, statistics help researchers analyze data, summarize findings, tell their stories, and provide a base for rational decision making and conclusion. In research including program evaluation, statistics illustrate the phenomena, relationships, or program activities and outcomes. They help to tell the stories in numbers and with evidence. Statistics use numbers, but they are not all about numbers. Statistics are a tool that helps people to summarize, make predictions, and learn about the world. Making sense of statistics starts with understanding a couple of basic dichotomies.

FIRST DICHOTOMY: PARAMETRIC VERSUS NONPARAMETRIC

Parametric is defined as a quantity, a quantifiable characteristic, a property, a feature, or a constant factor that describes the statistical population. For example, age, gender, and income can be the **parameters** for a population. They can be summarized as a quantity (e.g., mean, mode, and variance) or a constant factor that is often represented in a normal or bell curve distribution. The average midterm exam grade for a research class, 70 out of 100 points is an example of a parameter. Characteristics or properties of a sample are called **statistics**. The proportion of all older adults over the age of 65 in the City of Springfield that need to see a physician at least once every 6 months is a parameter. The proportion of a sample of older adults over the age of 65 in the City of Springfield needs to see a physician at least once in 6 months is a statistic. Note that the term statistics is both a name for a mathematical science and the characteristics of a sample.

DATA SOURCE	CHARACTERISTICS
Population	Parameters
Sample of the Population	Statistics

Yuliya is a very interesting person who does not appear to have a particular way of doing things or a firm opinion of anything. She is a bit of a mystery. Her friends can tell where she is but cannot tell what her next step will be. Her best friends describe her as "she is what she is." They have a difficult time to decide what birthday present to buy for her because they just don't know what she likes! They nicknamed her "nonparametric." Dmitri is Yuliya's fiancé. He is more "manageable" and much more predictable because he has some known characteristics. Although he could be deviant at times; he is mostly a "typical guy." He is "one of the guys" who likes to do average and stereotypical 'guys' things." They nicknamed him "parametric."

An old university professor of a very popular class has been asking his students at the end of the semester to write him a reflective paper about the class. He wants to use the papers to learn more about his teaching and his students. He does not give any instructions or guidelines for this paper. He claims that each paper will be judged on its own unique merits *(nonparametric)*. Students have been talking to each other trying to figure out what to do with this assignment, but no one know has any ideas. Over the past 20 years of this course, a large number of such papers have been written. One of his smart research assistants stumbled across a scattered collection of these papers a couple of years ago. Since then, with his approval, she has collected more graded papers directly from the students. Although each of these papers is unique and different, together, they form a large sample that common characteristics can be identified, quantified, and summarized *(parametric)*. Her analysis has revealed some general patterns and characteristics about the papers, the students, and the professor' teaching.

Essentially, in nonparametric, little is known about the study subjects or the variables. Therefore, no assumption is made about the general structure or distributional form (e.g., normal curve distribution) of the variables. Nonparametric statistics are also called parameter-free or distribution-free statistics. Nonparametric data are mostly nominal or ordinal data. Researchers present the characters of the data by stating their appropriate descriptive properties. Parametric statistics which are mostly interval measures, on the other hand, rely on the assumption of the normal distribution of the population and the properties of the samples to make inferences. Table 11.1 provides comparisons between parametric and nonparametric statistics. The normal curve distribution will be discussed and explained in Chapter 13.

Parametric or Nonparametric Tests for Parametric or Nonparametric Data

The analysis of nonparametric data requires the use of specific nonparametric tests, and specific parametric tests are used for parametric data. However, when the sample size of the nonparametric continuous data becomes large enough (e.g., 30 or larger), the application of parametric statistics for the analysis also becomes acceptable (see the old professor example).

The central limit theorem (CLT) is a statistics theory. It states that the distribution of the means of a sufficient number of samples will approximate a normal distribution. And that the mean of all samples would be close to the population

TABLE 11.1. Parametric and Nonparametric Statistics

	PARAMETRIC	NONPARAMETRIC
Information about the population	Information about the population is known	No information about the population
Characteristics	Quantifiable characteristics of a population (e.g., average age and height, GPA, IQ score)	Characterized by the appropriate descriptive properties of the data collected (e.g., number of clients seen each month, class ranking, gender)
Level of data	Interval or ratio data (e.g., mean, variance)	Nominal or ordinal data (e.g., median, frequency, percent, ranking)
Assumption	Assumption of the normal distribution, normality	No assumption of the general structure or distributional form, "distribution-free"
Tests	Use parametric tests (e.g., t-tests, ANOVA, Pearson's r, linear regression)	Use nonparametric tests (e.g., chi-square, U test, rank test, Spearman, logistic regression)
Samples and population	Use of samples to draw statistical conclusions about the population	Use of available data (population, immediate group, samples) for descriptions and statistical conclusions
Hypothesis testing	Hypothesis testing is based on the known population distribution or parameter	Hypothesis testing is not based on known distribution or parameter
Advantages and disadvantages	More efficient	Simple and easier to use
	Results can be misleading when normal assumption is not satisfied	Flexible and versatile. Not concerned about the normality assumption or knowledge of the population
	More powerful explanation	Less powerful explanation

mean, regardless the original data is normally distributed or not. How sufficient is sufficient? Generally speaking, 30 samples or more is considered a baseline. In other words, when a researcher draws 30 or more random samples from an immediate group (e.g., program participants), the distribution of the means of these samples will approximate a normal distribution. This condition will, therefore, allow the data to be further analyzed with parametric statistics. (CLT will be further explained in Chapter 13.)

Frost (2015) reported results of simulations conducted by Minitab, a private software and statistics education company, and concluded that "parametric tests can perform well with continuous data that are nonnormal if you satisfy the sample size guidelines" (para. 6). They proposed a sample-size guideline and suggested a sample size of greater than 20 for a one-sample t-test, each group greater than 15 for a two-sample t-test, and a sample size of greater than 15 to 20 for a one-way ANOVA.

Nonparametric statistical tests are very useful tools for data set that have nominal or ordinal data or when the sample size is small. They are also very useful when the median is the better measure for the data set (Frost, 2015). We often report median incomes instead of the mean income because the median is not affected by outliers. Several extremely rich residents in a neighborhood will raise the neighborhood's mean income but the median income would be unchanged or very minimally affected. A researcher may have a set of parametric data, but the nonparametric tests (median based) may be more suitable choices than the parametric tests (mean based), particularly when the outliers cannot be removed. The choice of using parametric or nonparametric statistics is not always a straightforward decision.

SECOND DICHOTOMY: DESCRIPTIVE VERSUS INFERENTIAL

The second important distinction in statistics is between descriptive statistics, which portrays the data, and inferential statistics, which makes predictions from the data. Both descriptive and inferential statistics use the same data set the researchers collected. Descriptive statistics summarize and present the features of the data as what they are in a meaningful way. Inferential statistics attempt to make conclusions about the population from the samples, forecast the results of the action, draw conclusions, give explanations, or make predictions. Inferential statistics also involve normal curve distribution, sampling, randomization, experimental designs, and hypothesis testing.

If a fair quarter was flipped end over end in the air, it would land on the ground as either heads or tails. If the coin flip came to rest as heads, the probability of having the head side up *is,* therefore, "one" (100:100, 100%) and the probability of the coin coming up as tails would be "zero" (0). However, before the coin is flipped, it is **predicted** that the probability of it being heads or being tails is the same (50:50 or 0.5:0.5).

In saying to someone, "it's heads," describes the result of the flip. That is the essence of *descriptive statistics*. It describes what happened. On the other hand, before the coin flip in a football game, the result could have been either heads or tails, each having an equal chance. However, the team captains both predict that the outcome should be to their advantages. That is the prediction or inference, the basis of *inferential statistics.*

Descriptive statistics merely describe the data the researcher has collected, there are no predictions or inferences. The probability for this data set is 100% or one. It is what the researcher collected. It is what is happening. Similarly, when a researcher describes her data set, it is a factual report of what she has collected. For example, "67% of the public believe that mowing lawn has a positive influence on their lives." Fictitious in this case, but that is what the researcher found in her study.

By itself, a descriptive statistic is an important and significant part of statistics. It is also the essential first step for other statistical analyses. All studies should have descriptive statistics reported in the text as grounds for the inferences to follow. Consider the following examples:

- Is this community bigger than that community?
- Is this university better than that university?
- Which restaurant has the best food in town?
- Do more people prefer the middle seat to the aisle seat on a plane?
- Which big U.S. corporate boards have more female board members?

All these questions require a comparison; something that descriptive statistics do not really do, at least in any meaningful sense. Descriptive statistics, however, provide the ground or foundation for such a comparison to take place. To determine if something is different than something else, is higher or lower, or better or worse than previous or other data is an extrapolation that requires inferential statistics.

So, can someone infer that Alabama Football is better than Auburn Football? Alumni argue that point incessantly, and the answer is always the same—"My alma mater is better!" In a statistical sense, the research question is, What is the probability that Alabama is better than Auburn? Both have a chance to be found as better, as the probability is very likely less than one ($p < 1$), perfect, certain, or 100%.

An inferential statistic is made much easier if there is only one variable that changes. For example, one population to a different population, one population to a sample, one sample to its population, one sample to a different sample, the same population before and after, or the same sample before and after. While more complex comparisons are possible and done all the time, it is beyond the scope of this book to discuss those complexities.

The most common forms of comparison are the similarity and difference between subjects. In statistics, the inference of similarity or difference is based on probability or chance. Inferential statistics attempt to answer the question, "Did it happen by chance or not?" More specifically, inferential statistics answer the following questions:

- Typical versus not typical
- Probable versus not probable
- Likely versus unlikely

Table 11.2 below summarizes and compares the common characteristics of descriptive statistics and inferential statistics. Descriptive statistics and inferential statistics work together to provide better understanding and analysis of the data.

TABLE 11.2. Descriptive and Inferential Statistics

DESCRIPTIVE STATISTICS	INFERENTIAL STATISTICS
Summarizes and presents the features of the data as what they are in a meaningful way	Makes conclusions about the population from the samples, forecasts the results of the action, draws conclusions, gives explanations, or makes predictions
Not concerning normal distribution, sampling, or hypothesis testing	Involves normal distribution, sampling, randomization, experimental designs, and hypothesis testing
Not based on probability. The probability is one—the population or the immediate groups	Based on probability. The probability varies
Is interested in the population or the immediate groups of data	Uses samples to make generalizations about the population
Describes what happened	Explains the chance of happening, makes prediction
Provides a foundation for inferential statistics	Builds upon descriptive statistics

Descriptive/Inferential and Nonparametric/ Parametric: Do They Mix?

Descriptive and inferential statistics both employ parametric and nonparametric tests. Dependent on the level of measurements (e.g., nominal, interval) and the distributions (e.g., normal distribution or distribution-free) different tests will be

TABLE 11.3. Descriptive/Inferential and Nonparametric/Parametric: Sample Statistics

	DESCRIPTIVE STATISTICS	INFERENTIAL STATISTICS
Nonparametric tests	Frequency, percentage, range, mean, mode, median	Chi-square, Mann-Whitney U test, Wilcoxon rank test, Spearman, Logistic regression
Parametric tests	Frequency, percentage, range, mean, mode, median, variance, standard deviation	Z-test, t-tests, ANOVA, Pearson's r, Linear regression

used for the analysis. Table 11.3 lists some of the tests that can be used in different situations.

BASIC FRAMEWORK FOR STATISTICS

So far, we have discussed the two dichotomies in statistics: parametric and non-parametric, as well as descriptive and inferential. The understanding of these two dichotomies, along with other factors, provides a framework for the researcher to decide what statistics are appropriate for data analysis. Table 11.4 summarizes some of the key components and statistical tests for both descriptive and inferential statistics.

Descriptive statistics aim to give information about the population or the immediate group of data in the following three areas:

1. *Presentation of data.* What is the data set like in numbers and graphic presentations?
2. *Measures of central tendency.* How do the data look when they come together or are summarized? What are the common denominators?
3. *Measures of dispersion.* How spread out are the data? What are the distributions?

Inferential statistics aim to make generalizations from the samples about the population, provide explanations, make predictions, or draws conclusions. It gives answers to two major questions:

1. *Test of correlation.* Are they related?
2. *Test of difference.* Are they different?

TABLE 11.4. Key Components of Descriptive and Inferential Statistics

Descriptive Statistics

Descriptive statistics summarize, present, and describe data as what they are, but do not make hypothesis-related conclusions.

I. Presentation of Data

Present the data as they are and their summaries

A. Frequency distributions
  o Frequency distributions
  o Percentage distributions
  o Cumulative

B. Graphic presentation
  o Bar graphs—nominal—height
  o Histograms—interval and ratio—height and width
  o Pie charts—nominal to ratio—segments of the whole
  o Frequency polygons—interval
  o Scattergrams—interval and ratio—association

II. Measures of Central Tendency

Summarizing the data or reporting on what attributes are "typical." They also provide a common denominator for comparing.

A. Mode tells which value in the distribution of values is observed most frequently. It is the most "popular" value and is used for nominal or higher level data. It is possible to have more than one mode.

B. Median divides any distribution of values into two equal parts or proportions. It is the "middle" point. It is least affected by extreme values and, therefore, is the most stable one. It is used for ordinal or higher level data.

C. Mean is the sum of all the values of a variable divided by the number of values. It is the "average." It is affected by extreme scores and used for interval or ratio level data.

We must consider reporting more than one measure of central tendency to provide a more comprehensive description.

III. Measures of Dispersion (Variability)

The way in which values scatter themselves (the spread or distribution of values) around a location or a measure of central tendency (mean, mode, or median).

A. Minimum is the lowest value

B. Maximum is the highest values

C. Range (maximum–minimum)

D. Variance is the dispersion of data around the mean. It is the mean of the squared difference (of the data away from the mean). The larger the variance, the greater the distribution

E. Standard deviation is a measure of the dispersion of data around the arithmetic mean in the original score units. It is the square root of the variance. The larger the standard deviation, the greater the spread of scores around the mean.

Conceptual and Practical Research and Statistics for Social Workers

Inferential Statistics

Inferential statistics attempt to infer from the samples about the population, draw conclusions, give explanations, or make predictions. In other words, test the hypothesis.

I. Test of Association/Correlation
It tests how things change together: positive or negative, high or low, strong or weak, statistically significant or not significant.
Examples: Chi-square, Spearman's Rho, Kendall's Tau, Pearson's r

II. Test of Differences
How significantly different?
Examples: Chi-square, Mann-Whitney U test, Wilcoxon signed-rank test Z-test, t-tests, F test, and ANOVA.

Related Concepts

I. Hypothesis Testing
Research hypothesis, alternative hypothesis, null hypothesis: reject or fail to reject

II. Statistical Significance
Rejection levels
One-tailed or two-tailed
Statistically significant versus meaningful findings

III. Parametric and Nonparametric Statistics

CHOOSING THE APPROPRIATE STATISTICS

Following the framework described in Table 11.4, the subsequent chapters will describe and explain some of the common statistical tests. One of the common challenges for social workers and students is to decide which test is the appropriate one to use. Two charts are being introduced here to assist researchers in deciding which tests to use. These charts only include major or common statistics that are often used by social workers. Each chart is by no means an exhausted list. They can be used as a general reference or a starting point in deciding what statistics should be considered.

1. The Common Statistics and Choice of Statistics Chart (Table 11.5)
2. Inferential Statistics Test Choice Flowchart (Figure 11.1)

TABLE 11.5. Common Statistics and Choice of Statistics Chart

A. **Descriptive Statistics:**

1. **Presentation of data.** Frequency distribution, percentage, graph, chart
2. **Measures of central tendency.** Mean, mode, median
3. **Measures of dispersion.** Minimum, maximum, range, variance, standard deviation

B. **Inferential Statistics:**

LEVEL OF MEASURE-MENT	TEST FOR SIGNIFICANT ASSOCIATION/CORRELATION	TEST FOR SIGNIFICANCE OF DIFFERENCES
	• To what extent are the two variables or attributes correlated?	• Is the difference between groups at a significant level? • Is the difference a result of chance or a result of the independent variable?
Nominal	**Nonparametric** **Chi-square, McNemar's test, Fisher's exact test, Chi-square Goodness of Fit test** • Two nominal variables • The correlation between programs (nominal variable: BSW or MSW) and success in obtaining a job (nominal variable: yes or no) o Is there a significant relationship between the level of education (BSW or MSW) and their success (successful or unsuccessful) in obtaining a job?	**Nonparametric** **Chi-square, McNemar's test, Fisher's exact test, Chi-square Goodness of Fit test** • Two nominal variables • The difference between BSW and MSW (independent variable) graduates' success (dependent variable) in obtaining jobs. o Is there a significant difference between BSW and MSW graduates in their success in obtaining a job following the completion of their studies?
Ordinal	**Nonparametric** **Spearman's rank correlation coefficient (Spearman's Rho), Kendall's Tau** • Test for correlation (strength, direction) between two groups on an ordinal scale	**Nonparametric** **Mann-Whitney U (independent samples), Wilcoxon signed test (related samples), Kolmogorov-Smirnov (goodness of fit)** • Test for difference (significant or not significant) between two groups on an ordinal scale

Conceptual and Practical Research and Statistics for Social Workers

TABLE 11.5. Common Statistics and Choice of Statistics Chart (*Continued*)

- Test for correlation between attitudes toward one's spouse pursuing graduate education (non-supportive, supportive, very supportive) and one's own level of education (graduate degree, college, high school).
  - o Is there a statistically significant correlation between attitudes toward one's spouse pursuing graduate education and one's own level of education?
- Test for regression (prediction) between two ordinal scales
- To what extent do clients' levels of satisfaction (low, moderate, high) have a correlation to clients' levels of participation (low, moderate, high)?
  - o Will clients who have a high level of participation also have a high level of satisfaction and vice versa?

Parametric

Interval and Ratio	**Pearson's product-moment correlation coefficient (Pearson's r), correlation coefficient (r), coefficient of determination (r²)**

- Test for correlation (degree of linear relationship) between two interval/ratio variables
  - o Is there a significant correlation between students' ages and their test scores for the course?
- Correlational coefficient (r) strength and direction: $-1 \leq r \leq +1$ (.3, .5, .7)
- Correlation of determination (r²) how well (certain) the regression line represents the data: $0 \leq r^2 \leq 1$ (.3 = 9%, .5 = 25%, .7 = 49%)

- Test for difference between husbands and wives (nominal variable) on an ordinal scale (non-supportive, supportive, very supportive) designed to measure spouse's attitudes toward each other on pursuing a graduate degree
  - o Is there a statistically significant difference between husbands and wives in their attitudes toward each other on pursuing a graduate degree?
- Does the level of satisfaction differ significantly between the clients with different levels (high or low) of participation?
  - o Are clients with a high level of participation significantly different from those with a low level of participation in their level of satisfaction?

Parametric

Z-test

- Test of difference between population means with normal distribution and with known variances/standard deviations
  - o **One-sample Z-test.** Is this client's resiliency score different from the population score?
  - o **Two-sample Z-test.** Is client A's resiliency score from Test A different from Client B's resiliency score from Test B?

One-sample t-test, independent (unpaired) t-test, correlated (paired) t-test,

- o **One-sample t-test.** Test for difference between the sample and the population on an interval/ratio variable
  - o Is the person (sample) really from this community (population)—a true representative?
  - o Is the person (sample) significantly different from the norm (population) that the independent variable may be responsible?

TABLE 11.5. Common Statistics and Choice of Statistics Chart (*Continued*)

- *Independent t-test.* Test for difference between two unrelated (independent) groups on an interval/ratio variable.
  - o Is there a significant difference in the test scores between Mr. Padilla's class and Mrs. Smith's class?
  - o Is there a significant difference between the treatment group and control group on their coping skills scores?
- *Correlated t-test.* Test for difference between two related groups on an interval/ratio variable.
  - o A pre and post comparison of students on their test scores after the tutoring program.
  - o A comparison between two comparable groups (two randomly selected, very similar, or matched samples) on the effects of a treatment approach.

ANOVA ("extended t-test"), **ANCOVA, F test**

- Test for statistically significant difference between two but usually three or more groups on an interval/ratio variable.
  - o Are there significant differences among BSW, MSW, and DSW (nominal) on their incomes (interval/ratio)? (ANOVA)

Comparison of …	Interval/Ratio (Parametric)	Ordinal (Nonparametric)
One group to a hypothetical value	One-sample t-test	One-sample Wilcoxon signed test
Two unrelated groups	Independent (unpaired) t-test	Mann-Whitney U test
Two related groups	Correlated (paired) t-test	Paired-sample Wilcoxon signed test
Three or more unrelated groups	One-way ANOVA	Kruskal-Wallis test
Three or more related groups	Repeated-measures ANOVA	Freidman test

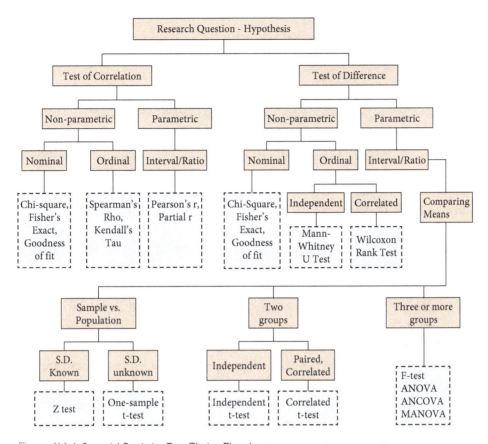

Figure 11.1. Inferential Statistics Test Choice Flowchart

The **Common Statistics and Choice of Statistics Chart** is a chart for the selection of statistics and a road map for the statistics discussions for this book. Simple examples are included. This chart takes into consideration the following:

- Levels of measurement
- Descriptive or inferential statistics
- Parametric or nonparametric statistics
- Test of correlation or test of difference

The **Inferential Statistics Test Choice Flowchart** is in effect a flowchart version of the inferential portion of the Common Statistics and Choice of Statistics Chart. It uses the following sequence of questions:

1. What is the research hypothesis?
2. Is it a test of correlation or test of difference?

3. Are the data parametric or nonparametric?
4. What levels of measurement (nominal, ordinal, interval/ratio) are the data involved?
5. If it is a test of correlation, pick the choice statistics (X^2, Rho, r, etc.)
6. If it is a test of difference, pick the choice statistics (X^2, U, Z, t, ANOVA, etc.) considering the relationship of comparison groups (independent or correlated) and the number of variables involved.

Details for each of the statistics mentioned in these charts will be discussed in the following chapters. As a result, we will be referring back to this chart often.

CONCLUSION

This chapter presented the basic concepts for data analysis. It explained the differences between parametric and nonparametric statistics, as well as descriptive and inferential statistics. The Common Statistics and Choice of Statistics Chart provides a guiding framework for the selection of appropriate statistics. The choices are based on the levels of measurement of the variables and whether they are tests for correlation or difference. The Inferential Statistics Test Choice Flow Chart further highlights the choices specifically for inferential statistics. These two charts serve as road maps for understanding and choosing these statistics. The following chapters will further explain and connect individual statistics that are included in these charts.

12

PRESENTATION OF DATA, CENTRAL TENDENCY, AND DISPERSION

As explained in the previous chapter, descriptive statistics are different from inferential statistics. Descriptive statistics simply present the data the researcher has collected, with no predictions or inferences. The data for a variable can be narrated by descriptive statistics in any or all of three main measures:

1. Presentation of data
2. Measures of central tendency
3. Measures of dispersion

In this chapter, we will discuss each of these measures with explanations and examples. However, after the data are collected and before they can be analyzed, they first have to be cleaned and organized. Not all data collected are usable data. Researchers need to use their professional judgment to decide which data are usable and which are not. The clean data then need to be organized and summarized in a manner that can give a clear impression of what the data are like. Presentation of data, which includes frequency distributions in numbers or in graphs, is the first step of this process.

PRESENTATION OF DATA: FREQUENCY, PERCENTAGE, AND CUMULATIVE PERCENTAGE

Yoriko collected the intake forms from her Family Resource Center every evening to prepare the daily report on the service recipients. With the help of a statistical software program, she input all the data into a

265

data file, which she could use for analysis. Among the information provided by the form are the family sizes of the recipients.

CLIENT ID	FAMILY SIZE	CLIENT ID	FAMILY SIZE	CLIENT ID	FAMILY SIZE	CLIENT ID	FAMILY SIZE
001	6	006	2	011	4	016	4
002	5	007	6	012	5	017	5
003	6	008	2	013	8	018	3
004	4	009	5	014	7	019	8
005	3	010	3	015	5	020	7

Yoriko ran an analysis and had the following data output, which included the variable name (family size), frequency, percent, and cumulative percent. Frequency is the actual count of the happening or occurrence of the attributes. Percent means the proportion of that attribute per the total number of cases. Cumulative percent is incremental aggregation of percentages.

FAMILY SIZE	FREQUENCY	PERCENT	CUMULATIVE PERCENT
2	2	10	10
3	3	15	25
4	3	15	40
5	5	25	65
6	3	15	80
7	2	10	90
8	2	10	100
Total	20	100	

This analysis provided Yoriko with the information that there were a total of 20 (N = 20) service recipients that day. Their family sizes range from two to eight. More of them had a family size of five people (n = 5, 25%), and 65% of the 20 families have a family size of five or less.

GRAPHIC PRESENTATION: BAR GRAPH, PIE CHART, HISTOGRAM, FREQUENCY POLYGON, SCATTERPLOT

To present her data visually, Yoriko constructed a bar graph and a pie chart to demonstrate the data. Both the bar graph and pie chart are suitable for nominal data. The length of each bar in the bar graph (Figure 12.1) represents the frequency of occurrence of the category or attribute. Therefore, the longer the bar the higher the frequency. Note that because the data are nominal and not continuous (interval), bars in the bar graphs are separated and not (continuously) connected. The pie chart (Figure 12.2) looks like a pie that is made up by the different segments of the total. Together, they constitute the total, which is 100%. The proportion of each of the slices of the pie represents the frequency of occurrence of the category or attribute.

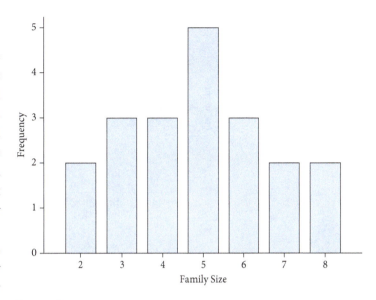

Figure 12.1. Bar Graph of Family Size of Service Recipients

To construct a bar graph, one can use the following steps:

1. Draw and label the horizontal axis (X) and vertical axis (Y).
2. Use x-axis for the categories and the y-axis for the frequency of occurrence.
3. Draw the bar for each of the categories to the height that represents the frequency.

To construct a pie chart, one can use the following steps:

1. Calculate the proportion of each of the attributes (categories) of 360 degrees (a circle is 360 degrees): (Number of cases in the attribute/Total number of cases) × 360 = Proportion.
2. Use a protractor to plot the different proportions onto a circle.
3. Label each section and add supplemental information to improve readability.

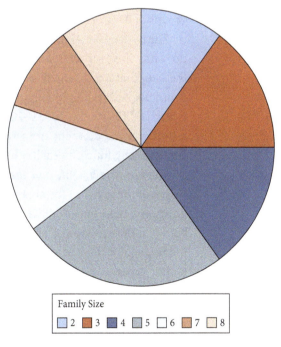

Figure 12.2. Pie Chart of Family Size of Service Recipients

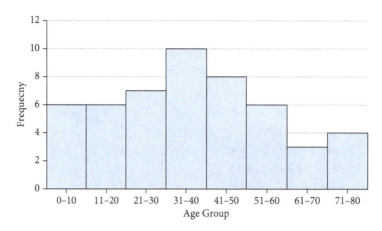

Figure 12.3. Histogram of Ages of Service Recipients

Yoriko analyzed the ages of 50 recipients. She grouped them by every 10 years (a *Bin*) and ran a frequency analysis, along with a histogram (see Figure 12.3). A ***bin*** or a class interval is about sorting data in groups, categories, or ranges. Literally, it is like throwing data into the different designated bins. In this current example, it is the age groups of 0–10, 11–20, etc.

The histogram (Figure 12.3) is designed for grouped ordinal, interval, and ratio data. The (vertical) y-axis shows the frequency and the (horizontal) x-axis has the data that are grouped in ranges (bins). The x-axis is made up by a sequence of contiguous bins. The bins represent an inherent order of a continuous data set, for example, "11–20, 21–30, 31–70" or "low-risk, medium-risk, high-risk." As a result, a histogram is different from the bar graph in that the adjacent bars are lined up continuously touching each other.

The bin, the height, and the width. The histogram uses both the width and the height of the bar (i.e., the area) to reflect the number of cases in that bin. Some histograms will have bins of different sizes (e.g., 0–40, 41–60, 61–90) that result in having bars of different widths. Therefore, the height of the bar does not necessarily reflect the frequency of occurrence. It is the area of the bar that counts. Similarly, taller bins do not necessarily hold more volume than shorter bins.

However, the widths of the bins for ordinal data are all equal, but the width of interval and ratio data may have different widths. There are many computer software programs that can easily produce well-constructed histograms. However, different computer programs usually have default settings for their graphic presentations. For

Conceptual and Practical Research and Statistics for Social Workers

example, by default, the current SPSS will produce a histogram of the bins that are of equal width.

AGE GROUP	FREQUENCY	PERCENT	CUMULATIVE PERCENT
0–10	6	12	12
11–20	6	12	24
21–30	7	14	38
31–40	10	20	58
41–50	8	16	74
51–60	6	12	86
61–70	3	6	92
71–80	4	8	100
Total	50	100.0	

A frequency polygon (Figure 12.4) could be constructed by connecting the middle point of the top of each bar (bin). It will show the distribution of the data in a line. While a frequency polygon could be used by itself, it is clearer to the readers if it is used with the histogram (Figure 12.5). Frequency polygons and histograms together set up the foundation for our discussions of the normal curve distribution in the following section.

A frequency polygon can be used to compare results of different data sets (Figure 12.6). It provides an instant graphic comparison of different data sets. In the example that follows, the age range distributions of two groups are compared side by

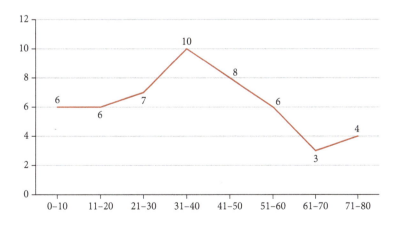

Figure 12.4. Frequency Polygon of Ages of Service Recipients

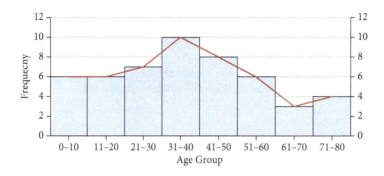

Figure 12.5. Frequency Polygon and Histogram of Ages of Service Recipients

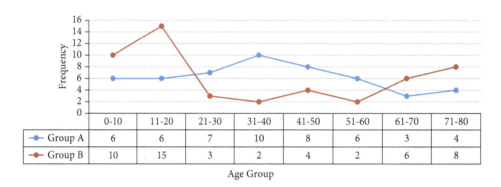

	0-10	11-20	21-30	31-40	41-50	51-60	61-70	71-80
Group A	6	6	7	10	8	6	3	4
Group B	10	15	3	2	4	2	6	8

Age Group

Figure 12.6. Frequency Polygon-Comparison of Ages of Two Groups of Service Recipients

side. Both Group A and Group B have members ages ranging from younger than 10 to older than 71. However, Group A has more young to middle-age adults; Group B has more children and teens, as well as older adults.

A scatterplot is a commonly used graphic presentation that shows the relationships between two variables. In Figure 12.7, the number of hours used in studying was correlated with the test scores of 10 students (assuming they all were at the same level prior to studying). A scatterplot will help to show the connection between these two variables. A "trendline" (the straight line running through the data point) helps us to see the trend and direction of the relationship. In this case, it shows a positive relationship that the more hours students put into studying the higher scores they got on the test.

A scatterplot is also a tool that is used when conducting correlational analysis. It helps to show the pattern and the distribution of the data to better understand the statistical outcomes. In the example in Figure 12.7, there is a positive correlation between

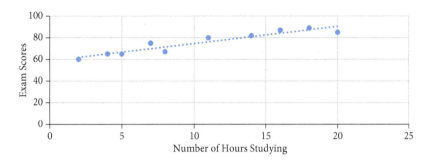

Figure 12.7. Scatterplot of Age of Service Recipients

hours of study and test scores. However, it does not tell which variable brought about the other one. Did more hours of study help students get better grades or did students who got better grades spend more time studying? The relationship between correlation and causation will be discussed in Chapter 15.

Hours Studying	2	4	5	7	8	11	14	16	18	20
Test Score	60	65	65	75	67	80	82	87	89	85

MEASURES OF CENTRAL TENDENCY

Measure of central tendency is also called measures of center or measures of central location. It is a central value, which is like the town center or a hub where the data congregate toward it. A point where the others come together. A central tendency measure summarizes and depicts the crucial characters as well as the overall picture of the whole data set. As shown in Chapter 11 (Table 11.4 and Table 11.5), mean, mode and median are the three main measures of central tendency. Each of these measures summarizes different characters of the data set. It is advisable that researchers use more than one measure to provide a more complete picture of the data.

1. Mode—The most frequently occurring score or category
2. Median—The statistical middle
3. Mean—The average score

Mode is the score or category that is most popular or frequently appeared. It can be used for data of nominal, ordinal, interval, or ratio level. A data set can have one or more modes. A frequency distribution analysis will identify the mode(s). The following are scores in ascending order for two 100-point statistics tests:

65, 75, 75, 82, 88, 91, 92, 95, 96—The mode is 75 because it happened more often.

65, 75, 75, 75, 88, 91, 95, 95, 95—The modes are 75 and 95 (bimodal).

Median is the middle number, the person who stands in the middle of a lineup, or at the 50th percentile. It splits the data set into two equal halves. It is either the middle score (for an odd number data set) or the average of the middle two scores (for an even number data set). It is also a measure that is *not affected by the outliers* or the extreme scores. When the U.S. Department of Census reports about incomes, usually it reports the median incomes not the mean incomes. Example: a social worker lives in a neighborhood that has an annual median household income of $50,000. If a family with a $60,000 income moved out and was replaced by a family with an income of $1,000,000, the median income for the neighborhood would remain unchanged, still $50,000. However, the mean income would become much higher. Use the statistics class test scores example from earlier to find the median:

65, 75, 75, 82, 88, 91, 92, 95, 96—The median is 88. It has four scores to its left and four to its right.

65, 75, 75, 82, 88, 90, 91, 92, 95, 96—The median is 89, because (88 + 90)/2 = 89.

5, 75, 75, 82, 88, 90, 91, 92, 100—The median is still 88, in spite of extreme cases of 5 and 100.

Mean (μ or $\bar{X}$) is the average number. The **arithmetic mean** is the sum (Σ) of all the scores divided by the number of scores (cases) on the data set. The formulas for the population mean and sample mean are listed next.

With the statistics class test example, the average of the nine students who took the test is 84.

(65 + 75 + 75 + 82 + 88 + 91 + 92 + 95 + 96)/9 (cases) = 84.

The mean is an important measure that is instrumental for inferential statistics; it is, however, susceptible to outliers or extreme cases. Say if one of the students in

TABLE 12.1. Population Mean and Sample Mean

POPULATION MEAN	SAMPLE MEAN (STATISTICS)
$$\mu = \frac{\sum X_i}{N}$$	$$\bar{X} = \frac{\sum X_i}{n}$$
μ = Population mean	$\bar{X}$ = Sample mean
Σ = The sum score	Σ = The sum score
X = individual scores	X = individual scores
N = Number of cases in the population	N = Number of cases in the sample

the example got five points instead of getting 65, the mean score for the whole class would drop from 84 to 78.

$(5 + 75 + 75 + 82 + 88 + 91 + 92 + 95 + 96)/9$ (cases) = 78.

The mean is the balancing point of the distributions of the data set. The data distribute around the mean and they balance each other off. The sum of the data above the mean equals the sum of the data below the mean. Students can balance their statistics book on one figure at the mean point of the weight distributions (i.e., the center of gravity).

The **trimmed mean** is the mean score of the data set after a small percentage of the data are trimmed from both the upper end and the lower end. This is done to eliminate the possible negative effect of the extreme cases.

Mean: $(5 + 75 + 75 + 82 + 88 + 91 + 92 + 95 + 96 + 255)/10$ (cases) = 95.40
Trimmed Mean: $(5 + 75 + 75 + 82 + 88 + 91 + 92 + 95 + 96 + 255)/10$ 8 (cases) = 86.75

MEASURES OF DISPERSION

While measures of central tendency describe how the data come together, measures of dispersion describe the spread or the variability of the data. Different sets of data may have the same mean but have different distributions of data (see Figure 12.8). Two psychoeducational groups may have the same mean score for their learning outcomes; could the social worker assume members of the two groups have the same degree of understanding of the materials?

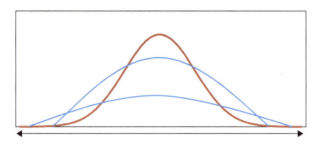

Figure 12.8. Same Mean Different Dispersion

As shown in Table 11.4 and Table 11.5, the common measures of dispersion are maximum, minimum, range, variance, and standard deviation. They all provide information on the characteristics of the spread of the data around the central value (i.e., mean). A lesser degree of dispersion means a greater degree of homogeneity. The data are more alike or uniformed.

Range is the difference between the maximum and minimum (i.e., Range = Maximum – Minimum). Maximum is the largest number of a data set and minimum is the smallest number. Say the oldest member of a support group is 55 (maximum) and the youngest member is 23 (minimum). The age range for members of this support group is, therefore, 22 (i.e., 55 – 23 = 32). This range is what everyone normally finds in most textbooks. It is the most commonly used general range, and it is called exclusive range.

22　→　55
Range = (Max. – Min.)
　　　= (55 – 23)
　　　= 32

There is also the inclusive range, whereas the formula is Range = Maximum – Minimum + 1.

22　→　55
Range = (Max. – Min.) +1
　　　= (55 – 22) +1
　　　= 33

Range is a measure of difference between the highest and lowest scores for interval or ratio data. The exclusive range reflects the number of intervals between two scores. Between 22 and 55, there are 32 intervals (scores). It is the commonly used range. The inclusive range, however, includes all the scores in the data set. Between 22 and 55, there are 33 different intervals. Say an elementary school has classes from first grade to sixth grade. Would you say the school has a class range of 5 or 6? It is safe to say that the school has classes range from first to sixth and, therefore, the range is $(6 - 1) + 1 = 6$. Range is a measure that could be easily calculated; it is also easily affected by extreme scores. The interquartile range addresses this concern of the presence of extreme cases.

Interquartile range is a measure of dispersion only involving the data between 25th percentile and 75th percentile. It is the numerical difference between the first quartile (Q_1) and the third quartile (Q_3). Therefore, it only includes the middle section that makes up half (50%) of all the scores or observations. Its use can eliminate the effect of extreme values (scores) that affect the general range. In responding to a questionnaire that employs a scale, such as the Likert type scale, some respondents may mechanically mark one end of the answers for all or most of the questions. The interquartile range helps minimize the effect of such extreme or incorrect responses, as well as errors made during data entry. The interquartile range for the ages of the member of the support group is 11, which is the difference between Q_3 and Q_1.

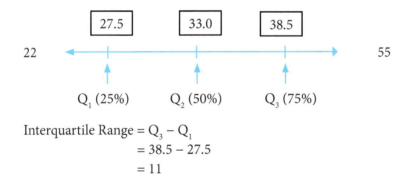

Interquartile Range = $Q_3 - Q_1$
$$= 38.5 - 27.5$$
$$= 11$$

Variance (σ^2) is the average of the squared differences (deviations) from the mean. It shows how the data are dispersed around the mean. If everyone in a class gets the same grade that, means there is no variability of grades, and the variance is zero. Everyone is situated on the same spot. When the scores are not the same, then there are variabilities, and we would wonder what the spreads are like. Two classes have an average (mean) grade of 80. The highest and lowest scores for class A are 99 and 50, while scores for class B are 85 and 75. Obviously, the spread of grades for class A is greater than that for class B. While the mean score fails to tell the whole story, the measures of dispersion (e.g., variance) adds clarity to the description of the spread of the data. Variance by itself, however, does not necessarily give the readers a lot of usable information. Variance is related to another very import measure of dispersion: standard deviation, which is a more versatile statistic.

$$\sigma^2 = \frac{\sum (X - \mu)^2}{N}$$

Standard deviation (σ) is also a measure of the dispersion of data around the mean in the original score units. It is the square root of the variance. It shows how tightly or spread out the data are around the mean. It is the square root of the variance. The larger the standard deviation, the greater the spread of scores around the mean.

The standard deviation of a probability distribution allows the researchers to take advantage of inferential statistics to make prediction and generalization. The probability distribution will be discussed further under normal distribution in Chapter 13. However, as a preview here, the normal distribution has some predictable statistical characteristics. Sometimes, the bell curve is more pointed, sometimes flatter, sometimes narrower, and sometimes very wide. Most importantly, it has a bell shape. It is normal for scores to deviate around the mean in a predetermined or standardized manner. That standardized manner of the scores away from the mean score is called the standard deviation. It is an expected deviation.

Formula for standard deviation

$$\sigma = \sqrt{\frac{\sum (X - \bar{X})^2}{N}} \; ,$$

where
  Σ = Sum,
  x = A particular score,
  μ = Mean of the population (mu),
  N = Number of scores.

The following shows how variance and standard deviation are calculated and how they are related. Formulas for calculating the mean, variance, and standard deviation are listed and illustrated. Say you have five houses (N) that are built around the town center. Measuring their direct (aerial) distance from city hall at the town center in miles are 10, 8, 6, 4, and 2. Because the mean ($\bar{X}$) is six, the sum of the "difference from the mean" is zero (the very nature of the mean). However, if we square the "difference from the mean," we will have a score of 40 instead of zero. From there we are able to calculate the variance and the standard deviation.

X	X − X̄	(X − X̄)²	(X − X̄)²
10	10 − 6 = 4	4²	16
8	8 − 6 = 2	2²	4
6	6 − 6 = 0	0²	0
4	4 − 6 = −2	−2²	4
(N = 5) 2	2 − 6 = −4	−4²	16
Σx 30	0		40

- Mean $(\mu \text{ or } \overline{X}) = \dfrac{\sum X}{N} = \dfrac{10 + 8 + 6 + 4 + 2}{5} = \dfrac{30}{5} = 6$

- Variance (Population) $(\sigma^2) = \dfrac{\sum (X - \overline{X})^2}{N} = \dfrac{\text{Sum of Square}}{N} = \dfrac{40}{5} = 8$

- Variance (Sample) $(\sigma^2) = \dfrac{\sum (X - \overline{X})^2}{N-1}$

- Standard Deviation (Population) $(\sigma) = \sqrt{\dfrac{\sum (X - \overline{X})^2}{N}}$

  Sum of square (difference)

  Sum of difference

  $= \sqrt{\dfrac{40}{5}} = \sqrt{8} = 2.83$

- Standard Deviation (Sample) (S.D.) $= \sqrt{\dfrac{\sum (X - \overline{X})^2}{N-1}}$

Why squared and unsquared? Let's try to explain this from a nonstatistical perspective. These houses (scores) are not built along a straight line from the town center (the central value, mean) but are scattered around in the general area. There are no roads that are straight and directly connect these houses to the town center. Like any street roads, they curve, loop, turn, and are built following the landscape. At the end, while the direct distance between a house and the town center is 4 miles, the driver may have to drive around and cover an expanse of area for 10 square miles to arrive at the town center. In some ways, the variance takes into the consideration of the whole area (square) instead of just a straight line between two points. Besides, when the sum of differences equals zero, there is not much one can do with a zero and further analysis is very limited. Squaring the "dispersion from the mean" may seem to be a fine idea! As the variance allows the researchers to capture the dispersion by area (square), there is also a need to narrow down the differences to a number that is somewhat along the straight line while reflecting the area covered. That number along the straight line will be the standard deviation, and its relationships with the normal curve will be discussed in the next chapter.

CONCLUSION

This chapter described the basics of descriptive statistics. It included the three main categories: presentation of data, measures of central tendency, and measures of dispersion. The concepts of standard deviation and variance are the jumping-off points for students to segue from descriptive statistics into inferential statistics.

Inferential Statistics

13 NORMAL DISTRIBUTION AND Z STATISTICS

As researchers move up from using descriptive statistics to describe the data to using inferential statistics to make predictions, they need a common standard or a system of reference for such projections. This chapter discusses such a standard called a normal distribution, along with its formulation, properties, and utilities. The associated Z statistics will also be explained. Key concepts that are fundamental to the understanding and use of inferential statistics will be discussed.

THE NORMAL DISTRIBUTION

A normal distribution is also known as a normal curve or a bell curve because this shape is normally or naturally found in nature through science and it resembles a bell. If a thousand grains of sand were dropped one after another to the bottom of an hourglass, the shape would "normally" look like a pyramid with rounded corners. See Figure 13.1 and note that it has a bell shape. Most of the grains of sand are in the middle of the bell and some have rolled off to either side. Significantly, the sand has done so in a very predictable or regular manner-so much so that scientists have decided this shape is "normal."

This happens predictably and not just with sand. Most people are of average or near-average intelligence, some are intellectually challenged, and some are geniuses. Everyone is represented by a grain of sand in this diagram. Similarly, most people are of average driving ability while others are poor drivers or good drivers. Even fewer are of exceptional driving ability but others on another extreme are so bad their licenses

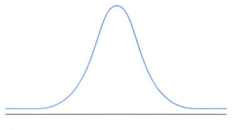

Figure 13.1. A Normal Curve

should be suspended. While many people feel that other drivers around them are bad drivers, they are actually few in number and that number is predictable because the curve has a known, constant distribution—normal.

A normal distribution contains the probability distributions of a continuous random variable. A continuous random variable has values that result from a random phenomenon. These values are continuous because they could be any possible value. For example, a person's height can be 45.25 inches, 45.25678 inches, 63.21 inches, or whatever number. A continuous random variable could have any values, but a discrete random variable could only have certain values. For example, the number of children in a family are discrete and could only be 1, 2, 3, etc., but not 1.25. Because of the normal distributions' properties of approximating many natural phenomena, it is often used as a frame of reference or a common standard in understanding, describing, comparing, and making predictions for probability related problems. The total area under the normal distribution is "one," as it includes all the probabilities for a random variable. It is under this roof and within this family that everything happens, from mundane to extraordinary on both extremes, and from expected to surprising.

If the life of light bulbs is the variable, then the normal curve would include the possible lengths of life of all light bulbs. The keys for the researchers to unlock this light bulb length of life "universe" are *the mean (μ) and standard deviation (σ or SD)* (i.e., the average and the distribution of scores away from the mean) of the normal distribution. Once they have these two crucial parameters (i.e., a quantity or a quantifiable characteristic of the statistical population), researchers could use them to estimate or infer the probability of the length of life of the light bulb population and the light bulb samples that they have on hand. For example, if the average life of a light bulb is 1,000 hours and the standard deviation is 150 hours, the researchers can reasonably predict the likelihood of having a light bulb that lasts for 1,300 or whatever hours.

The U.S. Social Security Administration, based on historical statistics, compiles actuarial life tables that estimate the average life expectances of people of different ages and backgrounds. This information can be used for retirement planning and social security benefit calculations. Life insurance companies use this information to develop mathematical models to estimate the risks and, therefore, the insurance rates. After all, under this normal curve of life expectances, the mortality rate equals one, and we all will reach our ultimate age and pass on. Until then, the probability or

Conceptual and Practical Research and Statistics for Social Workers

likelihood of each of us living to a certain age can be estimated or predicted. Literally speaking, you can bet your life on a normal curve!

NORMAL DISTRIBUTION AND STANDARD NORMAL DISTRIBUTION

The normal curve is a mathematical equation that models reality. It is also called Gaussian distribution (named after mathematician Karl Friedrich Gauss) or, in its specific form, a standard normal distribution. Its properties are constant, notably articulated by its standard deviations. It is useful for researchers for its ability to test and to demonstrate the relationships among samples and particularly between samples and the population through the use of inference.

Normal distributions are a family of probability distributions, and they do not have the same means and standard deviations (see Figure 13.2). It is therefore difficult to compare across different normal distributions. Statisticians decided to convert the normal distribution units into standardized deviation units by using the Z transformation (see the z formula next and Figure 13.3).

$$Z = \frac{x - \mu}{\alpha}$$

This produces a particular type of normal distribution which is called standard normal distribution that has *a mean of zero ($\mu = 0$) and a standard deviation of one ($\sigma = 1$)*. Essentially, a standard normal distribution is a normal distribution standardized by the Z transformation. This allows different normal distributions to

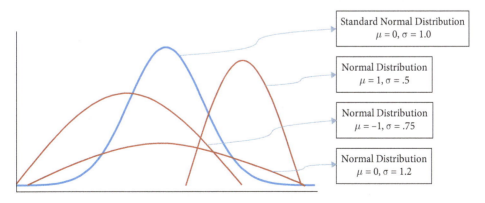

Figure 13.2. Normal Distributions With Different Mean and Standard Distributions

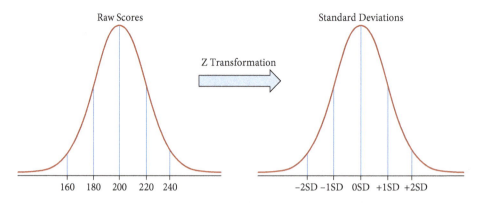

Figure 13.3. Standardizing a Normal Distribution to a Standardized Normal Distribution

be understood within a common distribution for comparisons and making inferences. This is roughly similar to adopting the metric system of measurement for transnational use and communication or using a common language for meaningful exchanges among people with different linguistic backgrounds.

NORMALITY AND CENTRAL LIMIT THEOREM

A normal distribution is a probability distribution of values in a symmetrical fashion with most values gathered around the mean, fewer values at both tails, and half of the values on each side. Again, the dropping of grains of sand that forms a bell-shaped curve in an hourglass illustrates the formulation of the normal distribution. The word "normal" itself suggests that these distributions are more typical. But as we will see, not everything is normally distributed.

Non-normal Distribution

While the distribution of samples of many naturally occurring phenomena would produce a normal distribution; there are still situations in which the population distribution is non-normal. The distributions may be affected or skewed by extreme cases or outliers. They may be bimodal or multimode in that they have more than one peak. Insufficient data could also contribute to the non-normal distribution. Take school grades as an example. Most of the grades are scattered in grades A, B, or C, and then a smaller number of them are in D and F. If school grades are normally distributed, there will be many more students who will receive grades D and F. Income

Conceptual and Practical Research and Statistics for Social Workers

is another example that features disparity and unequal distributions with the high numbers clustered on both ends representing the high numbers of the very poor and the very rich (U.S. Census Bureau, 2016). Unique requirements for inclusion into the population also produces a non-normal distribution. Mandatory draft age of 18 in certain countries makes the age distribution of military personnel more heavily represented by the young 18- and 19-year-old new recruits.

Central Limit Theorem

Among the many ways that non-normal distributions could be transformed to resemble a normal distribution is the use of the central limit theorem (CLT). CLT states that if sufficiently large samples are drawn randomly with replacement from the population then the distribution of the sample means will be approximately normally distributed and they will be very close to the population mean (Central Limit Theorem, n.d.; Paret & Martz, 2009) (Figure 13.4). This transformation allows a large enough sample from a population that is skewed or not normally distributed, such as income or school grades, to use the more precise and higher statistical power parametric statistics for analysis.

- In other words, as the sample size increases, the sampling distribution of the means of sufficiently large size samples (i.e., 30 or more) will approach normality, regardless of the shape (i.e., normal or non-normal distribution) of the data set from which the samples are drawn.

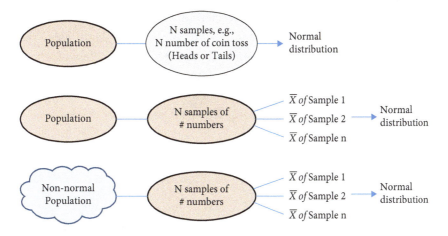

Figure 13.4. Central Limit Theorem and Normal Distribution

- The number of 30 is a result of many lengthy Monte Carlo simulations that determine n = 30 is sufficient to achieve a "normal approximation" and to have a "normal-like" distribution.
- As a result, statistics associated with normal curve distribution could be applied.

For example, a group of child welfare social work researchers want to know the average length of stay in foster care. They could collect the length of stay for all children in foster care dating back to the beginning of the child welfare system. Theoretically, most of the cases would cluster nearby the average (mean) length of stay and the rest of them would scatter around stretching to both ends. The distributions would resemble a normal curve. Unfortunately and obviously, this task is way too extensive and not feasible. The researchers then elect to only study the current cases and conduct the following activities.

- They decide to sample many randomly selected small groups (e.g., 10 children in each group). They calculate the mean length of stay for each group and find the *distributions of these means somewhat resemble the normal distribution*. The data are somewhat more spread out and the curve is more flat and wide (i.e., leptokurtic).
- As the size (i.e., sample size) of the sampled groups increases (e.g., 100 in each group), the distribution of the means more and more closely resembles "normal," and the shape of the curve becomes more compact and narrow (i.e., platykurtic).
- They realize that the outcome of the distribution of the sample means resembles the hypothetical population means distribution. This happens even when the sampled groups' original distributions are not normally distributed. The averages (mean, $\bar{X}$) of n samples is normally distributed, regardless of whether the original distribution of the n samples is normal or not.
- In other words, researchers could still take advantage of the utilities of normal curve distributions to test their ideas for variables that do not follow the normal distribution.

PROPERTIES OF NORMAL DISTRIBUTIONS

There are many different normal distributions. They all have two key parameters, the mean (μ or $\bar{X}$) and the standard deviation (σ or SD). The simplest normal distribution

Conceptual and Practical Research and Statistics for Social Workers

where the mean equals zero and a standard deviation of 1—i.e., ($\mu = 0$, $\sigma = 1$)—is known as the *standard normal distribution*. This is the base for the application of a statistical method called z-test (see z transformation and z statistics).

Nonetheless, all normal distributions adhere to the following rules:

1. Because the shape of the curve (bell shaped) is NORMAL (or STANDARDIZED), the area under the curve is predetermined. That is to say that the two dimensions of each area (height and width) are described or represented by the curve.
2. The base of a normal curve distribution can be divided into six equal segments that cover about 99.7% of all the variations that exist for that variable.
3. Each of the segments equals exactly one standard deviation (1σ).
4. The empirical rule, which is also known as the 68–95–99.7 rule or the three-sigma rule, reflects how the variations or values lie under different standard deviations.

In Figure 13.5, 34.13% of all scores of a data set are under the curve from zero to +1SD. From +1SD to +2SD are 13.59% of all scores, while 2.14% are between +2SD to +3SD, and 0.13% are from +3SD to beyond. In this standard normal distribution, *zero SD is also the mean, median, and mode* of the data set. The bell curve is

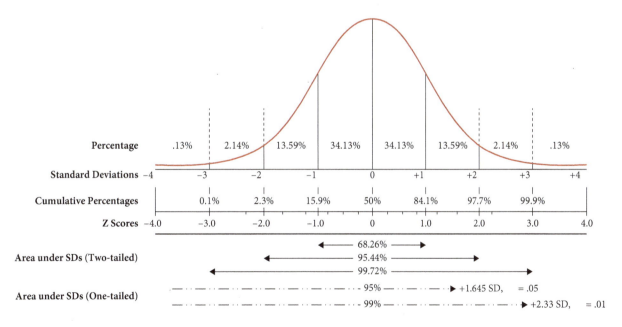

Figure 13.5. Properties of the Normal Distribution

symmetrical so all of the percentages under each section of the curve are identical on the negative side of the bell (from 0 to −3SD).

When the positive and negative standard deviation areas are combined, the following results are observed. They are also the bases for the 68–95–99.7 rule.

- Around 68% (i.e., 34.13% + 34.13% = 68.26%) of all data are between −1SD and +1SD.
- Around 95% (i.e., 13.59% + 34.13% + 34.13% + 13.59% = 95.44%) of all data are between −2SD and +2SD.
- Around 99.7% (i.e., 2.14% + 13.59% + 34.13% + 34.13% + 13.59% + 2.14% = 99.72%) of all scores are between −3SD and +3SD.

Because of these combined values, most researchers use approximately plus or minus two standard deviations (+/−2SD) as a general cutoff point for what is considered normal or typical for roughly 95% of all data (95.44% to be exact!) falls within that boundary. Approximately 5% (i.e., .05) (100% − 95.44% = 4.56% to be exact!) will fall outside of that +/−2SD boundary. The combined probability of data being beyond the barrier (left or right) for "being normal" is .05 or 5%.

In hypothesis testing, the exact values are used. For a one-tailed test, 1.645 SD covers 95% of the areas from one end of the curve, whereas 2.33 SD covers 99% of the areas (see Figure 13.5).

Normal Distribution and Intelligence Abilities

Scientists use the bell-shaped curve to determine cutoff scores for intelligence abilities (i.e., IQ). See Figure 13.6.

- As the mean is standardized at 100 with a standard deviation of 15, people of average intelligence would have scores between 85 and 115 (−1SD to +1SD). That is about 68%, the majority of the population.
- Scores between 70 and 85 (−1SD to −2SD) are considered low average (13.59% of the population).
- Scores at or below 70 (below−2SD) are classified as having an intellectual disability (2.27% of the population).
- Scores between 115 and 130 (+1SD to +2SD) are considered high or above average (13.59% of the population).

Conceptual and Practical Research and Statistics for Social Workers

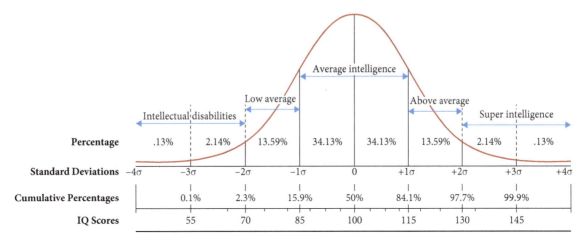

Percentage	.13%	2.14%	13.59%	34.13%	34.13%	13.59%	2.14%	.13%
Standard Deviations	-4σ	-3σ	-2σ	-1σ	0	$+1\sigma$	$+2\sigma$	$+3\sigma$	$+4\sigma$
Cumulative Percentages		0.1%	2.3%	15.9%	50%	84.1%	97.7%	99.9%
IQ Scores		55	70	85	100	115	130	145

Figure 13.6. IQ Scores and the Normal Distribution

- Genius or super intelligence is usually measured at or above +2SD, which is around 130–145 and above, encompassing the upper 2.27% of the population.

Many measures, besides intelligence, are standardized, which allows comparisons between various groups and/or observations at various times. For example, standardized tests for education, such as the ACT, SAT, GRE, and others, allow colleges to choose between students from different high schools, in different school districts, over the years. If the president of a university wants to increase the diversity of the student body, he/she could adjust the different standardized measures such as ACT, family incomes, and others to identify and attract qualified and diverse applicants. Many other fields use standardized scores. Medicine has standardized its laboratory values. For example, hemoglobin (the measure of the blood's oxygen-carrying ability) has a healthy range of 14–18 gm/100 ml for adult males and 12–16 gm100/ml for adult females. Variations from these values may be indicative of out of the ordinary or normal range.

UNDERSTANDING Z STATISTICS

Using the z-score transformation, normal distributions are converted into the *standard normal distribution*. Data values of a normal distribution are therefore standardized into z-scores or standard scores. This z-score represents how far the data value is away from the mean measured by the unit of standard deviation. In other words, it shows the position of the data value in relation to the mean by the number of standard deviations. The z-score is in effect a horizontal scale for the standard normal distribution.

As with the three-sigma or empirical rule (68%–95%–99.7%) discussed earlier, z-scores or standard scores reflect the corresponding area percentages on the standard normal distribution (see Figure 13.5). The area percentages are also called proportions or probabilities. Z-scores range mostly from −3.4 to +3.4 and with 0 (zero) situated at the mean of the distribution. A negative z-score indicates that it is located at the left side of the mean, and a positive z-score is at the right side of the mean. To find out exactly what area percentages of the z-scores represent, researchers have to use the z-score table (see Table 13.1). Readers should note that the z table only reflects half of the areas under the normal distribution. Researchers need to include the "missing" half (i.e., adding 50%) to the area percentage from the table to reach the final area percentage. However, if researchers and students are using statistical software programs for analysis, they will find the exact area percentages are provided in the statistical printouts.

Thora is a clinical social worker in a mental health clinic. Two potential clients came to the agency on the same day requesting immediate service. Both of them are from out of state and both had been tested for anxiety disorder but with different tools. Thora had a problem because she only had one opening. She had to choose the more severely affected one for immediate service and the less severely affected one would have to wait for the next available clinician. She asked both potential clients—Susan and Tom—for their prior assessment test results. Susan had a score of 78 from Anxiety Scale A and Tom had a score of 66 from Anxiety Scale B. Thora was familiar with both tests and was able to locate the means and standard deviations for both tests. She used the raw scores, means, and standard deviations and applied the z-score formula to calculate the z-scores for Susan and Tom.

$$Z = \frac{\text{Raw Score} - \text{Mean}}{\text{Standard Deviation}} \quad \text{or} \quad Z = \frac{X - \bar{X}}{\text{S.D.}}$$

Table 13.2 displays the information of Thora's calculations and the results. Susan's raw score (78) is higher than Tom's raw score (66). After standardizing, Susan's z-score (.80) shows that her corresponding area percentage is at the 78.81 percentile, while Tom's z-score (1.33) is at the 90.82 percentile. That means Susan's anxiety level is higher than 78.81% of the population (the general public), but Tom's anxiety level is higher than 90.82% of the population. In other words, Tom has the higher level of anxiety and is more in need of immediate service.

TABLE 13.1. Percent of Area Between the Mean and the Z-Score Under the Standard Normal Curve

z	Percent of Area Between the Mean and the Z-Score Under the Standard Normal Curve									
	0	0.01	0.02	0.03	0.04	0.05	0.06	0.07	0.08	0.09
0	0.00%	0.40%	0.80%	1.20%	1.60%	1.99%	2.39%	2.79%	3.19%	3.59%
0.1	3.98%	4.38%	4.78%	5.17%	5.57%	5.96%	6.36%	6.75%	7.14%	7.53%
0.2	7.93%	8.32%	8.71%	9.10%	9.48%	9.87%	10.26%	10.64%	11.03%	11.41%
0.3	11.79%	12.17%	12.55%	12.93%	13.31%	13.68%	14.06%	14.43%	14.80%	15.17%
0.4	15.54%	15.91%	16.28%	16.64%	17.00%	17.36%	17.72%	18.08%	18.44%	18.79%
0.5	19.15%	19.50%	19.85%	20.19%	20.54%	20.88%	21.23%	21.57%	21.90%	22.24%
0.6	22.57%	22.91%	23.24%	23.57%	23.89%	24.22%	24.54%	24.86%	25.18%	25.49%
0.7	25.80%	26.12%	26.42%	26.73%	27.04%	27.34%	27.64%	27.94%	28.23%	28.52%
0.8	28.81%	29.10%	29.39%	29.67%	29.95%	30.23%	30.51%	30.78%	31.06%	31.33%
0.9	31.59%	31.86%	32.12%	32.38%	32.64%	32.89%	33.15%	33.40%	33.65%	33.89%
1	34.13%	34.38%	34.61%	34.85%	35.08%	35.31%	35.54%	35.77%	35.99%	36.21%
1.1	36.43%	36.65%	36.86%	37.08%	37.29%	37.49%	37.70%	37.90%	38.10%	38.30%
1.2	38.49%	38.69%	38.88%	39.07%	39.25%	39.44%	39.62%	39.80%	39.97%	40.15%
1.3	40.32%	40.49%	40.66%	40.82%	40.99%	41.15%	41.31%	41.47%	41.62%	41.77%
1.4	41.92%	42.07%	42.22%	42.36%	42.51%	42.65%	42.79%	42.92%	43.06%	43.19%
1.5	43.32%	43.45%	43.57%	43.70%	43.82%	43.94%	44.06%	44.18%	44.29%	44.41%
1.6	44.52%	44.63%	44.74%	44.84%	44.95%	45.05%	45.15%	45.25%	45.35%	45.45%
1.7	45.54%	45.64%	45.73%	45.82%	45.91%	45.99%	46.08%	46.16%	46.25%	46.33%
1.8	46.41%	46.49%	46.56%	46.64%	46.71%	46.78%	46.86%	46.93%	46.99%	47.06%
1.9	47.13%	47.19%	47.26%	47.32%	47.38%	47.44%	47.50%	47.56%	47.61%	47.67%
2	47.72%	47.78%	47.83%	47.88%	47.93%	47.98%	48.03%	48.08%	48.12%	48.17%
2.1	48.21%	48.26%	48.30%	48.34%	48.38%	48.42%	48.46%	48.50%	48.54%	48.57%
2.2	48.61%	48.64%	48.68%	48.71%	48.75%	48.78%	48.81%	48.84%	48.87%	48.90%
2.3	48.93%	48.96%	48.98%	49.01%	49.04%	49.06%	49.09%	49.11%	49.13%	49.16%
2.4	49.18%	49.20%	49.22%	49.25%	49.27%	49.29%	49.31%	49.32%	49.34%	49.36%
2.5	49.38%	49.40%	49.41%	49.43%	49.45%	49.46%	49.48%	49.49%	49.51%	49.42%
2.6	49.53%	49.55%	49.56%	49.57%	49.59%	49.60%	49.61%	49.62%	49.63%	49.64%
2.7	49.65%	49.66%	49.67%	49.68%	49.69%	49.70%	49.71%	49.72%	49.73%	49.74%
2.8	49.74%	49.75%	49.76%	49.77%	49.77%	49.78%	49.79%	49.79%	49.80%	49.81%
2.9	49.81%	49.82%	49.82%	49.83%	49.84%	49.84%	49.85%	49.85%	49.86%	49.86%
3	49.86%	49.87%	49.87%	49.88%	49.88%	49.89%	49.89%	49.89%	49.90%	49.90%

Source: Original data from Pearson, K. (Ed.). (1930). Tables for Statisticians and Biometricians, (3rd ed.). London: Cambridge University Press.

TABLE 13.2. Using the Z-Score to Compare Results From Two Different Scales

	ANXIETY SCALE A	ANXIETY SCALE B
	SUSAN	TOM
Raw score	78	66
Mean	70	50
SD	10	12
Z-score	78 − 70/10 = .80	66 − 50/12 = 1.33
Z table	28.1%	40.82%
	50% + 28.81% = 78.81%	50% + 40.82% = 90.82%

The z-score permits the sample scores (Susan's and Tom's scores) to find their positions in the standard normal distribution. It, therefore, allows the scores to be compared with those of the population and with each other as well as locating the area percentages, or probabilities, that they represent.

THE INTENDED AND UNINTENDED "DEVIANT OUTLAWS" AND THE "COMMONERS"

When scores come from any standardized test or any data set known to be normal, serious deviations from the norm (i.e., scores in the tails of the bell curve) are unlikely to happen. For example, if the population is repeatedly sampled (say 100 times), about 95% (95.44% to be exact) of the time those sample means will be within +/−2SD of the population mean—the commoners. Sample means that show up in the tail areas are unusual and not common ($p < .0466$ or 4.66% of the time; about 5%). The z-score is one of the statistics that can help researchers determine where the test statistic is located in relation to the population mean. It helps to determine whether it is a commoner or a deviant outlaw, which is exceptional, unusual, and rare. Z-scores can also be compared to each other in relation to the population, just like the Susan and Tom example earlier.

Independent Variable and Standard Deviation

In a situation where an independent variable (e.g., intervention, treatment, stimulus) is introduced, the resulting test statistic (score) may fall within or outside −2SD to +2SD. If it is within, that means the score is just one of the 95.46% of possible "normal" scores; it really is not that unique—the commoner. If the score falls outside the −2SD to +2SD range, then it is in one of the tails—the exceptional. Scores found in those tails are unlikely, and the researcher assumes the larger deviation from the mean is attributable to the independent variable (i.e., the change agent). Because extreme scores—the intended and unintended deviant outlaws—can be caused by the independent variable (the intentional change agent), chance (unintentional co-incident), or some other variables. Replication or controlled study designs are often necessary to establish true validity of the intervention.

In hypothesis testing that will be discussed more completely in the next chapter, researchers will use the exact measurement. They will move beyond the empirical rule approximation to the more precise measurements involving the significant level (α) and confidence level (CL). If a researcher does 100 replications of her work with-out a change agent (i.e., independent variable), the means of her work statistics will be under the bulk of the normal curve around 95 times with only about five samples/ times being in the tails because of chance. If she is to introduce an independent vari-able to invoke change, she will expect the mean of the outcomes to be very different from the normal range (i.e., 95%), and the new value will be in the tails. By using the CL, she can confidently make the claim that the independent variable has made a difference and produced the change, although there is still a 5% probability that it is due to chance (α).

Using an everyday example, an effective change agent, such as ibuprofen, is given to people who have complained of having headaches and other pains. By having received the independent change agent (i.e., ibuprofen), most people will get relief from the pain that they have experienced. People will, therefore, claim success at-tributable to the independent variable with a certain degree of confidence. The ones who do not get the relief may be the result of random chances or other confounding factors.

Desirable results are unlikely to happen without the help of the change agent. Researchers who get extreme scores are allowed to claim success attributable to the independent variable. The logic and the statistics are not complicated and can be easily obtained. It is what questions are being asked, or how they are asked, that determine how the values that fall within or outside the expected range are being interpreted or desired.

The Z-Score Formula

Again, the following is the z-score formula:

$$Z = \frac{X - \bar{X}}{\sigma} \quad \text{or} \quad Z = \frac{\text{Raw Score} - \text{Mean}}{\text{Standard Deviation}}$$

In simple English, a z-score is

$$Z = \frac{\text{This score} - \text{Normal score}}{\text{Normal range}} = \frac{\text{This study's range}}{\text{Normal range}}$$

Put it another way;

$$Z = \frac{\text{How much does the Sample Mean differ or deviate from the Population Mean}}{\text{In relation to the way the population NORMALLY deviates around its mean (i.e., its standard deviation)}}$$

Z-SCORE FOR COMPARISON AND THE EFFECT OF THE INDEPENDENT VARIABLE

Ultimately, statistics answer the question, Does this study's result deviate normally after the introduction of the independent variable? If the answer is no, the researcher concludes that the independent variable had no effect. If yes, the researcher concludes that the study is different from normal and, therefore, the independent variable of the study may have caused the difference.

While mathematically correct, *the following example is an intuitive, but not statistically accurate*, explanation of this formula. Let's say you have a job and the first thing you do on payday is to pay your bills. Normally, after the bills are paid, you have $35 left to spend. But because you work irregular hours, and your utility bills fluctuate each month, the range of money leftover is $15–$55 (i.e., $40 range). So you have an average of $35 leftover each month with a normal range of ± $20 ($55 − $35 and $35 − $15). Today, all the bills are paid, and you have $110 left. You think you're rich. But are you? Plugging in the numbers to the *intuitive* z-score formula results in the following:

$$Z = \frac{110 - 35}{55 - 15} = \frac{110 - 35}{40} = \frac{75}{40} = 1.875$$

The math shows that Z = 1.875. It is interpreted as you are doing well but not yet being rich this month, even though you are $75 ($110 − $35 = $75) to the good. For a normally distributed data set (and a z-score requires a normal distribution) the final data would have to be greater than 2SD (i.e., $\geq$ 2 SD). Therefore, to be "rich" you would need at least $115 ($35 + $40 $\times$ 2) leftover or $80 more than the normal. Rich, but just barely. Intuitively, the formula is applied and can also be viewed as follows:

$$\frac{\text{Today's amount} - \text{Typical amount}}{\text{Typical range}}$$

It reads as "today's range compared to the typical range." In this intuitive example, the range was wider but not wide enough to be significant. Is what we observed typical or atypical? If atypical, how extreme or uncharacteristic is it?

CONCLUSION

The standardized normal distribution provides the basis for statistical inferences. It is the foundation for hypothesis testing, test of correlation, and test of differences. The subsequent chapters will further discuss these key statistics for social work researchers.

14

HYPOTHESIS AND HYPOTHESIS TESTING

"Have you ever imagined a world with no hypothetical situations?" is an old saying. The fact is that people hypothesize all the time, although many do not distinguish hypothesis from assumption. Hypothesis plays an important role in research and statistical testing. As explained in Chapter 6, based on the research design and the research questions, hypotheses may take on many different forms and focuses. This chapter will deliberate step by step on how these hypotheses are being tested. Key concepts such as null hypothesis (H_0) and alternative hypothesis (H_1), one-tailed and two-tailed hypotheses, confidence level (CL) and level of significance (α), critical values (*p-value*) and statistical significance/observed critical values (*p*), as well as Type I and Type II errors will be introduced. The process that researchers use to determine whether the research data support or do not support the tested hypotheses will be explained. Hypothesis testing essentially is a statistical analysis of probability (*p*) of the test statistics in relation to a preset level of significance (α).

NULL HYPOTHESIS AND ALTERNATIVE HYPOTHESIS

A research hypothesis (Hy) is an educated hunch to be tested by the research process to give answers to the research question. It pinpoints beforehand the specific speculated relationship between variables and provides a beginning point for empirical verification. Expanding from the research hypothesis, there is the null hypothesis (H_0) and its rival alternative hypothesis (H_a or H_1). The null hypothesis is a statement that there is no relationship or no difference between the variables (i.e., between the independent variable and dependent variable in a test of difference

TABLE 14.1. Different Formats of the Null Hypothesis

1. There is no difference between A and B; A equals B; A = B, A is similar to B, A − B $\simeq$ 0.
2. There is no correlation between A and B; A is unrelated to B; Correlation is zero or minimum, A : B $\simeq$ 0.
3. There is no supported relationship between A & B. No or minimum contribution to each other.

or between the predictor variable and criterion variable/response variable in a test of correlation and regression analysis.) An alternative hypothesis, on the other hand, indicates particular or expected relationships or differences between variables. It is usually the expected study outcomes. This is the hypothesis that the researchers set out to examine in the beginning. Alternative hypotheses can be directional (one-tailed) or non-directional (two-tailed) and will be further discussed in the following sections.

A null hypothesis states that there is no correlation, no difference, or supported relationship between the variables. The null hypotheses can be presented in different formats (see Table 14.1). They are, however, specific in identifying the relationship to be tested and the variables that are involved.

From Research Questions to Hypotheses: Not So Serious and Serious Examples

A research question defines the general focus and purpose of the research. The research question is then further narrowed down or operationalized into more specific and researchable research hypotheses. If you keep losing your eyeglasses and think that, of course, it is not your fault, you have probably developed some educated guesses regarding these incidents, including that a bogeyman has stolen your eyeglasses (Null Hypothesis, 2017). You decide to conduct your own investigation (research) to find out if this hypothesis is true. To take into consideration the confounding issues, including random chances that may contaminate the findings, you set up the following research hypothesis, null hypothesis, and alternative hypothesis:

Research question	Has a bogeyman stolen my eyeglasses?
Research hypothesis	A bogeyman has stolen my eyeglasses.
Null hypothesis	A bogeyman did not steal my eyeglasses. A bogeyman has nothing to do with the disappearance of my eyeglasses.
Alternative hypothesis	A bogeyman stole my eyeglasses when I was not watching. A bogeyman stole my eyeglasses during the full moon. A bogeyman has something to do with the disappearance of my eyeglasses.

As another example, silly as it may sound, one may wonder if the proverbial Jack and Jill are the same person and put together a research study with the following hypotheses:

Research question	Are Jack and Jill the same person?
Research hypothesis	Jack and Jill are two different persons.
Null hypothesis	Jack and Jill are the same; there is no difference between Jack and Jill.
Alternative hypothesis	Jack is not Jill; Jill is not Jack; Jack and Jill are different persons.

A research-minded student, Dalek, is trying to decide whether Dr. Hu is a good teacher and if she should take a class taught by Dr. Hu. She designs a study that has the following question hypotheses:

Research question	What kind of teacher is Dr. Hu?
Research hypothesis	Dr. Hu is a good teacher.
Null hypothesis	Dr. Hu is not a good teacher. Dr. Hu is no different from other teachers. There is no evidence that supports Dr. Hu is a good teacher.
Alternative hypothesis	Dr. Hu is very likely a good teacher. Dr. Hu is a good teacher in this subject. Dr. Hu is a good teacher in all subjects. Dr. Hu is far better than other teachers. Dr. Hu demonstrates sufficient characteristics of being a good teacher.

For a more serious example: Priyanka is studying conflict management approaches between medical social workers and nurses in hospitals. She develops the following hypotheses for her study:

Research question	Do medical social workers and registered nurses manage conflicts differently in hospital settings?
Research hypothesis	Medical social workers and registered nurses manage conflicts differently.
Null hypothesis	There is no difference in conflict management approaches between medical social workers and registered nurses. Professional background is not related to conflict management approaches.
Alternative hypothesis	Medical social workers have more confidence in their ability to manage conflicts. Registered nurses encounter more conflicts in hospital settings. Registered nurses are more effective in managing conflicts.

One-Tailed and Two-Tailed Alternative Hypotheses

Researchers may be only interested in knowing whether the variables are related or if differences exist. If they are not concerned about the direction of the relationship, then they would use a two-tailed test to examine their pre-determined two-tailed hypothesis. However, when researchers have a directional hypothesis that speculates a leading relationship (e.g., positive or negative), more or less, they will employ a one-tailed test. Table 14.2 shows the differences between the two.

TABLE 14.2. One-Tailed and Two-Tailed Hypothesis and Tests

TWO-TAILED	ONE-TAILED
Only interested in whether the variables are different or related	Interested in the leading relationship between variables
No expectation or indication of direction	Direction is expected and indicated
Describes the expected outcomes	Compares the expected outcomes
$A \neq B$ ($H_a \neq H_o$)	$A >$ or $<$ than B ($H_a >$ or $<$ than H_o)
More relaxed or conservative (requires less rigorous test statistics to establish)	More certain and affirmative (requires more rigorous test statistics to establish)
Divides the alpha value (α) into halves and place each on both tails of the normal distribution.	Puts all of the alpha value (α) on one tail of the normal distribution.
(Examples)	(Examples)
Students who study have grades that are different than those who do not	Students who study have better grades than those who do not
Amount of study is related to grade	Students who study more will get better grades
Clinical case management produces different treatment outcomes than the other approaches	Clinical case management produces better treatment outcomes than other approaches
Social connectedness is correlated to the presence of suicidal ideation	Social connectedness is negatively correlated to the presence of suicidal ideation
Family support is associated with older adults' abilities to stay in their own homes	Family support increases the likelihood of older adults' abilities to stay in their own homes longer

To explain the difference, imagine that someone asks you for your opinion of his or her new friend. Your two-tailed responses could be "Well, he is a character!" "She certainly is different!" "He reminds me of someone I know." "I could connect with her." However, your statements only describe your perceptions. It will need additional prompting to find out whether you like or dislike the new friend.

Conceptual and Practical Research and Statistics for Social Workers

However, you might tell your opinions about this new friend with conviction in one-tailed responses: "He is head and shoulders better than the rest!" "She is amazing! I am impressed!" Of course, there could also be other honest and direct responses, such as "The person is a dud!" "He is bad news! He scares me!"

Figures 14.1 shows a two-tailed test distribution, where α = .05 splits it between both ends of the distribution with α = .025 on each side. Figure 14.2 shows a one-tailed test distribution with α = .05 on the right side of the distribution, indicating a positive direction predicted. Figure 14.3 shows a one-tailed test distribution with p = .05 on the left side of the distribution, indicating a negative direction predicted.

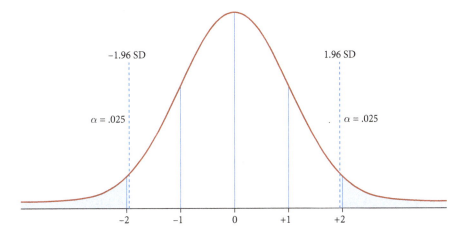

Figure 14.1. Two-Tailed Test Distribution With α = .05

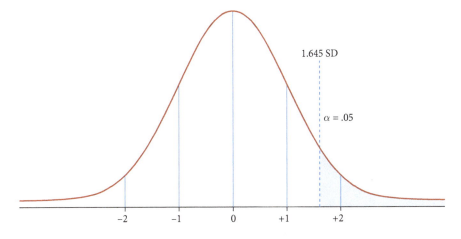

Figure 14.2. One-Tailed Test Distribution With α = .05, Positive Direction Predicted

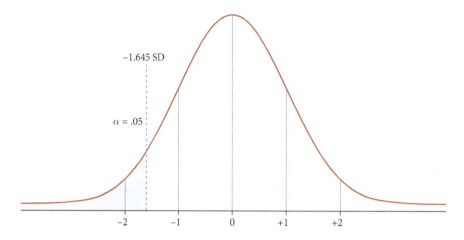

Figure 14.3. One-Tailed Test Distribution With α = .05, Negative Direction Predicted

TEST OF SIGNIFICANCE AND HYPOTHESIS TESTING

In hypothesis testing using tests of significance, the two important numbers are probability value (*p*-value) and level of significance (α). The values for both range from zero to one (Taylor, 2017). Through the comparison of these two numbers, researchers can determine whether to reject or fail to reject the null hypothesis. To understand this process, several key concepts need to be understood: confidence interval (CI), significance level (α), and probability value (*p*).

Confidence Interval (CI) and Level of Confidence (CL)

When drawing random samples from the population or having a large number of random samples, researchers wonder how much their samples approximate the population. One way to do this approximation is the use of the distribution of the sample means. A Confidence Interval (CI) is an estimated range of sample mean values (parameter) that is likely to contain the population mean. How likely is the true value of the population included in this range of values?

A student expects his course grade will be somewhere between B (85 points) and A (93 points). This is his CI because he estimates somewhere between 85 points and 93 points lies the mean course grade. As an average student, he believes his grade will be very close to the course average. How confident is he? If he is 95% confident, his CI would be +/−1.96 SD of the course grades distribution; that also means that there is a

5% chance that he is wrong. If he is only 90% confident, then his CI will be $+/-1.645$ SD, and his chance of being wrong rises to 10%. The percent of confidence (i.e., 90%, 95%) is the Level of Confidence (CL).

The CI is presented as the actual numerical interval, e.g., $+/-2$ SD, but the CL is presented as a percentage (e.g., 95%). The CI of $+/-1.96$ SD reflects a CL at 95%. The CI of $+/-1.96$ SD covers 95% of the normal distribution. In other words, researchers are 95% certain (level of confidence of 95%) that the values of the samples that possess the characteristics (parameter) of the population can be found within this confidence interval.

Significance Level (Level of Significance): α Value

The significance level (α) is the bottom-line probability number for researchers to determine whether the test statistics are significant. **Researchers set the alpha value before conducting any statistical tests**. The significance level reflects the researchers' standard in rejecting or not rejecting the study's null hypothesis. It is also the probability that the researchers will commit a Type I error of making an erroneous decision of saying "yes" when the answer is "no."

The significance level (α) is the opposite of the CL ($1 - α = CL$). Having a significance level (α) of .05 means having a CL of 95%. The researchers are 95% confident that the statistics is significant but there is a 5% chance that they could make an error. The significance level and CL are compliments to each other. Each looks at the same standard from a different perspective. If your boss has 95% confidence in you that also means there is a 5% chance that she could be wrong (which is significant!). This particular point or value (i.e., 5% or .05) that the CL and significance level meet is the critical value (p), which will be discussed immediately in the following section.

The alpha value of .05 (α =.05) is a commonly accepted standard, but it is not the only standard. For nonexperimental general studies such as a survey or program evaluation, a 90% CL or an alpha of .10 can be acceptable. On the other hand, experimental or more rigorous studies will need an alpha of .05 or .01 (α = .05 or α = .01). Situations that are more serious, such as using the service of an anesthesiologist or testing a new medical treatment, demand a higher CL. We strive to minimize the chance of making the wrong decision. In choosing an anesthesiologist, you probably want to have one who has an alpha of .00000000000000001 or even smaller, if you do not want to risk not waking up after surgery or feeling the surgery while it is in action!

CRITICAL VALUE AND PROBABILITY VALUE: THE P-VALUE

A critical value (*p-value*) is the point on the normal distribution for the chosen level of significance. Associated with the researcher preset alpha value (α), the critical value marks the cutoff point for hypothesis testing. When researchers set the significance level at .05 or the CL at 95%, they also set the critical value (*p*) at .05. It is a point on the scale of the test statistics probability that becomes the bar separating the significant and the not significant.

The observed critical value (observed/calculated *p-value*) is a probability value that shows the probability of the test statistics happening. This calculated probability value reflects the likelihood that the occurrence of the test result is due to random chance or something else (e.g., independent variable). When the observed/calculated *p*-value (i.e., the test statistics' *p-value*) is smaller than the critical value (*p*) or the significance level (α) value, the researcher will reject the null hypothesis. However, when the observed p-value is greater than the critical value, the researcher will fail to reject (i.e., not reject) and retain the null hypothesis. Figure 14.4 below shows the relationships among α value, *p* value, and observed/calculated *p* value in hypothesis testing.

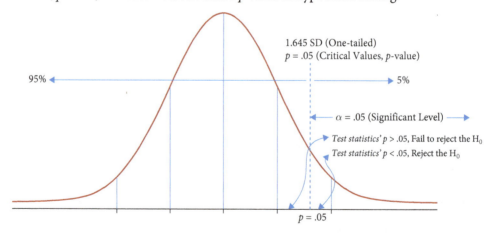

Figure 14.4. Hypothesis Testing, *p*-Value, α Value, and Test Statistics *p*-Value

STATISTICAL SIGNIFICANCE: *P*

"Significance is a statistical term that tells how sure you are that a difference or relationship exists" (StatPac, 2017, para 5). Statistically significant is the statistical

Conceptual and Practical Research and Statistics for Social Workers

BOX 14.1. HYPOTHESIS TESTING GETS A TEMPERATURE

The website WebMD (n.d.) reports that a normal body temperature for an adult is 98.2°F *(population mean)* but it could range between 97°F to 99°F *(CI)*. Age, activities, sex, health conditions, and many other factors contribute to different body temperature readings *(sample means)*. However, when a person's body temperature reaches 100.4°F *(critical value)* that would technically be considered as having a fever. The persons would start not feeling well and experience unpleasant symptoms that notably bother them *(significance level, α = .10)*. Some would try to shake it off on their own because it is not that serious *(null hypothesis)*. When they have a temperature of 103°F for more than 3 days *(higher significance level, α = .05 or .01)*; sore throat, vomiting, headache, and body pain have finally convinced the person that this is not just another day *(reject the null hypothesis)*; the person is sick *(alternative hypothesis)*. The occurrence of these troubling symptoms and high body temperature are just not normal and are so extreme *(probability value, p)* that it is something significant *(p < α)*. They are certain that this is not a random happening; something *(independent variable)* must be causing the problem. Maybe it is related to that delicious dinner at the local greasy spoon or the cold and rainy weather in recent days. Calling the doctor is certainly in order.

outcome because of something other than random chance or it is unlikely due to chance. That something else could be the independent variable(s) or just the very nature of the test variable. Statistical significance is the observed *p*-value or test statistics' *p*-value.

REJECT OR NOT TO REJECT: THAT IS THE QUESTION

To test whether a statistical test result is significant, researchers compare the test statistics' p-value against the preset α value.

a. If the test statistics' p-value is smaller than the alpha (i.e., p < α), researchers reject the null hypothesis (i.e., reject no relationship or no difference) and that they would entertain or consider the alternative hypothesis which indicates that there is a statistically significant difference or correlation.

b. If the test statistics' p-value is greater than the alpha value (i.e., p > α), researchers would say they fail to reject the null hypothesis (i.e., cannot support the idea that there is no relationship or difference) and they would retain the null hypothesis which says there is no difference or correlation.

TABLE 14.3. Reject or Fail to Reject the Null Hypothesis

IF ...	THEN ...	CONCLUSION
P < α	Reject the null hypothesis Entertain or adopt the alternative hypothesis	That there is a statistically significant difference or correlation
p > α	Fail to reject the null hypothesis Retain the null hypothesis	There is no difference or correlation

Presenting the p-Value: =, <, or >?

In presenting the statistical findings, some researchers would present the p-value as it is (e.g., p = .0123). Others would present the p-value in a way that reflects the conclusion (e.g., p < .05 or p < .05). In the case of p < .05, the researcher is saying the actual test statistics' p-value is smaller than .05. The researcher is also saying that anything that is <.05 is considered as significant. Alternatively, p > .05 means the researcher uses .05 as the cutoff point (i.e., critical value) for significance and the statistics observed is greater than .05 and the statistical finding is not significant. You may say that you have more than 95% (p < .05) confidence that you will pass a statistics class. Of course, you can also say that you have exactly 98.75% (p = .0125) confidence. Nonetheless, the p < .05 description already reflects your observed or calculated p-value is smaller than .05; although, it is not clearly written out.

TYPE I ERROR (α) AND TYPE II ERROR (β)

In setting the α values (significance level), researchers are declaring how much Type I error (risk) they are willing to take or how much confidence they have regarding their assertion whether there is a difference or there is a relationship. In other words, alpha (α) is the probability or likelihood of making a Type I error. Type I error is the error of a false positive. The p < .10 means researchers are correct (say yes to yes) 90% time (90/100) and the chance (probability) that researchers are wrong (having different results because of probability) is 10% (10/100). Type I error is when the researchers reject the null hypothesis but, in fact, the null is true. It is the error of saying yes to no. It is like the mistake of accepting a lousy job offer but turning down a wonderful job opportunity. The symbol for Type I error is also α—the same symbol as the significance level. Confusing huh?!

Then, what is Type II? Type II error is saying no to yes, a false negative. It is the probability of failing to reject the null hypothesis (not saying no to no relationship). Therefore treating the null hypothesis as true (thinking there is no relationship), but, in fact, the null hypothesis is false (it is incorrect to say there is no relationship) and the alternative hypothesis is true (because, in fact, there is a relationship). Researchers claim that there is no relationship, but there is one. One thinks this new job is not a good one, but, in fact, it is a wonderful one. The symbol for Type II error is β.

Type I and Type II errors cannot be avoided completely, but they can be minimized by increasing the sampling size and curtailing researchers or instruments bias (Banerjee, Chitnis, Jadhav, Bhawalkar, & Chaudhury, 2009). While there is a dilemma, in most situations, researchers chose to focus on minimizing the Type I error which has more serious consequences than the Type II error.

Type I Error and Type II Error Go to Court

The court proceeding of "proof beyond a reasonable doubt" is commonly used to illustrate the difference of type I and Type II error. Expanding from one such example (Rogers, 2006), Table 14.4 illustrates the hypothesis testing process, the Type I and Type II errors, and other related statistical concepts.

The Choice of Type I and Type II Errors

Table 14.5 explains the difference between Type I and Type II errors. Researchers have to decide which error they want to minimize.

The following is a commonly used example that explains Type I error and Type II error. Errors arise whenever the result of the measurement is different form the reality or the truth. A false positive (Type I error) or false negative (Type II error) cannot be completely avoided but can be minimized.

Type I error
(false positive)

Type II error
(false negative)

TABLE 14.4. Hypothesis Testing Goes to Court

The Problem/ Hypothesis	The reasons or suspension that got the person arrested and being sent to court.
	It is believed that the person is related to the problem.
The Null Hypothesis	The person is innocent and has nothing to do with the problem.
	When the problem arose, it was just a regular day for the person, nothing out of ordinary happened.
	The person has nothing to do with the problem.
The Alternative Hypothesis	The rivals of the null hypothesis.
	If the null hypothesis said you are not Californian, then the alternatives could be Alabamian, New Yorker, Minnesotan, or Hawaiians, etc.
	However, in consideration of the reason (the problem) of why we are in this discussion, the alternative hypothesis (or hypotheses) should be closely tied to the research hypothesis that researchers set out to prove in the first place. At time, it is the same but more specific to the research hypothesis (i.e., the person is related to the problem; the person is guilty as charged).
P-value, and α	P-value—The evidence against the laws, the courts, or society standards.
	α-Reasonable doubt. Maximum possibility that what happened was totally coincidental or random and has nothing to do with the person.
	To reject the null hypothesis—The person is not "not guilty"; the court needs to judge the person based on the evidence and its set standards (p values). It has to prove beyond a reasonable doubt that the test statistics' p-value (i.e., evidence) has to be = or < than the α.
Parametric and Non-Parametric and Statistics	The CSI—The evidence and the source of evidence.
	Nonparametric-personal accounts
	Parametric-preponderance of evidence, enough individual accounts, or specific scientific evidence that rule in/out of probability (e.g., DNA).
	Statistics is the tool used to summarize, differentiate, and correlate the data so that you can make your case.
Type I Error	Make an error and convict the innocent. Say yes to no. The α!
	The Innocence Project tries to correct this error by exonerating the wrongly convicted.
Type II Error	Let the guilty person go free. The β. Say no to yes. Hmm … the hand-glove does not fit.

All in all, choices between the two evils, researchers and the court systems prefer to avoid or minimize Type I error to Type II error. The legal system would rather let a guilty person go free (Type II error) than to convict an innocent person (Type I error) (take Type II error over Type I error). Clinical practice researchers would avoid making claim on the success of an intervention when, in fact, the result is inconclusive (Type I error), while they may mistakenly let a successful intervention slip away (Type II error) (take Type II error over Type I error). There are situations

Conceptual and Practical Research and Statistics for Social Workers

TABLE 14.5. Type I or Type II Error, Pick Your Poison!

TYPE I ERROR (α)	TYPE II ERROR (β)
Reject the null hypothesis (there is a relationship) when it is actually true (there is no relationship)	Fail to reject the null hypothesis (there is no relationship) when it is actually false (there is a relationship)
Falsely reject the null hypothesis	Falsely retain the null hypothesis
Saying no to there is no relationship (implies there is a relationship (yes) but, in fact, there is not (no)	Saying yes to there is no relationship (no) but, in fact, there is (yes)
False positive or alpha error	False negative or beta error
Say yes to no	Say no to yes
The likelihood or probability of mistaking a fake or untruth as a fact or true (buying a knockoff as the real thing)	The likelihood or probability of mistaking a fact or truth as a fake or untrue. (Calling a real thing a knockoff)
Err on the wrong side	Err on the safe side
If there is going to be an error, which one will you try to avoid or minimize?	
Convicting (yes) an innocent person (no)	Letting free (no) of a guilty person (yes)
Marrying (yes) the wrong partner (no)	Missing (no) the good catch (yes)
A shopkeeper sells tobacco (yes) to someone who is not yet 21 years old (no)	A shopkeeper refuses to sell tobacco (no) to someone who is over 21 years old (yes)
Telling a man that he is pregnant (yes), although he is not (no)	Telling a pregnant women (yes) that she is not pregnant (no)
Telling a patient he has cancer (yes), although he is not (no)	Telling a patient who does not have cancer (no), although he is (yes)
In Research Study	
Claiming a weak intervention as strong	Claiming a strong intervention as weak
Claiming a nonsignificant difference or relationship as significant and real	Claiming a significant relationship or difference that does not really exist

Reject (−) the Null Hypothesis (−) means Yes (+) to the alternative hypothesis: (−) (−) = (+)
Fail (−) to reject (−) the null hypothesis (−) means No (−) and the null hypothesis stays: (−) (−) (−) = (−)

that researchers or practitioners prefer to avoid Type II error more (take Type I error over Type II error). For example, a "pregnant" diagnosis would be a big surprise to a biological man and a false positive cancer diagnoses (Type I error) would indeed be devastating. However, a pregnant biological woman not seeking proper prenatal care because she thinks she is not pregnant (Type II error) and a person who has cancer who thinks he is not (Type II error) and leaves his health needs unattended will suffer consequences that are even more serious.

Reject and Fail to Reject – Type I Error and Type II Error

Research Question: Is A different from B? Is A related to B?
Hypothesis (H_y): A and B are different. A and B are related.

Null Hypothesis (H_0):
1. There is no difference between A&B; A equals B; A = B; A is similar to B; $A - B \simeq 0$
2. There is no correlation between A&B; A is unrelated to B; Correlation is zero or minimum; $A : B \simeq 0$
3. There is no supported relationship between A&B; No or minimum contribution to each other

Alternative Hypothesis (H_1): A is different from B; A is related to B; A is contributing to A, or vice versa.

(1) *Find out the test statistic's (x^2, U, t, F, etc.) calculated probability, probability value, or (p) =, <, or > the alpha (α)*

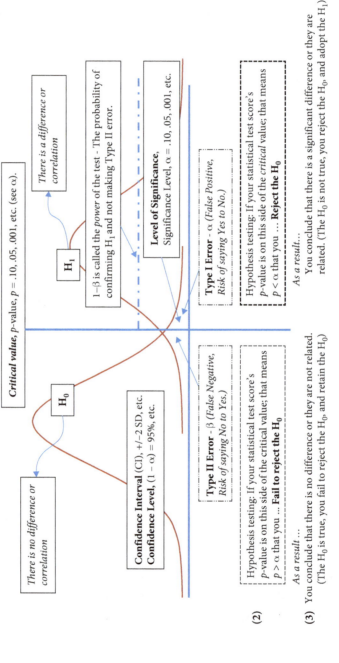

Critical value, p-value, $p = .10, .05, .001$, etc. (see α).

There is a difference or correlation

H_1

$1-\beta$ is called the *power* of the test - The probability of confirming H_1 and not making Type II error.

Level of Significance, Significance Level, $\alpha = .10, .05, .001$, etc.

Type I Error - α *(False Positive, Risk of saying Yes to No.)*

Hypothesis testing: If your statistical test score's p-value is on this side of the *critical value*; that means $p < \alpha$ that you … **Reject the H_0**

As a result …

(3) You conclude that there is a significant difference or they are related. (The H_0 is not true, you reject the H_0, and adopt the H_1)

There is no difference or correlation

H_0

Confidence Interval (CI), +/−2 SD, etc.
Confidence Level, $(1 - \alpha) = 95\%$, etc.

Type II Error - β *(False Negative, Risk of saying No to Yes.)*

Hypothesis testing: If your statistical test score's p-value is on this side of the critical value; that means $p > \alpha$ that you … **Fail to reject the H_0**

As a result …

(2) You conclude that there is no difference or they are not related. (The H_0 is true, you fail to reject the H_0, and retain the H_0)

Figure 14.5. Reject or Fail to Reject, α and p, Type I and Type II Errors

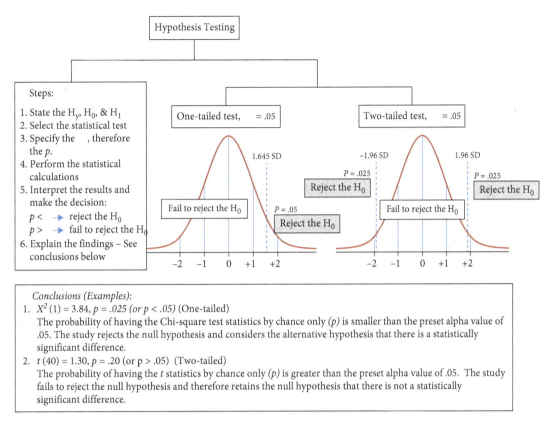

Figure 14.6. Hypothesis Testing Diagram

The diagram contains the following text elements:

Hypothesis Testing

Steps:

1. State the H_y, H_0, & H_1
2. Select the statistical test
3. Specify the , therefore the p.
4. Perform the statistical calculations
5. Interpret the results and make the decision:
   $p <$ → reject the H_0
   $p >$ → fail to reject the H_0
6. Explain the findings – See conclusions below

One-tailed test, = .05

1.645 SD

Fail to reject the H_0

$P = .05$

Reject the H_0

−2 −1 0 +1 +2

Two-tailed test, = .05

−1.96 SD

1.96 SD

$P = .025$

Reject the H_0

$P = .025$

Reject the H_0

Fail to reject the H_0

−2 −1 0 +1 +2

Conclusions (Examples):
1. $X^2 (1) = 3.84$, $p = .025$ (or $p < .05$) (One-tailed)
   The probability of having the Chi-square test statistics by chance only (*p*) is smaller than the preset alpha value of .05. The study rejects the null hypothesis and considers the alternative hypothesis that there is a statistically significant difference.
2. $t (40) = 1.30$, $p = .20$ (or $p > .05$) (Two-tailed)
   The probability of having the *t* statistics by chance only (*p*) is greater than the preset alpha value of .05. The study fails to reject the null hypothesis and therefore retains the null hypothesis that there is not a statistically significant difference.

Figure 14.5 summarizes the definitions and relationships among the key concepts that we have discussed so far.

The hypothesis testing process provides a systematic approach to examine the data collected. With the assistance of appropriate statistical tests, it checks whether the observed sample data is the result of chance or by other reasons, such as the independent variable. It also helps to decide how likely it is that the results can be generalized to a large population. Based on a schematic presentation on the steps of hypothesis testing (Evrard, 2015), Figure 14.6 summaries the key elements and processes involved in hypothesis testing.

CONCLUSION

Hypothesis testing involves the use of many concepts and conditions that allows researchers to make decisions about the results of their analysis. They include the research hypothesis, null hypothesis, alternative hypothesis, reject or fail to reject the null hypothesis, one-tailed or two-tailed test, critical p-value, observed critical p-value, and α value, as well as Type I and Type II errors. No wonder students find them to be confusing and convoluting, particularly when they are scattered throughout the textbook. This chapter aimed to lay out and connect these concepts in one place. It used charts, figures, and examples to explain and illustrate these concepts so that students can be prepared as they enter the discussion of tests of correlation and tests of difference in the following chapters.

Figure Credits

15

TEST OF CORRELATION

With the use of standard normal distribution and associated statistical concepts, researchers can go beyond the basic descriptive statistics and move into the use of inferential statistics. Inferential statistics allow researchers to test a hypothesis, identify relationships, and make predictions and inference. The key questions for inferential analysis are whether the variables are related and whether they are different. This chapter first clarifies concepts related to correlation and then explains correlational statistics for variables of different levels of measurement. It will be followed by the next chapter on the test of difference.

Depending on the variables' levels of measurement, different tests of correlational statistics will be used. The Common Statistics and Choice of Statistics Chart, introduced in a previous chapter, lists the choices of statistics as they relate to levels of measurement and tests of correlation and difference. In this chapter, the following tests of correlation statistics will be discussed.

LEVELS OF MEASUREMENT	STATISTICS	RELATED CONCEPTS
Nominal	• Chi-square • Fisher's exact test • Chi-square goodness of fit	• Contingency table • Degrees of freedom
Ordinal	• Spearman's rank correlation coefficient (Spearman's Rho) • Kendall's Tau	• Coefficient of determination
Interval/Ratio	• Pearson's product-moment correlation coefficient (Pearson's r)	

CAUSATION AND CORRELATION

"Aristotle's *Metaphysics* begins: All men by nature desire to know" (Lear, 1988, p. 1). The thirst to seek out causes and explanations and to understand appear to be part of our human nature. "Why" is a short word, but it has mighty power. Human service providers probably would like to know what causes a certain situation to happen and what causes a program to fail or succeed. One of the purposes for research, and particularly program evaluation is to assess which interventions have brought about (caused or contributed to) the desirable outcomes. A straightforward causal relationship in social science is often not that easily achieved. Contributing variables correlated or associated with the desirable outcomes are equally important and more likely to be identified and studied.

Causation and correlation (and association) are two key concepts in the discussions of explanation. They are important for general social research, program evaluation, and program planning. Research and evaluation help explain what happened in the program and intervention, and program planning applies these explanations to designing programs.

Simplistically, people like answers that allow them to see a clear causation that a particular cause (e.g., reason, need) directly explains a particular change (e.g., effect, result). However, in most social work practice situations, the clear and clean answer to the question "Why?" is not easy to obtain. Too many interrelated factors or conditions might have led to the presence of the client's situation.

Necessary and Sufficient Explanations

A *causal relation* can only be established in the presence of a "list of conditions which together are considered necessary and sufficient to explain the occurrence of the phenomenon in question" (Chafetz, 1978, p. 22). Chafetz further explains that "a *necessary explanation* is one in which the elements listed must be present to bring about the result in question" (p. 22). The presence of clouds is necessary to have any rainfall, but a cloud alone is not enough to cause rain. It is not possible to have rain under a clear blue sky, but it is possible to have a cloudy day with no rain in sight.

"A *sufficient explanation* is one in which the elements listed will always bring about the result in question" (Chafetz, 1978, p. 22). Always, a spoonful of cyanide is enough to kill a person if untreated. The presence of enough cyanide in a person's body can bring about death. Cyanide is a sufficient cause of death, but it is not necessary for anyone to use cyanide to die. While a cloud is a necessary but not sufficient condition for rainfall, cyanide is a sufficient but not necessary condition for death. Nevertheless, both are the important and key contributing factors that bring about the results of ***correlation*** in question.

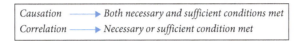

Figure 15.1. Causation and Correlation

Very often, social work practice may only be working with key contributing factors rather than the absolute root causes. These contributing factors are associated with or correlated to the presence of the clients' current conditions. By making changes to the contributing factors and with the ultimate end outcomes in mind, social workers attempt to affect the likelihood of the attainment of the desirable results and the elimination of the undesirable results.

Medical doctors, supported by rigorous scientific testing and clinical studies, can pinpoint a particular virus, bacteria, or biological agent that causes a particular disease. Specific medical interventions are therefore used to eliminate or control the cause of the disease in the patient. Unlike medical doctors, social workers do not deal with the causes of issues that behave like viruses or bacteria. They do not even necessarily know the exact causes for clients' situations or have the "magic pills" to cure the problem. Like medical professionals, social workers work with individuals, families, and communities to address issues and factors that affect their health and well-being (Yuen, 2006).

Contributing factors that affect the likelihood of achieving desirable outcomes probably are valuable and often more obtainable than the causal factors. Children who live in drug-and violence-prevalent communities have a higher likelihood of getting involved with the criminal justice system when they are growing up. The correlation between the community characteristics and legal involvement is a correlation that could be the focus of many studies and service plans. This connection does not mean a community with high drug and violence incidences causes its youth to become lawbreakers, or that children from this community are doomed to become criminals. Many successful youth from such communities have proven their resiliency and strength to excel and defy odds. The challenges and difficulties experienced by these children, however, point out the likely correlational or contributing effects of risk and protective factors.

In the process of making claims about affecting change, there is a need to distinguish between causation (causal relation) and correlation (including association). Intervention and service programs are designed to bring about changes, but it is difficult, if not impossible, to claim that the intervention directly and solely caused the change. To establish causation, as discussed previously, both necessary and sufficient conditions have to be present. A correlation or association, however, is more likely to be established by a service program than causation.

ASSOCIATION AND CORRELATION

Association refers to two things that relate to each other and change together; two variables make related moves at the same time. As a result, when researchers know the value of one variable, they know the likely value of the second variable. There is however no information on how vigorous (e.g., fast/slow or strong/weak) the changes are and in what direction (e.g., left/right or positive+/negative−). While association only indicates that two things vary together, correlation also indicates the strength (0 to 1.0) and direction (i.e., + and −) of the association. In addition, "there is *correlation* between the variables if the association is linear; this can be represented by a straight line on a scatter diagram" (MEI, 2007, p. 1). In this linear relationship, a correlation coefficient (see the discussions that follow) is used to measure the strength and direction of the correlation.

Correlation ⟶ Association + Strength (0 – 1) + Direction (+/−)

Figure 15.2. Correlation and Association

The In and Out of Correlation

Yuliya and Farah are colleagues in the same agency. It is not unusual to see both of them in the office at the same time, and it is also not uncommon that one is in the office and the other is not. When someone is looking for Yuliya and cannot find her, that person may ask Farah where Yuliya is. Farah may or may not know but is more likely than anyone else to know because they work together. They have shared and separate assignments; they also provide coverage for each other when needed. As colleagues or associates, they are related to and affect each other's work.

Whenever Yuliya enters the office, Farah follows into the office. If it happens enough times, people would connect Yuliya's presence in the office with the likelihood of Farah being in the office as well. When Yuliya is in the office, Farah also shows up in the office; that probably is a coincidence (i.e., chance) but it may possibly be a positive correlation. If it happens all the time (100% of the time or 100/100), the strength and direction of the correlation will be +1.0. If it happens only 70% of the times, then the correlation will be +0.7. Conversely, if 70% of the time, Yuliya comes in the office and Farah leaves, then they have a negative correlation of −0.7. If 100% of the time when Yuliya is in the office, Farah is away from the office, they have a perfect-1 correlation.

$$(-1) \quad \frac{+100 \text{ Yuliya}}{-100 \text{ Farah}} \longleftrightarrow \frac{\text{n Yuliya}}{\text{n Farah}} \longleftrightarrow \frac{+100 \text{ Yuliya}}{+100 \text{ Farah}} \quad (+1)$$

No matter what the correlation number is, one cannot tell whether Yuliya causes Farah to be in the office or Farah causes Yuliya to show up. All we can say is that if one sees Yuliya or Farah in the office, one may also likely (at different extent/strength) see the other one there (therefore, a positive correlation). The other way around, if one sees Yuliya or Farah in the office, it is unlikely (at different extent/strength) to see the other one there (therefore, a negative correlation).

CORRELATION COEFFICIENT: STRENGTH AND DIRECTION OF CORRELATION

A correlation coefficient is the statistic that measures the correlation, an index of relationship between two or more continuous (ordinal, interval, and ratio) variables. Any correlation results, both positive (+) and negative (−), less than 0.3 is considered a negligible correlation; between 0.3 and 0.49 is a weak one; between 0.5 and 0.69 is a moderate one, and a 0.7 or above is a strong correlation. Of course, a correlation of 0.0 means no linear correlation. Table 15.1 lists the strength of different size of correlation. Figure 15.3 and Figure 15.4 are scattergrams that display the positive and negative direction of the linear relationship between variables. Figure 15.5 shows that little to no relationship exists between variables. Note that a zero linear relationship does not mean a zero relationship. Other relationships such as a curvilinear relationship may exist.

TABLE 15.1. Different Strength and Size of Correlation Coefficient

Size of Correlation	−0.70 to −1.00	−0.50 to −0.69	−0.30 to −0.49	<−0.30	0.00	< 0.30	0.30 to 0.49	0.50 to 0.69	0.70 to 1.00
Direction	◄————————————————— 0.00 —————————————————►								
Strength of Correlation	Strong	Moderate	Weak	Negligible	None	Negligible	Weak	Moderate	Strong

Apply this correlation discussion to a program evaluation situation. Ahmad's mother puts him in a tutoring program; she believes it will increase his academic

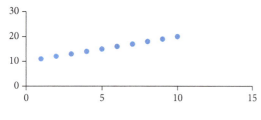

Figure 15.3. Positive Correlation

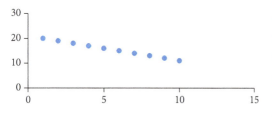

Figure 15.4. Negative Correlation

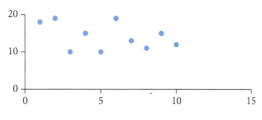

Figure 15.5. No Correlation

performance in school. Ahmad's last report card shows he has been doing better since his enrollment in the tutoring program. While it seems the tutoring program improves Ahmad's performance, it is not possible to claim the tutoring directly and single-handedly causes Ahmad's improvement. There are also other variables such as Ahmad's self-motivation or having the wonderful Mrs. Smith as his teacher this year. We can say there is a strong positive correlation between participating in the tutoring program and improved school performance. This by itself is an endorsement of the effectiveness of the tutoring program as a major and significant contributing factor.

Different research designs generate different types of data that affect what analysis can be used. Exploratory and descriptive researchers can provide data that test the correlation or association. The use of risk and protective factors in theory and in practice is based on the framework of correlation. Experimental research allows a researcher to identify the correlations as well as the possible causal relationships between variables.

CHI-SQUARE STATISTIC

A chi-square (X^2) statistic is a nonparametric statistic used to test the association and difference between two categorical variables (i.e., nominal or ordinal). It compares the distribution of responses (i.e., counts or tallies) between categorical variables to examine whether the association or difference is due to chance. The chi-square statistic is also called chi-square test of association and the chi-square test of independence. The chi-square test's suitability for categorical variables, its ease of use, and its versatility fit well with the reality of human services. It is a popular statistic test for social workers.

For example, a chi-square test can be used to test associations or to compare differences:

1. The successful and failed treatment outcomes (observed values for a categorical dependent variable) between the use of Intervention A and nonuse of Intervention A (values for a categorical independent grouping variable). The association between the use and nonuse of intervention and their outcomes.
2. The successful and failed treatment outcomes (observed values for a categorical variable) between Intervention A and Intervention B (categorical comparison group variable). The association between types of intervention (A or B) and treatment outcomes (Table 15.2).
3. The difference in the distribution between a sample and the population. It is used to test whether the sample is drawn from the population (Chi-square goodness of fit test).

The chi-square statistic is a test of independence because it tests whether the difference (in treatment outcome) is independent of (i.e., has nothing to do with) the Intervention (Intervention A vs. No Intervention A, Intervention A vs. Intervention B). In other words, by investigating the difference or correlation in distribution between groups/interventions, chi-square examines whether group membership, not chance, makes the difference. "That the distribution of responses 'depends' on the group" (LaMorte, 2016, para. 3).

Depending on the phrasing of the research hypothesis, the chi-square statistic can provide answers to questions regarding correlation, difference, or both. For example, studying or not studying may make a difference in having a pass or fail grade. Alternatively, it can be phrased as studying or not studying is correlated to having a pass or fail grade. Chi-square is a rather versatile statistic.

TABLE 15.2. Contingency Table

| | | TREATMENT OUTCOME | | |
		SUCCESSFUL	FAILED	TOTAL
Intervention	A	a	b	a + b
	B	c	d	c + d
Total		a + c	b + d	N

| | | TREATMENT OUTCOME | | |
		SUCCESSFUL	FAILED	TOTAL
Intervention	DBT	38	12	50
	Narrative	22	28	50
Total		60	40	100

Contingency Table

A contingency or a crosstab is a frequency distribution table that displays how the data of variables are located and related. Typically, the independent variable would be included in the column and the dependent variable would be placed in the row. Depending on the number of values that each of the variables has, it is also called a 2 × 2 table, a 2 × 3 table, and so on. For a two-way table (i.e., 2 × 2), its four cells are called a, b, c, & d. Table 15.2 is a very basic contingency table. Row and column percentage can be added to better understand the distribution.

CHI-SQUARE TEST

Essentially, the chi-square test is used to compare the observed (experimental, actual) values and the expected (theoretical) values. Applying the chi-square formula (see Box 15.1), a chi-square statistic is obtained. Based on the preset significant level (α value) and the degrees of freedom, the researcher can look up the chi-square score's probability value (p-value) using the chi-square distribution table (Table 15.3). Alternatively, if a computer software statistical program (e.g., SPSS) is used for the calculation, the exact p-value will be calculated and presented in the printout (e.g., $p = .0123$).

Application of Chi-Square Test

Chi-square statistic is often used in social work studies to find out if a statistically significant relationship exists. While a chi-square test itself is not a very powerful test, its results help to test the hypothesis and provide a starting point for further investigation. The following examples demonstrate the application of chi-square statistics in various practice situations.

BOX 15.1. CHI-SQUARE FORMULA

X^2 **(Chi-square)** $= \sum \frac{(O-E)^2}{E}$

Where: O = Observed frequency, the actual data for each of the cells
E = Expected frequency, the calculated probability for each of the cells
The expected frequency for a cell can be calculated using this formula:

$$E \text{ (Expected Frequency)} = \frac{(R)(C)}{N} = \frac{(\text{Row Total}) (\text{Column Total})}{\text{Grand Total}}$$

BOX 15.2. CHI-SQUARE—THE EFFECTIVENESS OF DBT

In a study of 50 clients on the effectiveness of the use of Dialectic Behavior Therapy (DBT) in treating mood disorders, it had the following hypothesis and had the following chi-square result:

H_0: There is no relationship between the use of DBT and treatment outcomes.
H_1: There is a relationship between the use of DBT and treatment outcomes.

| | | TREATMENT OUTCOME | | |
		SUCCESSFUL	FAILED	TOTAL
Use of DBT	Yes	23	5	28
	No	10	12	22
Total		33	17	50

$E \text{ (Expected Frequency)} = \frac{(R)(C)}{N}$

Cell a: $E = \frac{(a+b)(a+c)}{N} = \frac{(28)(33)}{50} = 18.5$ Cell b: $E = \frac{(a+b)(b+d)}{N} = \frac{(28)(17)}{50} = 9.5$

Cell c: $E = \frac{(c+d)(a+c)}{N} = \frac{(22)(33)}{50} = 14.5$ Cell d: $E = \frac{(c+d)(b+d)}{N} = \frac{(22)(17)}{50} = 7.5$

$X^2 \text{ (Chi-Square)} = \Sigma \frac{(O-E)^2}{E}$

$$X^2 = \frac{(23-18.5)^2}{18.5} + \frac{(5-9.5)^2}{9.5} + \frac{(10-14.5)^2}{14.5} + \frac{(12-7.5)^2}{7.5} = 7.39$$

    Looking up the Chi-square table (Table 15.3) or using the excerpt that follows, a score of 7.39 with one degrees of freedom (df = 1) for a two-tailed test can only be found between the values of .01 and .001. However, if the researchers are using a statistics software program to calculate the chi-square, they will likely get a printout like this one in which the exact p-value (p = .007) will be displayed.

    Either using the chi-square table to estimate the general area of the p-value (p < .01) or using the software program that produces the exact p-value (p = .007), the researchers will have the same statistical outcome. They can present the two-tailed finding in one of the following formats:

- $X^2 = 7.390$, df = 1, p < .01
- $X^2 = 7.390$, df = 1, p = .007

- X^2 (1) = 7.390, p < .01
- X^2 (1) = 7.390, p = .007

SPSS Printout-Chi-Square Tests

	VALUE	DF	ASYMPTOTIC SIGNIFICANCE (2-SIDED)	EXACT SIG. (2-SIDED)	EXACT SIG. (1-SIDED)
Pearson Chi-Square	7.390[a]	1	.007		
Continuity Correction[b]	5.845	1	.016		
Likelihood Ratio	7.511	1	.006		
Fisher's Exact Test				.015	.008
Linear-by-Linear Association	7.242	1	.007		
N of Valid Cases	50				

[a] 0 cells (0.0%) have expected count less than 5. The minimum expected count is 7.48.
[b] Computed only for a 2 x 2 table

The researchers are therefore to conclude that:

- The H_0 of no relationship between DBT use and treatment outcome is rejected.
- The probability of having this calculated chi-square statistic is less than 1% ($p < .01$).
- The H_1 that the use of DBT is related to treatment outcome (i.e., more likely to produce a successful outcome) should be considered.

TABLE 15.3. Distribution of Critical Values of X^2 Table

	CRITICAL VALUES OF χ^2					
	LEVELS OF SIGNIFICANCE FOR A ONE-TAILED TEST					
	0.1	0.05	0.025	0.01	0.005	0.0005
	LEVELS OF SIGNIFICANCE FOR A TWO-TAILED TEST					
DF	0.2	0.1	0.05	0.02	0.01	0.001
1	1.64	2.71	3.84	5.41	6.64	8.83
2	3.22	4.60	5.99	7.82	9.21	13.82
3	4.64	6.25	7.82	9.84	11.34	16.27
4	5.99	7.78	9.49	11.67	13.28	18.46
5	7.29	9.24	11.07	13.39	15.09	20.52
6	8.56	10.64	12.59	15.03	16.81	22.46
7	9.80	12.02	14.07	16.62	18.48	24.32
8	11.03	13.36	15.51	18.17	20.09	26.12
9	12.24	14.68	16.92	19.68	21.67	27.88
10	13.44	15.99	18.31	21.16	23.21	29.59

TABLE 15.3. Distribution of Critical Values of X² Table (*Continued*)

DF	LEVELS OF SIGNIFICANCE FOR A TWO-TAILED TEST					
	0.2	0.1	0.05	0.02	0.01	0.001
11	14.63	17.28	19.68	22.62	24.72	31.26
12	15.81	18.55	21.03	24.05	26.22	32.91
13	16.98	19.81	22.36	25.47	27.69	34.53
14	18.15	21.06	23.68	26.87	29.14	36.12
15	19.31	22.31	25.00	28.26	30.58	37.70
16	20.46	23.54	26.3	29.63	32.00	39.29
17	21.62	24.77	27.59	31.00	33.41	40.75
18	22.76	25.99	28.87	32.35	34.8	42.31
19	23.9	27.2	30.14	33.69	36.19	43.82
20	25.04	28.41	31.41	35.02	37.57	45.32
21	26.17	29.62	32.67	36.34	38.93	46.8
22	27.30	30.81	33.92	37.66	40.29	48.27
23	28.43	32.01	35.17	38.97	41.64	49.73
24	29.55	33.20	36.42	40.27	42.98	51.18
25	30.68	34.38	37.65	41.57	44.31	52.62
26	31.80	35.56	38.88	42.86	45.64	54.05
27	32.91	36.74	40.11	44.14	46.94	55.48
28	34.03	37.92	41.34	45.42	48.28	56.89
29	35.14	39.09	42.69	46.69	49.59	58.30
30	36.25	40.26	43.77	47.96	50.89	59.70
32	38.47	42.59	46.19	50.49	53.49	62.49
34	40.68	44.90	48.60	53.00	56.06	65.25
36	42.88	47.21	51.00	55.49	58.62	67.99
38	45.08	49.51	53.38	57.97	61.16	70.70
40	47.27	51.81	55.76	60.44	63.69	73.40
44	51.64	56.37	60.48	65.34	68.71	78.75
48	55.99	60.91	65.17	70.20	73.68	84.04
52	60.33	65.42	69.83	75.02	78.62	89.27
56	64.66	69.92	74.47	79.82	83.51	94.46
60	68.97	74.40	79.08	84.58	88.38	99.61

Source: Original data from Table IV (p. 47) of R.A. Fisher and F. Yates (1963). *Statistical Tables for Biological, Agricultural, and Medical Research. (6th ed.).* New York: Hafner Publishing Co.

Several more Chi-square examples to illustrate the use of the chi-square statistics in various practice situations:

BOX 15.3. CHI-SQUARE—OLDER ADULT FINANCIAL ABUSE

A county Adult Protective Services wanted to know if the incidents of confirmed financial abuse against older adults last month was higher than the statewide statistics. In other words, are older adults in the county more or less likely to be the victims of financial abuse compared to the statewide statistics? Because whether it is "financial abuse" or "not financial abuse" and "county" or "state" are both nominal measurements, the researchers used the chi-square statistics to test their hypotheses.

| | | FINANCIAL ABUSE | | |
		YES	NO	TOTAL
Location	County	25 (35.71%)	45 (64.29%)	70 (100%)
	State	475 (43.38%)	620 (56.62%)	1095 (100%)
Total		500	665	1165 (100%)

The above contingency table displays the tabulation of the data collected. Chi-square analysis showed the following result: $X^2 = 1.577$, df = 1, $p = .209$.

Because the calculated p-value is greater than the preset p-value of .05, the researchers concluded that the result was not significant and that location was not correlated to the prevalence of financial abuse. In other words, the county figure was not significantly different from the state figures.

By listing the actual p-value only (i.e., $p = .209$), readers may not know where the α value was set. The researchers can display the result as $X^2 = 1.577$, df = 1, $p > .05$. In this format, whether the p-value is greater or smaller than the preset α value (.05) is clearly indicated.

BOX 15.4. CHI-SQUARE—SEXUAL HARASSMENT PREVENTION TRAINING IN SCHOOL

A school social worker was interested in knowing if gender was associated with the gain of knowledge about sexual harassment after her 8-week, in-class training for the school's eighth graders. Her post-training evaluation generated the following data for a chi-square analysis:

		GAIN IN SEXUAL HARASSMENT KNOWLEDGE			
		A LOT	SOME	NO CHANGE	TOTAL
Gender	Male	40 (36.36%)	40 (36.36%)	30 (27.28%)	110 (100%)
	Female	90 (64.29%)	30 (21.43%)	20 (14.28%)	140 (100%)
Total		130	70	50	250 (100%)

H_0: There is no relationship between gender and knowledge gained.

H_1: There is a relationship between gender and knowledge gained. More specifically, female students gained more than male students.

Statistical result:

$$X^2 = 19.337, df = 2, p < .05 \ (p = .000063) \ (\text{Direction predicted})$$

Conclusion:

The null hypothesis is rejected. Gender is related to knowledge gain in sexual harassment training. The frequency distributions in the contingency table reflect that female eighth graders demonstrated more significant gain than male students.

BOX 15.5. CHI-SQUARE—PEER-MENTORING FOR SOBRIETY STUDY: MORE IS BETTER

Is having a trained post-treatment peer-mentor associated with successes in maintaining an early sobriety that lasts at least 12 months? A trained peer-mentor is a volunteer who is in recovery and has been sober for at least 5 years. They also have completed a one-week, peer-mentorship training. A residential alcohol treatment agency collected such data for its clients 12 months after completion of their treatment program. Upon discharge, clients can choose to have a mentor or not to have a mentor. The following is the data for one of the agencies' treatment facilities and its statistical findings:

		EARLY SOBRIETY		
		YES	NO	TOTAL
Have a Peer Mentor	Yes	30	15	45
	No	20	20	40
Total		50	35	85

H_0: There is no association between the use of a peer-mentor and early sobriety.

H_1: There is an association between the use of peer-mentor and early sobriety.

$X^2 = 2.4286, df = 1, P > .05$ (Direction predicted) [*Note: the exact p-value = .1191*]

Conclusion: Because the calculated p-value (.1191) is greater than the preset α value of .05, the agency failed to reject the null hypothesis. It concluded that the effect of the use of a peer mentor could not be determined or supported.

Upon gathering similar data from its several treatment facilities, the agency achieved the following larger data set for analysis:

		EARLY SOBRIETY		
		YES	NO	TOTAL
Have a Peer-Mentor	Yes	300	150	450
	No	200	200	400
Total		500	350	850

H_0: There is no association between the use of a peer-mentor and early sobriety.
H_1: Peer mentoring contributed to the attainment of early sobriety.
$X^2 = 24.2857$, df = 1, p < .001 (Direction predicted) [*Note: the exact p-value = .00001*]

Conclusion: Because the p-value is smaller than the preset α value of .01, the agency rejected the null hypothesis of no association. It concluded that there was a statistically significant association between the use of a peer mentor and early sobriety. In other words, with more than 99% confidence, peer mentoring was effective in contributing to the attainment of early sobriety.

Sample Size Matters

As one can see the second analysis in the sobriety study had a data set that was 10 times larger than that of the first one. While the smaller sample size failed to detect the correlation, the larger sample was able to capture the relationship. A larger sample minimizes sampling error and has higher statistical power to identify relationships that exist. As a result, it is advisable for researchers to employ a larger sample size for their analysis and be aware of this reality when replicating a study with different sample sizes. Chi-square statistic is sensitive to sample size and it is usually recommended to be used for a sample that is larger than 50 cases. When the sample size is smaller than 50, researchers may wish to consider using Fisher's Exact Test, which we'll discuss just ahead.

Limitations to (Assumptions for) the Use of Chi-Square

There are some limitations to the use of Chi-square statistics. These limitations reflect the underlying assumptions for the use of chi-square statistics. If any of the limitations that follow are encountered, researchers should consider the use of Fisher's exact test instead.

1. Chi-square can be used for categorical variables such as nominal or ordinal variables that are mutually exclusive (e.g., belonging to one or the other group, not both).
2. Chi-square can only be used for actual frequency counts, not percentages, or ratios.
3. Each observation should be independent from each other. An observation should belong to one category only and one observation per subject.
4. For a 2 × 2 table, the expected minimum count for each of the cells should not be less than 5
5. For tables larger than 2 × 2, no more than 20% of the expected counts are less than 5

If a chi-square analysis is conducted with the above limitations, the chi-square statistic would be inaccurate and misleading. To be sure no one cell has less than 5 counts, it becomes obvious that the sample size has to be large enough (e.g., 50 cases or larger) for Chi-square to be an appropriate analysis. Again, if any of the limitations are encountered, one should consider Fisher's exact test.

FISHER'S EXACT TEST OF INDEPENDENCE

Fisher's exact test of independence is a nonparametric statistical test of significance for two nominal variables. It is a more accurate alternative to the chi-square test when the sample sizes are smaller or when one of the cells has an expected frequency that is less than 5.

Fisher's exact test explores whether the proportions (i.e., possible distribution) of one variable is different among values of the other nominal variable. The statistics may show that the percentage of pregnant teens who have at least one supportive adult in life and have graduated from high school (12 out of 15, or 80%) is higher than those who don't have a supportive person but still graduated from high school (6 out of 12, or 50%). Fisher's exact test can determine whether the difference between 80% and 50% is statistically significant (McDonald, 2014).

Fisher's exact test is most commonly used for a 2 × 2 table. In certain statistics programs such as SPSS, Fisher's exact test is included in the results of a chi-square

BOX 15.6. FISHER'S EXACT—ROLE PLAY IN SOCIAL WORK TRAINING

In a study of the effectiveness of using role-play in social work skills training, the following results were obtained from two undergraduate practice classes totaling 37 students. This seems to be a perfect set up for a chi-square analysis with two nominal variables. The problem is that one of the cells has less than 5 expected cases. Fisher's exact test was used instead because it does not have such assumptions and the expected frequency can be a very small number.

		SOCIAL WORK SKILLS DEVELOPED		
		YES	NO	TOTAL
Use of Role Play	Yes	16	2	18
	No	5	14	19
Total		21	16	37

Result: Fisher's Exact, $p < .0001$, (one-tailed).

H_0: There is no association between the use of role-play and skills development.

H_1: Role-play contributed to the development of social work skills.

Conclusion: Because the p-value is smaller than the preset α value of .01, the study rejected the null hypothesis of no association. It concluded that there was a statistically significant association between the use of role-play and skills development. The researcher has more than 99% confidence that the difference is due to actual dissimilarity (related to the independent variable—role-play) but not due to random chances. Role-playing was effective in contributing to the attainment of social work skills.

analysis that involves a 2 × 2 table and has a cell that has less than five (5) cases. Fisher's exact test does not produce a score. It only shows the p-value of the analysis.

DEGREES OF FREEDOM

The degrees of freedom (df) is the number of variations of values that a calculation can have in the estimation of the parameter. It is a complicated modeling concept that is used in many fields. In statistics, "it provides a way to put different fitting procedures on equal footing" (Tibshirani & Taylor, 2012, p. 1203). A fitting procedure refers to how well a statistical model best fits the observed data set. The degrees of freedom is important in that it helps to compare procedures that involve different sample sizes. As a result, it is included and reported in statistical analysis findings. Detailed discussions on the nature and calculation of degrees of freedom for various statistical tests are beyond the scope of this book. The following is a simple portrayal of the significance and functions of the concept of degrees of freedom.

In a calculation of estimating the statistical distribution (of a parameter such as a mean), degrees of freedom is the number of values of a data set that can be chosen freely. Let us assume we have a calculation of $1 + 2 + 3 + x = 10$. The x is, therefore, 4 (i.e., $1 + 2 + 3 + 4 = 10$). When the x is a fixed value, then the other three numbers can be any value, as long as they total 6 (i.e., $4 + 6 = 10$). These values could be 1, 2, & 3; 2, 2, & 2; 1, 1, 4, and so on. The data set of four has three numbers that are free to vary (i.e., df = 3). In this calculation, the degrees of freedom is, therefore, one less than the total number of items (i.e., df = n − 1 = 3).

The formulas for the degrees of freedom differ from statistics to statistics. The following are the most common ones (Table 15.4):

TABLE 15.4. **Common Degrees of Freedom**

DATA SET	FORMULA	SAMPLE STATISTICS	EXAMPLE
One sample	df = n − 1	One sample t-tes Correlated t-test t	X = 11, 12, 13, 14, 15, 16 (n = 6) df = 6 − 1 = 5
Two samples	df = $(n_1 + n_2) - 2$	Independent t-test Pearson's r Spearman's Rho	X = 11, 12, 13, 14, 15, 16 (n_1 = 6) Y = 31, 32, 33, 34 (n_2 = 4) df = (6 + 4) − 2 = 8
Two types of data	df = (Number of Columns 1) x (Number of Rows 1); or simply df = (C − 1)(R − 1)	Chi-square	For a 2 × 2 crosstab df = (2 − 1)(2 − 1) = 1 × 1 = 1 For a 2 × 3 crosstab df = (2 − 1)(3 − 1) = 1 × 2 = 2 For a 3 × 4 crosstab df = (3 − 1)(4 − 1) = 2 × 3 = 6

Why do we subtract one (1) from the total number of cases or levels? Let's try a simple example by examining the calculation of "$1 + 2 + 3 + X = 10$" again. Once the first three values 1, 2, and 3 are chosen, the fourth number (X) would be a fixed one and has to be 4. Look at this in another way, only a fixed number of value (i.e., one) could be missing and still the calculation could be completed. One could easily figure out the one x in "$1 + 2 + 3 + X = 10$" is 4. The calculation would be difficult when more than one are missing (e.g., "$1 + 2 + X_1 + X_2 = 10$"). The X_1 can be 0, 1, 2, 3, or 4 while the X_2 is 4, 3, 2, 1, or 0. For a calculation with one sample, the degrees of freedom is limited to the total number of items minus the fixed one.

TABLE 15.5. Example of Degrees of Freedom and the Associated *p*-Values

CHI-SQUARE	DEGREES OF FREEDOM	P-VALUE (ONE-TAILED)
$X^2 = 7.390$	1	p < .010
$X^2 = 7.390$	2	p < .025
$X^2 = 7.390$	3	p < .050

Degrees of Freedom and Critical Value

Mathematically, as the degrees of freedom increase (larger), the test statistics' critical values become less stringent. Using the earlier chi-square example and the chi-square distribution table, one can see the same chi-square value of 7.39 will have different *p*-values when the degrees of freedom increase (Table 15.5). The larger the sample size (therefore the greater the degrees of freedom), the smaller the *p*-value for getting a significant result.

CHI-SQUARE GOODNESS OF FIT TEST

The goodness of fit test is also called **single variable chi-square, one sample chi-square, Pearson's chi-square goodness of fit, or chi-square goodness of fit**. It is used to measure the compatibility between the observed values of a nominal variable in the sample with the expected values of a theoretical model or a hypothesized distribution. It assesses whether the distribution of cases in a single categorical variable (e.g., political party affiliation that can have categories such as Democratic, Republican, and Independent) follows the theoretical or known distribution (e.g., record of party affiliation according to county voter registration). Is the percentage of Democrats in the study sample different from the percentage of Democrats in the county?

Essentially it asks whether the sample data observed is representative of (or similar or dissimilar to) the actual data in the population. Later, we will introduce the one-sample t-test, which will perform the same function. As Weinbach and Grinnell (2015) point out the one-sample t-test employs the mean scores for the analysis, but the goodness of fit test uses the percentages of cases in given attributes.

The single variable chi-square is different from the regular chi-square. It only involves one categorical variable that has different groups such as political party affiliations described above. If researchers want to cross-tabulate that with the voters' gender, then two variables are involved and a regular chi-square test should be used. Although there is a difference between the goodness of fit test and the chi-square test, the goodness of fit test needs to meet the same chi-square test assumptions described earlier to generate valid test results. In that sense, the goodness of fit test compares the proportionalities between the expected number (of the population) and the actual/observed number (of the sample). The frequency counts are used in the calculation.

The goodness of fit test uses the regular chi-square statistics formula, $X^2 = \Sigma(O - E)^2/E$ to identify the chi-square and its associated p-value to determine its statistical significance. The degrees of freedom is $k - 1$ where k is the number of categories.

Examples of Goodness of Fit Test

The goodness of fit test is used to test the compatibility between the sample and the hypothesized population or model. The following examples further explain the use of this statistic:

BOX 15.7. GOODNESS OF FIT—HOSPITALITY WORKER CLIENTS

An agency is serving a neighborhood in which 45% of the residents (n_1) are employed in the hospitality industry. When reviewing the randomly selected service data of 100 service recipients for the past 12 months, the social worker notices that only 10% of the service recipients (n_2) are hospitality workers. Is the difference just a matter of random chance? Is the disparity so out of proportion that it is significant enough to warrant further investigation? The researchers employ the chi-square goodness of fit (i.e., $X^2 = \Sigma(n_1 - n_2)^2/n_2$) to answer these questions.

The expected frequency count of 100 hospitality workers in the community: 100 x .45 = 45
The observed frequency count of 100 hospitality workers in the sample: 100 x .10 = 10

	OBSERVED	EXPECTED	DIFFERENCE	DIFFERENCE SQ.	DIFF. SQ./EXP FR.
Hospitality	10	45	−35.00	1,225.00	27.22
Not Hospitality	90	55	35.00	1,225.00	22.27
					49.495

Result: $X^2 = 49.495$, df = 1, p-value < .001

H_0: The sample distribution is consistent with the population distribution
(There is no difference between the sample distribution and population distribution)

H_1: The sample distribution is not consistent with the population distribution
(There is a statistically significant difference between the sample distribution and population distribution)

The degrees of freedom = k − 1, where k = 2 (Hospitality workers and nonhospitality workers), that 2 − 1 = 1.

Conclusion: Reject the H_0 and consider the H_1. The sample distribution is significantly different from the population distribution. The percentage of hospitality worker clients is not in proportion to the percentage in the neighborhood. Many reasons may have contributed to this difference and further investigation is needed to better understand this disproportion.

BOX 15.8. GOODNESS OF FIT—RACIAL DIVERSITY OF THE STUDENT POPULATION

The racial composition of a local community is 45% Latino, 25% white, 20% black, and 10% Asian. (That is, for every 100 residents, there will be 45 Latino, 25 white, 20 back, and 10 Asians). The ethnic composition of a random sample of 100 students in a local elementary school is 15% Latino, 30% white, 10% black, and 45% Asian. (That is 15 Latino, 30 white, 10 black, and 45 Asian students). The researchers are wondering whether the elementary school student body truly represents the community's racial makeup.

   H_0: The race distribution in school is consistent with the race distribution in the community.
   (There is no difference between the school distribution and community distribution)

   H_1: The race distribution is not consistent with the race distribution in the community.
   (There is a statistically significant difference between the school distribution and community distribution)

The degrees of freedom = k − 1, where k = 4, that 4 − 1 = 3.

	OBSERVED FQ	EXPECTED FQ	DIFFERENCE	DIFFERENCE SQ.	DIFF. SQ./EXP FQ.
Latino	45	15	30.00	900.00	60.00
White	25	30	−5.00	25.00	0.83
Black	20	10	10.00	100.00	10.00
Asian	10	45	−35.00	1225.00	27.22
				X^2	98.05

Result: $X^2 = 98.05$, df = 3, p-value < .001

Conclusion: Reject the H_0 and consider the H_1. The student racial distribution in the school is significantly different from the racial distribution in the community.

PEARSON'S PRODUCTION-MOMENT CORRELATION COEFFICIENT

Correlation is a statistical method that assesses the linear relationship between two variables. **Pearson's product-moment correlation coefficient** (Table 15.6) or simply Pearson's r (named in honor of its developer Karl Pearson) is one of the most commonly used correlation coefficients for interval and ratio variables. Table 15.7 shows the distribution of the critical values for Pearson's r. Its nonparametric counterpart for ordinal variables is Spearman's Rho, which we'll discuss just ahead. Because it tests the linear relationship of the variables, researchers often use the scatter plot to assess the linear nature of the data set.

A product, simplistically speaking, is the result of multiplying. For example, 10 is the product of 2 and 5 ($10 = 2 \times 5$). "Statistical products are, generally, information … that describe, estimate, forecast, or analyze the characteristics of groups" (OECD, 2007, para 1). A moment is a quantitative measure of a set of data. There are many orders of moment in statistics. The mean $\Sigma(X - \bar{X})$ and variance $\Sigma(X - \bar{X})^2$ are the first two statistical moments. They describe the location and variability of a data set. A product moment is the product or the mix (multiplication) of the moments (means, variance) of the variables involved.

TABLE 15.6. Formula for Pearson's Product-Moment Correlation Coefficient

There are several ways to calculate Pearson's correlation coefficient and they are mathematically equivalent. This is the basic formula for the Pearson's correlation coefficient of variables X and Y:

$$r = \frac{\sum (X - \bar{X})(Y - \bar{Y})}{\sqrt{\sum (X - \bar{X})^2 (Y - \bar{Y})^2}}$$

Where: r = correlation coefficient
Σ = sum of values
X = n values of X
Y = n values of Y
$\bar{X}$ = Mean of X
$\bar{Y}$ = Mean of Y

For this book, the following Pearson's correlation coefficient formula will be used:

$$r = \frac{N\sum XY - \left(\sum X\right)\left(\sum Y\right)}{\sqrt{\left[N\sum X^2 - \left(\sum X\right)^2\right]\left[N\sum Y^2 - \left(\sum Y\right)^2\right]}}$$

BOX 15.9. PEARSON'S CORRELATION COEFFICIENT—HOME AND SCHOOL

A school social worker is wondering if the number of self-reported conflicts with adult guardians at home is correlated to the number of behavioral problems in school resulting in disciplinary actions. Over the last month, she has collected such data from seven (N = 7) of her students. Because this is a study of correlation involving interval/ratio variables, she chooses to analyze that data using the Pearson's correlational coefficient.

Research hypothesis (H_y): There is a positive correlation between conflicts at home and behavioral problems in school.

Null hypothesis (H_0): There is no correlation between conflicts at home and behavioral problems in school.

Alternative hypothesis (H_1): Conflict at home is positively correlated to behavioral problems in school.

Predictor variable: Number of conflicts at home (X)

Criterion variable: Number of disciplinary actions for behavioral problems in school (Y)

Degrees of freedom: N – 2 = 7 – 2 = 5

Analysis:
$$r = \frac{N\Sigma XY - (\Sigma X)(\Sigma Y)}{\sqrt{[N\Sigma X^2 - (\Sigma X)^2][N\Sigma Y^2 - (\Sigma Y)^2]}}$$

$$= \frac{(7)(563) - (62)(59)}{\sqrt{[(7)(600) - (62)^2][(7)(555) - (59)^2]}}$$

$$= \frac{3941 - 3658}{\sqrt{[4200 - 3844][3885 - 3481]}} = \frac{283}{\sqrt{[356][404]}}$$

$$= \frac{283}{\sqrt{143824}} = \frac{283}{379.24}$$

$$= .7462$$

STUDENT ID	CONFLICT AT HOME (X)	PROBLEMS IN SCHOOL (Y)	X²	Y²	XY
01	13	10	169	100	130
02	8	9	64	81	72
03	4	3	16	9	12
04	10	12	100	144	120
05	7	6	49	36	42
06	11	8	121	64	88
07	9	11	81	121	99
Total	62	59	600	555	563

Result: $r(5) = .7462$, $p < .05$ (Direction predicted)

Conclusion: The null hypothesis is rejected, and the alternative hypothesis is supported. Conflicts at home have a strong and statistically significant positive correlation to behavioral problems in school.

TABLE 15.7. Distribution of Critical Values of r Table

	CRITICAL VALUES OF r				
	LEVEL OF SIGNIFICANCE FOR A ONE-TAILED TEST				
	0.05	0.025	0.01	0.005	0.0005
	LEVEL OF SIGNIFICANCE FOR A TWO-TAILED TEST				
N	0.1	0.05	0.02	0.01	0.001
5	0.8054	0.8783	0.9343	0.9587	0.9912
6	0.7293	0.8114	0.8822	0.9172	0.9741
7	0.6694	0.7545	0.8329	0.8745	0.9507
8	0.6215	0.7067	0.7887	0.8343	0.9249
9	0.5822	0.6664	0.7498	0.7977	0.8982
10	0.5494	0.6319	0.7155	0.7646	0.8721
11	0.5214	0.6021	0.6851	0.7348	0.8471
12	0.4973	0.576	0.6581	0.7079	0.8233
13	0.4762	0.5529	0.6339	0.6835	0.8010
14	0.4575	0.5324	0.6120	0.6614	0.7800
15	0.4409	0.5139	0.5923	0.6411	0.7603
16	0.4259	0.4973	0.5742	0.6226	0.7420
17	0.4124	0.4821	0.5577	0.6055	0.7246
18	0.4000	0.4683	0.5425	0.5897	0.7084
19	0.3887	0.4555	0.5285	0.5751	0.6932
20	0.3783	0.4438	0.5155	0.5614	0.6787
21	0.3687	0.4329	0.5034	0.5487	0.6652
22	0.3598	0.4227	0.4921	0.5368	0.6542
27	0.3233	0.3809	0.4451	0.4869	0.5974
32	0.2960	0.3494	0.4093	0.4487	0.5541
37	0.2746	0.3246	0.3810	0.4182	0.5189
42	0.2573	0.3044	0.3578	0.3932	0.4896
47	0.2428	0.2875	0.3384	0.3721	0.4648
52	0.2306	0.2732	0.3218	0.3541	0.4433
62	0.2108	0.2500	0.2948	0.3248	0.4078
72	0.1954	0.2319	0.2737	0.3017	0.3799
82	0.1829	0.2172	0.2565	0.2830	0.3568
92	0.1726	0.2050	0.2422	0.2673	0.3375
102	0.1638	0.1946	0.2301	0.254	0.3211

Source: Original data from Table VII (p. 63) of R.A. Fisher and F. Yates (1963). *Statistical Tables for Biological, Agricultural, and Medical Research. (6th ed.).* New York: Hafner Publishing Co.

One may note the relationship between products and moment in the Pearson's product-moment correlation coefficient formula. Gerardinco (n.d.) points out the following:

$$r = \frac{\sum \text{Cross product of X \& Y}}{\sqrt{\sum(\text{Deviation score of X})^2 \sum(\text{Deviation score of Y})^2}}$$

$$= \frac{\text{Degree to which X and Y vary together}}{\text{Degree to which X and Y vary independently}}$$

$$= \frac{\text{Covariance of X \& Y}}{\text{Variance of X \& Y}}$$

BOX 15.10. PEARSON'S CORRELATION COEFFICIENT—MISSED APPOINTMENTS AND TRANSPORTATION

An agency is interested in knowing whether the number of missed appointment (no show) is related to clients' transportation challenges, which are measured by a scale ranging from no difficulty (0) to extreme difficulty (10). Because they are testing the correlation between interval/ratio variables, they have chosen the Pearson's r for the analysis. After collecting data from 20 randomly selected clients who have met the threshold of missing at least 5 appointments during the last 3 months, they have the following results.

Research hypothesis (H_y): There is a positive correlation between missed appointments and transportation challenges.

Null hypothesis (H_0): There is no correlation between missed appointments and transportation challenges.

Alternative hypothesis (H_1): Transportation challenges are positively correlated to missed appointments.

Predictor variable: Difficulty in accessing transportation scale (X)

Criterion variable: Number of missed appointments (Y)

Degrees of freedom: $N - 2 = 100 - 2 = 98$

Data: X = 9, 8, 7, 6, 8, 6, 7, 6, 8, 9, 8, 10, 8, 9, 7, 8, 6, 7, 8, 8
Y = 8, 7, 6, 6, 9, 8, 8, 6, 8, 7, 9, 9, 7, 10, 9, 8, 7, 7, 9, 10

Result: r (98) = .5287, $p < .05$ (direction predicted)

Conclusion: The null hypothesis is rejected, and the alternative hypothesis is supported. Transportation challenges have a moderate and statistically significant positive correlation to missed appointments.

Pearson's product-moment correlation coefficient is the result of the interactions (product) of how X and Y vary (moment) together and independently.

In reporting the result, the degrees of freedom for the correlation coefficient is included in parentheses after the r symbol. One can find out the *p*-value from the table of critical values for Pearson's r (Table 15.7). As discussed before, tests of association give information about the correlation or contributory factors but they do not establish causation. In the Box 15.9 example, researchers can verify that conflict at home is positively (+) and strongly correlated (.7462 is > .7) with problems in school. There is, however, no suggestion that conflict at home causes problems in school or vice versa. Box 15.10 provides another example of correlation between missing appointment and transportation.

COEFFICIENT OF DETERMINATION

The coefficient of determination or R square (R^2 or r^2) is another way to determine the relationship between the X and Y variables in a correlation coefficient analysis. It is the square of the correlation coefficient (r) of the independent (predictor) variable (X) and dependent (criterion) variable (Y), hence r^2. If the correlation coefficient such as Pearson's shows an r = .80, then the coefficient of determination is $(.80)^2$ which equals .64 or 64%.

Coefficient of determination (R^2) = (Correlation coefficient)^2 = $(.80)^2$ = .64 = 64%

The coefficient of determination shows the percentage of how the predicator variable (X) can explain the variation in the criterion variable (Y). For example, to what extent, do hours of studying (X) explain the variation of grade (Y)? The numbers range from 0.00 (0%) to 1.00 (100%). One can use the regression line to understand the correlation. If the regression line goes through every one of the values of Y on a scatterplot, the R^2 will be 1.00. In other words, 100% of the Y values fall on the regression line (Figure 15.6). If 2 of the 5 Y values fall on the line, the R^2 would be 0.40 or 40% (Figure 15.7). Of course, if the regression line

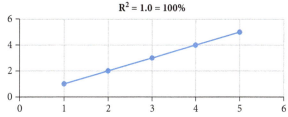

Figure 15.6. Coefficient of Determination = 1

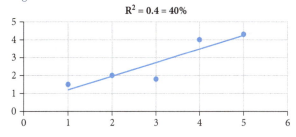

Figure 15.7. Coefficient of Determination = .40

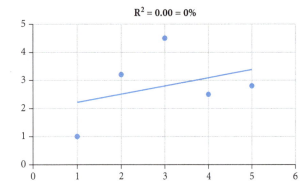

R² = 0.00 = 0%

Figure 15.8. Coefficient of Determination = .00

goes through none of the Ys then the R^2 would be 0% (Figure 15.8).

$R^2 = 64\%$ means 64% of the variation in the course grade is explained or affected by the number of hours spent studying. At the same time, 36% of the variation can not be explained (by hours of study). The coefficient of determination reflects the covariation between variables that take place; how they change together. Some like to visualize it as overlapping. $R^2 = 0.64$ means the X and Y overlap each other 64% of the time.

A higher R^2 means a better capacity of the predictor variable to forecast the criterion variable. The model employed (i.e., predictor variable) can do a good job in estimating what would be observed (criterion variable). Turning it around, it also means the observation is rather close to the model. It is not a causation but only a correlation. In the hours of study and course grade analysis, the r = .7462 and therefore an $R^2 = (.7462)^2 = .5568$. That means the hours of study could explain 55.68% of the course grade received.

A low R^2 is not necessarily a bad thing. It means simply that the observations do not fit the model employed; other factors should therefore be considered. In the transportation challenges and missed appointments study, the r = .5287 and therefore an $R^2 = (.5287)^2 = .2795$. Transportation could, therefore, explain 27.95% of the variation in missed appointments. The relatively low R^2 only means some other factors (e.g., childcare, employment, local transportation system, time of appointment, and others) should also be considered.

SPEARMAN RANK CORRELATION COEFFICIENT

Spearman rank correlation is a test of correlation coefficient between two ordinal variables. It is named after its inventor Charles Spearman and is denoted by either the Greek letter of Rho or r_s. Do people's love of chocolate at different degrees (e.g., very much, somewhat, none) correlate to their different degrees (e.g., very much, somewhat, none) of love of coffee? Because the data involved in this example are by nature not strictly linear and continuous but with the nonlinear properties and of ordinal level variables, their correlation could be analyzed with the Spearman rank correlation.

Since correlation coefficient is used to analyze *linear* data, what happens if the data is nonlinear? Items in linear data are related to each other in a sequential manner similar to children line up in a queue. Items in nonlinear data are connected through many points and are not necessarily in sequence, similar to a tree with many branches or a flow chart. For example, the crime rate of a city is likely related to the city's population density in a nonlinear manner. One of the ways to **transform nonlinear data into linear data** (see Table 15.8) is to **use the ranks of the value instead of the real values** (Zar, 1998). There are also times that interval level data could benefit from being analyzed at the ordinal level. For example, outcomes of Likert scale data analyzed as interval data could be further validated by being analyzed as ordinal data.

Although Pearson's r formula could be employed to calculate Spearman rank correlation (MEI, 2007, Zar, 1998), the "more algorithmic" (MEI, 2007, p. 4) formula is the following (Table 15.9):

TABLE 15.8. Converting Data into Ranks

NEIGHBOR SAFETY (NARRATIVE) (NONLINEAR)	I AM SCARED	PROBABLY	SAFE	NO PROBLEM	NOT REALLY
Safety score (1–100 points) [Higher number = safer]	25	70	82	95	55
Rank of safety (Ranking) [Higher rank = safer]	5	3	2	1	4

TABLE 15.9. Formula for Spearman Rank Correlation Coefficient

$$r_s = 1 - \frac{6\sum d^2}{n(n^2 - 1)}$$

Where: r_s = Spearman rank correlation coefficient

$\sum$ = Sum of values

d = Difference in ranks between the two variables

n = sample size

BOX 15.11. SPEARMAN RANK CORRELATION COEFFICIENT—INDEPENDENT LIVING AND SELF-EFFICACY

A child welfare agency provides an independent living training for youth who are aging out of the system. It assesses youth mastery of such skills by using a generic assessment form that scores from 0 to 100. It also uses an agency developed scale to assess youth's sense of self-efficacy that ranges from 0 to 100.

Research hypothesis (H_y): There is a positive correlation between independent living skills and sense of self-efficacy.

Null hypothesis (H_0): There is no correlation between independent living skills and sense of self-efficacy.

Alternative hypothesis (H_1): Competency in independent living skills is positively correlated to sense of self-efficacy.

Predictor variable: Independent living skills (ILS) score (X)

Criterion variable: Sense of self-efficacy (SSE) score (Y)

Degrees of freedom: N − 2 = 10 − 2 = 8

Analysis:
$$r_s = 1 - \frac{6\Sigma d^2}{n(n^2 - 1)}$$
$$= 1 - \frac{(6)\,(22)}{10\,(10^2 - 1)} = 1 - \frac{132}{10\,(99)} = 1 - \frac{132}{990} = 1 - 0.1333$$
$$= .8667$$

YOUTH ID (N) = 10	ILS (X)	SSE (Y)	ILS RANK	SSE RANK	DIFFERENCE IN RANK (d)	d²
01	75	66	7	7	0	0
02	66	59	8	10	2	4
03	58	62	10	9	1	1
04	79	74	6	6	0	0
05	86	87	4	1	3	9
06	59	64	9	8	1	1
07	87	75	3	5	2	4
08	92	82	2	3	1	1
09	94	85	1	2	1	1
10	82	76	5	4	1	1
Total						22

Result: $r_s(8) = .8667$, $p < .01$ (direction predicted)

Conclusion: The null hypothesis is rejected, and the alternative hypothesis is supported. Independent living skills have a strong and statistically significant positive correlation to one's sense of self-efficacy.

In an older adult service agency, there is always a question of whether clients' ability of hearing is correlated to clients' rate of participation in social activities organized by the agency. The ability of hearing is rated at different levels: 1= no hearing problems, 2 = occasional hearing problems, and 3 = frequent hearing problems. The rate of participation is also reflected by different levels: 1 = often, 2 = occasionally, 3 = seldom.

Research hypothesis (H_y): There is a correlation between hearing ability and rate of participation

Null hypothesis (H_0): There is no correlation between hearing ability and level of participation

Alternative hypothesis (H_1): Older adults' ability to hear is related to their rate of participation in activities.

Predictor variable: Ability to hear (AH) – (X)

Criterion variable: Rate of participation (RP) – (Y)

Degrees of freedom: N – 2 = 8 – 2 = 6

Analysis: $r_s = 1 - \dfrac{6\Sigma d^2}{n\,(n^2 - 1)}$

$$= 1 - \frac{(6)\,(50.50)}{8\,(8^2 - 1)} = 1 - \frac{303}{8\,(63)} = 1 - \frac{303}{504} = 1 - 0.6012 = .3988$$

ID	LEVEL OF HEARING	LEVEL OF PARTICIPATION	HEARING RANK	PARTICIPATION RANK	d	d²
01	3	3	6.5* (5 + 6 + 7 + 8)/4	7 (6 + 7 + 8)/3	.5	.25
02	2	3	3.5 (3 + 4)/2	7 (6 + 7 + 8)/3	3.5	12.25
03	1	2	1.5 (1 + 2)/2	4 (3 + 4 + 5)/3	2.5	6.25
04	3	3	6.5 (5 + 6 + 7 + 8)/4	7 (6 + 7 + 8)/3	.5	.25
05	3	1	6.5 (5 + 6 + 7 + 8)/4	1.5 (1 + 2)/2	5	25
06	1	1	1.5 (1 + 2)/2	1.5 (1 + 2)/2	0	0
07	3	2	6.5 (5 + 6 + 7 + 8)/4	4 (3 + 4 + 5)/3	2.5	6.25
08	2	2	3.5 (3 + 4)/2	4 (3 + 4 + 5)/3	.5	.25
Total						50.50

* *Note:* When two numbers in the data set are the same, researchers could add the next two ranks together and divide them by 2. For example, there are two 1's under Hearing. They cannot both be rank #1. Instead adding rank #1 and rank #2 together and dividing them by 2, we have 1.5 for both. The procedure is the same where there are 3 or more of same numbers. This calculation is included in the paraphrase in the table above. Also note that the manually calculated result may be slightly different from the software generated results. Some attribute it possibly to the different algorithms employed and the small sample size.

Result: $r_s(6) = .3988$, $p < .05$ (Two-tailed)

Conclusion: The null hypothesis is rejected, and the alternative hypothesis is supported. Older adults' hearing ability has a weak but statistically significant correlation to their level of participation in activity.

CORRELATION WITH MORE THAN TWO VARIABLES

Correlation Matrix

With the help of statistics software programs, researchers nowadays could run correlation analysis with several variables at once. A correlation matrix will be generated to display how each of the variables correlate to other variables. This matrix provides a comprehensive view of the relationship among the variables involved and where the major correlations reside. This table looks like a spreadsheet and could be constructed differently to meet the unique needs of the study. Table 15.10 is an example of a common correlation matrix showing the correlations among the six variables for a study of youth offenders.

TABLE 15.10. **Common Correlation Matrix Youth Offenders Study Correlation Table**

	1	2	3	4	5	6
Age	–					
Number of offenses	.47*	–				
Years of education	−.63**	.05	–			
Years of AOD use	.54**	.91***	.14	–		
Family support score	.49*	−.54**	.82***	−.57**	–	
Peer support score	.58**	−.45*	.93***	−.46*	.74***	–

*$P < .05$. **$P < .01$. ***$P < .001$.

This correlation matrix presents the following statistical findings:
- Age is significantly correlated to Number of offenses, years of education, years of AOD use, family support, and peer support
- Number of offenses is significantly correlated to age, years of AOD use, family support, and peer support but not with years of education
- Years of education is significantly correlated to age, family support, and peer support; but not with years of education and years of AOD use
- Years of AOD use is significantly correlated to all the other factors except years of education
- Family support and peer support are significantly correlated to all the other factors

Partial r

Partial r is a linear correlation coefficient that measures the strength and direction of two continuous variables while controlling the third continuous variable that is also called a covariate. It is a measure for interval and ratio variables. Controlling means holding a variable (a covariate or a confounding variable) constant to reduce its effects on the other test variables. This will allow the study to get a clearer and better understanding of the relations between the two test variables.

BOX 15.13. PARTIAL r—PRACTICE COURSE, INTERNSHIP, AND PRIOR HUMAN SERVICE EXPERIENCE

To what extent, do social work students' practice class grades correlate to their internship grades? Would students' prior human service experience affects this correlation? Partial r could be used to control the years of prior human service experience and then explore the relations between practice course grades and internship grades.

Research hypothesis (H_y): There is a correlation between practice course grades and internship grades

Null hypothesis (H_0): When controlling the prior human service experience, there is no correlation between practice course grades and internship grades

Alternative hypothesis (H_1): When controlling the prior human service experience, there is a correlation between practice course grades and internship grades

Control variable 1: Practice course grades—(X)

Control variable 2: Internship course grades—(Y)

Covariate: Years of prior human service experience

Data: Practice course grade-86, 90, 82, 75, 93, 84, 93, 90, 88, 80
Internship course grade-90, 92, 80, 85, 96, 88, 95, 91, 90, 85
Years of prior human service experience (HSExp)-3, 4, 1, 0, 6, 3, 8, 2, 1, 2

SPSS Output:

CORRELATIONS			PRACTICE	INTERNSHIP	HSExp
CONTROL VARIABLES					
-none-[a]	practice	Correlation	1.000	.849	.764
		Significance (2-tailed)	.	.002	.010
		df	0	8	8
	Internship	Correlation	.849	1.000	.782
		Significance (2-tailed)	.002	.	.008
		df	8	0	8
	HSExp	Correlation	.764	.782	1.000
		Significance (2-tailed)	.010	.008	.
		df	8	8	0
HSExp	practice	Correlation	1.000	.626	
		Significance (2-tailed)	.	.072	
		df	0	7	
	Internship	Correlation	.626	1.000	
		Significance (2-tailed)	.072	.	
		df	7	0	

[a.]Cells contain zero-order (Pearson) correlations.

Result: When controlling human service experience, r(7) = .626, $p < .10$ (two-tailed)

Conclusion: All three variables are positively correlated with one another with r = .849, .764, and .782 respectively. When controlling prior human service experience, there is a decreased but significant correlation (r = .626, $p < .10$) between practice course grades and internship grades.

CONCLUSION

This chapter explored the various inquiries of how variables are related to each other. Chi-square (X^2) statistics, Fisher's exact test, and chi-square goodness of fit test are common tests that examine the correlational relationship for nominal level variables. Spearman correlation coefficient (r_s or Rho) is suitable for ordinal variables. Pearson's product-moment correlation coefficient (r) is the statistic for interval and ratio variables. Related concepts, including degrees of freedom and coefficient of determination, were explained. Partial r can be used to study the correlation for more than two variables. Readers may wish to further explore other multivariate analysis approaches, such as multiple R, factor analysis, and regression for more advanced studies.

16 TESTS OF DIFFERENCE

The ability to differentiate and to integrate plays an important role in our cognitive development as well as our capacity for problem solving. One of the most common forms of questioning on a test paper typically begins with "compare and contrast." In social work practice research, practitioners often need to compare the differences between groups, between tests, and between attributes. These findings could be used for many purposes including assessing the outcomes of interventions, identifying varying needs within and between groups, and making evidence-based inferences.

Comparisons could be made based on the different parameters of the datasets that are at the ordinal, interval, or ratio levels of measurement. The most basic comparison is based on the original raw value. Vera gets 20 points for her exam and Jisu gets 30 points from hers. On the surface, Jisu gets more points than Vera as there is a 10 point difference ($30 - 20 = 10$). However, the truth may be a very different story: Vera gets 20 out of 50 points from her statistics class but Jisu gets 30 out of 100 points from a different statistics class. Percentage-wise, Vera is doing better. Straight comparison of raw values is simple and easy, but the result could be misleading. Certainly using other parameters such as percentage would be a more reliable option. It would be an even better and clearer comparison if the researchers would use more refined parameters such as mean, standard deviation, or variance. This chapter will examine the use of these parameters to test the differences between data sets and to assess their statistical significance.

STANDARD ERROR OF THE MEAN

Standard error (SE, $\sigma_{\bar{x}}$) describes the variability and distribution of a sample parameter such as a mean or a median. It reflects the extent to which this parameter changes or is different from sample to sample. **Standard error of the mean** is an estimate of the distribution of the sample means (parameter) around the estimated population mean.

Researchers want to know more about the ages of the graduating social work students in their school. It is a large program with 300 graduating Bachelor of Social Work candidates. They randomly sample 50 graduating students from the population (i.e., 300 students) and ask them their age. They repeat the same process for another 99 groups of randomly selected 50 students. As expected, due to sampling error, each group is a bit different from each other and from the population although they are randomly selected. The researchers calculate the mean for each of the 100 groups (samples) and plot these sample means on a histogram. A **sampling distribution of the sample means** is so formed. The standard deviation of this sampling distribution of the sample means is, therefore, the **standard error of the mean**.

The standard error of the mean is affected by the sample size. Researchers could increase the number of these randomly sampled groups from 100 groups of 50 students to 500 groups of 50 students. They could also increase the size of each of these 100 groups from 50 students to 200 students. With the increase of sample size, the "mean of the sample means" will be getting closer to the "true population mean." The sampling distribution of the sample means will also approach the normal distribution. Using a common example from many kitchens, the chance of getting a better taste of the full complexity of a bowl of chili could be better achieved by a big enough bowl or sufficient number of tastings than just one try with a small spoon. The more you try, the more accurate you get with less error. *The larger the sample size the smaller the sampling error.* A regular standard deviation for a normal distribution, however, would not be affected significantly by the sample size.

Researchers use samples to estimate the properties of the population. When there is a sample, there is a chance for error (of being different from the population). The parameter (i.e., mean) of samples therefore, with some degree of confidence (or error), could give researchers an estimate or a range of how likely they could represent the population. This range is the confidence interval (CI). This interval is an estimate within which the population mean is likely to be located. For example, how confident are you after overhearing someone speaking English in Germany and predicting this person is an American from the South? The standard error of the mean is a statistical concept that is crucial in hypothesis testing. It is related to the confidence interval (CI) that plays an important role in statistical analysis and their interpretations such as the significance level of the finding.

Standard Deviation and Standard Error of the Mean

A standard deviation is a measure of the actual spread or distribution of the original data around the population mean in a normal distribution. Whereas, a standard error of the mean is the likely spread or distribution of the sample means around the estimated population mean. Just like the standard deviation, the standard error of the mean could help to assess whether sample means are representative of the population mean. Table 16.1 summarizes the differences:

TABLE 16.1. Standard Deviation and Standard Error of the Mean

STANDARD DEVIATION	STANDARD ERROR OF THE MEAN
1. A measure of the dispersion of the *original values* or samples in a normal distribution	1. A measure of the dispersion of the *sample means* in the sampling distribution
2. It is "a measure of the variability of the sample" (McHugh, 2008, p. 7)	2. It is "a measure of the variability of the sampling distribution" (McHugh, 2008, p. 7)
3. A normal distribution of the sample values around the population mean	3. A standard deviation distribution of the sample means around the estimated population mean
4. Helps to assess whether the original data or samples are representative of the population	4. Helps to assess the preciseness or exactness of an estimate representing the population mean based on the sample means
5. Is a descriptive statistic of the actual distribution of original values	5. Is an inferential statistic based on the probability of the standard errors
6. Not affected by the sample size, the standard deviation remains constant	6. Affected by the sample size. The larger the sample size the smaller the standard error to the point that it could reach zero

The following is the formula for the standard error of the mean. Mathematically, as the sample size (N) gets larger the resulting standard error of the mean gets smaller.

$$\sigma_{\bar{x}} = \frac{\sigma}{\sqrt{N}}$$

Where:

$\sigma_{\bar{x}}$ = Standard error of the mean

σ = the original standard distribution $\bar{x}$

N = the sample size

USING T-STATISTICS IN TEST OF DIFFERENCE

A major test of difference between means is the t-test and it is related to the Z test that we discussed in the previous chapter. There are several types of t-test: one-sample t-test, independent t-test, correlated/paired/matched t-test, and ANOVA (a.k.a. extended t-test). Table 16.2 provides a summary of these tests.

William Gosset introduced t-statistics in 1908 under the pseudonym of "Student" to test the quality of Guinness stout in Ireland (hence, Student's t-test). It was used for the purpose of quality control to monitor the quality of the productions. A t-test could be used to make sure the samples are consistent with, or are not different from, the production standards (population mean, norm, or known value). In any production, if one batch of the products (dependent variable) were significantly different from the norm or another batch, then the cause (independent variable) of the difference would need to be identified.

Basic Assumptions for t-Statistics

As inferential statistics, all of these tests aim to explore "whether there is a significant difference?" and "If so, is it due to chance or something else, i.e., an independent variable?" They are also based on the following assumptions:

1. The dependent variable is a continuous variable (interval/ratio).
2. The observations of the dependent variable are independent from each other (assumption of independence), except for the correlated t-test.
3. The dependent variable should be normally distributed, or the sample size is large enough to assume normality (assumption of normality).

4. Outliers for the dependent variable may affect the statistical outcomes.
5. Many also assume the variances across groups for the dependent variables are equal (assumption of homogeneity).

Confidence Interval

As discussed before, a confidence interval is an estimated range of sample mean values (parameter) that also contains the population mean. It is a normally anticipated range. This is similar to our expectations that most first-year MSW students would have professional competencies that are within the normal range for first-year students.

Conversely, a confidence interval could also be calculated for a range of *"mean differences."* Every student performs, on an average, differently from each other (mean difference) and these mean differences could form a range. Most of the time, professors would expect that the differences are within the range (confidence interval). When one of the mean-differences is so out-of-range then it may be considered as significantly different.

The t-statistic is calculated based on the *"difference of the means."* The t-distribution curve, therefore, is a distribution of the *"differences of the means"* around the center, which is a zero (0). The t-statistic uses the t-distribution just as the Z statistic uses the standard normal distribution. All t-tests generate t-scores and with their associated p-values; they allow researchers to compare different scores in a standardized structure. Table 16.3 is the table of the distribution of the critical values of t.

ONE-SAMPLE t-TEST

One-sample t-test compares the sample mean to the known population mean or a known value. A known value could be the standard that is being tested against and is also known as the test value. It could be the historical mean or a hypothesized population mean. A t-test tests whether the sample is different from the population or a set standard. Practically every sample, even those randomly formed, will be different from each other and from the population. The question is whether it is so different that it is out of the range of the confidence interval. The one-sample t-test allows the researcher to measure this difference and the significance of this difference. The t-test result could determine whether the sample is from or belongs

TABLE 16.2. Testing for Difference between Means

TYPE OF TEST	COMMON USE (AND SPECIFIC ASSUMPTIONS)	FORMULA AND DEGREES OF FREEDOM (df)	SUMMARY QUESTIONS/ DESCRIPTIONS AND HYPOTHESIS
Z-test	Compare two samples on a standard normal distribution. Are the means ($\bar{X}$) of two data sets significantly different? Given the variance (σ^2), [therefore, S.D. (σ)], is known.	$z = \dfrac{x - \bar{x}}{\sigma}$ df: Not applicable	"*Converting and comparing oranges and apples on a standardized scale as fruits.*" $H_0: \bar{X}_1 = \bar{X}_2$ ¦or¦ $\bar{X}_1 - \bar{X}_2 = 0$ $H_1: \bar{X}_1 \neq \bar{X}_2$ (Two-tailed) $H_2: \bar{X}_1 > \bar{X}_2$ ¦or¦ $\bar{X}_1 < \bar{X}_2$ (One-tailed)
One-sample t-test (student's t-test)	Test the statistically significant mean difference between a sample mean ($\bar{X}$) and the population mean (μ) or a known value using a t-distribution. Given the population variance is unknown	$t = \dfrac{\bar{X} - \mu}{S/\sqrt{n}}$ df = n − 1 Where: s -Sample standard deviation	"*Are you one of us?*" "*Are you the same or different than us?*" $H_0: \mu = \bar{X}$ ¦or¦ $\mu - \bar{X} = 0$ $H_1: \mu \neq \bar{X}$ (Two-tailed) $H_2: \mu > \bar{X}$ ¦or¦ $\mu < \bar{X}$ (One-tailed)
Independent t-test (two-sample t-test)	Test of statistically significant mean difference between two independent (distinct) groups using a t-distribution. Assuming independent groups, normality of distribution, and homogeneity of variances (i.e., equal variances)	$t = \dfrac{(\bar{X}_1 - \bar{X}_2) - (\mu_1 - \mu_2)}{s_p^2 \sqrt{\dfrac{1}{n_1} + \dfrac{2}{n_2}}}$ df = $n_1 + n_2 - 2$ or N − 2 Where: s_p^2 -Pooled estimate of variance	"*Are these two independent groups different from each other?*" $H_0: \bar{X}_1 = \bar{X}_2$ ¦or¦ $\bar{X}_1 - \bar{X}_2 = 0$ $H_1: \bar{X}_1 \neq \bar{X}_n$ (Two-tailed) $H_2: \bar{X}_1 > \bar{X}_2$ ¦or¦ $\bar{X}_1 < \bar{X}_2$ (One-tailed)

Conceptual and Practical Research and Statistics for Social Workers

TABLE 16.2. Testing for Difference between Means (*Continued*)

TYPE OF TEST	COMMON USE (AND SPECIFIC ASSUMPTIONS)	FORMULA AND DEGREES OF FREEDOM (*df*)	SUMMARY QUESTIONS/ DESCRIPTIONS AND HYPOTHESIS
Correlated t-test (Paired t-test, Matched t-test, Dependent t-test)	Test of statistically significant mean difference between two correlated groups using a t-distribution. The groups could be repeated measures or two methods of measurement of the same subjects. They could also be specifically matched pairs. Essentially it is a one-sample t-test comparing $\bar{X}_1$ to $\bar{X}_2$ instead of $\bar{X}_1$ or $\bar{X}_2$ to μ.	$$t = \frac{\sum d}{\sqrt{\dfrac{n\left(\sum d^2\right) - \left(\sum d\right)^2}{n_1}}}$$ $df = n - 1$ Where: d-difference between two observations on the same subject, i.e., $\bar{X}_1 - \bar{X}_2$	*"The pre and post comparison – Has there been a change"* *"The twins study – Are they somehow different?"* $H_0 : \bar{X}_1 = \bar{X}_2$!or! $\bar{X}_1 - \bar{X}_2 = 0$ $H_1 : \bar{X}_1 \neq \bar{X}_2$ (Two-tailed) $H_2 : \bar{X}_1 > \bar{X}_2$!or! $\bar{X}_1 < \bar{X}_2$ (One-tailed)
One-way ANOVA	Test of statistically significant mean difference between two or more independent groups using an F-distribution. Assuming homogeneity of variance (i.e., equal variance)	$$F = \frac{\text{Mean Square between}}{\text{Mean Square within}}$$ $$F = \frac{MS_{Between}}{MS_{Within}}$$ $df_{between} = K - 1$ $df_{within} = n - K$ $df_{total} = n - 1$	*"Host, please, party for two or more. Some of us want to sit around one table but some want to be at separate tables."* $H_0 : \mu_1 = \mu_2 = \mu_3 = \mu_n$ $H_1 : \mu_1 \neq \mu_2$ (Two-tailed), at least one of the group means (e.g., μ_3) is different from the other group means (e.g., μ_1 & μ_2).

Where:
N- Number of cases,
X- Raw value
$\bar{X}$- Sample mean
μ- Population mean
σ- Population standard deviation or S.D.
σ^2- Population variance
s- Sample standard deviation
s^2- Sample variance
s_p^2- Pooled estimate of variance

TABLE 16.3. Table of the Distribution of the Critical Values of t

	CRITICAL VALUES OF t					
	LEVELS OF SIGNIFICANCE FOR A ONE-TAILED TEST					
	0.1	0.05	0.025	0.01	0.005	0.0005
	LEVELS OF SIGNIFICANCE FOR A TWO-TAILED TEST					
df	0.2	0.1	0.05	0.02	0.01	0.001
1	3.078	6.314	31.821	31.821	63.657	636.619
2	1.886	2.920	4.303	6.965	9.925	31.598
3	1.638	2.353	3.182	4.541	5.841	12.941
4	1.533	2.132	2.776	3.747	4.604	8.610
5	1.476	2.015	2.571	3.365	4.032	6.859
6	1.440	1.943	2.447	3.143	3.707	5.959
7	1.415	1.895	2.365	2.998	3.499	5.405
8	1.397	1.860	2.306	2.896	3.355	5.041
9	1.383	1.833	2.262	2.821	3.250	4.781
10	1.372	1.812	2.228	2.764	3.169	4.587
11	1.363	1.796	2.201	2.718	3.106	4.437
12	1.356	1.782	2.179	2.681	3.055	4.318
13	1.350	1.771	2.160	2.650	3.012	4.221
14	1.345	1.761	2.145	2.624	2.977	4.140
15	1.341	1.753	2.131	2.602	2.947	4.073
16	1.337	1.746	2.120	2.583	2.921	4.015
17	1.333	1.740	2.110	2.567	2.898	3.965
18	1.330	1.734	2.101	2.552	2.878	3.922
19	1.328	1.729	2.093	2.539	2.861	3.883
20	1.325	1.725	2.086	2.528	2.845	3.850
21	1.323	1.721	2.080	2.518	2.831	3.819
22	1.321	1.717	2.074	2.508	2.819	3.792
23	1.319	1.714	2.069	2.500	2.807	3.767
24	1.318	1.711	2.064	2.492	2.797	3.745
25	1.316	1.708	2.060	2.485	2.787	3.725
26	1.315	1.706	2.056	2.479	2.779	3.707
27	1.314	1.703	2.052	2.473	2.771	3.690
28	1.313	1.701	2.048	2.467	2.763	3.674
29	1.311	1.699	2.045	2.462	2.756	3.659
30	1.310	1.697	2.042	2.457	2.750	3.646
40	1.303	1.684	2.021	2.423	2.704	3.551
60	1.296	1.671	2.000	2.390	2.660	3.460
120	1.289	1.658	1.980	2.358	2.617	3.373

Source: Original data from Table III (p. 46) R.A. Fisher and F. Yates (1963). *Statistical Tables for Biological, Agricultural, and Medical Research. (6th ed.).* New York: Hafner Publishing Co.

to the population. In cases where the value of the sample is supposedly changed by the independent variable, a t-test could help to assess the significance of the change.

Let's consider the following scenarios. Rami found out she has become the administrator for a large inheritance from a rich granduncle who had no children. As she has expected, several new people whom she has never met have come forward and claimed to be blood relatives of her granduncle. They want to have a share of the inheritance. The first question that comes to mind for Rami is "Are you one of us? Are you truly my long-lost cousin?" Rami has her job cut out for her. However, if this can be done statistically, she probably will use the one-sample t-test. She will try to find out whether the samples (claimers) are truly from the population (Granduncle's relatives) or are they completely out of the range.

Nqobile works in an under-performing school district. Children in the district face many challenges that have negatively affected their academic performance. To her surprise, not everything is gloom and doom. Some children actually have overcome challenges and done extremely well academically. Nqobile decides to conduct a study to identify what factors have contributed to these children's successes. The one-sample t-test would be among the many statistical tests that she would employ to complete her study. She uses the one-sample t-test to find out if these outstanding performances are just a fluke, due to chance, or due to something else. By controlling that "something else," she could use the one-sample t-test to check if the difference continues to exist.

BOX 16.1. ONE-SAMPLE T-TEST—BEREAVEMENT RISK ASSESSMENT

Ofentse runs a grief and loss intervention group in a community center. All such groups are closed groups, but they employ an open-enrollment approach when the group is formed with no eligibility requirements for participation. Group participants however are asked to complete a one-page questionnaire at the beginning stage to assist program planning. The questionnaire includes a short bereavement risk assessment form which produces a Bereavement Risk Score (BR Score) ranging from 0 to 10. A score of 5 or below represents "normal" bereavement adjustment capacities according to two prior large-scale studies. Ofentse wants to know if his summer group that had 10 members was representative of the general population.

H_0: The summer group's bereavement risk is not different from that of the general population (H_0: $\bar{X} = \mu$)

H_1: The summer group's bereavement risk is greater than that of the general population (H_1: $\bar{X} > \mu$)

Members' BR Scores: 4.5, 9.2, 6.9, 3.9, 8.8, 7.8, 4.3, 8.6, 6.7, and 6.8.

Degrees of Freedom = N − 1 = 10 − 1 = 9

Test-value = 5

Ofentse input the data into SPSS and received the following printout:

One-Sample Statistics

	N	MEAN	STD. DEVIATION	STD. ERROR MEAN
Bereavement Risk Score	10	6.750	1.942	.614

One-Sample Test

	TEST VALUE = 5					
					95% CONFIDENCE INTERVAL OF THE DIFFERENCE	
	T	DF	SIG. (2-TAILED)	MEAN DIFFERENCE	LOWER	UPPER
Bereavement Risk Score	2.850	9	.019	1.750	.360	3.139

Statistical Findings: $t = 2.85$, df = 9, $p < .05$ (one-tailed) or $t(9) = 2.85$, $p < .05$ (one-tailed)

The mean BR score for the sample is 6.75. The SPSS result shows a p = value of .019 for a two-tailed test. Ofentse converted that into a one-tailed p-value by dividing it by 2. With .019/2 = .0095, Ofentse could, therefore, list the test statistic's p value as p = .0095, or p < .05 or even p < .01.

Conclusion: Ofentse would reject the null hypothesis and consider the alternative hypothesis. His summer group had greater bereavement risk than the general population.

BOX 16.2. ONE-SAMPLE T-TEST—HEIGHTS AMONG MALE YOUTHS

Lutfana is a social worker in a community action agency. She has noticed that on average youth who have grown up in this economically challenged neighborhood are shorter than youth from other neighborhoods. She is not quite sure if that is true at all. She however suspects that if this observation is true, the lack of resources and access to a nutritional diet and physical activities may be the culprits. She wants to use this data to be the starting point for her community organizing to promote community health and access to healthy foods and other resources.

She collected the heights of a random sample of 30 adult males aged 20 to 29 who have lived in the neighborhood because they were children. She wants to compare this data with the United States Center for Disease Control and Prevention (CDC) 2016 report that the mean height for males aged 20 to 29 is 68.90 inches (Anthropometric Reference Data for Children and Adults: United States, 2011–2014, Table 11, p. 15, https://www.cdc.gov/nchs/data/series/sr_03/sr03_039.pdf).

H_0: The mean height of the sample is not different from that of the general population (H_0: $\bar{X} = \mu$)

H_1: The mean height of the sample is shorter than that of the general population (H_1: $\bar{X} < \mu$)

Degrees of Freedom = $N - 1 = 30 - 1 = 29$

Population mean = 68.90

Lutfana input the data into SPSS and received the following printout:

One-Sample Statistics

	N	MEAN	STD. DEVIATION	STD. ERROR MEAN
Height	30	63.40	6.30	1.15

One-Sample Test

					TEST VALUE = 68.90	
					95% CONFIDENCE INTERVAL OF THE DIFFERENCE	
	T	DF	SIG. (2-TAILED)	MEAN DIFFERENCE	LOWER	UPPER
Height	−4.781	29	.000	−5.500	−7.852	−3.147

Statistical Findings: $t(29) = -4.781$, $p < .001$ (one-tailed)

The mean height for the sample is 63.40 inches. The SPSS analysis supplies a result of p = .000, which means the p value is smaller than .0005 for a two-tailed test. A one-tailed test will be even smaller (i.e., half) than .0005 or the preset α of .001.

Conclusion: Lutfana would reject the null hypothesis and consider the alternative hypothesis. Her suspicion that young males in this neighborhood are shorter than the population average is confirmed. The reasons for the difference, however, are a subject for further studies.

INDEPENDENT t-TEST

The independent t-test is also called the two-sample t-test and the unpaired t-test. It is used to test a statistically significant mean difference between two independent or unrelated groups using a t-distribution. The t-score or t-value is achieved by dividing the difference between means with the standard error of difference between the groups. *The larger the t-value the greater the difference between groups; the smaller the t-value the more the similarity between groups.*

For a classic experimental design, the difference of the results between the experimental group and the control group could be tested by using the independent t-test. The independent t-test aims to answer the question of whether there is a difference. If so, is it due to chance or due to the independent variable? As with many social work studies, researchers *may not have any knowledge of the population mean and its variance or standard deviation.* The independent t-test allows these to remain unknown and still be able to make the comparison.

Assumptions

There are several key assumptions underlying the use of the independent t-test.

1. *Independent groups.* Categorical groups involved should be unrelated and independent from each other. "Membership" in each of the groups should be exclusive, so that belonging to one group excludes one from belonging to another group. A fifth grader is not a sixth grader, and vice versa. In a playful way to say it, the independent variable for an independent t-test should be groups that are independent from each other!
2. *Normality.* The independent variable should be approximately normally distributed. If not, a similar test for ordinal level variables such as the Mann-Whitney U test should be used instead. However, the independent t-test is a rather robust statistical test that it can tolerate minor deviation from normality. It is particularly true when the sizes of the comparison groups are similar.
3. *Homogeneity.* The variances of the two groups or datasets involved should be equal (i.e., equal variance assumed). If not a different reading (i.e., equal variance not assumed) of the t-statistics should be used (see examples, explanations, and Table 16.4).

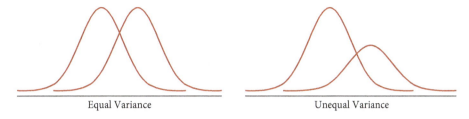

Equal Variance   Unequal Variance

Figure 16.1. Homogeneity of Variance

TABLE 16.4. Levene's Test of Equality and Choice of t-statistics

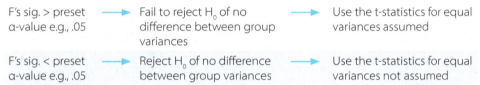

F's sig. > preset α-value e.g., .05	→	Fail to reject H_0 of no difference between group variances	→	Use the t-statistics for equal variances assumed
F's sig. < preset α-value e.g., .05	→	Reject H_0 of no difference between group variances	→	Use the t-statistics for equal variances not assumed

An independent t-test assumes homogeneity that the variances for the two samples are equal, and **Levene's test of equality** is commonly used to test this assumption. Statistical software such as SPSS would automatically run this analysis for independent t-test. It also provides two different t-statistics based on the analysis' F score and its level of significance to decide whether homogeneity (equal variances) is assumed.

If the F score's level of significance is greater than the researcher's p value such as .05, the researcher fails to reject the null hypothesis that there is no difference between means. In other words, the variances are assumed equal and the assumption for homogeneity is satisfied. The t-statistics for "equal variances assumed" would be used.

However, if the F score's level of significance is smaller than the p-value, then the researcher rejects the null hypothesis that there is no difference between means. There is a significant difference between the variances and "equal variances not assumed."

Simply speaking *"F's sig > α, equal variance assumed; F's sig < α, equal variance not assumed"* or *"Greater assumed, smaller not assumed."* Statistical analysis software such as SPSS would provide statistically adjusted t-statistics with modified degrees of freedom for such analyses. More specifically, it will involve a reduction of the t-statistics and the degrees of Freedom.

Sometimes, negative t-scores are indicated in the analysis. The sign of the t-statistics is somewhat irrelevant. A negative score has no bearing on the significance of the difference between the groups tested. Researchers could interpret the negative or positive t-test in the same manner. Negative or positive t-values reflect whether the t-value is smaller or larger than the hypothesized t-value. It could be the outcome of the order or arrangement of the numeric values.

Practice Examples

There are many situations in which the independent t-test could be used to make the comparison. It will measure whether there is a difference; if so, is it a significant difference? The following social work practice examples demonstrate the usage and procedures involved in using the independent t-test. Again, it is assumed that researchers are using statistical software such as SPSS for the analysis.

In collaboration with the teachers, a school social worker organized an after-school math-tutoring program run by college students for the fifth graders. The targeted participants were students whose math grades were at, or lower than, the 40th percentile of the school standards. At the end of the school year, they pulled the math grades of students who met the inclusion criteria at the beginning of the school year. They compared those who had regularly participated in the tutoring program with those who had not. Because they were comparing two independent groups (students who were in tutoring and students who were not) on a continuous variable (course grade), they decided to test the effectiveness of the tutoring program by using an independent t-test.

A County Adult Protective Service social worker has been wondering if the caseload for staff who have an MSW is somehow different from other staff who do not have an MSW. She gathers the necessary data on MSW degree (independent variable, nominal variable) and caseload (Dependent variable, continuous variable) for the comparisons using the independent t-test. She also suspects that there is a difference in caseload (Dependent variable, continuous variable) between two difference office locations (independent variable, nominal variable). She again uses the independent t-test to test her hypothesis. Box 16.3 and Box 16.4 below show the use of the independent t-test and how the statistical findings are being interpreted.

A minority outreach social worker, Dorji, wants to find out if there is a significant difference in the attitudes toward mental illness (dependent variable) by Bhutanese American adults aged 20 to 25. He suspects that having their formative years in the United States (independent variable) may be related to the difference if there is any. He recruited two groups of Bhutanese American adult respondents of suitable ages who are either recent immigrants (n = 20) or born and raised in the United Sates (n = 22). He used the newly developed Bhutanese American Attitudes toward Mental Illness scale for his study. The 30-item scale produces a numeric Bhutanese American Attitudes toward Mental Illness (BAAMI) score between 1 and 100. A higher number reflects higher acceptance and positive attitudes toward mental illnesses. Dorji uses the independent t-test to find out if there is a difference, and if so, is it significant?

H_0: There is no difference in attitudes toward mental illness among immigrant and U.S. born Bhutanese Americans ($H_0 : \overline{X}_1 = \overline{X}_2$)

H_1: There is a significant difference in attitude toward mental illness between immigrant and U.S. born Bhutanese Americans ($H_1 : \overline{X}_1 \neq \overline{X}_2$)

Degrees of Freedom = $n_1 + n_2 - 2 = 20 + 22 - 2 = 40$

Dorji input the data into SPSS and received the following printout:

Group Statistics

	US BORN & RAISED	N	MEAN	STD. DEVIATION	STD. ERROR MEAN
BAAMI	Recent immigrant	20	72.60	10.359	2.316
	US born & raised	22	85.59	7.202	1.536

Independent Samples Test

		LEVENE'S TEST FOR EQUALITY OF VARIANCES		T-TEST FOR EQUALITY OF MEANS					95% CONFIDENCE INTERVAL OF THE DIFFERENCE	
		F	SIG.	t	df	SIG. (2-TAILED)	MEAN DIFFERENCE	STD. ERROR DIFFERENCE	LOWER	UPPER
BAAMI	Equal variances assumed	1.770	.191	−4.755	40	.000	−12.991	2.732	−18.513	−7.469
	Equal variances not assumed			−4.675	33.513	.000	−12.991	2.779	−18.642	−7.340

Levene's Test for Equality: The F score for Levene's test is 1.770 with a sig. (or p) = .191 which is larger than the pre-set alpha (α) of .05 (p > .05). That means the researcher failed to reject the null hypothesis of no difference between variances. The assumption of homogeneity is satisfied and that there is no difference for the variances. The researchers should, therefore, use the t statistics from the row of "Equal variances assumed."

Statistical Findings: $t(40) = -4.755$, $p < .001$ (one-tailed)

The mean BAAMI scores are significantly different between the immigrated and American born Bhutanese Americans.

The SPSS analysis supplies a p-value of .000. That means the p-value is in fact smaller than .0005 for a two-tailed test. The p-value for a one-tailed test will be half of .0005 and, therefore, even smaller.

Conclusion: Dorji would reject the null hypothesis and consider the alternative hypothesis. His suspicion that there is a difference due to the length of time in the US is supported.

BOX 16.4. INDEPENDENT t-TEST—FAMILY WELLNESS VOTING STUDY

Hadiya is a social worker for a legislative advocacy organization. Her agency has set a goal to lobby aggressively for legislation that supports family wellness. To pinpoint her efforts, she studied the voting records of the current State Assembly legislators on family related issues. She got this educated hunch that female legislators (n = 33), in spite of political party affiliation, were more likely to support family related legislations than their male colleagues (n = 47). She, however, was wondering whether this assertion was true or if it was somewhat stereotyping the legislators based on gender. Hadiya identified 20 family-related legislative measures from the last two years and tallied up how many times each male and female legislator had voted "yes" for these 20 bills.

H_0: There is no difference in voting pattern between male and female legislators on family wellness related bills. $(H_0 : \overline{X}_1 = \overline{X}_2)$

H_1: There is a significant difference in voting pattern between male and female legislators on family wellness related bills. $(H_1 : \overline{X}_1 \neq \overline{X}_2)$

Degrees of Freedom = 55.225

Hadiya input the data into SPSS and received the following printout:

Group Statistics

	GENDER	N	MEAN	STD. DEVIATION	STD. ERROR MEAN
Yes Vote #	Male	47	9.77	1.631	.238
	Female	33	16.27	2.226	.387

Independent Samples Test

		LEVENE'S TEST FOR EQUALITY OF VARIANCES						t-TEST FOR EQUALITY OF MEANS			
										95% CONFIDENCE INTERVAL OF THE DIFFERENCE	
		F	SIG.	t	df	SIG. (2-TAILED)	MEAN DIFFERENCE	STD. ERROR DIFFERENCE	LOWER	UPPER	
Yes Vote #	Equal variances assumed	5.861	.018	−15.095	78	.000	−6.507	.431	−7.365	−5.649	
	Equal variances not assumed			−14.310	55.225	.000	−6.507	.455	−7.418	−5.596	

Levene's Test for Equality: The F score for the Levene's test is 5.861 with a sig. of .018 which is smaller than the pre-set alpha of .05 (p < .05). That means the researcher should reject the null hypothesis of no difference for the assumption of homogeneity of variances. In other words, the variances are not equal. The research should, therefore, use the data from the row of "Equal variances not assumed."

Statistical Findings: $t (55.22)= −14.31, p < .001$ (one-tailed)

The mean number of votes that supported family wellness are significantly different between the male and female legislators. The SPSS analysis supplies a p-value of .000. That means the p-value is in fact smaller than .0005 for a two-tailed test. The p-value for a one-tailed test will be half of .0005 and, therefore, be even smaller.

Conclusion: Hadiya would reject the null hypothesis and consider the alternative hypothesis. Female legislators have been more supportive of family wellness related legislative measures than their male counterparts have, in spite of political party affiliation.

CORRELATED t-TEST

The correlated t-test is a test of the mean difference between two correlated groups or sets of observation. It is set up to test if the mean difference between two observations equals zero ($\bar{X}_1 − \bar{X}_2 = 0$), even when the population mean and standard deviation are unknown. It is **basically a one-sample t-test** comparing sample means ($\bar{X}_1$ to $\bar{X}_2$) instead of comparing sample mean(s) to a population mean ($\bar{X}_1$ or $\bar{X}_2$ to μ). It is also called a *repeated measures t-test, matched t-test, paired t-test, or dependent t-test*. It can be used in a variety of situations to check if there is a difference and if the difference is significant.

1. The paired samples are the same group or same set of respondents that are being measured twice (repeated measure), once at a pretest and again in a posttest. For

example, members' social anxiety scores before and after the 6-week intensive group therapy. An observation for one subject at the pretest should have corresponding observation for that subject in the posttest. These observations are dependent of each other (hence, dependent t-test). This is the before and after observations on the same subjects.

2. The test could be used to compare two methods of measurement on the same subjects. For an elementary Spanish language proficiency assessment, a list of verb phrases was read to the subjects. They are asked to spell out the verb phrases in writing and act out or explain their meaning at the same time. Researchers want to find out if there is a difference in demonstrating one's language proficiency through different methods of measurement.

3. The comparing groups may be matched pairs which are identical (such as twins), randomly drawn (therefore presumed equal), or intentionally created with corresponding key characteristics tightly matched. For example, two teams of students that are selected randomly from the same population. Alternatively, two elementary schools that serve communities that are comparable in school performances, socioeconomic background, racial composition, or other measures.

Missing Overlapping Data

Researchers using the correlated t-test often encounter a common problem of missing overlapping data. Respondents from the pretest may decide to drop out or, for whatever reasons, fail to complete the posttest. Corresponding data that are supposed to be overlapping from pretest to posttest are, therefore, missing. Researchers have the following options:

1. Exclude the incomplete data pairs
2. Use the independent t-test instead
3. Continue to use the correlated t-test if the problem of missing data is not serious. Derrick, Toher, and White (2017) suggest, "If the amount of missing data is relatively small, the bias is likely to be inconsequential" (p. 121). They also note "the literature suggests that up to 5% of observations missing is acceptable (Graham, 2009; Schafer, 1997). There are some that take a more liberal stance in the literature suggesting that up to 20% of data missing may be acceptable (Schlomer, Bauman, & Card, 2010)" (p. 121).

Breno is interested in finding whether an audio or visual presentation makes a difference in teaching the adolescents in his youth center on recognizing abusive relationships and their severity. He identifies four (4) incidents of abusive relationships. Each of these incidents is presented both in audio and in pictures. Breno recruited 10 adolescents to participate in this study by rating the presentation and severity on a scale from 1 to 20. The higher the number the more severe the situation. To minimize experimental bias, these four incidents were presented to five of the adolescents in audio while the other five were shown in pictures. A month later, these adolescents were presented with these four incidents again but in the opposite presentation format. This is not a pre/post-test on the adolescents but a comparison of two methods of measurement (audio or pictorial) on the same group of respondents (10 adolescents) for a continuous variable (severity rating). Breno chooses to use the correlated t-test.

H_0: There is no difference in the severity rating by adolescents when the incidents are presented either in audio or in picture. ($H_0 : \overline{X}_1 - \overline{X}_2 = 0$)

H_1: There is a difference in the severity rating by adolescents when the incidents are presented either in audio or in picture. ($H_1 : \overline{X}_2 > \overline{X}_1$)

Severity rating for audio: 15, 14, 13, 18, 11, 9, 17, 12, 11, and 16

Severity rating for picture: 16, 14, 14, 18, 15, 13, 16, 13, 11, and 16

Degrees of Freedom = N − 1 = 10 − 1 = 9

Breno input the data into SPSS and received the following printout:

Paired Samples Statistics

	MEAN	N	STD. DEVIATION	STD. ERROR MEAN
Severity Audio	13.60	10	2.914	.921
Severity Picture	14.60	10	2.011	.636

Paired Samples Correlations

	N	CORRELATION	SIG.
Severity Audio & Severity Picture	10	.823	.003

Paired Samples Test

	PAIRED DIFFERENCES							
				95% CONFIDENCE INTERVAL OF THE DIFFERENCE				
	MEAN	STD. DEVIATION	STD. ERROR MEAN	LOWER	UPPER	T	DF	SIG. (2-TAILED)
Severity Audio-Severity Picture	−1.000	1.700	.537	−2.216	.216	−1.861	9	.096

Statistical Findings: $t(9) = -1.861$, $p > .05$ (two-tailed)

The mean severity rating for the audio presentation is 13.60 and the pictorial presentation is 14.60. The SPSS result shows a p-value of .096 for a two-tailed test, which is larger than the present α value of .05.

Conclusion: Breno would fail to reject the null hypothesis. There is no statistically significant difference in the rating of severity when the incidents are presented in audio or in pictorial format.

ANALYSIS OF VARIANCE (ANOVA)

The **one-way analysis of variance** (ANOVA) compares the means of two or more groups (K) to test if there is a significant difference among them using the F distribution. It is *one-way because it only has one independent variable (factor)*. For that reason, it is also called *single factor analysis of variance*. Often, researchers refer ANOVA as an *extended t-test* for its similar but additional function to t-tests. While t-test compares means between two groups, ANOVA can test across two or more groups. There are several main assumptions for using the ANOVA. They include the assumption of independence, normality, and homogeneity (see description for Table 16.1).

The one-way ANOVA has one nominal level independent variable or *factor* that has different ***groups or levels***. For example, professional social work training could be an independent variable that has three levels: Bachelor, Master, and Doctoral degrees. A respite program for caregivers will have different activities (individual, group, or community) for promoting self-care. A substance abuse program may measure one's sobriety at different time-periods (e.g., 1 month, 3 months, and 6 months).

Similarly, the one-way ANOVA only has one continuous (interval/ratio) dependent variable. Social workers employ three different types (groups—e.g., CBT, DBT, psychosocial) of intervention (independent variable) to treat anxiety (dependent variable—degree of success). Youth from four job-training (independent variable) programs (groups) would participate in the same mock job interview to see if their job readiness levels (dependent variable—assessment grades) are different or have changed.

A researcher may study whether there is a pay difference among home-help workers in three neighboring cities that have similar characteristics. This one-way ANOVA involves one nominal independent variable that has three levels or independent groups, i.e., cities. The dependent variable is the associated amount of pay, which is a continuous variable.

Hypothesis Testing and the Logic of F-statistics

The ANOVA is to test whether the means of different groups (K) are different. Therefore, its null hypothesis is that there is no difference among group means or the group means are equal. It hypothesizes the equality of K groups means. Its alternative hypothesis is that at least one of the group means (e.g., μ_1) is different from the other group means (e.g., μ_n).

$$H_0: \mu_1 = \mu_2 = \mu_3 = \mu_n$$
$$H_1: \mu_1 \neq \mu_n$$

The ANOVA is a type of *omnibus* (Latin for "All") test in that it points out whether there are general departures from the null hypothesis (no differences). It tells whether the differences are significant, but it does not tell where the differences are placed. Researchers, therefore, have to follow up with *post hoc* (Latin for "after this") tests to find out which mean is different. The **Tukey post hoc test** is one of the more commonly used post hoc tests, as demonstrated below.

David anxiously looked at his mother after she took a couple bites of his "imitation" of her famous stuffed turkey dinner. His mom looked up and said, "That is different?" (ANOVA). "Good or bad? How different? What's the difference?" David eagerly asked. His mom said, "Oh, that's good. I really like the stuffing and the tenderness of the turkey, they are delicious!" (post hoc).

TABLE 16.5. Sequences for ANOVA Testing

INDEPENDENT VARIABLE THAT HAS DIFFERENT INDEPENDENT GROUPS/ LEVELS	ASSOCIATED GROUP MEANS FOR THE DEPENDENT VARIABLE	HYPOTHESIS TESTING BASED ON THE F-STATISTICS	POST HOC
Group 1 $\longrightarrow$	μ_1	Are they equal or different?	Where is the difference?
Group 2 $\longrightarrow$	μ_2		
Group n $\longrightarrow$	μ_n	$H_0: \mu_1 = \mu_2 = \mu_3 = \mu_n$	

Degrees of Freedom

There are three different types of degrees of freedom for a one-way ANOVA: the between group degrees of freedom, the within group degrees of freedom, and the total degrees of freedom. Their formulas are listed below, where "K" refers to the number of groups, and "n" refers to the total number of cases or objects.

$df_{between}$ = Degrees of freedom between, $df_{between} = K - 1$
df_{within} = Degrees of freedom within, $df_{within} = n - K$
df_{total} = Total degrees of freedom within, $df_t = df_{between} + df_{within} = (K - 1) + (n - K) = n - 1$

The Formula and the Logic for ANOVA

The following is the basic formula for a One-way ANOVA in various expressions. It uses the F statistics to test the differences among groups. The F statistic formula is presented below first, and the subsequent paragraphs explain the logic behind this formula. Different statistical terms are also introduced to illustrate the formation of the formula.

$$F = \frac{\text{Between group variance}}{\text{Within group variance}} = \frac{\text{Sum of squares between groups (SS}_{\text{Between}})}{\text{Sum of squares within (SS}_{\text{Within}})} \quad \text{or}$$

$$F = \frac{\text{Mean Square between (MS}_{\text{Between}})}{\text{Mean Square within (MS}_{\text{Within}})}$$

The fundamental idea of an ANOVA calculation is comparing the **between groups variance (sum of squares between groups) and the within group variance (sum of squares within)**. The ratio between these two variances is the F statistic that reflects the findings of the analysis. Variance means variations from one sample data to another sample data. From the same population, different randomly selected samples will be different from each other; this variation is also called error.

Sum of squares (SS) is a variation index. It is the sum of the squared differences between the values and their means:

SS = Σ (value – mean)^2
SS$_{\text{Between}}$ = Σ (individual group mean value – overall group mean)^2
SS$_{\text{Within}}$ = Σ (individual observation value – Individual group mean)^2

Mean square (MS) is the result of converting the sum of squares by dividing it with the between (groups) or within (group) degrees of freedom. Mean square is the variance of sample means.

$$MS_{\text{Between}} = \frac{SS_{\text{Between}}}{df_{\text{Between}}}$$

$$MS_{\text{Within}} = \frac{SS_{\text{Within}}}{df_{\text{Within}}}$$

$$\text{As a result, } F = \frac{MS_{\text{Between}}}{MS_{\text{Within}}} = \frac{SS_{\text{Between}}/df_{\text{Between}}}{SS_{\text{Within}}/df_{\text{Within}}}$$

Conceptual and Practical Research and Statistics for Social Workers

A researcher is testing the mean happiness scores between three groups of randomly selected people with her Happy Face intervention technique. Group 1 is the experimental group that gets the happy face treatment, Group 2 is the control group that gets the placebo, and Group 3 is the library-time group. Statistically speaking, all three groups were equal in their happiness score at the beginning of the experiment. What happens after they receive the intervention? ANOVA helps to provide the answers.

The *within group variance* is the difference among members in each of the groups. This difference is just part of the naturally occurring difference and should have nothing to do with the independent variable or the interaction with other groups. That is the internal difference for each of the three groups in the experiment.

The *between group variance* is the difference among individual groups. This difference may have something to do with the effect of the independent variable (the presence of the intervention), the **treatment effect**. It could also be the result of the interactions between groups. At the beginning of the experiment, all three groups were supposedly to be equal with some naturally occurring differences within each group and between themselves. However, after the intervention, the differences between them may be more than naturally occurring errors but in fact the effect of the treatment.

Based on this, the F statistics, as a ratio, could be understood as the following:

$$F = \frac{\text{Between group variance}}{\text{Within group variance}} = \frac{\text{Error (variance)} + \text{Treatment effect}}{\text{Error (variance)}}$$

When the between group variance is equal or very close to the within group variance, one could conclude that the independent variable has no effect on the groups. However, when the between group variance is greater than the within group variance, then the means are not equal. The independent variable or the interaction between groups may have attributed to the difference. Depending on the ratio, i.e., F-statistics, researchers could determine whether the difference is significant. The Happiness study researcher certainly would be happy to see a greater F-value that shows there are differences among the three groups.

$$F = \frac{\text{Between group variance}}{\text{Within group variance}} = \text{smaller F-value} = \text{No or minimum treatment effect}$$

$$F = \frac{\text{Between group variance}}{\text{Within group variance}} = \text{larger F-value} = \text{Possible significant treatment effect}$$

Post Hoc Tests

The F-ratio tells the researchers the overall difference exists and post hoc tests help to tell what and where. There are many post hoc tests for different research needs. The most common ones are the Tukey's Honesty Significant Difference (Tukey's HSD) test and the Least Significant Difference (LSD). Others include Student-Newman-Keuls test, Bonferoni adjustment, Dunnett's C, etc. Post hoc tests work pretty much like t-tests comparing the means of each pair (pairwise comparisons). However, they also take into consideration multiple comparisons involving more than two means. It is similar to running a multitude of t-tests with added statistical corrections. It is not surprising that post hoc tests are also called multiple comparison tests.

On the statistical printout, the mean differences between groups are listed including their level of significance (sig. or p). When the p-value is smaller than the preset alpha (α), which is usually .05, that would mean the difference is significant. At the same time, mean pairs that have no significance (P > .05) would also be identified.

BOX 16.6. ONE-WAY ANOVA–SOCIAL SKILLS ENRICHMENT FOR YOUTH WITH DEVELOPMENTAL DISABILITIES

A nonprofit agency for youths with developmental disabilities plans to implement a social skills enrichment program for the youths in three of its centers. Program staff are wondering if youths in these three locations, on an average, have the same level of social skills competency. To answer that, the staff randomly select 10 youth from each of the centers. With appropriate assistance from the agency staff, each selected youth completes a short Social Skills Assessment form. Because the study attempts to compare the means among three groups, the staff has chosen One-Way ANOVA for the analysis.

H_0: There is no difference in the social skills competency mean scores by youths in three different centers. (H_0: $\mu_1 = \mu_2 = \mu_3$)

H_1: At least one of the groups' social skills competency mean scores is different from the other groups' mean scores. (H_1: $\mu_1 \neq \mu_n$)

Social Skills Competency Score: (SS Competency)

Center A: 11, 12, 14, 12, 13, 11, 9, 10, 14, 10

Center B: 14, 15, 16, 14, 15, 16, 18, 15, 16, 14

Center C: 17, 16, 14, 18, 15, 17, 16, 15, 17, 14

Degrees of Freedom

$df_{between} = K - 1 = 3$ (groups) $- 1 = 2$

$df_{within} = n - K = 30$ (cases) $- 3$ (groups) $= 27$

$df_{total} = (K - 1) + (n - K) = n - 1 = 30 - 1 = 29$

Program staff input the data into SPSS and received the following printout:

Descriptives

					95% CONFIDENCE INTERVAL FOR MEAN			
	N	MEAN	STD. DEVIATION	STD. ERROR	LOWER BOUND	UPPER BOUND	MINIMUM	MAXIMUM
Center A	10	11.60	1.713	.542	10.37	12.83	9	14
Center B	10	15.30	1.252	.396	14.40	16.20	14	18
Center C	10	15.90	1.370	.433	14.92	16.88	14	18
Total	30	14.27	2.392	.437	13.37	15.16	9	18

SS COMPETENCY

ANOVA

SS COMPETENCY

	SUM OF SQUARES	DF	MEAN SQUARE	F	SIG.
Between Groups	108.467	2	54.233	25.510	.000
Within Groups	57.400	27	2.126		
Total	165.867	29			

Multiple Comparisons (Post Hoc Tests)

DEPENDENT VARIABLE: SS COMPETENCY

TUKEY HSD

(I) CENTER LOCATION	(J) CENTER LOCATION	MEAN DIFFERENCE (I-J)	STD. ERROR	SIG.	95% CONFIDENCE INTERVAL	
					LOWER BOUND	UPPER BOUND
Center A	Center B	−3.700*	.652	.000	−5.32	−2.08
	Center C	−4.300*	.652	.000	−5.92	−2.68
Center B	Center A	3.700*	.652	.000	2.08	5.32
	Center C	−.600	.652	.632	−2.22	1.02
Center C	Center A	4.300*	.652	.000	2.68	5.92
	Center B	.600	.652	.632	−1.02	2.22

*The mean difference is significant at the 0.05 level.

Statistical findings. $F_{(2, 27)} = 25.51$, $p < .001$ (Two-tailed)

The social skills competency score is significantly different between the three centers. It is a two-tailed test because F-ratio does not tell which direction the difference is placed

Tukey's HSD post hoc test. There are statistically significant differences between Center A and both Center B and Center C ($p = .000$). The difference between Center B and Center C is not significant ($p = .632$).

Conclusion. The social skills competency for the youth in the three centers are not equal. Center A is significantly different (lower than) from Centers B and C. Whereas there is no difference between Center B and Center C.

BOX 16.7. ONE-WAY ANOVA—SUMMER CAMP CHORES

In a weeklong summer camp, adolescents learned how to be responsible, taking care of themselves and others. Each camper was expected to complete 10 equally demanding chores from a list of 30 during that week. Campers were randomly divided into four groups.

- In Group A, each member received individual assignments directly from the camp counselor, no substitution was allowed.
- Members in Group B also received individual assignments from the camp counselors, but they were allowed to swap tasks with each other.
- Group C members could individually choose which 10 chores they wanted to do.
- Group D members chose their own assignments, but each had 10 passes that they could use to skip doing the chores.

Once the assignments were made, no follow-up reminders were given. On the last day of the camp, campers tallied up how many of their assigned or chosen chores were actually completed. Counselors are interested in knowing if there are differences in chore completion among these four groups that had different ways of getting the chores assigned.

H_0: There is no difference in chore completion by campers of different groups. (H_0: $\mu_1 = \mu_2 = \mu_3 = \mu_4$)

H_1: At least one of the groups' chore completion mean scores is different from the other groups' mean scores. (H_1: $\mu_1 \neq \mu_n$)

Summer Camp Chore Completion Rate:

Group A: 5, 6, 4, 5, 5, 4, 6, 4, 5, 4
Group B: 6, 7, 5, 6, 7, 8, 5, 4, 6, 5
Group C: 8, 9, 8, 10, 8, 9, 10, 10, 9, 10
Group D: 7, 8, 7, 8, 7, 6, 5, 7, 6, 7

Degrees of Freedom

$df_{between} = K - 1 = 4$ (groups) $- 1 = 3$
$df_{within} = n - K = 40$ (cases) $- 4$ (groups) $= 36$
$df_{total} = (K - 1) + (n - K) = n - 1 = 40 - 1 = 39$

Camp counselors input the data into SPSS and received the following printout:

Descriptives

| | | | | | 95% CONFIDENCE INTERVAL FOR MEAN | | | |
	N	MEAN	STD. DEVIATION	STD. ERROR	LOWER BOUND	UPPER BOUND	MINIMUM	MAXIMUM
Group A	10	4.80	.789	.249	4.24	5.36	4	6
Group B	10	5.90	1.197	.379	5.04	6.76	4	8
Group C	10	9.10	.876	.277	8.47	9.73	8	10
Group D	10	6.80	.919	.291	6.14	7.46	5	8
Total	40	6.65	1.847	.292	6.06	7.24	4	10

ANOVA

CHORE COMPLETED					
	SUM OF SQUARES	**DF**	**MEAN SQUARE**	**F**	**SIG.**
Between Groups	100.100	3	33.367	36.400	.000
Within Groups	33.000	36	.917		
Total	133.100	39			

Multiple Comparisons (Post Hoc Tests)

DEPENDENT VARIABLE: CHORE COMPLETED						
TUKEY HSD						
					95% CONFIDENCE INTERVAL	
(I) CAMP GROUP	**(J) CAMP GROUP**	**MEAN DIFFERENCE (I–J)**	**STD. ERROR**	**SIG.**	**LOWER BOUND**	**UPPER BOUND**
Group A	Group B	−1.100	.428	.066	−2.25	.05
	Group C	−4.300*	.428	.000	−5.45	−3.15
	Group D	−2.000*	.428	.000	−3.15	−.85
Group B	Group A	1.100	.428	.066	−.05	2.25
	Group C	−3.200*	.428	.000	−4.35	−2.05
	Group D	−.900	.428	.172	−2.05	.25
Group C	Group A	4.300*	.428	.000	3.15	5.45
	Group B	3.200*	.428	.000	2.05	4.35
	Group D	2.300*	.428	.000	1.15	3.45
Group D	Group A	2.000*	.428	.000	.85	3.15
	Group B	.900	.428	.172	−.25	2.05
	Group C	−2.300*	.428	.000	−3.45	−1.15

*The mean difference is significant at the 0.05 level.

Statistical Findings: $F_{(3, 36)} = 36.40$, $p = .000$ (Two-tailed)

Reject the null hypothesis. There are statistically significant differences in the chore completion rates between the four camper groups.

Tukey's HSD Post Hoc test: There are statistically significant differences between Group A with Group C ($p = .000$) and Group D ($p = .000$). Group B is not significantly different from Group A ($p = .066$) and Group D ($p = .172$). Group C is significantly different ($p = .000$) from the other three groups.

Conclusion: Campers who chose their own chores (Group C) had the highest completion rate. Chores assigned by camp counselors with or without flexibility (Group A and Group B) were equally low in their completion rate. There is no difference between campers who chose their own chores but had passes (Group D) and campers who had assigned chores but had the option of swapping chores with other campers (Group B). Choices, autonomy, expectations, and accountability toward oneself appear to be important concerns in campers' self-management.

OTHER FORMS OF ANALYSIS OF VARIANCE

There are many other forms of analysis of variance. They serve different purposes and have different requirements. Between Group ANOVA tests the mean differences between the groups for the independent variable. Within-group ANOVA assesses the difference within the group. Two-way ANOVA tests two independent variables' effects on the dependent variable. MANOVA tests the difference of the independent variable on two or more dependent variables, while both ANCOVA and MANCOVA test the difference and at the same time controlling one or more covariates. Table 16.6 uses AOD relapse rate and self-efficacy (dependent variables) and various factors (independent variables) to summarize the key types of ANOVA.

NONPARAMETRIC TEST OF DIFFERENCE

Oftentimes social workers encounter data that are of an ordinal level: clients rated their satisfaction of service from unsatisfied, to average, or satisfied. People indicated their needs from service from no need to low need, moderate need, and high need. When the social work researchers want to compare these results between two groups or two populations, they will turn to the Mann-Whitney rank U test or Wilcoxon sign ranked test. These two tests are the parametric alternatives to independent t-test and correlated t-test.

MANN-WHITNEY U TEST

The Mann-Whitney U test (Mann-Whitney Rank Sum Test) is a test of differences between two independent groups on a dependent variable that is ordinal or continuous using the U statistic. Statistician Henry Berthold Mann and his student Donald Ransom Whitney proposed this test in their article "On a Test of Whether One of Two Random Variables Is Stochastically Larger Than the Other" (Mann & Whitney, 1947). This test is also called Mann-Whitney-Wilcoxon test. "In 1947 Mann and Whitney, acknowledging the previous work by Wilcoxon on the two-sample rank sum test (Wilcoxon, 1945), proposed an equivalent test statistic, U, based on the relative ranks of two samples" (Berry, Mielke, & Johnston, 2012, pp. 9–10).

TABLE 16.6. Major Types of Analysis of Variance

TYPE	KEY FEATURES	PURPOSES	NUMBER OF IV	NUMBER OF DV	SAMPLE QUESTIONS
One way ANOVA	Between group ANOVA	Cross-sectional test between two or more groups	1 (Income level)	1 (Relapse rate)	Do AOD relapse rates differ for low, middle, and high-income clients?
	Within group ANOVA (Repeated measures)	Test the same group repeatedly to study change within individuals in the group	1 (Time points)	1 (Relapse rate)	Do AOD post treatment relapse rates change overtime at 2, 4, and 6 months?
Two-way ANOVA	Two Independent variables	Test the mean differences between groups of different characteristics	2 (Gender and income)	1 (Relapse rate)	Do male and female clients of low, middle, and high-income levels differ in their relapse rate?
ANCOVA	ANOVA with Covariates	Test of mean differences while controlling for a continuous covariate IV	1 or more (Gender & Income) + 1 covariate (Education)	1 (Relapse rate)	Do male and female clients of low, middle, and high-income levels differ in their relapse rate after controlling for their level of education?
MANOVA	Multivariate ANOVA	Test of mean differences of two or more DVs while considering the correlation between the DVs	1 (Income level)	2 (Relapse rate and self-efficacy)	Do clients of low, middle, and high-income levels differ in their relapse rate and self-efficacy score?
MANCOCA	Multivariate ANOVA with Covariates	Test of mean differences of two or more DVs while controlling for one or more covariates	1 Income level + 1 Covariate (education)	2 (Relapse rate and self-efficacy)	Do clients of low, middle, and high-income levels differ in their relapse rate and self-efficacy score after controlling for their level of education?

The Mann-Whitney U test is a nonparametric alternative to an independent t-test when the assumptions for t-tests cannot be met. This includes the situation when the samples' observations are not normally distributed. The Mann-Whitney U test uses the groups' medians or rank-order positions for its computation. Because it relies on medians instead of means, it is not sensitive to extreme cases or outliers.

This test is often used in comparing attitudes or behaviors that are measured in an ordinal manner. For example, does having a family member who has a disability affect people's attitude toward the Americans with Disabilities Act (ADA)? Will they have a more or less favorable ranked attitude than people who do not have personal knowledge of someone with a disability? Do boys and girls like ice cream differently? Do boys like ice cream less, about the same as girls, or like ice cream more? Do social work students' ranking preferences of practice specializations differ by where they reside (rural vs. urban)?

Null and Alternative Hypotheses

Instead of comparing sample medians like the t-test comparing the sample means, the Mann-Whitney U test compares the distribution of scores for the two samples. The distribution of scores refers to the shape, size, spread, symmetry, or midpoint of the samples. The Mann-Whitney U test tests whether the two samples are coming from the same population (or populations with the same distributions) and, therefore, should have similar shapes. As a result, the hypotheses for the Mann-Whitney U test are different from those for the t-test:

It is not—H_0 = There is no difference between the medians of sample A and sample B.

It is— H_0 = There is no difference between two samples in their distribution of scores, or

H_0 = The two samples are equal in their distribution of scores, or
H_0 = The two samples have the same distributions (No difference).
H_1 = The two sample are not equal in their distribution of scores

The Mann-Whitney U test combines both samples' observations (scores) into one sample. It then uses the combined sample's distributions and rank-orders of scores from both samples to determine whether significant differences exist.

Formula for Mann-Whitney U Test

The following is the formula for the Mann-Whitney U test

$$U = n_1 n_2 + \frac{n_2(n_2 + 1)}{2} - \sum R$$

Where:

U = Mann-Whitney U test

n_1 = Sample size one

n_2 = Sample size two

R = Sum of the ranks in groups

Degrees of Freedom: Technically, the degrees of freedom for a Mann-Whitney U test is df = $n_1 + n_2 - 2$. However, it is normally not needed in estimating the critical values. It is often not included in statistical analysis package's reporting.

Practice Examples

While the direct calculation of the Mann-Whitney U test is not very complicated, this book uses the SPSS output to illustrate the use of the Mann-Whitney U test.

BOX 16.8. MANN-WHITNEY U TEST—ENHANCING EMOTIONAL INTELLIGENCE

Aadila had 10 second-grade students referred to her for issues related to on-going emotional outbursts in class. She, along with her supervisor and the school psychologist, believed that these students could improve their conditions if they were equipped with tools that improved their emotional intelligence (EI). These included recognizing the emotions, naming the emotions, and bringing their named emotions to teachers and caregivers for help. With collaboration from the teachers and parents, they also decided to break the 10 students randomly into two groups. The experimental group (Group A) received the EI facilitation from Aadila every morning in a group for 20 minutes for 3 weeks. During that time, the control group (Group B) had supervised playtime. After three weeks, the control group started receiving the EI facilitation. However, at week three, they asked students from both groups, with help from the facilitator, using a list of facial expression symbols, e.g. ,☺, ☹, etc., to rank their ability to properly name their emotions. These symbols represented a range of their abilities from "No, No, not able to do that" (1) to "Yeah, no problem, can do that easily" (10).

H_0: There is no difference in the ability to name emotions between two groups based on their score distributions. ($n_A - n_B = 0$).

H_1: There is a difference in the ability to name emotions between two groups. ($n_A - n_B \neq 0$)

Scores for the Experimental Group (A): 9, 10, 7, 8, and 5.

Median score for Groups A is 8 based on the scores of 5, 7, 8, 9, and 10.

Scores for the Control Group (B): 5, 4, 4, 6, and 3.

Median score for Group B is 4 based on the scores of 3, 4, 4, 5, and 6.

Aadila input the data into SPSS and received the following printout:

Descriptive Statistics

	N	MEAN	STD. DEVIATION	MINIMUM	MAXIMUM
Naming Emotion	10	6.10	2.331	3	10
Group	10	1.50	.527	1	2

Mann-Whitney Test

RANKS				
	GROUP	N	MEAN RANK	SUM OF RANKS
	Experimental Group	5	7.70	38.50
Naming Emotion	Control Group	5	3.30	16.50
	Total	10		

Test Statistics[a]

	NAMING EMOTION
Mann-Whitney U	1.500
Wilcoxon W	16.500
Z	−2.312
Asymp. Sig. (2-tailed)	.021
Exact Sig. [2*(1-tailed Sig.)]	.016[b]

a. Grouping Variable: Group
b. Not corrected for ties.

Statistical Findings: U = 1.50, $p < .05$ (two-tailed)

A tie is the same value happening more than one time in the samples. P-value adjusted/corrected for ties (.016) (see footnote "b" in the Test Statistics table above) is usually more precise. However, the unadjusted p-value (.021) (see footnote "a" in the Test Statistics table above) is more conservative and tends to be the larger value. Researchers have to make their pick based on their research needs. In this analysis, both are smaller than the alpha of .05.

Conclusion: Aadila would reject the null hypothesis. There is a statistically significant difference in the abilities of naming emotions by students who received the intervention ($Mdn = 8$) than students who did not receive the intervention ($Mdn = 4$), U = 1.50, Z = 2.312, $p < .05$.

WILCOXON SIGNED RANK TEST

The Wilcoxon signed rank test is a test of difference between two dependent group (correlated) samples in the median of a variable that is continuous. It is also called Wilcoxon signed rank sum test. Chemist and statistician Frank Wilcoxon introduced this two-sample test statistic in the article *Individual comparison by ranking methods* (Wilcoxon, 1945). This test is a nonparametric alternative to a one-sample t-test and correlated t-test when the assumptions for t-tests cannot be met. This includes the situation when the samples' data are not normally distributed. Just as discussed in the correlated t-test section, dependent groups mean paired groups or same subjects being tested twice.

The Wilcoxon signed rank test is used to test whether the average signed ranks of the two matched samples are equal. A part of the procedures for calculating for the test are included below, demonstrating the steps for how "signed rank sum" is developed.

1. Calculate the differences between the two assessments of each of the matched pairs resulting in a + or – score. (i.e., Test 2 – Test 1 = +/–score).
2. List the difference in its absolute value (i.e., ignore the +/–sign).
3. Arrange the absolute values of the difference in a ranked order.
   a. When two scores are equal and, therefore, the difference is zero, no rank will be assigned (i.e., subject 1 – both 13)
   b. Assign the average rank to the tied scores (Example below, subjects 2 and 7 both have the tied absolute value of 1. They are also tied for rank #2 and rank #3. Use the average of the two supposed ranks: (#1 + #2)/2 cases = rank #1.5.
4. Associate the +/–signs back to the values after they are ranked to show whether the values are + or–.
5. Calculate the sum of the positive signed ranks (Wilcoxon W+) and the sum of the negative signed ranks (Wilcoxon W–).
6. Apply additional calculations producing a W statistic that approximates a Z distribution for establishing the level of significance.

There are different ways to calculate the Wilcoxon signed rank sum test. Box 16.8 shows the steps of transforming ranks into signed ranks and then the calculation of the test result. Box 16.9 demonstrates the output of a Wilcoxon signed rank sum test using statistical software program such as SPSS for analysis. They also explain how the test results are to be interpreted. Statistical software programs commonly employ the Z statistics to determine the significance of the test statistics. For manual calculation, one may need to use the Wilcoxon Signed-Ranks Table (Table 16.7).

BOX 16.9. THE TRANSFORMATION OF SIGNED RANKS AND THE WILCOXON SIGNED RANK TEST

SUBJECT	(TEST 1) X_1	(TEST 2) X_2	STEP 1 $X_2 - X_1$	STEP 2 ABSOLUTE $X_2 - X_1$	STEP 2 CALCULATION OF RANKS	STEP 3 RANK OF ABSOLUTE $X_2 - X_1$	STEP 4 SIGNED RANK
1	13	13	0	0	—	—	—
2	12	11	−1	1	(Rank1 + Rank2)/2 = 1.5	1.5	−1.5
3	6	8	+2	2	(Rank3 + Rank4)/2 = 3.5	3.5	+3.5
4	19	17	−2	2	(Rank3 + Rank4)/2 = 3.5	3.5	−3.5
5	15	12	−3	3	(Rank5 + Rank6 Rank7 + Rank 8 Rank9)/5 = 7	7	−7
6	14	11	−3	3	(Rank5 + Rank6 Rank7 + Rank 8 Rank9)/5 = 7	7	−7
7	14	15	+1	1	(Rank1+ Rank2)/2 = 1.5	1.5	+1.5
8	18	15	−3	3	(Rank5 + Rank6 Rank7 + Rank 8 Rank9)/5 = 7	7	−7
9	14	11	−3	3	(Rank5 + Rank6 Rank7 + Rank 8 Rank9)/5 = 7	7	−7
10	19	16	−3	3	(Rank5 + Rank6 Rank7 + Rank 8 Rank9)/5 = 7	7	−7

Step 5
Sum of positive signed ranks (W_+) = (+3.5) + (+1.5) = 5
Sum of negative signed ranks (W_-) = (−1.5) + (−3.5) + (−7) + (−7) + (−7) + (−7) + (−7) = 40
Sample size (N): 10 − 1 (the pair of "13" for subject 1 that has no difference) = 10 − 1 = 9

Researchers could use the following formula to check whether the W_+ and W_- are calculated correctly.

$W_+ + W_- = \frac{1}{2}n\,(n+1)$
$5 + 40 = \frac{1}{2}9\,(9+1)$
$45 = \frac{1}{2}90$
$45 = 45$

With the confirmation that W_+ and W_- are correct, researchers would use the following options to decide which W is to be used to locate its test statistics.

For a two tailed test the test statistic is the smaller of W_+ and W_-

For a one tailed test, where the alternative hypothesis is that the median is greater than a given value, the test statistic is W_-

For a one tailed test, where the alternative hypothesis is that the median is less than a given value, the test statistic is W_+ (MEI, n.d., p. 9)

As the null hypothesis (H_0) is that Test 2 and Test 1 are not different (two-tailed), researchers should use the smaller of W_+ and W_-. In this case, it is the W_+, which is a 5 (see Step 5). According to the Wilcoxon signed-ranks test table (see Table 16.7), for n = 9 and alpha = .05, the critical value also happens to be 5.

Conclusion: Reject the H_0, there is a statistically significant difference between Test 1 and Test 2. (n = 9, $W = W_+ = 5$, p ≤ 5) (Two Tailed).

TABLE 16.7. Wilcoxon Signed-Ranks Table

The following table provides the critical values for two-tailed tests. For a one-tailed test, double the alpha value and use the table.

	ALPHA VALUES								ALPHA VALUES						
n	0.001	0.005	0.01	0.025	0.05	0.10	0.20	n	0.001	0.005	0.01	0.025	0.05	0.10	0.20
5	—	—	—	—	—	0	2	28	—	—	—	—	—	0	2
6	—	—	—	—	0	2	3	29	—	—	—	—	0	2	3
7	—	—	—	0	2	3	5	30	—	—	—	0	2	3	5
8	—	—	0	2	3	5	8	31	—	—	0	2	3	5	8
9	—	0	1	3	5	8	10	32	—	0	1	3	5	8	10
10	—	1	3	5	8	10	14	33	—	1	3	5	8	10	14
11	0	3	5	8	10	13	17	34	0	3	5	8	10	13	17
12	1	5	7	10	13	17	21	35	1	5	7	10	13	17	21
13	2	7	9	13	17	21	26	36	2	7	9	13	17	21	26
14	4	9	12	17	21	25	31	37	4	9	12	17	21	25	31
15	6	12	15	20	25	30	36	38	6	12	15	20	25	30	36
16	8	15	19	25	29	35	42	39	8	15	19	25	29	35	42
17	11	19	23	29	34	41	48	40	11	19	23	29	34	41	48
18	14	23	27	34	40	47	55	41	14	23	27	34	40	47	55
19	18	27	32	39	46	53	62	42	18	27	32	39	46	53	62
20	21	32	37	45	52	60	69	43	21	32	37	45	52	60	69
21	25	37	42	51	58	67	77	44	25	37	42	51	58	67	77
22	30	42	48	57	65	75	86	45	30	42	48	57	65	75	86
23	35	48	54	64	73	83	94	46	35	48	54	64	73	83	94
24	40	54	61	72	81	91	104	47	40	54	61	72	81	91	104
25	45	60	68	79	89	100	113	48	45	60	68	79	89	100	113
26	51	67	75	87	98	110	124	49	51	67	75	87	98	110	124
27	57	74	83	96	107	119	134	50	57	74	83	96	107	119	134

Source: Wilcoxon Signed-Ranks Table. (2018). Real Statistics, http://www.real-statistics.com/statistics-tables/wilcoxon-signed-ranks-table/

The following example includes two different cases. Case A represents a study involving a pre and post comparison. Case B represents a study comparing outcomes between two sites.

BOX 16.10. WILCOXON SIGNED RANK SUM TEST—SMOKING CESSATION PROGRAM

CASE A: PRE- AND POSTTEST

Jade ran a cigarette smoking cessation program in a health clinic for a group of expecting parents who are mostly late teens. She collected data on how often these parents experienced craving for cigarettes the week before the start of the program. During the first two meetings, Jade introduced several techniques that participants could use to minimize the craving. She asked them to apply the techniques and record the frequency of craving for a week. They reported the data to Jade after the week.

H_0: There is no difference in the ability of minimizing craving for cigarette smoking before and after the training $(Mdn_1 - Mdn_2 = 0)$

H_1: There is a difference in the ability of minimizing craving for cigarette smoking before and after the training $(Mdn_1 - Mdn_2 \neq 0)$

Frequency of craving before (Test 1): 13, 12, 6, 19, 15, 14, 14, 18, 14, and 19.

Frequency of craving after (Test 2): 13, 11, 8, 17, 12, 11, 15, 15, 11, and 16.

Jade input the data into SPSS and received the following printout:

Wilcoxon Signed Ranks Test

Ranks

		N	MEAN RANK	SUM OF RANKS
Test2-Test1	Negative Ranks	7a	5.71	40.00
	Positive Ranks	2b	2.50	5.00
	Ties	1c		
	Total	10		

a. Test2 < Test1
b. Test2 > Test1
c. Test2 = Test1

Test Statistics[a]

	TEST2-TEST1
Z	−2.114[b]
Asymp. Sig. (2-tailed)	.034
Exact Sig. (2-tailed)	.039
Exact Sig. (1-tailed)	.020
Point Probability	.008

a. Wilcoxon Signed Ranks Test
b. Based on positive ranks.

Statistical Findings: $Z = -2.114$, $p = .02$ (one-tailed)

The Exact. Sig is preferred when available. It is a more reliable approximation for smaller sample size.

Conclusion: Because the $p = .02$ is smaller than the alpha of .05, Jade would reject the null hypothesis. There is a statistically significant difference in participants' abilities of minimizing their craving after learning the special techniques. The mean rank for less frequent craving (negative rank) = 5.71, and the mean rank for more craving (positive rank) = 2.50.

CASE B: DIFFERENCE BETWEEN SITES

Jade's colleague Jasmine was also running the exact smoking cessation program for a group of expecting parents but in the county Juvenile Hall. She also collected data similar to Jade's data. Because both Jade and Jasmine's groups are almost identical in many aspects, they wonder whether there is a difference in outcome between sites based on the post-test scores.

H_0: There is no difference between two sites in the ability of minimizing craving for cigarette smoking after the training ($Mdn_1 - Mdn_2 = 0$)

H_1: There is a difference between two sites in the ability of minimizing craving for cigarette smoking before and after the training ($Mdn_1 - Mdn_2 \neq 0$)

Frequency of craving before (Test 1): 13, 12, 6, 19, 15, 14, 14, 18, 14, and 19.

Frequency of craving after (Test 2): 13, 11, 8, 17, 12, 11, 15, 15, 11, and 16.

Jade and Jasmine input the data into SPSS and received the following printout:

Wilcoxon Signed Ranks Test

Ranks

		N	MEAN RANK	SUM OF RANKS
Test2–Test1	Negative Ranks	6a	5.33	32.00
	Positive Ranks	3b	4.33	13.00
	Ties	1c		
	Total	10		

a. Test2 < Test1
b. Test2 > Test1
c. Test2 = Test1

Test Statistics[a]

	TEST2–TEST1
Z	−1.127[b]
Asymp. Sig. (2-tailed)	.260
Exact Sig. (2-tailed)	.289
Exact Sig. (1-tailed)	.145
Point Probability	.014

a. Wilcoxon Signed Ranks Test
b. Based on positive ranks.

Statistical Findings: $Z = -1.127$, $p = .145$ (one-tailed)

Conclusion: Jade and Jasmine would fail to reject the null hypothesis. There is no statistically significant difference between sites in participants' abilities of minimizing their craving after learning the special techniques. The mean rank for less frequent craving (negative rank) = 5.33, and the mean rank for more craving (positive rank) = 4.33.

EFFECT SIZE

In hypothesis testing, we seek answers to find out whether there is a significant difference or correlation between groups. Tests of difference and correlation tell researchers whether a significant difference or correlation (p value) exists, but they do not always tell how big the difference is nor the importance of the correlation. Intervention A is different than Intervention B, which produces better outcomes. But, how much better, how big is the difference? Adding ramps to the sidewalks improves accessibility for wheelchair users but how much improvement? Pre-and posttests show that clients have gained increased knowledge on positive parenting, but how substantial is the increase? To answer these questions, researchers turn to the measures of effect size.

Effect size (*d*) is a measure of the magnitude of the difference. It is about the extent of the difference or correlation. Literally, it is the size of the effect of the variable involved. Most things are different; but how different, that's the question. Similar to our discussions on the intermediate and end outcomes for the logical model, effect size asks more than "what change?" It indicates "how well," "how substantial," "how important," "what impact," and "so what?"

Many researchers have recommended that the effect size should be reported, along with the results of any test of difference or correlation. "The primary product of a research inquiry is one or more measures of effect size, not p values" Cohen (1990, p. 1310). Research is more than whether there is a change but also the size of the change.

There are many measures of effect size. "Effect-size measures include mean differences (raw or standardized), correlations and squared correlation of all kinds, odds ratios, kappas—whatever conveys the magnitude of the phenomenon of interest appropriate to the research context" (Cohen, 1990, p. 1310). The Pearson's r (*r*) and Spearman's Rho (r_s) that we discussed in the previous chapter also measure the effect size, i.e., strength and direction. Cohen's d (*d*) is the most common measure of effect size of the difference between two groups. The following is the formula for Cohen's d.

Effect size =

$$\frac{\text{Mean of Group A (experimental group)} - \text{Mean of Goup B (Control group)}}{\text{Standard Deviation}}$$

$$d = \frac{M1 - M2}{SD \text{ (pooled)}}$$

Essentially, effect size is just the standardized mean difference between the two groups. It is a way to quantify the difference. The standard deviation is the population's standard deviation and it is often not known. As a result, it is estimated based on the pooled value from the groups (Coe, 2002).

TABLE 16.8. Common Effect Size Indices*

INDEX	DESCRIPTION	EFFECT SIZE	COMMENT
Between groups			
Cohen's d	$d = M_1 - M_2/s$ $M_1 - M_2$ is the difference between the group means (M); s is the standard deviation of either group	Small 0.2 Medium 0.5 Large 0.8 Very Large 1.3	Can be used at planning stage to find the sample size required for sufficient power for your study
Odds ratio (OR)	$\dfrac{\text{Group 1 odds of outcome}}{\text{Group 2 odds of outcome}}$ If OR = 1, the odds of outcome are equally likely in both groups	Small 1.5 Medium 2 Large 3	For binary outcome variables Compares odds of outcome occurring from on intervention vs another
Relative risk of risk ratio (RR)	Ratio of probability of outcome in group 1 vs group 2; If RR = 1, the outcome is equally probable in both groups	Small 2 Medium 3 Large 4	Compares probabilities of outcome occurring from one intervention to another
Measures of association			
Pearson's r correlation	Range-1 to 1	Small ± 0.2 Medium ± 0.5 Large ± 0.8	Measures the degree of linear relationship between two quantitative variables
R^2 coefficient of determination	Range, 0 to 1; Usually expressed as percent	Small 0.04 Medium 0.25 Large 0.64	Proportion of variance in one variable explained by the other

* Sullivan, G. & Feinn, R. (2012)

Different effect size measures should be interpreted differently depending on what is being studied. Sullivan and Feinn (2012) constructed a table that shows different effect size measures and how they could be interpreted (see Table 16.8).

Statistical significance and effect size tell different aspects of the study findings. Statistical difference tells us whether significant difference or correlation exists, while effect size tells us how important or impactful they are. Researchers need to report both measures to allow readers to gain the full appreciation of the study findings.

Making comparisons is an ongoing human and professional task. In direct practice and in research, social workers use various tests of difference to analyze situations and generate useful evidence to inform practice and decision making. Based on the intent of the inquiry, level of measurement (i.e., nominal, ordinal, interval, or ratio) of the dependent variable, and whether the data is parametric or nonparametric, practitioners can choose the most appropriate test. The Common Statistics and Choice of Statistics Chart from an earlier chapter provides a quick reference to start the selection process.

This chapter explained the various inferential tests of difference, including three types of t-tests, ANOVA, Mann-Whitney U test, and Wilcoxon signed rank test. These inferential statistics help researchers to identify significant differences and differentiate outcomes. They ask, "Is there a difference? Is it statistically significant? Is the difference due to chance or something else, such as the independent variable?" The further inclusion of the use of effect size allows the research to measure the extent or the effect of those significant differences and correlations.

Credit

Table 16.1: Selections from Mary McHugh, "Standard Error: Meaning and Interpretation," Biochemia Medica, vol. 18, no. 1. Copyright © 2008 by Croatian Society of Medical Biochemistry and Laboratory Medicine (CC BY 4.0).

17 PREPARING RESEARCH REPORTS

Reporting of research findings is about the dissemination of information, an important part of the scholarly inquiry process. There are many ways to report. It could be a simple oral presentation, an executive summary, a poster presentation, a short oral or written summary, a full length written study report, or a carefully written manuscript for a refereed journal publication.

It takes researchers a great deal of time and effort to complete a research project—and they are excited to show others their research results. Unfortunately, some researchers end up writing a detailed, technical, verbose, and dry research report. The fact is that not all of us have the gift, talent, or training to be a good writer. Writing a good research report may not be easy for some of us but it is doable and an achievable task. Many writing experts have offered great ideas and techniques that researchers could use to improve the quality of writing and reporting. This chapter aims to provide a general guideline for preparing a written research report.

The heart of report writing is about storytelling. The researchers are telling the story of the research itself, the issues that it attempts to address, the people who are affected, and the implications for future inquiries. It is part of the researchers' collective efforts to have a positive impact and to move forward for the advancement of their causes.

RESEARCH REPORT OUTLINES

Many have observed that a research report has some similarities to a research proposal. It is true that they have many common components, but there are distinct differences as well. A proposal posts the research questions and ways to approach the questions; a report gives answers to the questions with supportive evidence gathered from the research process. A proposal focuses on what will happen; but for a report, the study had already completed, that it is about what had happened and what do they mean. Because of the nature and contexts for each of the researches are different that every report is different. However, in general, a research report should consider the sections listed in Box 17.1.

BOX 17.1. A GENERAL OUTLINE OF A RESEARCH REPORT

Title of the Study/Report (Authors of the Report)

Let potential readers know the focus and the scope of the study and the identity of the authors.

Abstract

This is a succinct summary of the report.

It is the shortest part of the report and the last section to be written.

It tells what the research is about, how it was done, and what the major findings are.

Readers often use the abstract to decide whether they want to read further.

There is no fixed length for an abstract but usually no longer than one page or in the range of 150 to 300 words.

Introduction

This is the opening statement for the study report.

It grabs the attention of the readers and gives an overview of the study on its importance, methods, and findings.

It segues the readers into the other contents of the report.

Purpose of the Study: Research Question

A purpose defines the reasons and the scope of the study.

The research question captures the essences of the purpose and put them in the form of an inquiry.

Background Information: Problem/Issue, Literature Review

Explain the social and academic contexts for the study and why it is needed.

Describe how the study is built up the current state of knowledge on the subject matter. Demonstrate how the relevant literature informs the formation and importance of the research question.

Research Design and Hypothesis

Describe the scheme and justifications of the research design chosen.

Explain why it is the most appropriate design.

Operationalize the research question into researchable hypotheses that guide the research approaches.

Human Subjects Considerations

Detail how human subjects and ethical considerations are being safeguarded and incorporated into the research.

Indicate approvals from appropriate human subjects or institutional review boards.

Target Population and Sampling Approach

Illustrate who were involved in the study, what are their backgrounds and characteristics, what were the inclusion and exclusion criteria, how they were identified and recruited.

What sampling methods were used, how they were conducted?

Describe the response rate.

Data Collection Approaches and Data Collection Tools

State the data collection approaches, justify why they were chosen, and how they were used.

Report the psychometric properties of the existing tools if they were used.

If new or research project-specific tools were developed, describe how they were developed, tested, and their psychometric properties, if available.

Describe the logic model and table of specifications if they were used.

Data Analysis and Results (also, see Box 17.2)

Identify the variables that are involved in the analysis.

Describe and justify the statistical procedures used in relation to the research questions and hypotheses.

Present the results of the analysis.

Study Findings

Provide a general summary of the findings.

Present succinctly the major and secondary findings, guided by the research questions and hypotheses and supported by the analysis results.

Employ various data presentation methods such as tables, charts, graphics, and quotes to illuminate findings to different audiences.

Discussions and Limitations

Summarize the study findings and provide deliberations or interpretations.

State practical, research, and theoretical limitations for the study and the use of the study results.

Conclusions and Recommendations

Reiterate the key factual findings (fact).

Expand and interpret the findings' implications and significance for the target population, the audience, the profession, and the society (opinions).

Reflect on the utilities and lessons learned from the study.

Generalize the findings to inform practice and scholarly inquiries .

References

REPORTING DATA ANALYSIS FINDINGS

In the business world, "ask the customers" is a sound practice. In the world of social work, practitioners often stress "client-centered" practice. Effective reporting is tailored to address the issues of greatest interest for the users of the report. Different users want different information. Consider who would be the chief audiences of your report. They may be the agency or university that sponsors the research, or the community or service recipients that are being affected, or the academic and professional communities. On the other hand, the nature and design of the research may dictate how the report should be formulated.

Dietz and Westerfelt (2010) proposed different report writing formats for different research designs. Modified from their proposed outline, Box 17.2 lists the outlines for quantitative studies. Subsequent Box 17.3 provides a general outline for a qualitative report and Box 17.4 highlights key elements for a program evaluation report.

BOX 17.2. OUTLINES FOR REPORTING QUANTITATIVE STUDIES

1. Individual variable analysis—descriptive statistics

    -   Presentation of data
    -   Frequency distribution and percentage
    -   Central tendency and dispersion
    -   Mean, mode, median
    -   Range, standard deviation

2. Determine what findings would best be presented in tables or graphs.

3. Group Comparisons

    -   Reflect if there are differences in an area (e.g., satisfaction) between the different categories (values) of a variable (e.g., Gender: male, female, and nonbinary).

VARIABLE	MALE	FEMALE
1. Number having school disciplinary actions	12	3
2. Average age	16.2	17.3
3. Percent witnessing violent acts	32%	44.3%
4. Median scores on Attitudes Toward Violence Scale	25	32

4. Test of significance: correlation/association and/or difference

    -   Report the results of the tests of correlation or difference of the research's hypotheses

5. Decide which findings to present in the report and determine the order in which they will be presented.

    -   Some prefer to begin with general findings and move to specific findings reflecting the focus of the study. Others prefer reporting the specifics first.
    -   Separate and present the findings as primary findings and secondary findings.
    -   The primary findings are directly related to the research question and the research hypotheses. They are the main focuses of the narrative and visual presentations.
    -   Secondary findings can be additional, auxiliary, incidental, or unexpected findings. These findings can be emerging and sometimes useful in many social science studies. They may highlight additional areas for future studies. However, they could also be evolving findings in medical or health studies that have significant ethical, legal, and methodological implications that their reporting requires serious debate.

6. Indicate plan for study findings dissemination.

BOX 17.3. OUTLINES FOR REPORTING QUALITATIVE STUDIES

1. List all the sources of data collected (e.g., interviews, field notes, demographics, and observation)
2. Describe your procedures for reducing the data. For example, conventional content analysis, Directed content analysis, summative content analysis (Hsieh & Shannon, 2005).
3. Identify themes (categories) in the data.
4. If available, report feedback from research participants regarding the initial themes, trends, and patterns identified.
5. Arrange themes to answer research questions

    - Grouping and organizing themes
    - Presenting themes in ways that make sense to the research

6. Data display

    - Select representative excerpts and anecdotal accounts from each main theme. Provide enough excerpts and illustrations so that the reader can "see" how you arrived at the findings.
    - Use quantitative data to help summarize findings
    - Use table or graphs to display data

BOX 17.4. KEY ELEMENTS TO INCLUDE IN A PROGRAM EVALUATION REPORT

Restate the Program Evaluation Objective

Restate the complete objective: what the community needed, what service activities were implemented to address the need, what were the anticipated outputs and outcomes, and what targets were set toward the anticipated outputs and outcomes. Here is where the purpose of the evaluation can be described and/or the evaluation questions restated.

Note Evaluation Activities in which the Researchers have Engaged

Refer to the evaluation plan developed. Describe the types of instruments used (e.g., survey, test, observation). Describe to whom, as well as how, each instrument was administered. Describe which, and how many individuals, completed each instrument. A description of evaluation activities in which the program has engaged might be stated in this manner:

Volunteers used a Homework Assignment Form to define and document successful homework completed for each student during a semester. Volunteers documented successfully completed homework assignments daily and gave copies of their forms to their supervisors weekly. Documentation was completed on all 80 students. Data from the previous semester regarding homework completion with reading literacy for each of the participating students was documented. It was used as baseline data for later comparison.

Describe Relevant Evaluation Data

Describe the results of the analysis based on the evaluation data collected. This should be related to the target standard set in the objective. What quantitative statistics did you find? What qualitative information did you find? What do these results imply about the success of the program services? A description of relevant evaluation data might look like this:

The objective target stated 60% of the 100 students who participated in the tutoring program successfully completed 95% of their homework during that semester. By the end of the semester, the program succeeded in assisting 60% of the students tutored to complete at least 80% of their homework assignments successfully, 15% less than the target the program hoped to reach. The lack of stable housing and a quiet location at home to complete homework assignments, as well as household responsibilities, are most frequently cited as reasons for not being able to complete assignments.

State Ideas for Program Improvement or Next Steps

How do the evaluation results inform the program in terms of next steps for program improvement? Should the program expand its service? Can the evaluation results be helpful to other stakeholders (e.g., the schools)? Can the evaluation results be used for other purposes? A description of reporting results might look like this:

The 60% students who successfully completed at least 80% of their homework also reported an increase in their overall GPA. The program plans to prepare 75% of students achieving the 95% homework completion rate during the next semester. The program will review how tutoring was provided to these students and consider additional volunteers support and format of the tutoring. The program will also work with the school social work team on issues of lacking stable housing and location for study at home as well as family responsibilities.

REPORTING STATISTICS IN APA STYLE

American Psychological Association (APA) style is the most commonly used writing style for social science disciplines including social work. Its 2010 *Publication Manual of the American Psychological Association* (6th ed.) provides specific guidelines on how to report statistics in documents. The following section summarizes some of the key guidelines. It also includes some of the common modified practices. Readers may find different publishers and publications employ slightly modified APA formats to meet their specific needs or layouts. Box 17.5 lists some of the common ways to report statistics in research reports.

BOX 17.5. COMMON FORMATS FOR REPORTING STATISTICS

Whole Number

For observations that could only be in a whole number, use the whole number without the decimal. For example, the group has 15 participants (N = 15); the client has four children (N = 4); the respondents have two options (N = 2). It is not 15.0, 4.0, or 2.0.

Rounding Numbers

Numbers greater than 100, round to the nearest whole number (e.g., 863 instead of 863.12)

Numbers between 10 and 100, round to one decimal place (e.g., 86.3 instead of 86.312)

Numbers between 0.10 and 10, round to two decimal places (e.g., 0.86 instead of 0.86312)

Numbers between 0.001 and 0.10, round to three decimal places (e.g., 0.086 instead of 0.0863212)

The p-Values

Typically, in reporting p-values, report the exact p-values, not the statement of inequality. It is $p = .0321$, not $p < .05$.

Yet, when the p-value is smaller than .001 using the statement of inequality. If it is $p = .00093$, it could be presented as $p < .001$.

Output by many statistical programs may show a $p = .0000$ as a result of it rounding off the number. Technically, p-values cannot equal zero. They should be reported as $p < .001$ instead.

However, it is also common to find that the p-value is being presented in relation to the preset alpha value (α), the statistical significance threshold.

Use the statement of inequality to show whether the statistics are significant or not in relation to the alpha value (α).

For example, $p < .05$ or $p \leq .01$ instead of $p = .0093$. It is to show the p-value is significant because it is smaller than the alpha value (α) of .05 or .01.

Similarly, a $p > .10$ instead of $p = .234$ shows the p-value is not significant because it is greater than the alpha (α) of .10.

This form of presentation could be useful for research that uses different alpha values (α) for different individual tests or hypothesis instead of a common $\alpha = .05$ for the whole research study.

Reporting the exact p-value may be a good practice that could avoid the possible interpretation problem.

Omit the Leading Zero

For statistics such as p-values, correlation coefficients (r, Rho), alpha value (α), and others, the leading zero is omitted (e.g., $p < .001$, instead of $p < 0.001$, r = .75 instead of r = 0.75).

In general, leading zero is omitted for any numbers that cannot be greater than 1 (*p-values* are always between 0 and 1).

Table 17.1 lists the common format in reporting statistics discussed in this book. The test statistics value (often rounded to two decimal point) usually is listed first, with the degrees of freedom and often the sample size in parenthesis, and then the significance level. Whether direction is predicated (i.e., one-tailed or two-tailed) could be indicated in parenthesis at the end. For example, $X^2(2, N = 78) = 24.28$, $p < .001$ (Direction predicted).

TABLE 17.1. Reporting Statistical Test Findings

STATISTICAL TEST	PRESENTATION OF STATISTICAL RESULTS
Chi-square	$X^2(2, N = 78) = 24.28$, $p < .001$ (Direction predicted)
Fisher's exact	Fisher's Exact, $p < .0001$, (one-tailed).
Chi-square Goodness of Fit	$X^2(1) = 49.495$, $p < .001$
Pearson correlation coefficient	r (5) = .74, $p < .05$ (Direction predicted)
Spearman rank correlation	$r_s(6) = .39$, $p < .05$ (Two-tailed)
Partial r	r(7) = .626, $p < .10$ (Two-tailed)
One-sample t-test	t(9) = 2.85, $p < .01$ (one-tailed)
Independent t-test	t(40) = −4.75, $p < .001$ (one-tailed)
Correlated t-test	t(9) = −1.86, $p > .05$ (two-tailed)
ANOVA	F (2,27) = 25.51, $p < .001$ (Two-tailed)
Mann-Whitney U test	U = 1.50, $p < .05$ (two-tailed)
Wilcoxon signed rank sum test	Z = −2.114, $p > .01$ (one-tailed)

DISCUSSIONS, CONCLUSIONS, IMPLICATIONS, AND RECOMMENDATIONS

At the final section of a research report, the researchers may want to offer readers the important takeaways of the study. This section may function as a highlight of the key findings and the meaning of these findings. It gives the readers a quick appreciation of the critical aspects of the study without going through and understanding all the detailed literature and statistical analyses. This section may include subsections that aim to elaborate on the key research findings, delimitate the study, give interpretations to the critical conclusions, and infer further actions and strategies.

Discussions summarize the study findings and provide deliberations or interpretations of those findings. Link this back to the study's original interest and speculations which have become the research questions and hypotheses. Authors should avoid presenting the research findings *(facts)* in their raw form without thoughtful organization and focus. "Data dumping" is no substitute for solid analyses and discussions—which are much more valuable to the consumer of the research study. Researchers may want to strategically provide their interpretation *(explanations and discussions)* of the findings in relation to the research questions and hypotheses. Their interpretations should ideally be consistent with the literature reviewed and the current base of knowledge in the field. Do the study findings show unique discoveries, particular trends, patterns, and directions? Are there any emerging findings, surprising findings, or unexpected outcomes? These are all helpful in putting the study into a useful context for the reader.

Limitations are a given when reporting on a study; they are part of any scientific inquiry. Having limitations does not lessen the significance of the study. In fact, it shows that the researchers are careful and critical about the rigor of the study. In general, there are limitations related to the following areas:

- Research methodology (e.g., restriction or availability of relevant literature or related studies, study design, sampling issues, validity and reliability issues, and procedure or ethical constraints).
- Statistics and data (e.g., nature and quality of the data, data collection and data analysis procedures, statistical model constraints, and interpretation of statistics).
- Research findings (e.g., generalizability of the findings, replicability, potential bias and errors, and effects of confounding variables).

Conclusions are a brief highlight of the study findings *(facts)* against your research questions and hypotheses. It is more succinct than the summary in the discussions section. It serves to transition into the concluding thoughts or generalizations *(opinions)*. They could be the further justification of the importance of the study; their contributions to the knowledge base and the better understanding of the subject matter; their meaning and significance to the issue, the profession, the service delivery system, the people, and the society. These are the implications that give answers to important questions such as "Why do other people and I care about this study and its findings? What is the significance? What impacts, if any, does it have? What generalization can be drawn?"

Recommendations expand from the conclusions section. The recommendations section presents actions, directions, solutions, predictions, and changes that could be considered. They may be related to the subject matter being studied; research design, methodology, and implementations; food for thought; and call for actions. If a social worker reads the research report, completely agrees with the conclusions, and wants to put some of the suggested ideas in action, what would the research suggest her to do? A social work student wants to further the study or develop a similar one. What advice would he find in the report? If the authors themselves want to do the study again, what changes would they make first?

CONCLUSION

Reporting writing can be the most exciting and trying part of the research process. Researchers are excited about the findings but also exhausted at the completion of their studies. They often have to rack up enough energy to put together a report that makes sense to readers. It is the end product of the rigorous and oftentimes difficult research process that may or may not offer answers to the research questions. "The more you know, the more you know you don't know." Research reports summarize major findings that contribute to the knowledge base. They also help researchers to further define and refine their inquiries, for they now have new perspectives and new questions to be answered.

EPILOGUE

This is the final section of this book on social work research and statistics—a reporting of this book project in its own right. We started the journey by examining the roles of research and statistics in social work. Then we dove into the key concepts and ethical considerations in conceptualizing, structuring, and implementing various research designs and their data collection methods. Different needs assessments and program evaluation methods helped us conclude the research section of the book. The statistics section of the book moved from descriptive statistics that show and summarize the data to inferential statistics that try to answer the key questions of difference and correlation. It is the hope of this author that, through this book, readers have developed the competencies to be consumers as well as producers of research and statistics. This will, in turn, contribute to the professional knowledge base and improve the effectiveness and quality of services.

Credit

REFERENCES

Chapter 1. Introduction to the Social Research Methods and Statistics

Atherton, C. R., & Klemmack, D. L. (1982). *Research methods in social work.* Lexington, MA: D.C. Heath.

Boehm, W. (1961). Social work: Science and art. *Social Service Review, 35*(2), 144–152. doi.org/10.1086/641041

Brekke, J. (2012). Shaping a science of social work. *Research on Social Work Practice, 22*(5), 455–464. doi.org/10.1177/1049731512441263

Council on Social Work Education (CSWE) (2015). Educational policy and accreditation standards for baccalaureate and master's social work programs. Retrieved from https://www.cswe.org/getattachment/Accreditation/Accreditation-Process/2015-EPAS/2015EPAS_Web_FINAL.pdf.aspx

Lalayants, M. (2012). Overcoming graduate students negative perception of statistics. *Journal of Teaching in Social Work, 32*(4), 356–375.

Maschi, T., Wells, M., Slater, G. Y., MacMillan, T., & Ristow, J. (2013). Social work students' research-related anxiety and self-efficacy: Research instructors' perception and teaching innovations. *Social Work Education, 32*(6), 800–817.

Morgenshtern, M., Freymond, N., Hong, L., Adamowich, T., Duffie, M. (2015). Researcher? Social worker? "Let us be both": Exploring the binaries that condition graduate social work research training. *Procedia—Social and Behavioral Sciences*, 191, 2002–2007.

National Association of Social Workers. (2008). Code of ethics of the national association of social workers. Retrieved from https://www.socialworkers.org/about/ethics/code-of-ethics/code-of-ethics-english

Pardeck, J. & Yuen, F. (2001). Family health: An emerging paradigm for social workers. *Journal of Health and Social Policy, 13*(3), 59–74.

Pham, D. & Tidd, M. (2014). *The challenges social work students face when taking research related courses* (Unpublished thesis). California State University, Sacramento.

Royse, D. (2011) *Research methods in social work* (6th ed.). Belmont, CA: Brooks/Cole.

Royse, D., & Rompf, E. L., (1992). Math anxiety: A comparison of social work and non-social work students. *Journal of Social Work Education, 28*(3), 270–277. Retrieved from http://connection.ebscohost.com/c/articles/9607251459/math-anxiety-comparison-social-work-non-social-work-students

Yuen, F. (1999). Family health and cultural diversity. In J. Pardeck & F. Yuen (Eds.), *Family health: A holistic approach to social work practice* (pp. 101–114). Westport, CT: Auburn House.

Yuen, F., Bein, A., & Lum, D. (2006). Inductive learning. In D. Lum (Ed.), *Culturally competent practice: A framework for understanding diverse groups and justice issues* (3rd ed., pp. 166–167). Pacific Grove, CA: Brooks/Cole.

Chapter 2. Research Question and Literature Review (the Purpose and the Quest)

Car Talk. (2014). The Andy scale. Retrieved from https://www.cartalk.com/content/andy-scale-0

Chapter 3. Human Diversity, Ethical Considerations, and Protection of Human Subjects

42 U.S.C. §241(d). (2011). Research and investigations generally. Retrieved from https://www.gpo.gov/fdsys/pkg/USCODE-2011-title42/pdf/USCODE-2011-title42-chap6A-subchapII-partA-sec241.pdf

45 CFR 46.102(i). (1991). Subpart A—Basic HHS Policy for Protection of Human Research Subjects. Retrieved from https://www.hhs.gov/ohrp/regulations-and-policy/regulations/45-cfr-46/index.html#46.102

Associated Press. (2017, May 10). Generations later, the effects of the Tuskegee syphilis study linger. State News. Retrieved from https://www.statnews.com/2017/05/10/tuskegee-syphilis-study/

Breault, J. (2006). Protecting human research subjects: The past defines the future. *The Ochsner Journal, 6*(1), 15–20. Retrieved from https://www.ncbi.nlm.nih.gov/pmc/articles/PMC3127481/ doi: 10.1043/1524-5012(2006)006[0015:PHRSTP]2.0.CO;2

Center for Disease Control and Prevention. (n.d.). U.S. Public Health Service syphilis study at Tuskegee. Retrieved from https://www.cdc.gov/tuskegee/

Committee for Protection of Human Subjects. (2016). Internet-based research. University of California Berkeley. Retrieved from http://cphs.berkeley.edu/internet_research.pdf

DuBois, J. M. (2008). *Ethics in mental health research: Principles, cases, and guidance.* New York, NY: Oxford University Press. Retrieved from https://sites.google.com/a/narrativebioethics.com/emhr/contact/the-tearoom-trade-study-1

Georgetown University. (n.d.). Significant event in human subject research. Retrieved from https://highschoolbioethics.georgetown.edu/units/cases/unit3_timeline.html

Gould, K. H. (1995). The misconstructing of multiculturalism: The Stanford debate and social work. *Social Work*, *40*(2), 198–205.

Harmon, A. (2010, April 21). Indian tribe wins fight to limit research of its DNA. *The New York Times*. Retrieved from http://www.nytimes.com/2010/04/22/us/22dna.html?pagewanted=all&_r=1

Hohman, M. (2013, September 10). Cultural humility: A lifelong practice. Retrieved from https://socialwork.sdsu.edu/insitu/diversity/cultural-humility-a-lifelong-practice/

Hook, J. N., Davis, D. E., Owen, J., Worthington, E. L., Jr., & Utsey, S. O. (2013). Cultural humility: Measuring openness to culturally diverse clients. *Journal of Counseling Psychology*, *60*(3), 353–366. http://dx.doi.org/10.1037/a0032595

Humphreys, L. (1970). *Tearoom trade: Impersonal sex in public places.* London, UK: Duckworth.

Kim, W. O. (2012). Institutional review board (IRB) and ethical issues in clinical research. *Korean Journal of Anesthesiology. 62*(1), 3–12. Retrieved from https://www.ncbi.nlm.nih.gov/pmc/articles/PMC3272525/ doi: 10.4097/kjae.2012.62.1.3

Leigh, J. (1983). The black experience with health care delivery systems: A focus on the practitioners. In A. E. Johnson (Ed.), *The black experience: Considerations for health and human services* (pp. 115–129). Davis, CA: International Dialogue Press.

National Commission for the Protection of Human Subjects of Biomedical and Behavioral Research, Department of Health, Education and Welfare (DHEW) (1978). *The Belmont report.* Washington, DC: United States Government Printing Office. Retrieved from https://videocast.nih.gov/pdf/ohrp_appendix_belmont_report_vol_2.pdf

National Congress of American Indians. (n.d.). Havasupai tribe and the lawsuit settlement aftermath. Retrieved from http://genetics.ncai.org/case-study/havasupai-Tribe.cfm

Ortega, R. M., & Coulborn Faller, K. (2011). Training child welfare workers from an intersectional cultural humility perspective: A paradigm shift. *Child Welfare*, *90*(5), 27–49.

Pedroni, J., & Pimple, K. (2001). *A brief introduction to informed consent in research with human subjects.* Poynter Center for the Study of Ethics, Indiana University USA. http://citeseerx.ist.psu.edu/viewdoc/download?doi=10.1.1.92.6284&rep=rep1&type=pdf

Science Museum, Brought to Life: Exploring History of Medicine (n.d.). Tuskegee syphilis study. Retrieved from http://www.sciencemuseum.org.uk/broughttolife/techniques/tuskegee

SexInfo. (n.d.). *The tearoom trade.* Retrieved from http://www.soc.ucsb.edu/sexinfo/article/tearoom-trade

Tervalon, M. & Murray-Garcia, J. (1998). Cultural humility versus cultural competence: A critical distinction in defining physician training outcomes in multicultural education. *Journal of Health Care for the Poor Underserved, 9*(2), 117–125.

U.S. Department of Health & Human Services. (n.d.). *Federal policy for the protection of human subjects ('common rule').* Retrieved from https://www.hhs.gov/ohrp/regulations-and-policy/regulations/common-rule/index.html

U.S. Department of Health and Human Services. (2009). *Code of federal regulations* [45 CFR 46.102(i)]. Retrieved from https://www.hhs.gov/ohrp/sites/default/files/ohrp/policy/ohrpregulations.pdf

Yuen, F. (2003). Critical concerns for family health practice. In F. Yuen, G. Skibinski, & J. Pardeck (Eds.), *Family health social work practice: A knowledge and skills case book* (pp. 19–40). Binghamton, NY: Haworth Press.

Chapter 4. Conceptualization and Measurement (Terms of Endearment)

Boslaugh, S. (2017). *Statistics in a nutshell* (2nd ed.). Safari Books Online. Retrieved from https://www.safaribooksonline.com/library/view/statistics-in-a/9781449361129/ch01.html

Content Validity. (n.d.). Lærd dissertation. Retrieved from http://dissertation.laerd.com/content-validity.php

Dudley, J. (2011). *Research methods for social work: Being producers and consumers of research* (updated ed.). Boston, MA: Allyn & Bacon: Cengage.

Haynes, S., Richard, D., & Kubany, E. (1995). Content validity in psychological assessment: A functional approach to concept and methods. *Psychological Assessment, 7*(3), 238–247. Retrievedfromhttp://citeseerx.ist.psu.edu/viewdoc/download?doi=10.1.1.452.5453&rep=rep1&type=pdf

Rubin, A & Babbie, E. (2017). *Research methods for social work* (9th ed.). Boston, MA: Cengage.

Shakespeare, W. (1914). *Romeo and Juliet*, Act II. Scene II. In W. J. Craig. (Ed.), *The Complete Works of William Shakespeare.* London: Oxford University Press. Retrieved from https://www.bartleby.com/70/3822.html line 47–48. New York: Bartleby.com (2000). (Original work published 1597).

Trochim, W. (2006a). Reliability. *Research methods knowledge base.* Retrieved from https://www.socialresearchmethods.net/kb/reliable.php

Trochim, W. (2006b). Theory of reliability. *Research methods knowledge base.* Retrieved from https://www.socialresearchmethods.net/kb/reliablt.php

Trochim, W. (2006c). Measurement error. *Research methods knowledge base.* Retrieved from https://www.socialresearchmethods.net/kb/measerr.php

U.S. Department of Health and Human Service. *Intellectual and developmental disabilities.* Retrieved from https://report.nih.gov/nihfactsheets/ViewFactSheet.aspx?csid=100

Chapter 5. Qualitative Research and Quantitative Research (Yin and Yang)

Bradford, A. (2017, August 4). What is science? *Livescience.* Retrieved from https://www.livescience.com/20896-science-scientific-method.html

Cantril, H. (1957, August). Perception and interpersonal relations. *The American Journal of Psychiatry, 114*(2), 119–126.

Creswell, J. (2009). *Research design: Qualitative, quantitative, and mixed methods approaches.* Los Angeles, CA: SAGE.

Finlay, L. (2009, September). Exploring lived experience: Principles and practice of phenomenological research. *International Journal of Therapy and Rehabilitation, 16*(9), 474–481.

Fisher, B. & Peterson, C. (1993). She won't be dancing much anyway: A study of surgeons, surgical nurses, and elderly patients. *Qualitative Health Research, 3*(2), 165–183.

Glaser, B., & Strauss, A. (1967). *The discovery of grounded theory: Strategies for qualitative research.* Chicago, IL: Aldine.

Grounded Theory Institute (2014, July 20). *What is grounded theory?* Retrieved from http://www.groundedtheory.com/what-is-gt.aspx

LeBar, M. (2011, July 25). What's real and what's in the mind [Blog post]. Retrieved from https://pileusblog.wordpress.com/2011/07/25/whats-real-and-whats-in-the-mind/

Moore, K. (1998). *Patterns of inductive reasoning: Developing critical thinking skills* (4th ed.). Dubuque, IA: Kendall/Hunt Publishing.

Norvelle, E. (2017, August 25). What are the differences between the philosophies of Socrates, Plato and Aristotle? Retrieved from https://www.quora.com/What-are-the-differences-between-the-philosophies-of-Socrates-Plato-and-Aristotle

Popik, B. (2015, March 28). Three umpires are sitting in bar … (baseball joke) [Blog post]. Retrieved from https://www.barrypopik.com/index.php/new_york_city/entry/three_umpires

Rowling, J. K. (2007). *Harry Potter and the deathly hallows*. New York, NY: Arthur A. Levine Books.

Sbaraini, A., Carter, S., Evans, R., & Blinkhorn, A. (2011). How to do a grounded theory study: A worked example of a study of dental practices. *BMC Medical Research Methodology, 11,* 128. https://doi.org/10.1186/1471-2288-11-128

Scott, H. (2009, November 1). What is grounded theory? Grounded Theory Online. Retrieved from http://www.groundedtheoryonline.com/what-is-grounded-theory/

Sommers-Flanagan, J. & Sommers-Flanagan, R. (2012). *Counseling and psychotherapy theories in context and practice: Skills, strategies, and techniques.* Hoboken, NJ: John Wiley & Sons.

TEDEd. (n.d.). *Socrates, Plato and Aristotle* [Video]. Retrieved from https://ed.ted.com/on/tb7gSI6b#digdeeper

Trochim, W. (2006). Experimental design. *Research Methods Knowledge Base.* Retrieved from https://www.socialresearchmethods.net/kb/qualdeb.php (para. 21).

Yuen, F., Bein, A., & Lum, D. (2006). Inductive learning. In D. Lum (Ed.), *Culturally competent practice: A framework for understanding diverse groups and justice issues* (3rd ed., pp. 166–167). Pacific Grove, CA: Brooks/Cole.

Chapter 6. Research Designs

Angell, B., & Townsend, L. (2011). *Designing and conducting mixed methods studies* [PowerPoint slides]. Retrieved from https://www.scribd.com/document/93212784/Designing-and-Conducting-Mixed-Methods-Studies

Atherton, C. R., & Klemmack, D. L. (1982). *Research methods in social work.* Lexington, MA: D.C. Heath.

Campbell, D. T., & Stanley, J. C. (1963). *Experimental and quasi-experimental designs for research.* Chicago, IL: Rand McNally.

Clarke, P. (2009). Understanding the Experience of Stroke: A Mixed-Method Research Agenda. *Gerontology, 49*(3): 293–302. Retrieved from: https://www.ncbi.nlm.nih.gov/pmc/articles/PMC2682172/ doi: 10.1093/geront/gnp047

Compton, B., & Galaway, B. (1984). *Social work processes* (3rd ed.). Chicago, IL: Dorsey Press.

Creswell, J. W., & Plano Clark, V. L. (2007). *Designing and conducting mixed methods research.* Thousand Oaks, CA: Sage.

Creswell, J. W., & Plano Clark, V. L. (2011). *Designing and conducting mixed methods research* (2nd ed.). Thousand Oaks, CA: Sage.

Creswell, J. W. (2014). Research design: qualitative, quantitative, and mixed methods approaches (pp. 3–23). Thousand Oaks, CA: Sage.

Dudley, J. (2011). *Research Methods for Social Work: Being Producers and Consumers of Research* (updated 2nd ed.). New York: Pearson.

Greene, J. C., Caracelli, V. J., & Graham, W. F. (1989). Toward a conceptual framework for mixed-method evaluation designs. *Educational Evaluation and Policy Analysis, 11*(3), 255–274.

Grinnell, R. & Unrau, Y. (2008). *Social Work Research and Evaluation: Foundations of Evidence-based Practice.* New York: Oxford University Press.

Haight, W. & Bidwell, L. (2016). *Mixed methods research for social work: Integrating methodologies to strengthen practice and policy.* Chicago, IL: Lyceum.

Johnson, B., Onwuegbuzie, A. & Turner, L. (2007, April). Toward a definition of mixed methods research. *Journal of Mixed Methods Research, 1*(2), 112–133. doi:10.1177/1558689806298224

Lammers, W. & Badia, P. (2005). *Fundamentals of Behavioral Research.* Belmont, CA: Thomson/Wadworth.

Miller, R., King, J., Mark, M., & Caracelli, V. (2016, June). The oral history of evaluation: The professional development of Robert Stake. *American Journal of Evaluation, 37*(2), 287–294. Retrieved from http://journals.sagepub.com/doi/10.1177/1098214015597314

Padgett, D. (2009). Qualitative and mixed methods in social work knowledge development. *Social Work, 54*(2), 101–105.

Royse, D. (2008). *Research Methods in Social Work.* (5th ed.). Belmont, CA: BrooksCole.

Rubin, A. & Babbie, E. (2015). *Essential Research Methods for Social Work* (4th ed.). Boston: Cengage Learning.

Tashakkori, A., & Teddlie, C. (Eds.). (2003). *Handbook of mixed methods in social and behavioral research.* Thousand Oaks, CA: Sage.

Townsend, L. Floersch, J., & Findling, R. (2009). The conceptual adequacy of the drug attitude inventory for measuring youth attitudes toward psychotropic medications: A mixed methods evaluation. *Journal of Mixed Methods Research, 4*(1), 32–55. doi.org/10.1177/1558689809352469

Trochim, W. (2001). *The research methods knowledge base* (2nd ed.). Cincinnati, OH: Atomic Dog Publishing.

Trochim, W. (2006). Experimental design. *Research Methods Knowledge Base.* Retrieved from https://www.socialresearchmethods.net/kb/desexper.php

Yegidis, B., Weinbach, R., and Myers, L. (2018). *Research methods for social workers* (8th ed.). New York, NY: Pearson.

Yuen, F. & Terao, K. (2003). *Practical grant writing and program evaluation*. Pacific Grove, CA: Brooks/Cole.

Chapter 7. Sampling (House of Representatives)

American Association for Public Opinion Research. (n.d.). Margin of sampling error/ Credibility interval. Retrieved from http://www.aapor.org/Education-Resources/Election-Polling-Resources/Margin-of-Sampling-Error-Credibility-Interval.aspx

Dudley, J. (2011). *Research methods for social work: Being producers and consumers of research* (updated ed.). Boston, MA: Allyn & Bacon: Cengage.

Lane, D. (n.d.) Sampling bias. Retrieved from http://onlinestatbook.com/2/research_design/sampling.html

Panik, M. J. (2005). *Advanced statistics from an elementary point of view*. Boston, MA: Academic Press.

Chapter 8. Data Collection Methods

Association of Social Work Board. (2017). Exam scoring. *About the Exams*. Retrieved from https://www.aswb.org/exam-candidates/about-the-exams/exam-scoring/

Atherton, C. R., & Klemmack, D. L. (1982). *Research methods in social work*. Lexington, MA: D.C. Heath.

Bly, N. (1887). *Ten days in a mad-house*. New York, NY: Ian L. Munro Publisher. Retrieved from http://digital.library.upenn.edu/women/bly/madhouse/madhouse.html

Bumgardner, M., Montague, I., & Wiedenbeck, J. (2017). Survey response rates in the forest products literature from 2000 to 2015. *Wood and Fiber Science*, *49*(1), 84–92. Retrieved from https://www.fs.fed.us/nrs/pubs/jrnl/2017/nrs_2017_bumgardner_001.pdf

Cheng, H. & Phillips, M. (2014, December). Secondary analysis of existing data: Opportunities and implementation. *Shanghai Archives of Psychiatry*, *26*(6), 371–375. Retrieved from https://www.ncbi.nlm.nih.gov/pmc/articles/PMC4311114/pdf/sap-26-06-371.pdf

College Board. (2017). SAT—Understanding scores. Retrieved from https://collegereadiness.collegeboard.org/pdf/understanding-sat-scores.pdf

Flanagan, J. C. (1954). The critical incident technique. *Psychological Bulletin*, *51*(4), 327–358.

Fook, J., & Askeland, G. (2007). Challenges of critical reflection: "Nothing ventured, nothing gained." *Social Work Education*, *26*(5), 520–555. https://doi.org/10.1080/02615470601118662

Johnston, M. (2014, September). Secondary data analysis: A method of which the time has come. *Qualitative and Quantitative Methods in Libraries (QQML)*, *3*, 619–626. Retrieved from http://www.qqml.net/papers/September_2014_Issue/336QQML_Journal_2014_Johnston_Sept_619-626.pdf

Kvale, S. (1996). *Interviews: An introduction to qualitative research interviews.* Thousand Oaks, CA: SAGE.

Lister, P. & Crip, B. (2007). Critical incident analyses: A practice learning tools for students and practitioners. *Practice: Social Work in Action, 19*(1), 47–60. https://doi.org/10.1080/09503150701220507

Masten, K. (2015). Adoption dissolution factors considering national data: A qualitative study. (Master's thesis). Retrieved from http://csus-dspace.calstate.edu/bitstream/handle/10211.3/139371/Final%20Thesis.pdf?sequence=1

Mcniff, K. (2017, April 25). "Are you really listening?" Tips for conducting qualitative interviews. NVIVO-QSR International. Retrieved from http://www.qsrinternational.com/nvivo/nvivo-community/blog/are-you-really-listening-tips-for-conducting-qual

National Research Center (2016, September 23). What's the average response rate for a citizen survey? Retrieved from http://www.n-r-c.com/whats-the-average-response-rate-for-a-citizen-survey/

Norm. (2017). *The free dictionary.* Retrieved from https://www.thefreedictionary.com/norming

Norm-Referenced Test. (2015, July 22). *The glossary of education reform.* Great School Partnership. Retrieved from http://edglossary.org/norm-referenced-test/

Open University. (2013, May 20). Conducting an interview. Retrieved from https://www2.open.ac.uk/students/skillsforstudy/conducting-an-interview.php

Rodriguez, M. (1997, January). *Norming and norm-referenced test score.* Retrieved from http://ericae.net/ft/tamu/Norm.htm

Spencer-Oatey, H. (2013) Critical incidents. A compilation of quotations for the intercultural field. *GlobalPAD Core Concepts.* Available at Global PAD Open House http://go.warwick.ac.uk/globalpadintercultural

SurveyGizmo. (2015, July 27). 3 ways to improve your survey response rates. Retrieved from https://www.surveygizmo.com/survey-blog/survey-response-rates/

University of Virginia. (n.d.). *Origins of eugenics: From Sir Francis Galton to Virginia's Racial Integrity Act of 1924.* Historical Collection at the Claude Moore Health Science Library. Retrieved from http://exhibits.hsl.virginia.edu/eugenics/2-origins/

Vector. (2017). *Merriam-Webster online dictionary.* Retrieved from https://www.merriam-webster.com/dictionary/vector

Yuen, F., Terao, K. & Schmidt, A.M. (2009). *Effective grant writing and evaluation for human service professionals.* Hoboken, NJ: Wiley & Sons.

Chapter 9. Data Collection Instruments and Development (the Tools)

Bureau of Labor Statistics. (2007, July). Consumer price index. Bureau of Labor Statistics. Retrieved from https://www.bls.gov/cpi/questions-and-answers.htm#Question_1

DeVellis, R. (2017). *Scale development: Theory and applications* (4th ed.). Los Angeles, CA: SAGE.

Nasdaq. (n.d.). Dow Jones Industrial Average. NASDAQ. Retrieved from http://www.nasdaq.com/investing/glossary/d/dow-jones-industrial-average

Trochim, W. (2006). Thurstone scaling. *Social Research Methods.* Retrieved from https://www.socialresearchmethods.net/kb/scalthur.php

Stephanie, G. (2016, June 29) What is Thurstone scale? *Statistics How To.* Retrieved from http://www.statisticshowto.com/thurstone-scale/

University of Davis (n.d.(a)) Thurstone scale. Retrieved from http://psc.dss.ucdavis.edu/sommerb/sommerdemo/scaling/enrich/thurstone.htm

University of Davis (n.d.(b)) Semantic differential. Retrieved from http://psc.dss.ucdavis.edu/sommerb/sommerdemo/scaling/semdiff.htm

Chapter 10. Needs Assessment, Program Planning, and Program Evaluation (What and What Happens)

Bradshaw, J. (1997). The concept of social need. In Gilbert, N, & Specht, H. (Ed.), *Planning for social welfare issues, task, and models* (pp. 290–296). Englewood Cliffs, NJ: Prentice-Hall.

GAO. (2005). *Performance measurement and evaluation: definitions and relationships.* GA)-05-739SP. Washington, D. C.: United States Government Accountability Office

Hatry, H. P. (1999). *Performance Measurement—Getting Results.* Washington, DC: Urban Institute Press

Kellogg Foundation. (2001). Logic model development guide: Logic models to bring together planning, evaluation & action. Battle Creek, MI: W.K. Kellogg Foundation.

Maslow, A. H. (1943). A theory of human motivation. *Psychological Review, 50*(4), 370–396.

Mayer, R. (1985). *Policy and program planning: A development perspective.* Englewood Cliff, NJ: Prentice-Hall.

Reviere, R., Berkowitz, S., Carter, C.C., Gergusan, C.G. (Eds). (1996). *Needs assessment: A creative and practical guide for social scientists.* Washington, DC: Taylor & Francis.

Rossi, P., Freeman, H., & Lipsey, M. (1999). *Evaluation: A systematic approach* (6th ed.). Thousand Oaks, CA: Sage.

Taylor-Powell, E., Jones, L., & Henert, E. (2002). *Enhancing program performance with logic models.* Retrieved from http://www1.uwex.edu/ces/lmcourse/

United Way of America. (1996). Measuring program outcomes: A practical approach. Arlington, VA: United Way of America. Retrieved from http://www.unitedway.org/outcomes/

Wyatt Knowlton, L. & Philips, C. (2009). *The logic model guidebook: Better strategies for great results.* Thousand Oaks, CA: Sage Publications, Inc.

Yuen, F. & Terao, K. (2003). *Practical grant writing and program evaluation.* Pacific Grove, CA: Brooks/Cole.

Chapter 11. Introduction to Data Analysis (the "CSI")

Council on Social Work Education (CSWE). (2015). Educational policy and accreditation standards for baccalaureate and master's social work programs. Retrieved from https://www.cswe.org/getattachment/Accreditation/Accreditation-Process/2015-EPAS/2015EPAS_Web_FINAL.pdf.aspx

Frost, J. (2015, February 19). Choosing between a nonparametric test and a parametric test. Retrieved from http://blog.minitab.com/blog/adventures-in-statistics-2/choosing-between-a-nonparametric-test-and-a-parametric-test

Chapter 12. Presentation of Data, Central Tendency, and Dispersion

No references

Chapter 13. Normal Distribution and Z Statistics

Central limit theorem. (n.d.). *Merriam Webster online dictionary.* Retrieved from https://www.merriam-webster.com/dictionary/central%20limit%20theorem

Paret, M. & Martz, E. (2009, August 26). Understanding the central limit theorem. *Quality Digest.* Retrieved from https://www.qualitydigest.com/inside/twitter-ed/understanding-central-limit-theorem.html#

Pearson, K. (Ed.). (1930). *Tables for statisticians and biometricians* (3rd ed.). London, UK: Cambridge University Press.

U.S. Census Bureau. (2016). *Table HINC-06. Income distribution to $250,000 or more for households: 2016.* Retrieved from https://www.census.gov/data/tables/time-series/demo/income-poverty/cps-hinc/hinc-06.2016.html

Chapter 14. Hypothesis and Hypothesis Testing

Banerjee, A., Chitnis, U. B., Jadhav, S. L., Bhawalkar, J. S., & Chaudhury, S. (2009). Hypothesis testing, type I and type II errors. *India Psychiatry Journal, 18,* 127–131. Retrieved from http://www.industrialpsychiatry.org/text.asp?2009/18/2/127/62274

Evrard, E. (2015). Hypothesis testing steps in hypothesis testing. Retrieved from http://slideplayer.com/slide/3791615/

Rogers, T. (2006). Type I and type II errors—Making mistakes in the justice system. Retrieved http://www.intuitor.com/statistics/T1T2Errors.html

StatPac (2017). Statistical significance. Retrieved from https://www.statpac.com/surveys/statistical-significance.htm

Taylor, C. (2017, July 24). What is the difference between alpha and p-values? Retrieved from https://www.thoughtco.com/the-difference-between-alpha-and-p-values-3126420

WebMD. (n.d.). What is normal body temperatures? Retrieved from https://www.webmd.com/first-aid/normal-body-temperature#1

Chapter 15. Test of Correlation

Chafetz, J. (1978). *A primer on the construction and testing of theories in sociology.* New York, NY: F. E. Peacock Publishers.

Fisher, R. A. & Yates, F. (1963). *Statistical tables for biological, agricultural, and medical research* (6th ed.). New York, NY: Hafner Publishing.

LaMorte, W. (2016, September 1). *Test for two or more independent samples, discrete outcome.* Boston University of Public Health. Retrieve from http://sphweb.bumc.bu.edu/otlt/MPH-Modules/BS/BS704_HypothesisTesting-ChiSquare/BS704_HypothesisTesting-ChiSquare3.html.

Lear, J. (1988). *Aristotle the desire to understand.* New York, NY: Cambridge University Press. https://books.google.com/books?id=hSAGlzPLq7gC&pg=PA1&source=gbs_toc_r&cad=3#v=onepage&q&f=false

Mathematics in Education and Industry (MEI). (2007). MEI paper on Spearman's rank correlation coefficient. Retrieved from http://mei.org.uk/files/pdf/Spearmanrcc.pdf

McDonald, J. H. (2014). *Handbook of biological statistics* (3rd ed., pp. 77–85). Baltimore, MD: Sparky House Publishing. Retrieved from http://www.biostathandbook.com/fishers.html

What is a null hypothesis (n.d.). In *Null Hypothesis: The Journal of Unlikely Science*. Retrieved 01 09 2017, from https://www.null-hypothesis.co.uk/straight-talking/.

Organisation for Economic Co-operation and Development (OECD). (2007, October). Statistical products. Retrieved from https://stats.oecd.org/glossary/detail.asp?ID=7343

Tibshirani, R, & Taylor, J. (2012). Degrees of freedom in lasso problem. *The Analysis of Statistics*, 40(2), 1198–1232. doi: 10.1214/12-AOS1003. Retrieved from https://projecteuclid.org/download/pdfview_1/euclid.aos/1342625466

Weinbach, R. & Grinnell, R. Jr. (2015). *Statistics for social workers* (9th ed.). Needham Height, MA: Allyn & Bacon.

Wilcoxon Signed-Ranks Table. (2018). Real statistics. Retrieved from http://www.real-statistics.com/statistics-tables/wilcoxon-signed-ranks-table/

Yuen, F. (2006). Family health social work practice and change. In F. Yuen (Ed.), *Social work practice with children and families: A family health approach* (pp. 1–20). Binghamton, NY: Haworth Press.

Zar, J. H. 1998. Spearman rank correlation. In Peter Armitage and Theodore Colton (Eds.), *Encyclopedia of biostatistics* (vol. 5, pp. 4191–4196). Chichester, England: John Wiley and Sons. Retrieved from ftp://biostat.wisc.edu/pub/chappell/800/hw/spearman.pdf

Chapter 16. Test of Differences

Berry, K. J., Mielke, P. W. Jr., & Johnston, J. (2012, December). The two-sample rank-sum test: Early development. *Electronic Journal for History of Probability and Statistics*, 8, 9–10. Retrieved from http://www.jehps.net/decembre2012/BerryMielkeJohnston.pdf

Center for Disease Control and Prevention (2016). Anthropometric Reference Data for Children and Adults: United States, 2011–2014. *Vital and Health Statistics*. 3(39). Retrieved from https://www.cdc.gov/nchs/data/series/sr_03/sr03_039.pdf

Coe, R. (2002, September). *It's the effect size, stupid: What effect size is and why it is important.* Annual Conference of the British Educational Research Association, University of Exeter, England. Retrieved from https://www.leeds.ac.uk/educol/documents/00002182.htm

Cohen J. (1990). Things I have learned (so far). *American Psychologist*, 45(12), 1304–1312. Retrieved from http://dx.doi.org/10.1037/0003-066X.45.12.1304

Derrick, B., Toher, D., & White, P. (2017). How to compare the means of two samples that include paired observations and independent observations: A companion to Derrick,

Russ, Toher and White (2017). *The Quantitative Methods in Psychology, 13* (2), 120–126. Retrieved from http://www.tqmp.org/RegularArticles/vol13-2/p120/p120.pdf

Fisher, R. A. & Yates, F. (1963). *Statistical tables for biological, agricultural, and medical research* (6th ed.). New York, NY: Hafner Publishing.

Mann, H. B., & Whitney, D. R. (1947). On a test of whether one of two random variables is stochastically larger than the other. *The Annals of Mathematical Statistics, 18*(1), 50–60. doi:10.1214/aoms/1177730491. Retrieved from https://projecteuclid.org/euclid.aoms/1177730491

Mathematics in Education and Industry (MEI). (n.d.). The Wilcoxon signed rank test. Retrieved from http://mei.org.uk/files/pdf/wilcoxonrerevised.pdf

McHugh, M. (2008). Standard error: Meaning and interpretation. *Biochemia Medica, 18*(1), 7–13. Retrieved from http://dx.doi.org/10.11613/BM.2008.002

Real Statistics. (2018, July). *Wilcoxon signed-ranks table.* http://www.real-statistics.com/statistics-tables/wilcoxon-signed-ranks-table/

Schlomer, G., Bauman, S., & Card, NA. (2010). *Journal of Counselling Psychology.* 57(1):1–10. Retrieved from http://citeseerx.ist.psu.edu/viewdoc/download?doi=10.1.1.703.9931&rep=rep1&type=pdf

Sullivan, G. & Feinn, R. (2012, September). Using effect size—or why the p value is not enough. *Journal of Graduate Medical Education, 4*(3), 279–282. doi: 10.4300/JGME-D-12-00156.1

Weinbach, R., & Grinnell, R. Jr. (2015). *Statistics for social workers* (9th ed.). Needham Height, MA: Allyn & Bacon.

Wilcoxon, F. (1945, December). Individual comparisons by ranking methods. *Biometrics Bulletin, 1*(6), 80–83. Retrieved from http://sci2s.ugr.es/keel/pdf/algorithm/articulo/wilcoxon1945.pdf. Stable URL: http://links.jstor.org/sici?sici=0099-4987%28194512%291%3A6%3C80%3AICBRM%3E2.0.CO%3B2-P

Chapter 17. Preparing Research Reports

American Psychological Association. (2010). *Publication manual of the American Psychological Association* (6th ed.). Washington, DC: Author.

Hsieh, H. & Shannon, S. (2005). *Qualitative Health Research.* 15 (9), 1277–1288. DOI: 10.1177/1049732305276687

Westerfelt, A. & Dietz, T. (2010). *Planning and conducting agency-based research* (4th ed.). Boston, MA: Allyn & Bacon.

INDEX

Bein, A., 72

bell curve. *See* normal distribution

Berra, Yogi, 140

bias, 67–68, 121–122

Bidwell, L., 111–112

Big Help Agency, 38–39, 201–202

Blackwell's Island, 145

Blinkhorn, A., 82

Bly, Nellie, 145

Boehm, W., 9

Bradshaw, J., 203–204

brand recognition, 132

Brekke, J., 9

C

California Achievement Test, 152

California Standardized Testing and Reporting program, 152

Campbell, D. T., 94

Candid Camera TV, 145

Cantril, Hadley, 78

Caracelli, V. J., 111

Car Talk, 16

Carter, S., 82

case study, 154–156

causal questions, 18

causal relation, 314–315

causation and correlation, 314–316

central limit theorem (CLT), 252–253, 285–286

checklist, 166

Children and Youth Assent Form, 39

child sexual abuse, 76

chi-square, 259

goodness of fit test, 260, 330–332

statistic, 317–319

chi-square test, 319–326

application of, 320

critical values, 322

effectiveness of dialectic behavior therapy (DBT), 321

formula, 320

limitations to and assumptions for use of, 326–327

sample size, 326

sexual harassment prevention training in school, 324–325

SPSS printout, 322

choice of instruments, 177

Clinton, Bill, 31

closed-ended questions, 129

cluster random sampling, 119–120

coefficient of determination (r^2), 261, 337–338

Cohen's d (d), 383–384

Common Core Initiative in 2010, 152–153

commoners, 292–294

common sense, 7

common statistics and choice of statistics chart, 260

comparative need, 204

competencies, 2–3, 8

composite resident, 138

Compton, B., 93

concept, 43–47

conceptual definition of variable, 47

conceptualizing observations, 142–143

conceptual statistics, defined, 250

conclusions, reports, 396

concrete definition of variable, 47

conducting interview surveys, 140–142. *See also* interview surveys

asking questions and more, 140

interviewer effects, 140–141

pilot study, 137

respondent-lead process, 137

social desirability bias, 139

steps for, 140

confidence interval (CI), 302–303, 346–347

confidence level (CL), 293

confidentiality, 32–33

confounding variable, 48–49

connotative, 174

consent

informed, 36–37

sample, 37–40

construct, 43–47

defined, 53

social constructionism, 81–82

consumer price index (CPI), 168

bar graph, 266–267

frequency polygon, 269–270

histogram, 266–267

pie chart, 266–267

scatterplot, 270–271

Greene, J. C., 111

grounded theory research, 82–84

Grounded Theory Institute, 82

group interviews (focus groups), 136

Guttman, Louis, 173

Guttman scaling, 173

H

Haight, W., 111–112

Havasupai Indian DNA study, 30–31

Havasupai Tribe, 30–31

hearing and participating, 341–343

hemoglobin, 289

Henert, E., 214

hidden observation, 145

hierarchy of human needs (Maslow), 203

histogram, 266–267

Hohman, M., 26–27

home and school, 334–335

homosexual sex, 32

Hook, J. N., 26

human diversity, 25–41

human immuno deficiency virus (HIV), 76

human subjects

ethical considerations and protection, 28–32

historical and significant events, 29–32

Human Subjects Review Committee (HSRC), 28, 34, 36

Humphreys, Laud, 31

hypothesis, 85–86

for descriptive designs, 90

for experimental/exploratory design, 91

hypothesis testing, 295–309

alternative hypothesis, 297–301

critical value, 303–304

null hypothesis, 297–301

probability value, 302–303

reject or not to reject, 305–306

test of significance and, 302–305

Type I error (α), 303–307

Type II error (β), 306–310

I

Imperial Japanese Army, 30

implications, reports, 395

in and out of correlation, 316–318. *See also* correlation

incentive, 132

inclusive range, 274

independent living and self-efficacy, 340–341

independent t-test, 262, 348, 356–361

independent variable, 48, 54

index, 166–168

inductive learning, 71–73

inferential statistics, 254–255, 257, 259–261, 313

test choice flowchart, 263–264

informed consent, 36–37

moral sense, 36

online/internet-based, 40–41

socio-legal sense, 36

in-person interview protocol/guide, 176–177

inputs, logic model, 218

Institutional Review Board (IRB), 28

instruments. *See also* tools, data collection

choice of, 177

existing, 178–179

pilot testing, 192–193

research developed, 179

survey. *See* survey instruments

intelligence abilities, 288–289

intended deviant outlaws, 293–295

internal consistency reliability, 63

internal validity, 59–62, 103

threats to, 60–61, 104

interquartile range, 275

inter-rater reliability, 62

interrupted time-series design, 95–96

interval variable, 50–53

intervention, 98, 314–315